From Artisan to Worker

From Artisan to Worker examines the largely overlooked debate on the potential reestablishment of guilds that occurred both inside and outside the French government from 1776 to 1821. The abolition of guilds in 1791 overturned a system of labor that had been in place for centuries. The disorder that ensued – from concerns about the safety of the food supply to a general decline in the quality of goods – raised strong doubts about their abolition and sparked a debate that continued for decades. The issue of the reestablishment of guilds, however, subsequently became intertwined with the growing mechanization of production. Under the Napoleonic regime, the government considered several projects to restore guilds in a large-scale fashion, but the counterargument that guilds could impede mechanization prevailed. After Bonaparte's fall, the restored Bourbon dynasty was expected to reestablish guilds, but its sponsorship of an industrial exhibition in 1819 signaled its endorsement of mechanization, and after 1821 there were no further efforts to reestablish guilds during the Restoration.

Michael P. Fitzsimmons is Professor of History at Auburn University Montgomery. His previous works include *The Parisian Order of Barristers and the French Revolution, The Remaking of France*, and *The Night the Old Regime Ended*, in addition to multiple articles published in scholarly journals.

From Artisan to Worker

Guilds, the French State, and the Organization of Labor, 1776–1821

MICHAEL P. FITZSIMMONS

Auburn University Montgomery, Alabama

CAMBRIDGE
UNIVERSITY PRESS

CAMBRIDGE UNIVERSITY PRESS
Cambridge, New York, Melbourne, Madrid, Cape Town, Singapore,
São Paulo, Delhi, Dubai, Tokyo

Cambridge University Press
32 Avenue of the Americas, New York, NY 10013-2473, USA

www.cambridge.org
Information on this title: www.cambridge.org/9780521193764

First published 2010

Printed in the United States of America

A catalog record for this publication is available from the British Library.

Library of Congress Cataloging in Publication data
Fitzsimmons, Michael P., 1949–
    From artisan to worker : guilds, the French state, and the organization of labor,
    1776–1821 / Michael P. Fitzsimmons.
        p.   cm.
    Includes bibliographical references and index.
    ISBN 978-0-521-19376-4 (hardback)
    1. Guilds – France – History.   2. Industrial policy – France – History.   3. Labor
    policy – France – History.   I. Title.
    HD6464.G85 2010
    338.6'32094409033–dc22   2009047100

ISBN 978-0-521-19376-4 Hardback

To my colleagues in the Department of History at Auburn University Montgomery

Contents

Acknowledgments

Before mentioning specific acknowledgments, I would like to express once again my warm appreciation for the collegiality of my colleagues in the field of the French Revolution. Perhaps it is the same in other areas – I hope so – but, as the beneficiary of extraordinary generosity of spirit on the part of fellow scholars, my passion for the subject is strengthened. Whatever differences of interpretation we may have, the spirit of *fraternité* remains strong.

Indeed, my debts of gratitude have expanded with this study, and the acknowledgments that follow cannot possibly convey the gratitude that I feel. Daniel Heimmermann, Kenneth Margerison, Michael Broers, and Robert Alexander read chapters, and James Livesey and Michael Sibalis read a complete draft of the work. All of them challenged me to refine my thinking and saved me from errors, and I thank them all for making this study better. Any deficiencies that remain are of course of my own making. Jeff Horn and Rafe Blaufarb kindly shared with me documents that they uncovered during the course of their own research. Jeff in particular unhesitatingly helped me to address a critical void and salvage what had been a frustrating trip to Rouen. Alan Forrest, William Doyle, and Isser Woloch supported this project, and I am deeply grateful for their encouragement and many years of friendship. Regrettably, geography has mandated that these friendships be nurtured from afar, but they are no less deep or warm as a result.

The Research Council of Auburn University Montgomery unwaveringly assisted this project with three Research Grants-in-Aid. It would not have been possible without the council's confidence and support. John Veres, the Chancellor of Auburn University Montgomery, made provision for me to receive a professional improvement leave that was critical to this work's completion. The study also benefited from a Newberry Library Short-Term Fellowship for Individual Research that allowed me to utilize its extraordinary French Revolution collection in a systematic manner, and I thank the Newberry Library for its support. As always, the entire staff of the Newberry was exceedingly helpful and went well beyond the norms of scholarly courtesy in dealing with my requests.

The staffs of the Archives Nationales, Archives de la Préfecture de Police, and the Bibliothèque Historique de la Ville de Paris were all unfailingly helpful in facilitating my research, particularly the first, which seems like a second home to me in Paris. Beyond Paris, I would like to thank the staffs of departmental and municipal archives and libraries for their assistance and courtesy, and beyond France, the International Institute of Social History in Amsterdam provided extraordinary hospitality.

I am equally grateful to my colleagues in the Department of History at Auburn University Montgomery. We have created a congenial and supportive environment that we value, and I want Jan Bulman, Lee Farrow, Steve Gish, Tim Henderson, Keith Krawczynski, Ben Severance, Michael Simmons, Wyatt Wells, and Qiang Zhai to know the high regard and personal affection in which I hold them. I did not anticipate that my career would be spent at Auburn University Montgomery, but I could not have asked for better colleagues. Janice Willis, our administrative associate, was endlessly patient with my technical backwardness and cheerfully converted material from my antiquated computer, with which I have a high comfort level, to a more modern format. She, too, has been a part of our cordial work atmosphere.

It has been a pleasure to work with the staff of Cambridge University Press. I would especially like to thank Eric Crahan, Jason Przybylski, Bindu Vinod, and the team at Newgen Imaging Systems for their careful attention in seeing this work through to publication. I deeply appreciate their courtesy and professionalism.

Lastly, others have provided various forms of support along the way – commiseration, editing, encouragement, friendship, goodwill, logistical support, and, usually unsuccessfully, but through no fault of their own, solace. In this regard, I would like to thank Robert Allen, William Cormack, Steven Daniell, Kelly Fitzsimmons, Theresa Fitzsimmons, Julian Jackson, Ralph Kingston, Pia Knigge and Anika Knigge Hutton, Pamela Long, Susie Paul, and Rochelle Ziskin.

Abbreviations

ACCIP	Archives de la Chambre de Commerce et d'Industrie de Paris
AD	Archives Départementales
AM	Archives Municipales
AN	Archives Nationales (Paris)
APP	Archives de la Préfecture de Police (Paris)
BHVP	Bibliothèque Historique de la Ville de Paris
BM	Bibliothèque Municipale
BN	Bibliothèque Nationale (Paris)
BNU Strasbourg	Bibliothèque Nationale et Universitaire de Strasbourg
IISH	International Institute of Social History (Amsterdam)

Introduction

Some of the work that has long been recognized as among the most innovative scholarship on the French Revolution centered on workers, particularly their politicization.[1] Paradoxically, however, as Haim Burstin noted some years ago, there is a lack of a history of work during the French Revolution.[2] Although Burstin himself has done as much as anyone to address this void, his observation is as valid now as it was then.[3]

The subject of work during the Revolution, of course, is large and multifaceted, but this study has as its focal point the organization of labor – more specifically, the issue of guilds and the Revolution. Guilds, or corporations, as they were also known, and the terms will be used synonymously, were abolished in 1791, destroying a structure of work that had been in place for centuries. Although they were never brought back in any comprehensive fashion, they remained the object of a vigorous and prolonged debate, with the advantages and disadvantages of their reestablishment considered. Their abolition was perceived by many as misguided, a view shared in some cases by deputies and administrators; others argued, more strongly, that their destruction had been a mistake and advocated for their restoration.

One reason that the debate on whether or not to restore guilds, which continued for decades, has attracted little attention may be due to the thematic focal points utilized by historians of French labor for the centuries flanking the Revolution and Empire. For understandable reasons, analyses of the

---

[1] Chief among these would be Albert Soboul, *Les Sans-culottes parisiens en l'an II: Mouvement populaire et gouvernement révolutionnaire, 2 juin 1793–9 thermidor an II* (Paris: Librairie Clavreuil, 1958); George Rudé, *The Crowd in the French Revolution* (Oxford: Oxford University Press, 1959); Kåre D. Tønnesson, *La Défaite des sans-culottes: Mouvement populaire et réaction bourgeoise de l'an III* (Oslo: Presses universitaires d'Oslo, 1959).

[2] Haim Burstin, "Problems of Work during the Terror," in *The French Revolution and the Creation of Modern Political Culture: The Terror*, Keith Michael Baker, ed., (Oxford: Pergamon, 1994), p. 271.

[3] Haim Burstin, *Le Faubourg Saint-Marcel à l'époque révolutionnaire: Structure économique et composition sociale* (Paris: Société des Etudes Robespierristes, 1983); Haim Burstin, *Une Révolution à l'oeuvre: Le faubourg Saint-Marcel (1789–1794)* (Paris: Champ Vallon, 2005).

eighteenth century concentrate on guilds, abolished in 1791 – the title of the most recent examination of the topic, *La Fin des corporations*, exemplifies this approach.[4] The issues that these studies engage end with the early period of the Revolution.

By the time of the Restoration, Paris had hundreds of thousands of workers; although no reliable number is available, a scholar of the period believed that an early 1823 figure of 244,000 workers, out of a total population of approximately 730,000–750,000, was credible.[5] This large, undifferentiated mass of workers forms the basis for most explorations of French labor history during the first half of the nineteenth century, focusing on what Louis Chevalier termed "the laboring and dangerous classes," a volatile element whose frustrations erupted during the June days in 1848.[6] Again, for equally understandable reasons, for studies with a nineteenth-century focus, the Restoration period, when concentrations of workers beyond such traditional locales as the *faubourg* Saint-Antoine or *faubourg* Saint-Marcel became more pronounced, is generally the point of departure.[7] In sum, for one important span of French labor history, the beginning of the Revolution marks the end, whereas for another significant period, the end of the Napoleonic Empire has generally marked the beginning. As yet, there is not, as Burstin broadly noted, any bridge between them.[8]

---

[4] Steven L. Kaplan, *La Fin des corporations* (Paris: Fayard, 2001). Some earlier examples, listed chronologically, include Etienne Martin Saint-Léon, *Histoire des corporations de métiers, depuis leurs origines jusqu'à leur suppression en 1791*, 3rd edition, (Paris: Librairie Felix Alcan, 1922); François Olivier-Martin, *L'Organisation corporative de la France d'ancien régime* (Paris: Sirey, 1938); Emile Coornaert, *Les Corporations en France avant 1789* (Paris: Les Editions ouvrières, 1941); Michael Sonenscher, *The Hatters of Eighteenth-Century France* (Berkeley, CA: University of California Press, 1987); Bernard Gallinato, *Les Corporations à Bordeaux à la fin de l'Ancien Régime: Vie et mort d'un mode d'organization du travail* (Bordeaux: Presses universitaires de Bordeaux, 1992).

[5] Guillaume de Bertier de Sauvigny, "Les Ouvriers d'industrie à Paris sous la Restauration," *Bulletin de la Société d'histoire moderne* 14 (1976), p. 26.

[6] Louis Chevalier, *Classes laborieuses et classes dangereuses à Paris pendant la première moitié du XIXe siècle* (Paris: Plon, 1958).

[7] Katherine A. Lynch, *Family, Class, and Ideology in Early Industrial France: Social Policy and the Working Class Family, 1825–1848* (Madison, WI: University of Wisconsin Press, 1988); outside of Paris, the Restoration starting point is equally apparent in Elinor Accampo, *Industrialization, Family Life, and Class Relations: Saint-Chamond, 1815–1914* (Berkeley, CA: University of California Press, 1989).

[8] There is the fine study of Raymonde Monnier, *Le Faubourg Saint-Antoine (1789–1815)* (Paris: Société des Etudes Robespierristes, 1981), but only two chapters are devoted to the organization of work and the scope of the book is limited to one neighborhood – albeit an important one – of Paris. In addition, there are classic studies of French workers during the first years of the Revolution, but they are devoted primarily to the political activities of workers rather than to the structure of work itself. These include Soboul, *Les Sans-culottes parisiens en l'an II*; Rudé, *The Crowd in the French Revolution*; Tønnesson, *La Défaite des sans-culottes*. In addition, there is an admirable work that, from its title, appears to be an exception, but it leaps from 1794 to the Restoration. William A. Sewell, *Work and Revolution in France: The Language of Labor from the Old Regime to 1848* (Cambridge: Cambridge University Press,

By the eighteenth century guilds had been a prominent feature of urban life for centuries, providing a structure to labor and, although the degree of success is open to debate, a measure of control over journeymen and apprentices – corporations were, in fact, regarded as an extension of the police. Although they were abolished during 1776, they were restored after only a few months because of unrest among journeymen. Consequently, by May 1789, as the Estates-General opened, with memories of 1776 still relatively fresh, the position of guilds seemed secure.

Just two months later, however, on August 4, 1789, the National Assembly – the body into which the Estates-General had evolved after a prolonged stalemate – unexpectedly launched a comprehensive attack on privilege, during the course of which it pronounced the dissolution of guilds, which were perceived as repositories of privilege. Even among the cascade of renunciations made during the meeting, which astonished both deputies and observers, the suppression of corporations seemed extraordinary. Indeed, their abolition was so stunning that the National Assembly appears to have had doubts about what it had done because it temporized – in the drafting of the August decrees summarizing the renunciations made during the session, the Assembly announced the reform of guilds rather than their abolition. Ultimately, however, the National Assembly did eliminate corporations, although relatively late in its tenure; their abolition came only after the destruction of provinces, the *parlements* and the nobility, and a fundamental reorganization of the Church. The dilatory approach by the Assembly testifies to the uncertainty and even apprehensiveness felt by deputies, but they honored the compact they had forged on August 4 and dissolved guilds.

In place of corporations and in the cause of liberty, the National Assembly enacted an occupational license (*patente*) that allowed its holder to practice any trade he wished. Problems quickly arose, so much so that for contemporaries the dissolution of corporations and the introduction of the occupational license became indelibly associated with a sharp decline in standards in both production and commerce.

As that descent continued, France declared war on Austria, initiating what would become nearly a quarter of a century of almost continuous war. Within a few months, serious reverses led to the overthrow and execution of Louis XVI, which in turn widened the conflict and placed France on the defensive. In response, the government, primarily the Committee of Public Safety acting on behalf of the National Convention, placed the country on a war footing. Among many measures, it enacted mass conscription, and supplying the hundreds of thousands of men taken into the armies required levels of production far beyond that of the traditional artisanal mode, leading the Convention to launch a large-scale manufacturing program.

1980). A notable exception, which addresses the effort to restore guilds in the context of French industrialization, is Jeff Horn, *The Path Not Taken: French Industrialization in the Age of Revolution 1750–1830* (Cambridge, MA: The MIT Press, 2006), pp. 262–266.

In terms of manufacturing capacity, the efforts undertaken by the Committee of Public Safety succeeded, especially in arms – Paris became the largest producer of muskets in the world. Ultimately, however, the government shut down the arms workshops, largely due to unrest among workers. Nevertheless, the endeavor essentially defined the issues that would frame the debate on the reestablishment of guilds that ensued.

On the one hand, the Convention's effort had revealed the possibilities of mass production, which would subsequently become attached to mechanization of production – the arms program had been driven mainly by a regimentation of labor, rather than mechanization. In the view of advocates of mechanization, any restoration of corporations would offer workers a platform from which they might impede mechanization.

On the other hand, the government had ended the system because of worker unrest, and proponents of guilds asserted that their reestablishment would bring an end to "insubordination." They also argued that it would restore quality and trust to manufacturing and commerce.

Moreover, guilds under the Old Regime had performed a number of functions, such as overseeing apprenticeships, conducting quality control and ensuring the safety of the food supply. After it abolished corporations, the National Assembly failed to provide for any of these responsibilities, and its successor bodies did not address these issues either. As skill, quality, and food safety declined precipitously, the issue for legislators, officials, and police was whether they should address abuses or problems with laws and regulations on an individual basis or seek a more comprehensive solution by reestablishing guilds, albeit in a reformed fashion.

As France emerged from the Terror, disaffection with the unregulated market and workplace was widespread, particularly in Paris. In a clear indication that sentiment favoring a return to corporations was more than idle longing, the commission appointed by the National Convention in 1795 to draft a new constitution believed it necessary to include an article maintaining the proscription of guilds. Two deputies from different parts of the political spectrum opposed the measure, but the Convention approved it and it became article 355 of the Constitution of the Year III that established the Directory.

Article 355 reinforced the abolition of corporations – it bolstered the statutory law of 1791 with constitutional status. Whereas a statutory measure could be repealed or overturned by the passage of a new law, to amend the constitution required a minimum of six years. The extraordinarily difficult winter of 1795–1796, the first after the installation of the Directory, provided additional impetus to the favorable recollection of guilds. Amidst dearth and severe hardship, most contemporaries associated the era of corporations with adequate supply, market stability, and good quality. Indeed, approximately a year after it was adopted, the deputy who claimed to have written and put forward article 355 expressed regret at having done so.

The easing of conditions diminished somewhat the positive outlook toward a restoration of guilds. Furthermore, in 1798 the Directory sponsored an

Exhibition of Products of French Industry, the first industrial exposition held in the Western world. The exhibition was successful, drawing large crowds despite inclement weather, and contributed to the creation of a favorable image of industry among the public.

The next year, in 1799, Napoleon Bonaparte overthrew the Directory, terminating the Constitution of the Year III and effectively reopening the possibility of more quickly restoring guilds. If, in fact, there was a moment during the revolutionary and Napoleonic epoch when corporations might have been reestablished, it was during Bonaparte's rule. The Council of State debated the question on several occasions until 1810, and under the Consulate the central government reorganized bakers and butchers of Paris into bodies strongly reminiscent of guilds. Furthermore, a secret counselor of Bonaparte repeatedly urged him to reestablish guilds.

Guilds were known and familiar, and it was recognized that they had provided services that were socially and economically beneficial. Their reestablishment seemed to some to be preferable to the partial solutions that had been attempted, the most notable of which was the law of 22 germinal year XI, with which there was dissatisfaction. The question that presented itself, then, was whether to accept limited results and continuing deficiencies or take the final step of restoring guilds.[9] Those who argued for their restoration emphasized the greater order and discipline that would result – values strongly embraced by the Napoleonic regime.

At the same time, manpower shortages resulting from conscription virtually mandated mechanization of production. Those who opposed any reestablishment of guilds asserted that they could become a platform from which opposition to mechanization could be mounted. For more than a decade, Bonaparte did not make a clear choice between the reestablishment of corporations and mechanized production, but a resolution occurred when the government undertook a major reorganization of the Ministry of the Interior in January 1812. A portion of the ministry's responsibilities were transferred to an entirely new entity, the Ministry of Manufacturing and Commerce. The restructuring signaled the triumph of mechanized, industrial production under the Napoleonic regime, but the formation of the new ministry coincided with a severe economic crisis that continued until the fall of Napoleon.

Bonaparte's defeat brought back the Bourbon monarchy, which was widely expected to undo the work of the Revolution. Only weeks after its return, the restored monarchy abolished the Ministry of Manufacturing and Commerce and reintegrated its functions into the Ministry of the Interior. This action, along with the expectation that it would reverse most reforms of the Revolution, fed a perception that the government of Louis XVIII would reestablish guilds. Both the Crown and the Ministry of the Interior received a number of requests to this end, and a lively debate, both in public and within

---

[9] Indeed, in contrast to the law of 22 germinal year XI, the reorganization of bakers and butchers was generally judged to have been successful.

the government, took place on the issue. A determination ultimately came in a somewhat indirect fashion – in 1819 the royal government sponsored an industrial exhibition in Paris, signaling a preference for industry and mechanization over a restoration of corporations.

The contradistinction between the reestablishment of guilds and mechanization reflects the terms of the arguments waged by contemporaries, particularly within the government but also in public. The oft-used phrase "freedom of industry" used in opposition to any reestablishment of guilds meant above all the freedom to innovate, and the primary connotation of innovation was mechanization of production. Although both proponents and opponents of the reestablishment of guilds may have had other objectives or motives,[10] the debate revolved principally around these issues, especially until 1819.

Through an examination of the debate on the reestablishment of guilds, this study seeks to demonstrate that the passage from the eighteenth-century regime of guilds to the working classes of the nineteenth century was neither irreversible nor automatic. Indeed, the decision to abolish guilds was questioned during succeeding years and at times maintained in the face of public discontent. The maintenance of the dissolution of corporations should in no way be taken for granted – their reestablishment was advocated and considered many times over the next thirty years. The proscription of guilds held, however, and in the end the change in the organization of labor altered its nature as well. After the abolition of corporations work would be regarded more as a commodity offered by independent workers than as a skill developed and ratified by artisans within a hierarchical, regulated system. The continued proscription of corporations also served to help set France on the path of industrialization that it would follow during the nineteenth century, with all of the consequences that would arise from this.

---

[10] Later in the nineteenth century, for example, some artisans viewed corporatism as a means to stem the development of capitalist production or marketing practices in their trade or as a vehicle for social reform. Christopher H. Johnson, "Economic Change and Artisan Discontent: The Tailors History, 1800–48," in *Revolution and Reaction: 1848 and the Second French Republic*, Roger Price, ed., (London: Croom Helm, 1975): pp. 87–114, especially pp. 108–110; Michael David Sibalis, "Shoemakers and Fourierism in Nineteenth-Century Paris: The Société Laborieuse des Cordonniers-Bottiers," *Social History/Histoire Sociale* 20 (1987): 24–49.

I

The Decline and Demise of Guilds, 1776–1791

Your committee believed that it should link the existence of this tax to a great benefit done for industry and commerce, the suppression of masterships and guilds that your good sense should abolish for the sole reason that they are exclusive privileges.

– d'Allarde, spokesman for the Committee on Taxation, to the National Assembly, February 15, 1791

During the eighteenth century many guilds became increasingly enfeebled because of external competition, internal divisions and other developments, but the decisive event in their decline was their dissolution in 1776, after which they fell away precipitously until their final suppression in early 1791. Although the Crown, after only a few months, retracted the edict of Controller-General Anne-Robert-Jacques Turgot that had abolished corporations, the reorganized bodies were left weakened and ill prepared to meet the challenges posed by the French Revolution, which brought about their final abolition.

GUILDS UNDER THE OLD REGIME

By the latter part of the eighteenth century, guilds had long been a prominent feature of urban life. Many of them had been in existence for centuries – in Paris the corporation of linen makers claimed to have statutes dating from 1278 and that of vinegar makers from 1294. The guild of bakers in Paris had statutes from 1290, but claimed foundations in the Gallo-Roman period.[1] Not all corporations could claim such venerable lineage, of course, but the entire system of guilds was deeply woven into the fabric of urban life, from large cities to smaller towns. In Lyon, even omitting workers in the silk industry,

---

[1] *Guide des corps des marchands et les communautés des arts et métiers, tant de la ville et faubourgs de Paris, que du royaume* (Paris: Veuve Duchesne, 1766), p. 295 (linen makers); p. 484 (vinegar makers); Steven Laurence Kaplan, *The Bakers of Paris and the Bread Question 1700–1775* (Durham: Duke University Press, 1996), p. 155.

which gave the city its unique character, the guild system encompassed tens of thousands of men.[2] In Grenoble, with a population of approximately 24,000 in 1776, there were 1,141 masters in forty-one guilds.[3] Including journeymen apprentices, who were not enumerated, the number of men associated with guilds probably approached 2,500, meaning that perhaps 25 percent of the active male population was connected to the guild structure.[4]

The scale of their presence gave guilds a substantial role in urban life, from municipal politics to policing, and was reinforced by the requirement of many corporations that members had to be born in the city in which the guild was located. Guilds served to oversee and regulate the behavior of masters and journeymen; indeed, during an age in which police structures were not well formed, they played a significant role as an auxiliary to the police.[5] In the final analysis, the primary function of each guild was to promote stability, both economic and social.

For this reason, workers outside of the guild system were often an object of suspicion and even fear.[6] In Nîmes, for example, unemployed silk workers threatened to riot and set fire to the town, leading the intendant to seek to employ them in a public works project tearing down the city walls.[7]

So prestigious was the corporate paradigm that in Paris and elsewhere non-skilled laborers sought to emulate it – even in the world of unskilled work, claims of a monopoly on certain tasks existed, although the basis of such assertions was "unformalized custom." As Haim Burstin noted, "these rights assumed the status of property. Even the water-carriers, upon retiring from

---

[2] Maurice Garden, *Lyon et les Lyonnais au XVIIIᵉ siècle* (Grenoble: Allier, 1970), pp. 315–320.

[3] AD Isère 2 C 88, documents 47–92; the population figure is from *Histoire de Grenoble*, Vital Chomel, ed., (Toulouse: Privat, 1976), p. 150.

[4] In the same vein, Edwin J. Shephard, Jr., "Social and Geographic Mobility of the Eighteenth-Century Guild Artisans: An Analysis of Guild Receptions in Dijon, 1700–1790," in *Work and Revolution in France: Representation, Meaning, Organization and Practice*, Steven Laurence Kaplan and Cynthia Koepp, eds., (Ithaca, NY: Cornell University Press, 1986), pp. 97–130, presents a portrait of the importance and pervasiveness of the guild structure in the similarly sized city of Dijon. For a profile of a stratum of guilds in a city, see Daniel Joseph Heimmermann, "Work and Corporate Life in Old Regime France: The Leather Artisans of Bordeaux (1740–1791)," (Ph.D. dissertation, Marquette University, 1994). On corporations in Caen, Jean-Claude Perrot, *Genèse d'une ville moderne: Caen au XVIIIᵉ siècle*, 2 vols. (The Hague: Mouton, 1975), I: 320–327. For a wider perspective on a single trade, Michael Sonenscher, *The Hatters of Eighteenth-Century France* (Berkeley, CA: University of California Press, 1987).

[5] BM Orléans Ms. 1422, section 7, (Commerce); Alan Williams, *The Police of Paris 1718–1789* (Baton Rouge: Louisiana State University Press, 1979), pp. 118–119; Steven Kaplan, "Réflexions sur la police du monde du travail, 1700–1815," *Revue historique* 256 (1979): 26–27; Bernard Gallinato, *Les Corporations à Bordeaux*, pp. 197–200.

[6] William H. Sewell, Jr., *Work and Revolution in France: The Language of Labor from the Old Regime to 1848* (Cambridge: Cambridge University Press, 1980), p. 24; Dean T. Ferguson, "The Body, the Corporate Idiom, and the Police of the Unincorporated Worker in Early Modern Lyons," *French Historical Studies* 23 (2000): 545–576, especially p. 553.

[7] AN H¹ 1023, documents 27, 30.

their occupation, would sell their business to a comrade."[8] In part, the adoption of the corporate model was a survival strategy in the extraordinarily difficult conditions of Paris for unskilled workers, but it also testified to the preeminent place of the guild structure. In Grenoble, horse-renters formed themselves into a corporation, but it had no statutes or regulations.[9] Similarly, in Bordeaux, shoemakers outside of the guild sustained a commitment to the corporate system of labor until the end of the Old Regime.[10]

The forming by unskilled laborers of a corporate configuration underscores a fundamental aspect of the guild system: It was not merely an economic institution, perhaps not even primarily an economic institution, but a social taxonomy that clearly demarcated one's place in the social hierarchy. Each guild also had a strong moral dimension that ranged from religious devotion to charitable relief.[11]

Guilds were vested with an array of privileges, the most important of which was a monopoly on production, and the privileges of each corporation were enforced by municipal authorities, who for example often accompanied representatives of a guild as they searched for those who were practicing its trade outside of the corporation. Such searches could sometimes become fearsome in nature.[12] Known as "false workers," *chambrellans* or other designations, non-guild workers were ubiquitous, and their products, despite the efforts of guilds to enforce their monopoly, substantially undermined that monopoly.

An important source of such goods were the suburbs or neighborhoods of most major cities that were nominally outside of the guild or municipal jurisdiction – the *faubourg* Saint-Antoine in Paris is the best known, but others included the *sauvetats* of Saint-André and Saint-Seurin in Bordeaux.[13]

---

[8] Haim Burstin, "Unskilled Labor in Paris at the End of the Eighteenth Century," in *The Workplace before the Factory: Artisans and Proletarians, 1500–1800*, Thomas Max Safley and Leonard N. Rosenband, eds., (Ithaca, NY: Cornell University Press, 1993), pp. 70–72, with the quotation from p. 71.

[9] AD Isère 2 C 88, document 90.

[10] Daniel Heimmermann, "The Guilds of Bordeaux, les métiers libres, and the sauvetats of Saint-Seurin and Saint-André," *Proceedings of the Annual Meeting of the Western Society for French History* 25 (1998): 30.

[11] Garden, *Lyon et les Lyonnais*, pp. 552–555; Sewell, *Work and Revolution in France*, pp. 34–35; Heimmermann, "Work and Corporate Life in Old Regime France," pp. 73–85; Sydney Watts, *Meat Matters: Butchers, Politics, and Market Culture in Eighteenth-Century Paris* (Rochester: University of Rochester Press, 2006), pp. 98–100.

[12] AN T 1373, dossier Martin (Philibert), *Mémoire au Roi concernant la communauté des maîtres perruquiers...*, which related the physical violence associated with seizures against unauthorized practitioners. For more on the violence associated with guilds, see Leonard Rosenband, "Jean-Baptiste Réveillon: A Man on the Make in Old Regime France," *French Historical Studies* 20 (1997): 481–510. See also Judith Coffin, *The Politics of Women's Work: The Paris Garment Trades, 1750–1915* (Princeton: Princeton University Press, 1996), pp. 24–25.

[13] Raymonde Monnier, *Le Faubourg Saint-Antoine*; Steven L. Kaplan, "Les corporations, les 'faux ouvriers,' et le Faubourg Saint-Antoine au XVIIIᵉ siècle," *Annales: Economies, Sociétés, Civilisations* (1988): 353–378; Heimmermann, "The Guilds of Bordeaux."

Indeed, it appears that consumer goods, particularly shoes, produced by artisans in Saint-André and Saint-Seurin – outside the jurisdiction of guilds – dominated the Bordeaux market.[14] The legal existence of a monopoly on production, then, should not necessarily be taken to represent the actual situation.[15]

Another feature of the monopoly on production, and an aspect of guild privilege that did have a broader effect, was that each guild determined both the method and volume of production, so, for example, the confection process was closely guarded by the corporation and was one of the "mysteries" of the trade.[16] The ability to govern fabrication and determine the quantity of a product to be officially manufactured – designed to assure stability within the guild – served to discourage innovation. In fact, during the revolutionary and Napoleonic eras, the period of guilds was pejoratively referred to as one of "routine." What Robert Darnton observed of Montpellier – that during the eighteenth century the city produced the same items that it had fabricated since the late Middle Ages and on the same scale[17] – would have been true of many other cities and towns of France and accounts, at least in part, for the centrality of guilds in most urban areas.

Despite, or perhaps because of, their commanding position, during the eighteenth century corporations became an object of criticism by liberal economic theorists, who assailed in particular the regulatory apparatus at the heart of the guild system.[18] A key figure – the first in France to suggest the abolition of guilds – was Jacques Vincent de Gournay, who emerged during the 1750s. He believed that human labor formed the basis of national wealth and that it should be encouraged by the deregulation of work and production, including the abolition of guilds, freedom in fabrication, shorter apprenticeships and facilitating artisanal innovations.[19] Gournay died in 1759, but his doctrines gained adherents in France. Ultimately, however, although critiques of guilds had become more pointed by the mid-eighteenth century, and despite divisions within and among guilds, there was little to indicate the devastation that lay immediately ahead.[20] Rather, guilds appeared to be a permanent fixture in French society.

[14] Heimmermann, "The Guilds of Bordeaux," pp. 25–27.

[15] James R. Farr, *Artisans in Europe, 1300–1914* (Cambridge: Cambridge University Press, 2000), pp. 81–82.

[16] *Ibid.*, p. 135.

[17] Robert Darnton, *The Great Cat Massacre and Other Episodes in French Cultural History* (New York: Basic Books, 1984), p. 114.

[18] Simone Meysonnier, *La Balance et l'horloge: La genèse de la pensée libérale en France au XVIIIᵉ siècle* (Paris: Editions de la Passion, 1989), pp. 66–70; Catherine Larrère, *L'Invention de l'économie au XVIIIᵉ siècle: Du droit naturel à la physiocratie* (Paris: Presses universitaires de France, 1992), pp. 100–101.

[19] Meysonnier, *La Balance et l'horloge*, pp. 200–202. See also Steven L. Kaplan, *La Fin des corporations*, pp. 7–49, especially pp. 24–26.

[20] Kaplan, *La Fin des corporations*, p. 79.

TURGOT AND THE SIX EDICTS

During the eighteenth century corporations were weakened both internally and externally. Internally, masters who violated paternalistic guild regulations in pursuit of their own interests or challenges to the authority of senior officials by junior officers threatened the fraternal ethos of guild solidarity. Externally, financial difficulties – whether as a result of the costs of litigation or the expenses incurred when corporations sought to repurchase offices that the Crown had sold – further debilitated guilds.[21]

Although guilds were in a weakened state, the catalyst for their enfeeblement came in February 1776 when Turgot, a disciple of Gournay and Controller-General of Finances, as part of an ambitious program of reform known as the Six Edicts, issued a proclamation suppressing guilds. The edict was registered during a *lit de justice* – a special session to override magistrates' objections – at the *parlement* of Paris on March 12.[22] The decree denounced the privilege accorded to artisans of assembling into a single body and justified the abolition of guilds as an act that would allow the king's subjects to enjoy their rights. Turgot also cited the stifling effect of guilds on industry. These two issues, in fact, would frame the debate on guilds for the next fifty years – the conflict between corporate privilege and industrial development would dominate during the Revolution, whereas the restrictions that guilds could place on industry were predominant during the Napoleonic and Restoration eras.

The edict abolishing guilds was the longest of the Six Edicts; in the words of an early scholar of the subject, "the reforms to be effected were so radical and far-reaching that it was imperative to make them clearly defined and specific."[23] Indeed, a modern scholar characterized the contemporary perception of the abolition of guilds by Turgot as "a sort of carnivalization of social relations, an invitation to taxonomic chaos, social disarray, and political mutiny."[24]

Although a wave of disorder followed the guilds' abolition, the scope and intensity of the unrest are difficult to ascertain. Whatever its scale, however, it unnerved contemporaries accustomed to a hierarchical, ordered society.[25] Furthermore, the measures that the Lieutenant-General of Police in Paris took in response to the agitation left workers and journeymen disillusioned, although they were the putative beneficiaries of the edict.[26]

---

[21] Steven L. Kaplan, "The Character and Implications of Strife among the Masters Inside the Guilds of Eighteenth-Century Paris," *Journal of Social History* 19 (1986): 631–647; Daniel Heimmermann, "The Bordeaux Shoemaker's Guild and the End of the Old Regime," *Selected Papers of the Consortium on Revolutionary Europe 1750–1850* (2001): 211–219.

[22] On the abolition of guilds through the Six Edicts, Robert Perry Shepherd, *Turgot and the Six Edicts* (New York: Columbia University Press, 1903); Douglas Dakin, *Turgot and the Ancien Régime in France*, reprint ed. (New York: Octagon Books, 1972), pp. 231–251; Sewell, *Work and Revolution in France*, pp. 72–77; Kaplan, *La Fin des corporations*, pp. 79–85.

[23] Shepherd, *Turgot and the Six Edicts*, p. 126.

[24] Kaplan, *La Fin des corporations*, p. 78.

[25] On problems of perception and the disorders themselves, Kaplan, *ibid.*, pp. 95–97.

[26] *Ibid.*, pp. 97–101.

As a result, amidst intrigues at court and with public confidence shaken by the unrest the edicts had generated, Turgot's position quickly became tenuous, and in early May Louis XVI dismissed him.[27] If the Six Edicts had denoted the success of liberal critiques of guilds by Gournay and his successors, the fall of Turgot signaled their failure, and the brevity of the reforms made that failure appear monumental. Indeed, to the degree that economic arguments against corporations were never again as prominent, the debate surrounding guilds all but ended – after 1776, guilds were not a major object of public discussion or debate. The issue was revived only during the Revolution, and then not for economic reasons but as a result of the revolutionary process itself.

By June there were rumors in Paris that guilds would be restored, albeit in modified form.[28] On August 28 the Crown did, in fact, reestablish guilds.[29] As Steven Kaplan noted, the reorganization of guilds "signified the reaffirmation of the traditional model of social classification and representation" – a concern articulated by the *parlement* of Paris in its remonstrance against the edict of March 12. Furthermore, Kaplan correctly observed that even as the Crown reinstated the old social order, it did not emphasize any commitment to that order. Rather, seeking not to be perceived as reactionary or beholden to special interests, the Crown focused on reform.[30]

The claim of reform advanced by the Crown was not without foundation, because the reestablishment of guilds was not a simple reversion to the *status quo ante*. In Caen, when the Crown reestablished corporations, accessibility to trades was made easier.[31] The guild of butchers in Paris was likewise opened somewhat more to outsiders.[32] Among other changes enacted were the opening of many trades to women, although they could not take part in the governance of a guild, as well as the right of individuals to practice more than one profession and a ban on all litigation between corporations.[33]

Most significantly, however, the reorganization substantially reduced the number of guilds, both through consolidation and suppression. Although the number of guilds in Paris before 1776 is difficult to ascertain with certainty,

[27] Edgar Faure, *12 Mai 1776: La Disgrâce de Turgot* (Paris: Gallimard, 1961), especially pp. 480–517.

[28] Kaplan, *La Fin des corporations*, p. 105.

[29] On the unrest and the reestablishment of guilds, Kaplan, "Réflexions sur la police du monde du travail," pp. 27–30.

[30] Kaplan, *La Fin des corporations*, p. 109. This echoes the earlier judgment of Sewell, *Work and Revolution in France*, pp. 76–77.

[31] Perrot, *Genèse d'une ville moderne*, I: 338.

[32] Watts, *Meat Matters*, p. 102.

[33] Kaplan, *La Fin des corporations*, p. 109; Sewell, *Work and Revolution in France*, p. 77; Claire Crowston, *Fabricating Women: The Seamstresses of Old Regime France, 1675–1791* (Durham, NC: Duke University Press, 2001), pp. 211–212. See also AN F¹² 786, edict of king concerning arts and trades of cities under jurisdiction of parlement of Rouen, April 1779. The reforms enacted may also have served to stifle the debate on guilds after 1776.

it was clearly well over a hundred.[34] Whatever the precise number was, it was reduced considerably, to fifty.

Furthermore, guilds were not automatically reconstituted – in the reorganization there were three categories of membership and former masters had to pay new fees to be admitted to a reorganized guild, a stipulation that made the reestablishment of guilds unpopular.[35] In addition, the property of many of the abolished corporations had been sold,[36] and each guild had to receive new statutes in order to reestablish itself. All this put guilds in a provisional state – one that extended for many years – and left them weak and divided.[37]

Outside of Paris, regulations for reestablishing corporations were promulgated later,[38] and detailed records on the reorganization of guilds in Lyon provide insight into the manner in which the reconstruction led to a state of fragility in many of the new corporations. During January 1777, the Crown issued an edict authorizing the creation of forty-one guilds in Lyon, and the reorganization consolidated many formerly separate guilds into new entities. The formerly discrete corporations of leather workers, tanners, leather dressers, skin dressers and glovemakers, belt makers and parchment makers, for example, were fused into a single guild. Likewise, the formerly separate corporations of hatmakers, nap cutters, furriers, and feather dealers were combined into a single body, and bricklayers, plasterers, stonecutters, marble workers, and pavers were also forged into a sole entity. The extent of amalgamation is evident in the fact that the forty-one guilds encompassed 132 trades, a circumstance that would have been unthinkable before the issuance of the Six Edicts.[39]

Although the consolidations through "parity of functions," as the officers of a restored corporation characterized it,[40] may have appeared more efficient from an administrative point of view – civil authorities, for example, would have fewer bodies with which to deal – the reorganization generated enormous practical problems. In many instances, the trades that were unified had formerly been bitter rivals, often quarrelling over work rights or responsibilities at job sites, in workshops, or in the streets.[41] Their awkward fusion made for a disconcerting situation, and the new corporations were not nearly as cohesive as the separate guilds had been.

---

[34] Shepherd, *Turgot and the Six Edicts*, p. 123, uses the number of 113 guilds in Paris; Kaplan, *La Fin des corporations*, p. 642, through a contemporary description of Paris, offers a figure of 124, whereas Crowston, *Fabricating Women*, p. 210, states "over 120." A contemporary guide to guilds published in 1766 lists a total of 112 guilds. *Guide des corps des marchands et les communautés des arts et métiers.*

[35] Kaplan, *La Fin des corporations*, pp. 111–112.

[36] AN Y 9509, undated list of premises of *corps et communautés*, which lists many buildings as sold; Kaplan, *La Fin des corporations*, p. 102.

[37] Kaplan, *La Fin des corporations*, pp. 252–261.

[38] Crowston, *Fabricating Women*, p. 212.

[39] AN F¹² 763, edict of king for communities of arts and trades of city of Lyon, January 1777.

[40] AN F¹² 763, letter of syndics of corporation of haberdashers of Lyon to Tolozan, July 24, 1784.

[41] *Ibid.*

The masters of the newly formed corporations were charged with drawing up the statutes of the new bodies. Ultimately, then, masters of dissolved guilds were forced to work together to draft new rules, and, not surprisingly, the process was hindered by the adhesion of many masters to "old customs" and an inability "to reconcile themselves with the provisions" of the new edict.[42]

Furthermore, because of the commingling of trades, some of the new guilds were large and unwieldy. The new guild of hatmakers had 300 masters and 1,500 journeymen or workers, and the officers of the guild had to be apportioned among the formerly separate occupations.[43] Grocers, wax makers, and candle makers were formed into a corporation that had 400 masters, and its officers had to be apportioned among the occupations as well.[44] It would take years for many of these new bodies to begin to coalesce and to assume a new sense of identity, which left them ill prepared to meet fresh challenges.

Indeed, during September 1779 the *intendant* in Lyon wrote to Jacques Necker, the Director-General of Finances, to ask for an extension until April 1, 1780, citing the uncertainty that prevailed in the formation of the new guilds, along with the slowness of decision-making that prevented masters from becoming members of them.[45] The Crown granted the extension, but during December 1781, nearly five years after the edict reestablishing guilds had been promulgated, the *intendant* complained about the efforts of the masters of the reestablished guilds to reconstitute the corporations. The *intendant* had convened a committee of magistrates and others to assist him in examining the statutes presented to the municipal government by the new bodies. From the outset, however, the process had been largely ineffectual, with many useless or inconsequential articles among the statutes submitted. Furthermore, many of the proffered rules were overly long, threatening to "recreate the spirit of the old regulations" and thereby, among a host of other difficulties, breed confusion and disorder. The proposed regulations advanced by the corporations, the *intendant* asserted, offered little for the common good or to advance commerce and manufacturing.[46]

The reorganization of guilds also moved only gradually in lesser cities. In the medium-sized cities under the jurisdiction of the *parlement* of Rouen, including Caen, Alençon, Bayeux, and smaller cities such as Dieppe, Evreux and Le Havre, the Crown proclaimed the reestablishment of guilds only in April 1779. The edict stated that the Crown sought to achieve a balance between the number of corporations and charges for rights of admission to them and the size of the cities and towns in which they were situated. Consequently, the edict established thirty-four guilds in Caen, and twenty-

[42] AN F[12] 763, undated draft of royal edict concerning royal edict of April 1777.
[43] AN F[12] 763, list of communities of arts and trades of city of Lyon.
[44] *Ibid.*
[45] AN F[12] 763, letter of intendant to Necker, September 5, 1779.
[46] AN F[12] 763, letter of intendant to Villevault, December 22, 1781.

three guilds in Alençon, Bayeux, and the smaller towns, although the smaller towns had lower admission charges.[47] At the same time, in smaller towns also there were difficulties in reestablishing corporations. In Langres, reorganization did not occur until late February 1781, nearly four years after the promulgation of the edict.[48]

Although guilds were slow to reorganize and were reduced in number, they once again became a ubiquitous and prominent feature of urban life, particularly in the enforcement of their privileges. During 1781, shortly after the reorganization of their guild, shoemakers in Issoudin sought enforcement of their monopoly on the production of shoes against merchants and street vendors who were selling shoes not turned out by the guild.[49]

In Paris, the reorganization of guilds proceeded slowly, even in the critical area of food supply. The corporation of butchers had its statutes approved only on December 10, 1782, and those of the guild of bakers were not promulgated until April 1, 1783.[50] The guild of lace makers–embroiderers, merged into that of ribbon weavers and ribbon makers, was reestablished only in August, 1784.[51] Some of these consolidations, including that of lace makers and embroiderers, were explicitly intended to end seizures and contestations that had arisen when the trades were separately organized.[52]

Despite the delays, guild members reverted to conflicts over privilege, including resort to seizures. During 1784 and 1785, for example, members of the vinegar and lemonade sellers' guild came into conflict with the corporation of fruit and cream sellers over the right to sell mustard. Members of the vinegar and lemonade sellers' guild had seized merchandise from the fruit sellers, which resulted in the arrest of members of the vinegar and lemonade sellers' corporation. Although they were acquitted on all charges after arguing that their seizures had been cleared by the police, their arrest signaled a lower threshold of tolerance for extralegal measures.[53]

The Crown continued to dispense privileges through the guild system. During February 1788, for example, the Lieutenant-General of Police of Paris

---

[47] AN F¹² 786, edict of king concerning communities of arts and trades of cities under jurisdiction of parlement of Rouen, April, 1779.

[48] AN F¹² 761, dossier 22, letters of lieutenant-general of police to Villevault, December 19, 1780; February 22, 1781.

[49] AN F¹² 761, dossier 18.

[50] AN AD XI 13, letters-patent of king, supplying statutes and regulations of guild of ... butchers for city and outskirts of Paris, June 1, 1782, registered in parlement December 10, 1782; AN AD XI 14, letters-patent of king conveying statutes and regulations for guild of ... bakers for city of Paris, given at Versailles, April 1, 1783.

[51] AN AD XI 14, letters-patent of king, conveying suppression of guild of master lace makers and embroiderers and their joining with corporation of merchant ribbon makers and ribbon weavers of Paris, given at Versailles August 5, 1784 and registered in parlement August 20, 1784.

[52] *Ibid.*

[53] AN Y 9530, interrogation and judgement of Lallemant, Rigny, Beauvais, Boron, and others, April 21, 1785.

reviewed and endorsed letters-patent of the king establishing a privilege for four butcher stalls.[54] By the late 1780s, then, corporations throughout France were once again functioning and participating in the system of privilege in which they were a major component, even if most guilds were not as united or cohesive as they had been before 1776.

THE ADVENT OF MECHANIZATION

At the same time, however, the 1780s saw the acceleration of a development that would ultimately become the inverse of the guild system of artisans – mechanization of production. On the French side, one of the motives in negotiating the Eden–Vergennes Treaty of 1786 to promote trade between Great Britain and France had been to hasten modernization among French manufacturers by compelling them to improve technology and manufacturing processes, and there is evidence that it succeeded in that goal.[55] In fact, it was the French who had been the driving force in concluding the treaty in the face of British reluctance.[56]

As Jeff Horn observed, the signing of the treaty was not an act of fatuousness or arrogance.[57] Rather, it was a carefully considered policy with diplomatic and economic objectives. The French Crown hoped that a commercial treaty would improve Anglo-French relations and increase the industrial and commercial position of France.[58] Furthermore, there was an expectation in France that government would take the lead in bringing about mechanization of production, particularly through the dissemination of machines.[59]

Unfortunately, the conclusion of the treaty coincided with a sharp recession, and many contemporaries conflated the two, attributing the economic difficulties to the treaty. In fact, the economic downturn was well underway in 1786, whereas the treaty did not take effect until May 1787.[60] Even if it did not cause the economic crisis, however, the treaty ultimately exacerbated

---

[54] AN Y 9500, opinion of police for establishment of privilege of four butcher stalls, February 22, 1788.

[55] Orville T. Murphy, *The Diplomatic Retreat of France and Public Opinion on the Eve of the French Revolution, 1783–1789* (Washington: The Catholic University of America Press, 1998), p. 67; on the success of the effort Alain Becchia, *La Draperie d'Elbeuf (des origines à 1870)* (Rouen: Publications de l'Université de Rouen, 2000), p. 441. Indeed, Becchia cites the treaty as a dividing line in the history of French manufacturing. *Ibid.*, p. 332.

[56] Orville T. Murphy, "DuPont de Nemours and the Anglo-French Commercial Treaty of 1786," *The Economic History Review* (New Series), 19 (1966), pp. 574–575; Marie Donaghay, "Calonne and the Anglo-French Commercial Treaty of 1786," *The Journal of Modern History* 50 (on-demand supplement) (1978), D 1166.

[57] Jeff Horn, *The Path Not Taken: French Industrialization in the Age of Revolution 1750–1830* (Cambridge: The MIT Press, 2006), pp. 66–69.

[58] *Ibid.*, pp. 65–67.

[59] *Ibid.*, pp. 57–58, 71, 79.

[60] On the lack of causality between the treaty and the economic crisis, *ibid.*, pp. 64–70.

it and led to great hardship, particularly in textile-producing areas. During December 1787, for example, the royal drapers convened to discuss the putative destruction resulting from the treaty as well as to ameliorate conditions for the unemployed.[61] Indeed, mechanization emerged especially, though not exclusively, in the textile and textile-related sectors.

In Rouen, garters, braids, edging, and lace had been woven by artisans, but during the 1780s these trades were threatened by mechanical production. The Chamber of Commerce of Rouen, among others, denounced the treaty, but also recognized that new methods of production were necessary to counter British economic dominance.[62]

Indeed, French producers, particularly in Normandy, but also elsewhere, sought to meet British competition with vigorous programs of their own. In 1786 a cotton manufacturer in Louviers, Alexandre de Fontenay, became one of the first French manufacturers to mechanize production.[63] In 1788, the provincial assembly of Normandy established a "Bureau of Encouragement for Agriculture, Commerce and the Public Good" and the Chamber of Commerce of Rouen allotted considerable funds for the purchase and dissemination of machines.[64] The Crown also allocated funds and donated machines, again demonstrating the manner in which government was expected to take the lead in modernization.[65]

Similarly, in Dauphiné, mechanization had begun in the cotton industry by late 1787, but Swiss cotton, even with a tariff on its entry into France, hindered its development. One manufacturer, however, believed that by procuring machines and placing a substantially higher tariff on Swiss cotton, Dauphiné could become a major center for cotton spinning.[66] Clearly, French producers sought to respond to the challenge of mechanization.

For their part, artisans did not remain passive as mechanization of production advanced. During the eighteenth century French workers resorted to destroying machines far less frequently than their English counterparts, but episodes of machine-breaking became more widespread during the 1780s. In Saint-Etienne, Falaise, Rouen, and Troyes, workers attacked machines to protest mechanization.[67]

---

[61] Murphy, *The Diplomatic Retreat of France*, p. 74.

[62] *Ibid.*, p. 75; Marc Bouloiseau, *Cahiers de doléances du tiers état du bailliage de Rouen*, 2 vols. (Paris: Presses universitaires de France, 1957), I: xlix–l; Horn, *The Path Not Taken*, pp. 72–74.

[63] Robert Legrand, *Révolution et Empire en Picardie: Economie et finances* (Abbeville: F. Paillart, 1985), p. 19.

[64] *Ibid*; William M. Reddy, *The Rise of Market Culture: The Textile Trade and French Society* (Cambridge: Cambridge University Press, 1984), pp. 54–57.

[65] Horn, *The Path Not Taken*, p. 82; Margaret C. Jacob, *Scientific Culture and the Making of the Industrial West* (Oxford: Oxford University Press, 1997), pp. 167–168, 177.

[66] AD Isère 2 C 90, state of different industries in Dauphiné 1787.

[67] Jeff Horn, "Machine-Breaking in England and France during the Age of Revolution. (Controversy/Controverse)," *Labour/Le Travail* 55 (2005): 143–166, especially pp. 154–166; Horn, *The Path Not Taken*, pp. 109–110, 114–115.

Although Paris was a major center for consumer consumption, mechanization in the Paris region was limited in scope, impaired in part by the financial crisis that overtook France during the 1780s.[68] Furthermore, to the degree that there was an inverse relationship between mechanization and the strength of guilds, the relative lack of mechanization in Paris testified to the major role played by guilds in the capital.[69]

The conflict and tension between the process of mechanization and the guild system in Paris is particularly evident in the experience of Jean-Baptiste Réveillon, the wallpaper manufacturer who had his residence and factory sacked during late April, 1789.[70] Réveillon had become a merchant mercer,[71] but mercers were prohibited from manufacturing items, which brought him into conflict with guilds when he sought to produce wallpaper, particularly flocked paper, when the Seven Years War ended the importation of English wallpaper. Recognizing the feuds that his enterprise would provoke with Parisian corporations, Réveillon moved his operation to Normandy, but the venture was not profitable, leading him to move back to Paris. He did not seek guild membership, but did purchase the right to practice the trade of copperplate printer, albeit from a body whose jurisdiction was often contested by Parisian corporations.[72] Despite his putative acquisition of the privilege to practice the trade of copperplate printer, the guild of printers sought to seize Réveillon's presses, although they were enjoined in their effort. Nevertheless, conflict with several corporations continued.

The conflicts led Réveillon to move to the *faubourg* Saint-Antoine on the outskirts of Paris – a region of "free" work over which Parisian guilds allegedly had no jurisdiction.[73] Some of the corporations with which Réveillon was in conflict, however, either entered the area or claimed some degree of authority over it, so he was not entirely beyond the reach of their claims.[74] As his business and his profits increased, largely on the strength of workers outside of the Parisian corporations, disputes with guilds grew.

To become more competitive beyond the borders of France, Réveillon needed to improve the quality of his products, the key to which was better

[68] Bertrand Gille, *Documents sur l'état de l'industrie et du commerce de Paris et du département de la Seine (1778–1810)* (Paris: Imprimerie municipale, 1963), p. 9.

[69] On the correlation, David S. Landes, *The Unbound Prometheus: Technological Change and Industrial Development in Western Europe from 1750 to the Present*, 2nd ed. (Cambridge: Cambridge University Press, 2003), p. 134.

[70] What follows is based on Leonard N. Rosenband, "Jean-Baptiste Réveillon," and Christine Velut, "L'Industrie dans la ville: Les fabriques de papiers peints du faubourg Saint-Antoine (1750–1820)," *Revue de l'histoire moderne et contemporaine* 49 (2002): 115–137.

[71] On the guild of mercers, Carolyn Sargentson, *Merchants and Luxury Markets: The Marchands Merciers of Eighteenth-Century Paris* (London: Victoria and Albert Museum, 1996).

[72] Rosenband, "Jean-Baptiste Réveillon," pp. 487–488.

[73] Kaplan, "Les Corporations, les 'faux ouvriers' et le Faubourg Saint-Antoine au XVIIIᵉ siècle," pp. 353–378; for a profile of the neighborhood, Monnier, *Le Faubourg Saint-Antoine*.

[74] Rosenband, "Jean-Baptiste Réveillon," p. 488; Velut, "L'Industrie dans la ville," pp. 133–134.

paper. To this end, he purchased a paper mill outside Paris, but this acquisition compounded his problems with labor, because paper-workers were notoriously independent. Despite difficulties with workers, the quality of paper improved, and his wallpaper business thrived.

The newly combined, post-1776 guild of bookbinders, wallcovering and paper suppliers, and hangers, along with the corporation of painters, sculptors, gilders, and marble-cutters became Réveillon's major adversaries, each claiming a portion of his production process as their privilege. The latter seized tools from Réveillon's shops, but Réveillon prevailed upon the Lieutenant-General of Police, who supervised corporations, to end the actions.[75]

In an effort to protect himself against further guild actions, Réveillon sought royal manufactory status, which would place him beyond the reach of the guild system. In 1783 both his paper mill and wallpaper works received the distinction of royal manufactory, thereby freeing him from guild inspections. His business thrived, and Louis XVI awarded him a gold medal for his contributions to the useful arts.[76]

On April 23, 1789, Réveillon addressed the electoral assembly of his home district and apparently spoke of reviving trade and manufacture. Although his remarks are unknown and may have been taken out of context, the contemporary perception was that he had called for a reduction of wages to 15 sous per day, which was approximately the price of a loaf of bread.[77]

During the evening of April 28 a mob burst into the grounds of Réveillon's residence and wallpaper works and sacked both; when the police arrived they fired on the looters, resulting in heavy casualties. In the view of Leonard Rosenband, the sacking of Réveillon's residence and business was, in part, the revenge of the guildsmen from whom he had always set himself apart.[78]

The experience of Réveillon with Parisian corporations demonstrated the inherent hostility between guild privilege and the nascent process of mechanization, modernization, and innovation and the memory of it lingered for decades. Réveillon retired in 1791 – Jacquemart and Bénard revived his manufactory that same year – but the enterprise remained a large and successful establishment well into the Napoleonic era.[79]

THE ENCOUNTER OF GUILDS WITH REVOLUTION

It was reflective of how deeply embedded corporations were in French society that, outside of Paris, the primary assemblies in urban areas to prepare for the meeting of the Estates-General were held by guilds.[80] In Paris, however, where

---

[75] Rosenband, "Jean-Baptiste Réveillon," pp. 496–497.
[76] *Ibid.*, pp. 498–499, 502.
[77] *Ibid.*, p. 503.
[78] *Ibid.*, p. 509.
[79] Velut, "L'Industrie dans la ville," p. 132.
[80] To give but one example, see AN B[a] 12, *liasse* 7, dossier 7, documents 1, 8.

voting was carried out by district rather than by corporation, a tax requirement for participation in assemblies limited the presence of artisans.[81]

Among the general *cahiers* – the final distillation of the *cahiers* drawn
up in primary assemblies – the attitude toward corporations was mixed.
According to Beatrice Hyslop, among general *cahiers*, forty-six supported
the maintenance of guilds in some fashion. The most unequivocal expression
of support came from the Third Estate of Brest, which not only advocated
the maintenance of current guilds, but also the extension of the guild system
to all arts and trades in which it did not exist.[82] At the same time, however,
a far greater number of *cahiers* advanced criticisms of guilds, although only
a small number sought outright suppression, and many were willing to make
exceptions for large towns or particular industries. According to Hyslop,
eighty-two *cahiers* requested the abolition of corporations in some manner.[83]
Curiously, the issue of guilds, whether advocating preservation or suppression, appeared overwhelmingly in the *cahiers* of the nobility – it was not a
major concern for the Third Estate.[84] Although criticism was directed against
guilds, most of the objections attempted merely to reform corporations by
reducing or eliminating charges or other such measures. Furthermore, with
615 general *cahiers*, the topic of guilds was dealt with in any manner in
only a minority of them – fewer than 21 percent.[85] Among artisans, *cahiers*
called for protection against mechanization and expressed hostility toward
machines.[86] Ultimately, however, the issue of corporations came before the
National Assembly not because of their presence as an issue in the *cahiers*,
but in an entirely unanticipated fashion – as a result of the meeting of the
night of August 4.

The Estates-General, called to address the fiscal crisis that had developed,
opened during May, 1789, and immediately fell into a deadlock that continued for weeks.[87] On June 17, the commons – a term the Third Estate used
to designate itself during the stalemate – took the title of National Assembly.
Three days later, on June 20, finding itself locked out of its meeting room, the
National Assembly moved to a nearby tennis court and took an oath not to
disband until it had given France a constitution. A week later, on June 27, Louis
XVI appeared to accept the National Assembly when he asked the recalcitrant
members of the clergy and the nobility who had refused to join it to do so.

[81] Peter Jones, *Reform and Revolution in France: The Politics of Transition, 1774–1791*
(Cambridge: Cambridge University Press, 1995), p. 166.
[82] Beatrice Fry Hyslop, *French Nationalism in 1789 According to the General Cahiers*, reprint
edition (New York: Octagon Books, 1968), pp. 127–128.
[83] *Ibid.*, p. 133.
[84] *Ibid.*, p. 270.
[85] *Ibid.*
[86] Peter McPhee, *Living the French Revolution, 1789–99* (Basingstoke: Palgrave Macmillan,
2006), p. 28.
[87] On the period of June–July, 1789, Michael P. Fitzsimmons, *The Remaking of France: The
National Assembly and the Constitution of 1791* (Cambridge: Cambridge University Press,
1994), pp. 33–52.

Seeking to forge a sense of identity and to move forward with an agenda, the Assembly, in accordance with its resolution on June 20, undertook to write a constitution. It created the Committee on the Constitution to act as a steering committee for the Assembly, and on July 27 the committee made its first presentation to the Assembly.

The first committee member to speak, Jean-Baptiste-Marie Champion de Cicé, archbishop of Bordeaux, summarized its deliberations. Champion de Cicé stated that the committee believed itself obligated to take constituents' views as expressed in the *cahiers* into account, and offered an initial chapter of the constitution.

Another committee member, Stanislas-Marie-Adélaïde, Comte de Clermont-Tonnerre, followed with a presentation that summarized the *cahiers* on the issue of a constitution. He told the Assembly that although the *cahiers* were unanimous in their desire to see a reorganization of the kingdom, they did not agree on the extent of that reorganization. Some *cahiers* sought merely to reform abuses and to repair the "existing constitution," whereas others sought a new constitution altogether.[88]

Because the matter at hand was that of drawing up a constitution, the question of guilds never arose. But the restrained approach of the committee made it unlikely that the issue of guilds would have been addressed at all.[89] Just eight days after the July 27 report by the Committee on the Constitution, however, the scope of the work of the National Assembly increased exponentially as a result of the historic meeting of the night of August 4. In the aftermath of that meeting, the National Assembly committed itself to a complete remaking of the French polity, including the world of work, through its promised abolition of guilds.[90]

Scholars have observed that the deputy who appears to have raised the issue of guilds during the meeting was a well-known opponent of them, but this is less important than the fact that their suppression was entirely consistent with the renunciation of privilege and the abolition of the corporate structure that propelled the relinquishments that evening. Although historians have disagreed on whether the deputy proposed reform or abolition of guilds, the preponderance of evidence indicates that it was abolition that he proffered.[91]

---

[88] *Procès-verbal de l'Assemblée nationale*, no. 33 (July 27, 1789), 8; *Archives parlementaires* 8: 280–285; BN Mss. Nouv. acq. fr. 4121, fol. 90.

[89] On the cautious approach of the National Assembly during the period from May to August, 1789, Michael P. Fitzsimmons, "From the Estates-General to the National Assembly, May 5 – August 4, 1789," in *The Origins of the French Revolution*, Peter R. Campbell, ed., (Basingstoke: Palgrave Macmillan, 2006): pp. 268–289.

[90] For a more extensive consideration of the night of August 4 and its results, Michael P. Fitzsimmons, *The Night the Old Regime Ended: August 4, 1789, and the French Revolution* (University Park, IL: Pennsylvania State University Press, 2003).

[91] The confusion that long surrounded the issue is evident in Albert Mathiez, "Les corporations ont-elles été supprimées en principe dans la nuit de 4 août 1789?" *Annales révolutionnaires* 8 (1931): 252–257.

To be sure, the minutes of the National Assembly for the August 4 meeting mention reform – a principal source of the confusion that surrounds the issue – but they were drawn up several days after the meeting.[92] The more contemporaneous writings of deputies, in those instances in which guilds are mentioned, are nearly unanimous in stating that abolition had been decreed.[93] Furthermore, newspaper reports and other printed items, especially handbills that began circulating before the measures appeared in an official decree – many of which would have been shouted in urban centers by street hawkers anxious to gain the public's attention – announced the suppression of corporations, creating a perception that they would soon be abolished.[94]

One Parisian newspaper, for example, published an item on August 13, 1789, in which the suppression of guilds was treated as if it was already an accomplished fact and praised the imminent transformation of the workplace.[95] In similar fashion, another Parisian newspaper reported that guilds had been abolished during the meeting of August 4, but the next day noted that the article decreeing their abolition was "susceptible to modification."[96] The retreat by the

[92] *Procès-verbal de l'Assemblée nationale*, No. 40 bis (August 4, 1789), p. 41; see also AN C 30, dossier 250, document 44.

[93] More contemporaneous refers to letters written or entries made before the official decree was formulated. See, for example, AM Bayonne AA 51, no. 23; AD Ain 1 Mi 1, letter of August 6, 1789, fol. 183; AM Strasbourg AA 2003, fol. 120; BHVP Ms. N.A. 108, fol. 193; [Jacques-Samuel Dinochau], *Histoire philosophique et politique de l'Assemblée nationale, par un député des communes de B*****, 2 vols. (Paris: Deveaux, 1789) II: 24; Adrien-Cyprien Duquesnoy, *Journal sur l'Assemblée constituante, 3 mai 1789–3 avril 1790*, Robert de Crevecoeur, ed., 2 vols. (Paris: Alphonse Picard et fils, 1894), I: 269; Saint-Just, *Chronique intime*, pp. 108, 119; *Etats-Généraux. Bulletin de la correspondance de la députation du tiers-état de la sénéchaussée de Brest* (Brest: n.p., 1789–1790), p. 235; *Etats-Généraux. Bulletin de la correspondance du Tiers-Etat, arrêté au Bureau de Rennes*, August 12, 1789; *Code de la Patrie et l'Humanité, ou des droits & des devoirs de l'homme et du citoyen*, August 6, 1789.

[94] On newspaper reports, *Affiches des Evéchés et Lorraine*, August 13, 1789. For handbills that proclaimed their abolition, see *Séance de la nuit du 4 au 5 août 1789, pour former la constitution* (BN L^{c29} 103); *Sommaire des articles convenus le 4 août 1789, pour former la constitution* (BN L^{c29} 104); *Articles de l'arrêté de l'Assemblée nationale du 4 août 1789, depuis neuf heures du soir, à deux du matin & dont le décret sera passé ce matin* (Grenoble: Allier, 1789) [Newberry Library, Case FRC 694]; *Arrêté par l'Assemblée nationale du 4 août 1789, depuis deux heures du soir à deux heures du matin. Contenant vingt articles de constitution connues par un courier extraordinaire, envoyé à Lyon le 7 du courant par les députés aux Etats-Généraux* (Marseille: F. Brebion, 1789) [Newberry Library, Case FRC 639]. On the manner in which they circulated, see the example of Bourges in Harvard University Fr 1380.20*, fols. 288–289. For other indications that the abolition of guilds was expected, see the journal of the bookseller Hardy, BN Mss. *Fonds Français* 6687, fol. 422. See also BN Mss. *Fonds Français* 13713, fol. 116; AN T* 1562/1, fol. 50. On the importance of oral transmission of major developments, Bronislaw Baczko, *Ending the Terror: The French Revolution after Robespierre* (Cambridge: Cambridge University Press, 1994), p. 3.

[95] *Journal d'Etat et du citoyen*, August 13, 1789.

[96] *Journal de la ville, par Jean-Pierre-Louis de Luchet*, August 6, 1789, August 7, 1789. Similarly, *Le Point du jour*, generally regarded as reliable, indicated that their reform was envisaged, but also made clear that the initial goal had been their suppression. *Le Point du jour*, August 7, 1789.

National Assembly on the issue of guilds is also evident in the correspondence of the deputy Théodore Vernier with the municipal officials of Lons-le-Saulnier. In his initial account of the results of the meeting, he wrote categorically of the "abolition of guilds and masterships in all cities of the kingdom," but in his next letter he amended his description to "guilds suppressed, or reformed."[97]

Indeed, the increasing sense of uncertainty that arose over the intentions of the Assembly is reflected in a spirited pamphlet debate that broke out during August 1789. A defender of corporations, citing newspaper reports and announcements in other public papers that they were going to be suppressed, mounted a defense of them, stating that their abolition would be detrimental to commerce in France. The writer asserted that the Six Corporations of Paris had lobbied the National Assembly and had been promised that the suppression of guilds would not be inserted into the constitution.[98]

The pamphlet provoked a response that argued that every member of society had the right to subsist and that this right should not be sold as it had been through the system of masterships. This writer applauded the abolition of guilds and masterships and expressed doubt that the Assembly would have been swayed from such a just measure by the Six Corporations of Paris.[99]

During this same period yet another Parisian newspaper expressed outrage that wigmakers – one of the more politically astute communities in Paris – had reorganized their guild, asking how a community could dream of reorganizing itself when corporations had just been abolished. The newspaper observed, however, that the original article decreeing the abolition of guilds – which had been included in early handbills – had been suppressed during the drawing-up of the formal decree, a development that the newspaper stated it could not understand.[100]

Why did the National Assembly quickly and almost furtively retreat from its intention to abolish corporations?[101] The strongest evidence on the question is to be found in an exchange of letters between the deputy Jean-François Begouen-Demeaux and his constituents in Le Havre during August 1789. After receiving the official decrees of August 4–11 from Begouen-Demeaux, his constituents complimented him on "this excellent work" that, they wrote, they had not even dared to ask for in their *cahiers*, but they inquired as to why guilds had not been mentioned in the official text.[102] Begouen-Demeaux wrote back on August

---

97 AD Jura 1 Mi 167, letters of August 3, 1789 [sic] and August 4, 1789.

98 *L'Oracle françois, dédié à l'Assemblée Nationale, au Roi et à toute la Nation* (Paris, n.d.).

99 (M. de Jabin), *Liberté du commerce, abolition des maîtrises et jurandes, suppression des moines* (Paris: Laurens, n.d.).

100 *Chronique de Paris*, September 4, 1789.

101 Much to the consternation of one unnamed deputy who complained in the Assembly about the dropping of the article on guilds by the committee charged with drawing up the decrees. *Bulletin de l'Assemblée Nationale*, August 8, 1789.

102 AM Le Havre D² 1, fol. 99 v°. Their question again underscores the attention that the unofficial lists of renunciations had received.

20 that "guilds have been deliberately set aside as demanding scrutiny and the taking of various precautions. Thus, nothing was decided on their account."[103] Indeed, still reeling from continuing turmoil in the countryside – evident in a decree on August 10 calling for the restoration of order – the National Assembly, mindful, perhaps, of the disorder and confusion that had occurred in 1776 after Turgot's abolition of corporations, did not wish to put forward a measure that had the potential to incite additional unrest in cities and towns.

Furthermore, during August 1789 labor unrest was rife in Paris and during mid-August rumors circulated that workers in Montmartre were planning to stage a revolt, leading Lafayette to address them in an effort to ease tensions.[104] The volatile situation in cities other than Paris is equally evident in the admonition of the Minister of War to the commandant of Lille, advising the latter to resign himself to the existence of bourgeois militias because in the current state of affairs it was impossible to enforce the law. Moreover, the minister stated, prudence demanded that the commandant "close his eyes" to minor infractions that occurred in the city.[105] In such a setting, the prospect of liberating journeymen from the perceived disciplinary strictures of guilds was unnerving, and this may have played a role in the Assembly's decision to defer action on the matter of guilds until some future date.

On August 11 the Assembly explicitly reaffirmed its desire not to eliminate guilds. A deputy presented article X of the proposed decree proclaiming the results of the meeting of August 4, an article that pronounced the suppression of all of the special privileges of the "Provinces et municipalités, des villes, corps et communautés." A member of the Assembly noted that unless the words *"d'habitants"* were added to *"corps et communautés,"* the suppression of corporations would be enacted. The Assembly immediately added the words, meaning that the decree applied to small villages or hamlets rather than to guilds – it was tantamount to a specific exemption for guilds.[106]

Despite the National Assembly's attempt to defer the issue, the incertitude surrounding corporations increased in late August with the promulgation of the Declaration of the Rights of Man and Citizen. Article one, of course, proclaimed the equality of men, an ideal particularly damaging to guilds, as Turgot's abolition of them had demonstrated.[107] Furthermore,

---

[103] AM Le Havre D³ 38, no. 40, letter of August 20, 1789. This development accords with the revision of articles mentioned by the *Journal de la ville, par Jean-Pierre-Louis de Luchet* and with the readjustment of goals specified by *Le Point du Jour*. For more on the internal debate in the National Assembly, see the letter from the deputy Baco to the bureau of correspondence in Nantes in *Etats-Généraux. Journal de la Correspondance de Nantes*, 10 vols. (Nantes, 1789–1791), II: 134. On the continuing nature of this internal division, see AM Strasbourg AA 2005ª, fol. 19.

[104] *Démarches patriotiques de M. de La Fayette, à l'égard des ouvriers de Montmartre* (Paris, n.d.).

[105] AN M 667, dossier 17, letter 8. The letter is dated September 15, 1789.

[106] *Bulletin de l'Assemblée Nationale*, August 11, 1789. It was almost certainly this action that led to the puzzlement expressed in newspapers and pamphlets.

[107] Steven Laurence Kaplan, "Social Classification and Representation in the Corporate World of Eighteenth-Century France: Turgot's 'Carnival,'" in *Work in France*, pp. 186–88.

article four pronounced that each man's exercise of his natural rights had no limits but those guaranteed to all other members of society and stated that such limits could be determined only by the law. Against the backdrop of the delegitimization of privilege that the August 4 meeting had initiated, these articles made the position of guilds disputable.[108] As a result, the events of August 1789 – the confusion produced by the August decrees compounded by the principles put forward in the Declaration of Rights – inaugurated a period of deep uncertainty for guilds throughout France.

THE REACTION OF GUILDS

In his memoirs, Jean-Sylvain Bailly, the former mayor of Paris, recalled that because their abolition had been expected, a wave of unrest swept through guilds during the weeks after August 4.[109] Only days after the promulgation of the August decrees, on August 16, the Commune of Paris – the municipal government – received reports of irregularities brought about by anticipated interpretations of decisions taken by the National Assembly, and in particular that regulations within the guild of butchers were being ignored by itinerant butchers eager to sell their products. After careful consideration, the Commune decreed that because only positive and sanctioned laws could overturn laws that had always been respected and were still in force, the established regulations for all corporations, but especially that of butchers, should be followed in both letter and spirit.[110] Nevertheless, in September 1789 itinerant butchers in Paris were still selling their meat two days per week, at the expense of masters of the butchers' guild.[111]

One scholar of corporations has written that the typical form of protest during the eighteenth century was not the food riot or strike, but the lawsuit, and it is indicative of journeymen's awareness of their legal rights that such contestations began almost immediately.[112] Only two days after the decree concerning the guild of butchers, the master tailors of Paris appeared before the Commune to seek relief from a work stoppage by their journeymen, who

---

[108] See AM Bordeaux D 85, fol. 107v°; AN D IV 32, dossier 767, document 14; AN D IV 49, dossier 1400, document 7; *Chronique de Paris*, September 4, 1789.

[109] Jean-Sylvain Bailly, *Mémoires d'un témoin de la Révolution*, 3 vols. (Paris: Baudouin, 1822), II: 275.

[110] APP DB 402, extract from minutes of Assembly of representatives of Commune of Paris, August 16, 1789; *Actes de la Commune de Paris pendant la Révolution*, Sigismond Lacroix, ed., 7 vols. (Paris: L. Cerf, 1894–1898), I: 235. On problems in the guild of butchers, AN F[12] 781[A], dossier 3, undated petition of butchers and proprietors of stalls of Paris to Legislative Assembly; Watts, *Meat Matters*, pp. 161–162.

[111] *Chronique de Paris*, September 14, 1789. It appears that the new and uncertain situation was one that contemporaries found disquieting. See *Chronique de Paris*, September 27, 1789. On the butcher trade in general, Hubert Bourgin, *L'Industrie de la boucherie à Paris pendant la Révolution* (Paris: Ernest Leroux, 1911).

[112] Michael Sonenscher, "Journeymen, the Courts and the French Trades 1781–1791," *Past and Present* 114 (February 1987): 77–109, especially pp. 86–90.

were seeking a wage increase and making other unspecified demands.[113] Although Bailly indicated that this action was an outgrowth of the August 4 meeting, work stoppages were a traditional form of protest so this occurrence was not particularly unusual. Indeed, whereas the situation with the corporation of butchers had a sense of urgency because of the implications for public health, the Commune acted somewhat less vigorously in relation to tailors, simply citing its decree of two days earlier.[114]

If guilds no longer possessed the same degree of power, however ineffective it may often have been, to enforce their exclusive control of their trade, they did retain, at least initially, the support of municipal authorities in protecting their monopolies. During September 1789 officers of the guild of wigmakers presented 3,000 livres to the municipal government and asked it to maintain discipline among journeymen wigmakers and to end "insubordination" by enforcing regulations. The corporation had been facing unrest since mid-August, when its journeymen had voted to lower the registration fee they paid from twenty *sols* to eight, and had further demanded that half of the eight *sols* be used to provide care for journeymen wigmakers who fell ill and could not care for themselves.[115] By late August the journeymen wigmakers had retained a barrister to put forward their demands.[116]

Bailly replied to the guild officials that the municipality intended to adhere to existing laws until the National Assembly deemed it appropriate to order a reform.[117] In fact, during December 1789 the Châtelet continued to enforce the wigmakers' monopoly by seizing the tools of individuals who had established themselves in the trade outside of the guild.[118] In similar fashion, on September 9, 1789, the booksellers and printers' guild of Paris met in order to vote a gift of 20,000 livres to the National Assembly – an action aptly characterized as a "symbolic overture to the new sovereign" – and followed on November 12 with an appeal to the Keeper of the Seals to suppress unlicensed printing shops.[119]

Concern about the status of corporations was not limited to Paris; the degree of uncertainty confronting them is evident in a letter written by the corporations of Toulouse. During September 1789 they appealed to the National Assembly to preserve their privileges and argued against proclaiming the right of each individual to work freely in any trade.[120]

[113] BHVP Ms. 894, fols. 38v°–39; *Actes de la Commune de Paris*, I:268; Bailly, *Mémoires*, II: 276–277.
[114] *Actes de la Commune de Paris*, I: 268.
[115] BHVP Ms. 894, fol. 38v°.
[116] BHVP Ms. 894, fols. 45–45v°.
[117] *Actes de la Commune de Paris*, II: 80; BHVP CP 4867, letter of Leclerc, August 3, 1789; letter of wigmakers' guild to mayor and representatives of commune, September 3, 1789; *Chronique de Paris*, October 2, 1789. See also AN D IV 65, dossier 1957, document 3, for a similar request to the National Assembly from the wigmakers of Castres.
[118] AN Y 13016ᴮ, entry of December 12, 1789.
[119] Carla Hesse, *Publishing and Cultural Politics in Revolutionary Paris, 1789–1810* (Berkeley, CA: University of California Press, 1991), p. 51.
[120] AN C 98, dossier 128, document 30. This document is undated, but it is mentioned in *Procès-verbal de l'Assemblée nationale*, No. 81 (September 22, 1789), pp. 2–3.

A particularly unusual situation developed in Grenoble during the fall of 1789. On November 26 municipal authorities allowed carpenters to separate themselves from the guild of masons, plasterers, and stonecutters and to form a corporation of their own. This was done because there were as many carpenters as there were masons in the corporation and its meetings had become virtually unmanageable due to the large number of men in attendance. The carpenters were henceforth to form their own corporation in order to govern themselves and to address their own concerns.[121] At the same time, however, during February 1790, in an indication of the guilds' pervasive sense of insecurity, the guild of masons, plasterers, and stonecutters decided unanimously not to elect officers for the coming year until the National Assembly had rendered a decision on corporations – a decision with which, they declared, they would fully comply.[122]

The sense of indeterminacy is equally apparent in a *mémoire* that the master locksmiths of Aix-en-Provence submitted to the National Assembly in early January 1790. They noted that they had been organized in a corporation since 1587 and had, during the intervening years, consistently paid various taxes to the government. The guild had been abolished by Turgot's edicts of 1776, when the government had sought to make all professions free but, the locksmiths asserted, "the disadvantages of this freedom were not long in making themselves felt [and] soon necessitated the return of the current regime." The locksmiths then noted that the same freedom had initially been announced as one of the benefits for which the nation would be indebted to the members of the National Assembly but, they argued, the wisdom of the deputies had led them to suspend their judgment on such a sensitive article. The *mémoire* went on to present a series of arguments against the abolition of guilds, particularly that of locksmiths.[123]

The locksmiths did not mention any tradesmen who had attempted to establish themselves as locksmiths outside of the corporation, indicating that their guild's authority was not under any direct challenge. At the same time, however, the apprehension of the locksmiths – one of the corporations that could legitimately lay claim to *sui generis* status, given its particularly pivotal role in urban life – attests to the general level of concern about the possible abolition of guilds. Nevertheless, to all appearances, at the beginning of 1790 the guilds, although apprehensive, were relatively secure in their position and generally continued to enjoy the support of local authorities.

One should not, however, infer that corporations in France were altogether passive or cowering fearfully as they awaited a decision from the National Assembly. During early January 1790 in Grenoble, for example, officers of the different guilds of the city met to protest the daily wage rate set by municipal authorities for the upcoming municipal elections. The municipality had fixed the local daily wage rate at fifty *sols*, which the guild officials claimed would

---

[121] AM Grenoble FF 56, fols. 567–570v°.
[122] *Ibid.*, fols. 571–571v°.
[123] AN D IV 20, dossier 412, documents 1–2.

prevent about two-thirds of citizens from participating. Indeed, claiming the fundamental principles of the Revolution as their own, the guild officials stated that the threshold set by the municipality was "the greatest injustice in a government where all men are equal in rights," and asked that the wage rate be set instead at twenty-five *sols*.[124]

As this episode attests, members of corporations felt no conflict between their status as members of a guild and their loyalty to the principles of the Revolution – indeed, in their communication to the municipal government and without irony, the guild officers in Grenoble had praised the National Assembly for "opening all occupations."[125] Likewise, although the desire to ingratiate itself with the National Assembly must be taken into account – it was requesting measures to assist their enterprise – the corporation of cloth producers of Bédarieux effusively hailed the decrees of the National Assembly, characterizing them as "the profound wisdom of enlightened politics."[126] Again, even allowing for the desire to curry favor with the Assembly, as well as for flattery and hyperbole, the letter indicates the degree to which there was little perception of a conflict between being a member of a corporation and a supporter of the Revolution. In addition, the statement by many guilds that they would submit to whatever decision the Assembly rendered underscores the perceived harmony between being a member in good standing of a corporation and being a good revolutionary.

In Paris during late 1789 the guilds, although somewhat dispirited, continued to operate in the usual fashion.[127] On November 9, 1789, for example, the guild of bakers conducted the election of its officers in a routine manner, with a commissioner from the Châtelet present, and the guild of tanners did the same on November 14.[128] The guild of tailors gathered on November 25 for the election of officers, but the unrest that had begun in August continued to roil the corporation – many of its members walked out of the election.[129] Moreover, various corporations continued to accept new members in 1789, albeit at a diminished rate.[130]

A good example of the indeterminate status of guilds as a result of the new ideals proclaimed by the National Assembly is to be found in Bordeaux where, during May 1790 the municipality, concerned about public order, adopted an ordinance concerning journeymen wigmakers in the city. Observing that "thoughtlessness and impatience to enjoy the fortunate effects of the decrees

---

[124] AM Grenoble LL 162, deliberation of syndics of corporations of city of Grenoble, January 10, 1790.

[125] *Ibid.*

[126] AN F¹² 652, letter of guild of cloth producers of Bédarieux to unnamed recipient, December 5, 1789; *mémoire* of cloth producers of town of town of Bédarieux to National Assembly, December 5, 1789.

[127] On the dispirited state of guilds in Paris, BHVP Ms. 742, fol. 233.

[128] AN Y 14437ᴮ, entry of November 9, 1789; AN Y 11207ᴮ, entry of November 14, 1789.

[129] AN Y 12079ᴮ, *procès-verbal* of election of deputies of guild of tailors, November 25, 1789.

[130] AN Y 9334; Y 9395ᴮ.

of the National Assembly" had led to "insubordination" among journeymen of many trades in Bordeaux, the *procureur* of the commune urged the municipal council to bring this to a halt. He noted that at the news of the abolition of privileges, journeymen believed that corporations had been destroyed but, the *procureur* went on to note, the National Assembly had deferred action on the matter in what he called "a wise precaution" taken in the interest of both masters and journeymen. The *procureur* stated that it was among journeymen wigmakers that most agitation was occurring – they had flagrantly contravened the regulations of their corporation and were working in concert to take over the work of the masters.

The *procureur* asked the municipal council to follow the example of the Commune of Paris, which was experiencing similar difficulties. The representatives of the Commune in Paris had ordered the enforcement of the regulations and statutes of the wigmakers' guild until the National Assembly decreed new laws and regulations. A similar measure in Bordeaux, he asserted, would produce greater public order. On his recommendation, the mayor and municipal officers stipulated, among other measures, the continued enforcement in Bordeaux of the regulations and statutes of the wigmakers and a prohibition on journeymen wigmakers and those of other trades from gathering.[131]

Similarly, during June 1790 more than 300 individuals in Amiens wrote to the president of the National Assembly to argue that article ten of the Declaration of Rights implicitly entailed the abolition of corporations because it suppressed privileges of every sort. On this occasion, however, the *procureur* of the commune of Amiens – at the behest of guildsmen, in the opinion of the petitioners – had decreed that all men exercising a trade without a certificate had to acquire one. The workers had earlier written to the National Assembly seeking a decision on the legality of the ruling of the *procureur* and, fearing closure of their shops, renewed their request in their June letter.[132]

In other locales, the privileges of some guilds were dismantled, although in early 1790 such actions were the exception rather than the rule. In Grenoble, on March 13, 1790, the municipal council lifted all restrictions on the trade of butcher, provided that individuals observed certain rules decreed by the council. It also allowed inhabitants of the city to buy meat for themselves outside the city walls, although they would have to pay a tax on it at the city gates. The council proclaimed that the measure was being enacted so that the public could enjoy the benefits of freedom of commerce in relation to meat and to assure a steady supply.[133] The action effectively destroyed many of the reasons for the existence of the guild of butchers.

---

[131] AM Bordeaux D 85, fols. 107v°–109.

[132] AN D IV 64, dossier 1924, document 1. In actuality, it was the August decrees rather than the Declaration of Rights to which they were referring, but it is clear that they thought of them as of equal importance.

[133] AM Grenoble HH 18, proclamation of mayor and municipal officers of city of Grenoble, March 14, 1790. On similar contestations with guilds in Lille, Jean-Pierre Hirsch, *Les*

In general, however, corporations continued to function in a generally normal fashion until the latter half of 1790. Indeed, in some instances, they behaved in the same manner as in the past, seeking to protect their privileges, although now they appealed to the National Assembly rather than municipal authorities. During February 1790, for example, the Paris guild of booksellers and printers wrote to the Assembly about the number of printers who had proliferated outside of the guild. Calling the multiplicity of printers that had sprung up outside of the corporation an "abuse of freedom of the press," the guild argued that it had produced an even greater abuse – "an infinity" of individuals who could barely read had established shops in every neighborhood of Paris. Their commerce, the corporation asserted, consisted largely of pirated editions, libels, and pornography.

The booksellers and printers argued that their guild had always been exempt from the suppression of corporations, a reference to 1776. The reason for this, the guild claimed, was that the poor would become corrupted by subversive works if everyone were granted the right to trade in books. The guild asked the Assembly to fix the number of printers in Paris and the major cities of the kingdom and that no one be allowed to be a printer if he could not read Latin and Greek.[134] In a similar vein, during June 1790 a delegation from the butchers' guild of Paris appeared before the National Assembly seeking enforcement of its statutes, although it received little sympathy with respect to its complaint about individuals operating outside of the guild.[135]

In another indication that the daily routine of corporations continued, during March 1790 the guild of shoemakers in Paris reported that it was the victim of a burglary at its office.[136] Moreover, just as corporations had participated in civic processions under the Old Regime, in Paris members of guilds turned out *en corps* – on one occasion an enormous number of wigmakers showed up – to help prepare the Champ de Mars for the Fête de la Fédération in 1790.[137] It was, in fact, not unusual for each corporation to arrive at the Champ de Mars with its own flag.[138]

Outside of Paris as well, guilds generally maintained themselves throughout the year 1790. In Rouen, for example, the guild of tailors admitted journeymen during May and September 1790 and during October 1790 it undertook action against tailors practicing outside of the guild.[139] At the same

Deux rêves du commerce: Enterprise et institutions dans la région lilloise (1780–1860) (Paris: Editions de l'Ecole des Haute Etudes en Sciences Sociales, 1991), pp. 238–240.

[134] AN D XIII 1, dossier 12, documents 1–2.

[135] *Courier de Madon*, June 1, 1790; *Journal des décrets de l'Assemblée Nationale, pour les habitans des campagnes*, May 29-June 4, 1790; *Procès-verbal de l'Assemblée Nationale*, No. 306 (June 1, 1790), p. 23.

[136] AN Y 11208ᴬ, entry of March 12, 1790.

[137] AD Jura 1 Mi 167, letter of July 7, 1790; *Chronique de Paris*, July 10, 1790; *Courier provincial*, July, 1790 (no. 12).

[138] *Journal des décrets de l'Assemblée Nationale, pour les habitans des campagnes,* July 10–16, 1790.

[139] On the admissions, AD Seine-Maritime 5 E 706, fols. 113vº-117; on the action against those outside of the guild, AD Seine-Maritime 5 E 680, entry of October 19, 1790.

time, however, the guild was not immune to unrest, and had difficulties with journeymen in May 1790.[140] Similarly, in November, 1790 the guild of glove makers and perfume makers in Rouen sought to compel the entry of a woman whose shop was already open and who had already gained a one-month delay on entering the guild.[141] In Bordeaux, the guild of joiners admitted journeymen during July 1790 in a ceremony before a municipal officer.[142]

In an indication of their vitality in Grenoble, on June 28, 1790, three dozen officers representing more than two dozen corporations of the city met for a collective deliberation. Almost certainly as a result of the decision of the municipal council on March 13 that had done away with all restrictions on the trade of butcher, the guild of butchers was not represented and had, in all probability, begun to disintegrate.[143] Other guilds, however, continued to operate in a normal fashion – on June 17, 1790, the guild of bakers elected officers and on September 2, 1790, it admitted a new master. Just over two weeks later it sought to improve relations with the newly elected municipal officials.[144]

If 1790 was a decisive year of transition, it is clear that, in Paris at least, the critical month for the guilds was July, although the reasons for this are not entirely clear. Possibly the Fête de la Fédération and the spirit of fraternity and common purpose that it generated delegitimized guilds, with their more circumscribed outlook.[145] Whatever the reason, the decline of corporations, especially in Paris, accelerated after July 1790. The record of admission of new members to guilds in the city in fact ceases in June 1790.[146] In a letter to journeymen tailors at Rennes, who had written to complain about corporations, the Breton deputies Jean-Denis Lanjuinais, Jacques Defermon and Joseph Lancelot asserted in late December 1790 that in Paris, with the exception of those of the goldsmiths, apothecaries and key makers, most guilds were moribund.[147] The registers of the booksellers and printers' guild of Paris, one of the few Parisian corporations whose records have survived, generally

---

[140] *Ibid.*, entries of May 3, 1790, May 19, 1790.

[141] AD Seine-Maritime 5 E 474, fol. 50v°.

[142] AM Bordeaux D 86, fol. 112v°. For additional evidence of the survival of guilds in outlying departments, see AN C* II 11, fols. 322v°, 392v°, 402v°; AN C* II 12, fols. 13, 67v°, 114v°, 128v°, 214, 247, 301, 311, 343, 376; AN C* II 13, fols. 21v°, 78, 130v°, 132, 142v°, 160v°, 167v°, 183, 237v°, 262v°, 306v°.

[143] *Délibération des différentes corporations de Grenoble* (Grenoble: Allier, 1790). Of forty-one guilds in Grenoble, twenty-nine were represented in the deliberation, suggesting that other guilds had begun to atrophy as well.

[144] On the election, AM Grenoble FF 56, fols. 571v°–572; on the admission of a new master, AM Grenoble FF 55, fol. 323; on the effort to improve relations with the municipal officials, AM Grenoble HH 13, letter of syndics of guild of master bakers to mayor and municipal officers of Grenoble, September 20, 1790.

[145] For an example of the erosion of the corporate outlook, see the speech by members of the *basoche* in Urbain-Réné Pilastre de la Brardière and J.B. Leclerc, *Correspondance de MM. les députés des communes de la province d'Anjou avec leur commettants relativement aux Etats-Généraux ... en 1789*, 10 vols. (Angers: Favie, 1789–1791), V: 567–568.

[146] AN Y 9334.

[147] *Journal des départements, districts et municipalités de la ci-devant province de Bretagne; et des amis de la constitution.* VIII: 377.

support this assertion. Although it continued to meet, the guild was in a state of atrophy, with the frequency of its meetings steadily decreasing.[148] The guild of parchment makers, which was small, remained in existence.[149]

It is indicative of the perceived ambiguity of the position of the National Assembly that other tradesmen who were beneficiaries of the Old Regime structure wrote to the Assembly asking it to protect their rights. During October 1790, for example, the guild of cabinet makers in Lille appealed to the National Assembly for the maintenance of its rights.[150] Likewise, the two authorized printers in the town of Dunkirk sought the Assembly's support against several printers who had set up presses there. Their letter reflects the clash of outlooks brought about by the Revolution. The printers buttressed their case with prescriptive tradition, citing edicts of January 10, 1719, March 31, 1739, and August 30, 1777, whereas the new printers cited the freedom of the press proclaimed by the National Assembly.[151]

Although printers were in a particularly sensitive sphere, their situation is a compelling illustration of the dilemma in which many guildsmen found themselves. Guild fidelity was not a reliable measure of political engagement, because many fervent supporters of corporations were equally fervent supporters of the Revolution. They endeavored to resolve what seems, in retrospect, a contradiction much greater than it appeared to many contemporaries.[152] Thus, in Bordeaux during January 1791 a deputation from the corporation of naval carpenters and another from that of wigmakers appeared before the city's municipal officers. The naval carpenters affirmed their love and respect for the constitution and renewed their oath to die for it. Two days later the wigmakers appeared in order to demonstrate their attachment to the constitution and to renew their civic oath.[153]

The manner in which the ideals unleashed at the August 4 meeting could undercut corporations is evident in a petition from the guild of goldsmiths in Paris to the National Assembly during September 1790. The corporation began by observing that many individuals had appeared before the National Assembly to renounce their privileges, but no corporate body had followed this example – instead, corporate bodies had stubbornly defended their privileges and monopolies. The corporation of goldsmiths, which professed to enjoy as many exclusive rights as other guilds, renounced its privileges and gave to the National Assembly, it claimed, the first signal of the reforms that should, by removing the hindrances placed on work and industry, bring about the completion of national freedoms.

---

[148] BN Mss. Microfilm 4884. On the records of the book guild, Hesse, *Publishing and Cultural Politics*, pp. 56–57.

[149] AN F¹² 652, *mémoire* for parchment makers, January 20, 1791.

[150] AN F¹² 761, dossier Lille, letter to Committee on the Constitution, October 13, 1790.

[151] AN D IV 46, dossier 1334, document 4. A similar situation had arisen earlier in Paris. See AN D XIII 1, dossier 12, documents 1–2.

[152] See, for example, AN D IV 65, dossier 1957, document 3.

[153] AM Bordeaux D 89, fols. 5, 15vᵒ.

The goldsmiths acknowledged the evils of the structure of guilds – they were monopolistic and restrictive, and enabled the basic right to work to be treated as a privilege. The goldsmiths asked that in return for their renunciation they be allowed to retain the rights of stamp and control on gold and silver.[154] The fact that the corporation of goldsmiths, which claimed more than a thousand members, was reduced to seeking to negotiate with the National Assembly less to assure its survival, which it appears implicitly to have conceded by agreeing to surrender its privileges, than to simply preserve some degree of jurisdiction over the trade, is a sign of how quickly and thoroughly the new principles generated by the August 4 meeting had advanced.

As a result of the indeterminate status of corporations, contestations of guild regulations continued unabated. From La Fere, in Picardy, during December 1790 a man named François Mourlet wrote to the National Assembly to appeal for its support against the guild of bakers there. Mourlet noted that through several of its decrees the Assembly had abolished all privileges, but in spite of that four or five bakers at La Fere, affirming themselves as a corporation by virtue of an edict of April 1777 sought to prevent him from practicing as a baker. It was not a question of his abilities, which he claimed they recognized, but that they demanded a large sum from him before they would allow him to open a shop. He was unable to meet it, and the putative guild continued to pursue him with legal proceedings. After denouncing the injustice of the guild, Mourlet appealed to the Assembly to allow him to practice freely with an open shop. He said that he would conform to all police ordinances and even offered to submit to an examination if the Assembly so desired.[155]

By contrast, during February 1791 the guild community of Bayonne sent an address to the Assembly seeking to preserve corporations and sent copies to guilds of other cities in an effort to orchestrate a larger movement. Asserting that an erroneous interpretation of article IV of the Declaration of Rights had allowed a host of workers of all trades to operate outside the guild structure, effectively destroying it, they asked the Assembly to address the situation of corporations.[156]

Indeed, the new structure of work that was evolving, however slowly, was an unsettling, even terrifying, prospect to many guildsmen. At a meeting of the corporation of joiners and cabinet makers of Rouen during February 1791 masters of the guild informed members that a large shipment of furniture of all types had arrived in the warehouses of a businessman in the city. The furniture could be sold at public auction or to anyone who presented himself to the businessman. The masters stated that, if this report were true, three-quarters of them would have to close their workshops, let their journeymen go and limit themselves to keeping in their shop the furniture produced since the

---

[154] AN AD XI 65, dossier Orfèvres, document 10.
[155] AN D IV 43, dossier 1192, document 2.
[156] AD Seine-Maritime 5 E 648.

Revolution. This, in turn, would render them unable to meet their obligations, jeopardizing their families and workers, thus it was necessary to anticipate the measures necessary to prevent such a disaster. The masters decided to present a request to the municipal officers of Rouen to ask that the furniture be sent to another city to avoid the ruin of a great number of families.[157]

THE REACTION OF PUBLIC AUTHORITIES

The uncertain course of the National Assembly with respect to corporations posed a particular problem for public authorities. On the one hand, the National Assembly had a reform agenda and had announced its intention to address the question of guilds, however tentatively it was doing so. On the other hand, across France corporations sought to preserve and maintain their rights and privileges, which, even if they seemed antithetical to the principles of the Revolution, had not been officially abrogated.

Consequently, even if they continued to function in a relatively normal manner, as time went on corporations were less able to enforce their monopolies and, as a result, throughout France irregular situations arose that demanded the attention of municipal or departmental authorities. In Rennes, for example, master joiners and shoemakers took action – with seizures, fines, and other measures – against journeymen who had begun to practice these trades freely, prompting the administration of the Department of Ille-et-Vilaine to write to the National Assembly for advice. The administrators averred that although no decree had explicitly abolished guilds, the exclusive privileges that guilds enjoyed seemed contrary to the rights of man and individual liberties. The administrators also feared greater violence if journeymen came to believe that they would not be able to find work, and asked the National Assembly to inform them of the course they ought to follow.[158]

The late summer and early fall of 1790 brought many changes that significantly altered the situation of guilds. In municipalities throughout France corporations of various trades were under assault, generating social tension. In yet another indication of the manner in which the guilds were on the defensive, local officials, rather than reflexively supporting corporations as had often previously been the case, sought guidance from the National Assembly on what action should be taken.

This shift resulted in part from a change in the structure of politics and power, from a system of privileged corporatism to a new ideal of the polity, defined by laws common to all. Whereas the local authorities in office in early 1790 had, for the most part, been products of the system of privileged

---

[157] AD Seine-Maritime 5 E 519, fols. 55–55v°.

[158] AN D IV 33, dossier 806bis, documents 4–5. The terms are taken from the petition, but the issue was clearly less that of the journeymen not being able to find any work than whether they would work in continued subordination or not. See also *Journal des départements, districts et municipalités de la ci-devant province de Bretagne*, VII: 96.

corporatism,[159] those in power during the summer and fall had assumed office as a result of elections based on the new ideal of the polity. These new public officials were also concerned with discipline in the workplace and the maintenance of public order, leading them initially to uphold the rights of guilds. As time passed, however, they became more inclined to adhere to the political ideals formulated at the August 4 meeting or in the Declaration of Rights. In those instances in which municipal officers were not receptive to their claims, workers often did not hesitate to invoke the authority of the National Assembly or approach it directly.

In Le Havre, for example, in early November 1790 the newly elected district tribunal wrote to the Committee on the Constitution to inform it that many individuals had presented themselves to the tribunal seeking to be admitted to various trades, claiming that, because of the abolition of privileges, guilds were effectively abolished, and that this was the case in Paris. Heretofore, the judges noted, municipal authorities had maintained the rights of guilds, and the judges were now writing to inquire whether they should continue to do so.[160]

Likewise, in Dieppe a group of tradesmen wrote to the Committee on the Constitution in October 1790 to argue that because the National Assembly had proclaimed all men equal in rights and had abolished privileges of every sort, corporations should no longer be allowed to levy charges on individuals for the right to practice a trade. The municipality backed the guilds, however, closing the shops of the authors of the letter and giving them one month to pay the charges. The men appealed to the committee for support.[161]

By the fall of 1790 the question of guilds had remained unsettled for more than a year, and the predicament in which public authorities found themselves was particularly evident in Paris. In early November 1790, the Committee on the Constitution replied to a letter from the mayor of Paris, Bailly, on the question of privilege, although the reply makes it clear that Bailly had focused on the question of corporations rather than the more general issue of privilege. Furthermore, the letter reflects the disarray present in the polity as the new principles put forward by the Assembly took root, as well as the confusion produced by the continuing inaction of the National Assembly. The committee stated that although many privileges had passed into oblivion as a result of the Declaration of Rights, it did not follow that the suppression of a given privilege ought to be left to each citizen to decide, because no citizen could anticipate what law might be passed. Consequently, without considering whether or not guilds ought to survive, the committee argued that their effects could be abolished only by a law.[162]

---

[159] There had, of course, been municipal revolutions during the summer of 1789 that had replaced some urban leadership, but officially, at least, those in office were products of the old system.

[160] AN D IV 61, dossier 1827, document 1.

[161] AN D IV 61, dossier 1827, document 2.

[162] AN D IV 6, dossier 85, document 5.

The letter clearly did little to clarify or resolve the confused situation of guilds in Paris or anywhere else in France. On the one hand, it sought to discourage individuals from anticipating the law and undertaking independent action. On the other, and perhaps more importantly, it was hardly the unequivocal endorsement of corporations and their rights the municipal authorities had been seeking. Indeed, the disclaimer about not examining whether or not guilds ought to survive, followed by the statement that the effects of guilds could be abolished only by a law, could be seen as a tacit acknowledgement that significant changes would be forthcoming.[163] The letter provided little incentive for Parisian authorities or those elsewhere either to enforce strictly the rights of corporations or to move decisively against those who called those rights into question.

Once again, however, the tension between the regulations of corporations and the new principles proclaimed by the National Assembly was particularly evident in Bordeaux. On October 29, 1790, Jean Savent, a journeymen wigmaker, was arrested at the request of the wigmakers' guild for having left the shop of his master nine days earlier in order to establish his own shop. After refusing a request by a group of masters to return to the shop of his master, Savent was arrested. Under questioning, he admitted that he knew he was in violation of the corporation's rules, but said that he did not recognize those statutes and regulations because they had been abolished by the Declaration of the Rights of Man.

The officers of the guild asserted that the Declaration of Rights had no application to his situation, but Savent replied that there was a major connection between the Declaration and his contestation with the guild because it was a question for him of obtaining the enjoyment of liberty common to all French enumerated in the document. He then read a report from the *Courier français* of October 13, 1790, and entered this into evidence.

The passage he read was an account of the visit of the deputation of Parisian goldsmiths to the National Assembly on October 11. It reported, apparently erroneously, that the visit had given rise to an examination of guilds as they had existed under the Old Regime, with the Assembly deciding that the present state of finances precluded any action at this time, but concluding with the statement that in the meantime the Assembly declared that the guideline for the behavior of each individual would be the Declaration of Rights, which allowed each member of society to exercise his talents as he saw fit.[164]

---

[163] It is clear that there was a strong belief that action against guilds was imminent. AN D IV 22, dossier 474, document 10; AN D IV 33, dossier 805bis, document 1; AN D IV 65, dossier 1957, documents 1, 2.

[164] For the passage, see *Courier français*, October 13, 1790. A search of other sources offers no corroboration for the remarks reported in the *Courier français*. See, for example, *Journal des débats et des décrets*, October 11–12, 1790; see also the account provided by members of the National Assembly in Pilastre de la Brardière and Leclerc, *Correspondance de MM. les députés du Département de Maine-et-Loire*, VI: 607.

The guild officials pointed out that the account did not mention a decree of the National Assembly that deferred such questions to current law, and stated that there were numerous decrees that continued guilds in their existing state until otherwise ordered. They added that Savent should feel it only just, for example, that the privileges of wigmakers be preserved because they had paid for their offices and that in the account he had read it appeared that the National Assembly did not wish to make any innovations in the trades because of the state of finances. Savent replied that he respected the decrees of the National Assembly to the point of no longer recognizing anything from the Old Regime, but that he would work as he had previously. In return for ceasing his independent practice and returning to the shop of his master, the charges against him were dropped.[165]

Clearly concerned by the arguments that Savent had made, however, the master wigmakers of Bordeaux sent an address to the National Assembly providing details of the state of their profession. They informed the Assembly that from the time that the Declaration of Rights had been promulgated their journeymen had interpreted it to allow them to do anything not prohibited by law. As a result, many had left the shops of their masters and opened their own. This had adversely affected the 200 master wigmakers in Bordeaux, and, after offering details of the hardships they had had to endure, the wigmakers asked the Assembly to reestablish order in their corporation and decree the maintenance of its rights.[166]

On December 20, 1790, the wigmakers received a favorable decision from the Committee on the Constitution. Although the committee noted that the National Assembly was preparing to rule on masterships and guilds, it stated that it was "indispensably necessary" to maintain regulations and statutes, and that the regulations of the wigmakers' guild therefore ought to be enforced because nothing had yet changed. The wigmakers quickly took the ruling to the municipal government, which posted it throughout the city.[167] Although the Committee on the Constitution and the municipal government had ruled very narrowly, citing only wigmakers, the proclamation forbidding non-master wigmakers from practicing the trade heightened tension among all journeymen in the city.[168]

---

[165] AM Bordeaux I 81, no. 56.
[166] AN D IV 32, dossier 767, document 14.
[167] AM Bordeaux D 88, fols. 130v°–131.
[168] *Le Spectateur national et le modérateur*, January 30, 1791. The situation of wigmakers throughout France was a special one, because they had often been forced to buy a large number of brevets from the Crown. As a result, their financial condition was often weak, and it is possible that municipal governments, for fiscal reasons, may have been more protective of them. For a situating of guilds in the fiscal structure of the Old Regime, see Gail Bossenga, *The Politics of Privilege: Old Regime and Revolution in Lille* (Cambridge: Cambridge University Press, 1991), p. 127, for the wigmakers. See also AN D IV 49, dossier 1400, document 7. The National Assembly ultimately granted them special consideration by not using the 1771 valuation as the basis for the liquidation price of their office. For more on the National Assembly and the liquidation of venal offices, see William Doyle, "The Price of Offices

The continuing uncertain position of guilds is evident in a letter written by the municipal officers of the town of Coutances to the National Assembly on January 1, 1791. After receiving a lengthy petition dated December 24, the officials implored the National Assembly to provide them with guidance with respect to various corporations in the town. For several months many merchants and workers had believed that, with all privileges suppressed, they were free to open shops and sell their merchandise or labor without having to satisfy the regulations prescribed by "the preceding regime." The existing merchants, for their part, claimed that they had had to meet those regulations before they could practice their profession.

These competing claims had led to many questions being brought before the municipality for resolution and, under the circumstances, it had postponed any ruling. Recently, however, the new merchants, who had been tolerated in the expectation of a decision from the National Assembly, had asked the municipality in the December 24 petition to determine their fate by conveying their wishes to the Assembly. When it was sent to the Assembly, the letter of the municipal officers, along with the petition, was reinforced by a letter from the administrators of the directory of the Department of Manche, who told the deputies that a prompt decision was vital to maintain peace and order in towns in which corporations were established.[169]

Similarly, in early January 1791 the municipal officers of Riom wrote to the National Assembly after it was reported in some handbills that the Committee on the Constitution had issued an opinion that because corporations had not been explicitly suppressed, the statutes that regulated them should continue to be enforced.[170] The news of this opinion had provoked investigations and legal proceedings against non-guild tradesmen in Riom. These tradesmen had presented themselves to the municipal authorities, invoking "the letter and spirit of our new laws, this freedom and equality that leaves to each man the natural use of his skills to satisfy his needs" as well as the proscription of privilege, which, they claimed, meant that ability was to be the only distinction in society. The authorities told the Assembly that these workers could not be persuaded that the Committee on the Constitution, which had contributed to breaking their chains, would not impose new ones. The municipal officers reported that the workers had said that it would be intolerable to return to a state of servitude after they had enjoyed "the charms of liberty."

For their part, the officials stated, guild masters valued the rights that they had bought and the privileges that had been secured by the old regulations, which had not been abolished. They believed that the reported opinion of the Committee on the Constitution favored their position.

---

in Pre-Revolutionary France," *Historical Journal* 27 (1984): 831–860, and William Doyle, *Venality: The Sale of Offices in Eighteenth-Century France* (Oxford: Clarendon Press, 1996), pp. 275–311.

[169] AN D IV 41, dossier 1102, documents 19–21.

[170] It is not entirely clear, but this almost certainly appears to be a reference to the opinion given by the Committee on the Constitution to the wigmakers of Bordeaux.

The municipal officers informed the National Assembly that this powerful clash of interests placed them in a difficult position as they sought to preserve peace and tranquility in Riom. Imbued, they said, with the principles of the constitution, they stated that they preferred to lean toward the rights of man, which, they said, gave to each individual the free exercise of his talents. They averred that a recent decree of the National Assembly reinforced their penchant, telling the deputies that newspapers had reported that journeymen wigmakers of Paris had won the freedom to work without constraint in their trade, despite the complaints and actions of the wigmakers' guild. If this decision were true, they stated, it would point the way out of the difficulties Riom was experiencing.

The officials asked the Assembly to inform them on the truth of the matter of the Parisian wigmakers, and to instruct them on what they should do to temper the impatience of the various guild masters in Riom. If their privileges, whatever they were, were to be maintained, or if they had not yet been abrogated by the dispositions implicit in the new laws, the authorities said that out of loyalty to the ideal of obedience to the law they would enforce those privileges. They closed their letter by observing that the situation in Riom was doubtless replicated in many other towns, making it a question of the tranquility and interests of a large number of citizens.[171]

A similar situation existed in Perpignan, and the municipal officers there likewise sought guidance from the National Assembly. Some merchants from outside the city had established shops and were openly selling their goods, but the city's guild had lodged a complaint with the municipal authorities, asking them to compel the newcomers to conform to the law. Torn, they said, between the public interest resulting from the freedom of commerce and the apparent justice of the masters' petition, they had decided to consult the Assembly before making a decision. They solicited answers to two questions: Did a French citizen from outside of a town in which corporations existed have the right to open a shop and, if he did not, should the municipality move against him by rigorously enforcing the regulations governing corporations?[172]

The administrators comprising the directory of the Department of Bas-Rhin in Strasbourg also wrote to the National Assembly in early January 1791 because of their uncertainty regarding the competing claims of laws or statutes that had not been suppressed versus the natural rights proclaimed in the Declaration of the Rights of Man. They, too, posed a series of questions and sought clarification from the Assembly, writing twice in fifteen days as the situation in Strasbourg became more unsettled. They pressed for a quick decision on an issue that they said affected the fate of many of their fellow citizens.[173]

[171] AN D IV 53, dossier 1540, document 1.

[172] AN D IV 55, dossier 1592, document 4.

[173] AN D IV 56, dossier 1654, document 2; AN D IV 55, dossier 1605, document 1. The problems with corporations in Strasbourg went on into the following month. AN C 54, dossier 537, document 12³.

Although it appears to have been sent directly to the National Assembly by workers rather than forwarded by municipal or departmental authorities, a much stronger petition, dated January 31, came from Lyon. It reveals, however, that the reason for the restiveness among workers was the lack of a determination by the National Assembly on the issue of corporations, and that this restiveness was of concern to public officials.

Also reacting to the news of the journeymen wigmakers of Paris to which the municipal officers of Riom had alluded, a large group of citizens from Lyon sent a petition to the National Assembly to ask for the abolition of all masterships and corporations. The petition opened by extolling the Declaration of the Rights of Man and then, in what was an apparent reference to the journeymen wigmakers of Paris, praised that city for proclaiming the free practice of one's skills, "even though the law that should abolish masters and guilds has not yet been passed." The Revolution, they said, was intended for all of France, and the citizens of the second city were still in the grip of what they termed the despotism of guilds. The workers asserted that daily outrages were committed against workmen by corporations seeking payment to allow them to practice a trade.

They asked for a law suppressing all guild structures, which they said divided men and made them enemies, as one persecuted the other. The only reason they had not written earlier was that they had long hoped that such a law would be forthcoming. They expressed confidence that their request would be granted, and claimed to have 2,316 signatures, collected from all sections of the city, affixed in support of it.[174]

THE REACTION OF THE NATIONAL ASSEMBLY AND ITS RESOLUTION OF THE ISSUE OF GUILDS

Despite the succession of appeals it received from guildsmen, ordinary citizens, and public officials, the National Assembly failed to respond or clarify its position throughout 1790 and into 1791. On October 11, 1790, after the visit by the deputation of Parisian goldsmiths, the Assembly decided to send the petition that the delegation presented to its Committee on Agriculture and Commerce, which had originally been charged to prepare a project on guilds. Some members of the Assembly were dissatisfied with this decision, however, because it was the committee's failure to produce a project that had largely been responsible for the Assembly's inaction and apparent equivocation. One member sought to have it referred instead to the recently formed joint committee of the Committee on the Constitution and Committee on Revision, but this motion was defeated. Instead, the petition was sent to both the Committee on Finances and the Committee on Agriculture and Commerce, which were to meet jointly.[175] The exchange

[174] AN D IV 57, dossier 1674, document 3.
[175] On the request of the goldsmiths, AN D XIII 1, dossier 1, undated address of goldsmiths to National Assembly; letter of Tournachoy(?), October 10, 1790. For the discussion in the

brought into the open, however, the dissatisfaction felt by many in the Assembly toward its Committee on Agriculture and Commerce.

This displeasure was not misplaced. The committee, which had come into existence in early September 1789, was comprised largely of obscure backbenchers and had only one Parisian deputy, Pierre Samuel Dupont (de Nemours), who was serving on eight committees before he resigned from nearly all of them in July 1790.[176] Dupont, an economic liberal, was the most prominent member and his departure served to push an already minor committee further into the background. Indeed, the committee's status would have been of little consequence if it were not responsible for the issue of corporations, and its inertia frustrated many deputies.

One deputy claimed during the spring of 1790 that the committee was reviewing Turgot's edict as well as thousands of *mémoires*, but a report on its agenda issued at almost the same time indicated that the question of corporations was not a major priority. Although the report mentioned in passing that the committee intended to prepare a law against exclusive privileges of different kinds, it made no specific mention of guilds.[177] As a result, although many members of the National Assembly envisaged the abolition of guilds – during the summer of 1790, for example, the Committee on Finances was attempting to estimate the cost of reimbursement for their suppression – the Committee on Agriculture and Commerce did not bring forward any project.[178]

Furthermore, it is evident that the Committee on Agriculture and Commerce had no intention of producing a report. In a committee meeting on September 13, 1790, a member, following up on several earlier efforts, again raised the question of preparatory work on the matter of guilds so that the committee would be ready to deal with the issue if it came up in the Assembly – another indication that the Assembly as a whole expected abolition. Other committee members, however, did not wish to take up the issue out of concern that it could increase unrest in France. The unnamed member who proposed the preparatory project stated that he was not suggesting that the matter be placed before the Assembly if the committee was not forced to do so, but that he simply did not want it to be caught off guard. The committee agreed with these views and charged the Marquis de Boufflers, a man with a reputation for indecisiveness, with the project.[179]

Assembly, AN C 45, dossier 415, document 4; *Procès-verbal de l'Assemblée nationale*, No. 438 (October 11, 1790), pp. 5–6.

[176] On the composition of the committee, Edna Hindie Lemay, *Dictionnaire des Constituants 1789–1791*, 2 vols. (Oxford: Voltaire Foundation, 1991), II: 953; on Dupont, *ibid.*, I: 314–316.

[177] For the letter of the deputy, AD Dordogne O E DEP 5004, no. 15, letter of de la Rocque to municipal officers of Perigueux, May 15, 1790; on the report regarding the committee's agenda, AN AA 29, dossier 901.

[178] On the Committee of Finances, Camille Bloch, *Procès-verbaux du Comité des Finances de l'Assemblée constituante*, Camille Bloch, ed., 2 vols. (Rennes: Oberthur, 1922–1923), I: 307, 313.

[179] AN AF I* 10, fols. 321v°–322. The characterization of the Marquis de Boufflers is found in Marie-Jean-Antoine-Nicolas Cantat, Marquis de Condorcet, *Mémoires de Condorcet*

This exchange, and particularly the statement by the anonymous deputy disavowing any desire to place the issue of corporations before the Assembly unless forced to do so, demonstrates that the committee deliberately withheld any project on guilds from the Assembly, but the reason for this is not clear. As a result, however, throughout the fall of 1790 the committee failed to act despite numerous petitions that offered it an opportunity to take action. Virtually all matters pertaining to guilds were assigned to the Marquis de Boufflers, who simply neglected them.[180]

As is the case with the committee, the reasons for Boufflers's inaction are not apparent, but he may have become disillusioned with the direction taken by the National Assembly. In June 1790 he protested the abolition of the nobility and the month after the National Assembly disbanded he emigrated. At the same time, however, he sought to promote mechanization of production and presented a report to the Assembly advocating subsidies to inventors of machines, suggesting that he was not necessarily favorably disposed toward guilds.[181] The best explanation does appear to be that the committee was concerned about unleashing unrest in urban areas if corporations were dissolved, and Boufflers therefore delayed any project.

Whatever the reason for the committee's inaction, deputies in the Assembly had to assume an ambiguous or even disingenuous stance when they received queries from constituents. In July 1790 the deputy Jean-François Fournier de Lacharmie responded to a question from the municipal officers of Perigueux about merchants from outside the town selling their goods. Fournier informed the officials that they certainly had the right to arrest the merchants and to prevent them from selling in the town because the laws concerning guilds had not been abrogated. At the suggestion of a committee he did not name, however, he urged the officials to "close their eyes" to the situation. He stated that the Committee on Agriculture and Commerce was preparing a project, but, he asserted, at a time of unrest, rigid enforcement of the rules should not be pursued.[182]

Similarly, in November 1790 the deputy Gabriel de Cussy, who represented Caen, advised the committee that, as a result of decrees of the National Assembly, many inhabitants of Caen in various trades had opened workshops independent of the guild structure. The municipal authorities had ordered the new workshops to close, causing severe harm and leading Cussy to ask the Committee on Agriculture and Commerce to take up the matter. Instead of seizing the opportunity to settle the question of guilds, however, the committee merely authorized its president to write to the municipality

---

sur la *Révolution française, extraits de sa correspondance et de celles de ses amis* 2 vols. (Paris: Ponthieu, 1824), II: 255.

[180] AN AF I* 10, fols. 331, 336, 386v°; AF I* 11, fols. 2, 27v°, 39v°, 43, 45v°, 61–61v°, 145–145v°.

[181] Lemay, *Dictionnaire des Constituants*, I: 128–129.

[182] AD Dordogne O E DEP 5004, no. 9, letter of Fournier to municipal officers of Perigueux, July 4, 1790. The committee in question was almost certainly the Committee of Agriculture

of Caen to urge its members to maintain peace and tranquility among "this class of citizens."[183]

As the year 1791 began, the situation of guilds remained uncertain. Many deputies in the National Assembly were ready to act,[184] but the Committee on Agriculture and Commerce was content to allow the continuation and enforcement of existing regulations. As petitions were sent to the committee during January 1791, from wigmakers and other trades asking for clarification on the situation of guilds, they were assigned to the Marquis de Boufflers, who took no action.[185]

It was clear to many members of the National Assembly that some resolution was necessary, but the question of corporations remained stalled in the Committee on Agriculture and Commerce. On February 4, 1791, in an apparent effort to break the stalemate, Pierre-Gilbert Leroy, Baron d'Allarde, a member of the Committee on Taxation, appeared before a meeting of the Committee on Agriculture and Commerce and presented a project concerning customs duties of towns that included a provision abolishing guilds and masterships. Characteristically, however, the Committee on Agriculture and Commerce did not adopt or even endorse the project; it deferred consideration of it to a future, unspecified date.[186] The committee continued to operate in this manner – a few days later, when letters from wigmakers in Pézenas and Marseille arrived, they were assigned to the Marquis de Boufflers, who again did nothing.[187]

The factor that ultimately led to a resolution of the issue of guilds by the National Assembly was the concern of deputies for revenue, a logical connection because guilds were closely tied to urban fiscal structures.[188] The Committee on

and Commerce, because Fournier's comment about the timing of its report being delayed because of unrest was doubtless a justification of its conduct.

[183] AN AF I* 11, fols. 49v°–50.

[184] *Journal des départements, districts et municipalités de la ci-devant province de Bretagne; et des amis de la constitution.* VIII: 377, in which Breton deputies, during late December, 1790, alluded to pending legislation on the *patente* and implied that significant changes regarding guilds would soon be forthcoming.

[185] AN AF I* 11, fols. 193, 203, 212v°–213, 222v°–223; Vardi, "The Abolition of Guilds," pp. 713–714.

[186] AN AF I* 11, fols. 234–240. In fact, it is possible that the appearance of d'Allarde before the Committee on Agriculture and Commerce may not have been altogether cordial. Although its meaning cannot be precisely known, a passage noting that d'Allarde had been invited to deliver a copy of his report to the secretariat of the committee is crossed out. It appears that the committee regarded d'Allarde's project an intrusion into its jurisdiction and did not intend to consider it at all. The Committee on Agriculture and Commerce was responsible for reforming customs duties, so there can be little doubt that the initiative of the Committee on Taxation was, in fact, an intrusion. See Kenneth Margerison, *P.-L. Roederer: Political Thought and Practice During the French Revolution* (Philadelphia, PA: The American Philosophical Society, 1983), p. 34. The papers of the Committee on Agriculture and Commerce, however, are limited to one carton, AN D XIII 1, and they shed no light whatsoever on the abolition of the guilds.

[187] AN AF I* 11, fol. 252.

[188] Gail Bossenga, "La Révolution française et les corporations: Trois exemples lillois," *Annales: Economies, Sociétés, Civilisations* 43 (1988): 406–407.

Taxation sought to eradicate customs duties of towns, but did not want to do so without first establishing an occupational license (*patente*), which would generate revenue to replace that lost by the termination of urban customs duties.[189]

Consequently, at the meeting of the National Assembly on February 15, 1791, the Committee on Taxation preempted the Committee on Agriculture and Commerce. On that day discussion was set on customs duties of towns, but Pierre-Louis Roederer, a member of the Committee on Taxation, rose and asked the Assembly to discuss customs duties only after considering the occupational license, on which the Committee on Taxation had prepared a report. The Assembly quickly adopted his motion, and Roederer yielded to Baron d'Allarde, who presented the report.[190] He proposed the suppression of guilds and masterships, arguing that each individual should be free to practice whatever trade he desired through the simple purchase of an occupational license, which would confer the right to practice a trade.

This proposal met with opposition. The deputy Begouen-Demeaux claimed that requiring a payment for the right to work would be a violation of the rights of man. He asserted, perhaps facetiously, that any such tax should be paid by the idle and unemployed. Antoine-Charles Gabriel, Marquis de Folleville, sought adjournment of the project and asked the committee to make known the manner in which masterships would be reimbursed. Louis-Alexandre, Duc de La Rochefoucauld, a member of the Committee on Taxation, did not address the method but answered that the total cost of compensation would be more than 140,000,000 livres. Antoine-Balthazar-Joseph d'André, also a committee member, asked that the occupational license proposal be approved in principle, and the Assembly voted to do so, but delayed consideration of the specific articles drafted by the committee until the next day.[191] Consideration of d'Allarde's project began the next day. Although the deputy Jean-François Reubell and others expressed concern about the implications for public safety of allowing individuals simply to purchase a license without passing some kind of test of their skills, the Assembly overrode their objections. During a lengthy debate, the Assembly decided to suppress corporations and to reimburse those who had purchased masterships. It went on to define the issuance of the occupational license, concluding the legislation on March 2.[192]

---

[189] *Journal des Etats-Généraux*, XXI: 336–338.

[190] It was, in fact, with only a few minor changes, the same report that he had presented earlier to the Committee on Agriculture and Commerce. Additional evidence of a jurisdictional strike against the inaction of the Committee on Agriculture and Commerce is the fact that on January 15, 1791, the Committee on Liquidation established a bureau to disband and redeem guilds and masterships. See AN D XI 1, composition of bureaus of liquidations, no. 8. I am grateful to William Doyle for bringing this document to my attention.

[191] AN C 54, dossier 537, document 10; *Procès-verbal de l'Assemblée nationale*, No. 563 (February 15, 1791), pp. 4, 5–6. See also Pilastre de la Brardière et Leclerc, *Correspondance de MM. les députés du Département de Maine-et-Loire*, VII: 176–177; *Courier de Madon*, February 15, 1791.

[192] *Journal des Etats-Généraux*, XXI: 356–357. See also AM Marseille 4 D 43, fol. 35; *Procès-verbal de l'Assemblée nationale*, No. 564 (February 16, 1791), pp. 5–7, 10–16, which does

The adoption of d'Allarde's project fulfilled the original but long-delayed promise of August 4 and brought about a major redefinition in the structure of work: Labor in France became more unfettered than it had been in centuries.[193] Indeed, within a few years nearly all distinctions between journeymen and masters had been blurred, beginning the formation of what would come to be known during the nineteenth century as the "working class."[194]

In political terms, the abolition of guilds settled one of the last remaining anomalies in the abolition of the corporate paradigm by the National Assembly. The law establishing municipal governments in France had specified that municipal assemblies could not be held by trade, profession or corporations, but only by neighborhoods or *arrondissements*.[195] This provision undercut a traditional function of guilds, which had played a central role in the political process right up to the opening of the Estates-General itself, but they had continued to exist. With the passage of the d'Allarde law, the anomaly of guilds – an integral part of the world of privileged corporatism – in a nation of citizens equal in rights was now resolved.[196]

In fiscal terms as well, the abolition of guilds settled a contradiction. The fiscal benefits that corporations had formerly offered to the state had become virtually meaningless in a nation in which the tax burden was to be borne according to one's means under direct taxation. In an egalitarian nation, one could only tax workers for performing a job, if the job was open for them to take. As a result, corporations no longer made fiscal sense.[197] Furthermore, because the payment for the occupational license was annual, whereas the

---

not, however, mention the committees involved; *Assemblée nationale, corps administratifs et nouvelles politiques et littéraires de l'Europe, réunis au Journal de Versailles, des départemens de Paris, de Seine et d'Oise*, February 16, 1791; Liana Vardi, "The Abolition of the Guilds during the French Revolution," *French Historical Studies* 15 (1988): 714–717. For the completion of this project, see the supplementary legislation in *Procès-verbal de l'Assemblée nationale*, No. 578 (March 2, 1791), p. 11; *Procès-verbal de l'Assemblée nationale*, No. 604 (March 28, 1791), pp. 14–18.

[193] Sewell, *Work and Revolution in France*, pp. 86–87.

[194] William H. Sewell, Jr., "Artisans, Factory Workers, and the Formation of the French Working Class, 1789–1848," in *Working-Class Formation: Nineteenth-Century Patterns in Western Europe and the United States*, Ira Katznelson and Aristide R. Zolberg, eds., (Princeton: Princeton University Press, 1986), pp. 45–70. Although it is true that to the degree that there remained a difference between craftsmen, often employers, who purchased an occupational license, and wage earners, who did not, the former distinction between master and journeyman perhaps continued, it was in an attenuated form. In the absence of the guild infrastructure that had enforced distinctions, within a few years most lines of demarcation between masters and journeymen withered.

[195] *Procès-verbal de l'Assemblée nationale*, No. 134 (November 25, 1789), p. 7.

[196] *Réflexions patriotiques, sur la suppression des jurandes & maîtrises, l'établissement du droit de patentes, et l'abolition des droits d'entrée des villes* (Toulouse: Imprimerie Nationale, 1791).

[197] *Ibid*. On the fiscal dimension of guilds under the Old Regime, René Nigeon, *Etat financier des corporations parisiennes d'arts et métiers au XVIIIᵉ siècle* (Paris: Bieder, 1934); Bossenga, *The Politics of Privilege*.

masterships generated revenue only at the time of their purchase, it was fiscally more advantageous.[198]

THE AFTERMATH OF THE ABOLITION OF GUILDS

Particularly in Paris, except among guildsmen themselves, reaction to the abolition of guilds was almost universally positive – it was widely perceived as the attainment of rights inherent in the Declaration of the Rights of Man. The *Journal des décrets de l'Assemblée nationale* offered a representative judgment:

These dispositions should be regarded as one of the greatest benefits that the legislature has yet extended to the nation. The guilds [enjoyed] exclusive privileges that deprived the vast majority of citizens of one of the foremost rights of man, that of working. In almost all of the towns of the kingdom, the practice of trades was concentrated in the hands of a small number of individuals joined in communities which, to the exclusion of their fellow citizens, produced or sold from a particular business for which they had the privilege. In order to obtain this privilege, it was necessary to undergo all the tests [and] all the exactions that fiscal genius could invent...

They have done away with these last vestiges of servitude; all men will have the means to make use of their skills; they will not need considerable sums to establish themselves...[199]

Likewise, the Jacobin Club of Angers wrote to the National Assembly to applaud the abolition of corporations and masterships and to praise the Assembly for restoring to men their right to practice the talents they had received from nature or had acquired through hard work.[200]

A cautionary note came from a surprising source, the radical Jean-Paul Marat.[201] Although he praised the freeing of citizens from the bonds that had stifled their talents, he also asserted that dispensation from apprenticeship to practice a trade or profession was problematic. Indeed, in what would turn out to be a prescient observation, he claimed that among the principal effects of the legislation would be the ruin of commerce and a decline in trades themselves. Without apprenticeships or any kind of proof of skill or capacity, trades would soon be susceptible to intrigue and roguery.

In the future, Marat argued, it would not be a matter of craftsmen producing excellent works but simply of seducing consumers by appearance, and if a worker was denounced in one neighborhood, he could simply move to another. The only way to make society flourish, Marat wrote, was to reward talent and conduct. He stated that it would not surprise him if, twenty years into the future, one could not find a single worker in Paris who would know

---

[198] BN Mss. Nouv. acq. fr. 1777, fol. 218.

[199] *Journal des décrets de l'Assemblée nationale, pour les habitans des campagnes*, February 16, 1791.

[200] *Affiches d'Angers*, March 8, 1791.

[201] On Marat, Louis R. Gottschalk, *Jean-Paul Marat: A Study in Radicalism*, revised edition (Chicago: University of Chicago Press, 1967).

how to make a hat or a pair of boots. He argued that the occupational license was humiliating, and predicted that the decline in trades would be swift.

Bitter experience, he argued, would soon force legislators to modify the decree on occupational licenses. Marat contended that it would have sufficed for the Assembly to abolish the jurisdiction of guilds, to do away with all charges for masterships and all rights of seizure, but to allow masters to report any workers in violation of standards to the law courts. In order for trades to flourish, Marat asserted that it was essential to subject aspirants to a rigorous apprenticeship lasting six to seven years.[202]

Marat dealt with the issue again the next day, repeating and emphasizing his stance. He asserted that unlimited freedom – granting each citizen the right to practice any trade he pleased and the ability to accumulate many of them without having to demonstrate his skill – would inevitably lead to a decline in the quality of trades, of workshops, of manufacturing and of commerce. He reiterated his contention that the National Assembly should simply have reformed guilds by doing away with abuses rather than abolish them altogether. He also reiterated the necessity of lengthy apprenticeships.[203]

Louis XVI approved the legislation concerning the *patente* on March 17, and the disbanding of guilds began in Paris the following day.[204] In fact, in Paris the guilds complied and dissolved themselves without incident.[205]

In towns and cities in outlying departments, where guilds had more successfully maintained themselves – the guild of vinegar merchants in Dijon had admitted journeymen as late as February 1791 and that of glovemakers and perfume makers in Rouen had elected new officers in January 1791 and the guild of apothecaries in Bordeaux had admitted a member in March that year – the abolition was felt more keenly.[206] In Rouen, the corporation of locksmiths assembled to discuss the dissolution and, after the first master to speak argued that the guild should conform to the decrees of the National Assembly,

---

[202] *L'Ami du peuple*, March 16, 1791.

[203] *L'Ami du peuple*, March 17, 1791.

[204] BN Mss. Microfilm 4884, fol. 44.

[205] AN AD XI 65, dossier *Maîtrises et Jurandes*, documents 3, 15. The process of reimbursement, however, continued for years. BHVP Ms. 793, fol. 88; *Courier républicain*, 18 brumaire year II (November 8, 1793); 30 brumaire year II (November 20, 1793).

[206] On the vinegar merchants of Dijon, see AD Côte d'Or E* 3473, fol. 68v°; for the glovemakers and perfume makers of Rouen, AD Seine-Maritime 5 E 474, fol. 51; on the apothecaries at Bordeaux, AM Bordeaux D 90, fol. 17v°. The greater vitality of guilds in the departments is evident not only in the reports of their harassment of journeymen, but in the petitions they sent to the National Assembly as well. See AN D IV 15, dossier 281, document 2; AN D IV 21, dossier 459, document 11; AN D IV 22, dossier 474, document 10; AN D IV 32, dossier 767, document 14; AN D IV 33, dossier 805bis, document 1; AN D IV 40, dossier 1092, document 4; AN D IV 40, dossier 1092, document 15; AN D IV 63, dossier 1909, document 1; AN D IV 65, dossier 1957, documents 1–2; AN C 124, dossier 404², document 74. On the corporation of apothecaries in Bordeaux, Angie Smith, "Weighed in the Balance? The Corporation of Apothecaries of Bordeaux, 1690–1790," *The Journal of the Social History of Medicine* 16 (2003): 17–37. See also *Extrait des délibérations du corps des cabaretiers-hôtelains de la ville de Douai. Du 14 janvier 1791* (Douai: Derbaix, n.d.).

all of the others concurred.[207] The dissolution produced tension in Strasbourg, at least one of whose deputies to the National Assembly had worked to preserve guilds.[208] Similarly, in Nancy and Bordeaux, some guilds briefly sought to resist the decree, but in vain.[209]

Apprehension or dismay at the legislation was not limited to guildsmen. In Saintes, one resident worried that although the suppression of guilds conformed to the principles of the Revolution, it would lead to deterioration in the quality of bread and meat.[210]

Nevertheless, corporations in the departments, in compliance with the decree, also soon began to dissolve themselves. The guild of saddle makers and carriage builders in Dijon gathered in the church at which they customarily met to hear a reading of the decree suppressing corporations. The members then withdrew the effects of their guild and ratified its dissolution.[211] Other guilds in Dijon simply surrendered their records to the municipality.[212] The guild of vinegar merchants dolorously noted the wave of change that had swept over its members during the preceding two years by alluding to "the former master vinegar merchants of the town of Dijon, former capital of the former province of Burgundy ..." as it dissolved itself.[213] In Rouen and Bordeaux municipal officers received the accounts of guilds and terminated their existence.[214] The National Assembly made the buildings and furnishings of guilds national property, and they were inventoried in the same manner as church lands.[215]

In Grenoble, all forty-one guilds quickly disbanded, although the wigmakers were dilatory in submitting their accounts.[216] There were debts to be liquidated, and the effects of different corporations were to be sold in order to pay creditors.[217] In the Department of Isère, and in cities and towns throughout France, after enduring for centuries, guilds ceased to exist.[218]

[207] AD Seine-Maritime 5 E 648, fols. 23v°–24.
[208] *Le Spectateur national et le modérateur*, March 1, 1791; on the effort to preserve them, AN C 54, dossier 537, document 12³; AM Strasbourg AA 2005ª, fol. 19.
[209] AN C 131, dossier 461, document 58; *Procès-verbal de l'Assemblée nationale*, No. 585 (March 9, 1791), p. 2; Heimmermann, "Work and Corporate Life in Old Regime France," pp. 625–626. For another example from an unknown location, AN D IV 63, dossier 1918, document 22.
[210] BM Saintes 25486 MAR, II: 91–92.
[211] AD Côte d'Or E* 3366, fols. 7–7v°.
[212] AD Côte d'Or E* 3370, entry of April 10, 1791; E* 3372, fols. 121–121v°; E* 3473, fol. 69.
[213] AD Côte d'Or E* 3473, fol. 69.
[214] AD Seine-Maritime 5 E 474; 5 E 648; AM Bordeaux D 91, fols. 80–80v°; Heimmermann, "Work and Corporate Life in Old Regime France," p. 625. As in Paris, the dismantling of guilds was a prolonged process in Lille. Hirsch, *Les Deux rêves du commerce*, p. 240.
[215] BN Mss. Nouv. acq. fr. 1777, fol. 230; AM Marseille HH 388, entry of December 13, 1791; AD Isère L 284, documents 4, 11.
[216] On the disbanding, AD Isère L 284, document 7; on the dilatoriness of the wigmakers, AM Grenoble LL 162, letter of *procureur-syndic* of district of Grenoble to mayor and municipal officers of Grenoble, March 19, 1792.
[217] AD Isère L 284, document 4; AM Grenoble LL 162, account of syndic-general of bodies of merchants, arts and trades, April 28, 1792.
[218] See, for example, the letter of the administrators of the directory of the district of La Tour du Pin in AD Isère L 284, document 12.

Workers quickly made the transition to the new system of occupational licenses, which came into effect on April 1, 1791.[219] From April to June that year the municipality of Paris issued nearly 14,000 licenses and in Bordeaux the municipality had to grant two extensions of the deadline for declaring for *patentes*, with over 6,000 declarations made.[220] Indeed, municipal officials were nearly overwhelmed and the implementation of occupational licenses in Paris and elsewhere gave rise to much confusion.[221] With men from smaller towns and villages having to go to the seat of a district to receive their license, the number of individuals desiring them sometimes led to delays and prolonged stays.[222] The new system did, in fact, produce significant revenue, with 10 percent going to the municipality and 90 percent to the state, and the government sought to enforce it strictly.[223]

There was dismay and discontent among some former guild members, with some in Paris allegedly refusing to perform guard duty in the aftermath of the dissolution of corporations.[224] From early on, counterrevolutionaries had made wigmakers – who, of course, had a particularly large noble clientele – a target of propaganda, and these efforts intensified after the guilds' abolition.[225]

At the time of abolition of corporations there had been some concern about possible abuses that could jeopardize the life or health of citizens.[226] Soon after their suppression there were, in fact, problems in the meat trade in Paris in May 1791, with the sale of meat from dead or diseased animals; commerce in meat remained a source of trouble in 1792.[227]

Some corporations, such as the goldsmiths of Paris, managed to continue briefly in a surreptitious fashion.[228] In one instance, at Bordeaux, during a minor provisioning crisis during July 1791 the municipal officers summoned the former officers of the dissolved guild of bakers to deal with the problem.[229] For the most part, however, the guild structure quietly disappeared.

---

[219] Indeed, the abolition of guilds opened a new and generally prosperous path for tailors during the Revolution and Empire, especially the Empire. Johnson, "Economic Change and Artisan Discontent," p. 91.

[220] AN H² 2176, statement on deliverance of *patentes*, August 3, 1791; AM Bordeaux D 91, fols. 28v°, 162, 191; D 139, fol. 91.

[221] AN H² 2103, supplement to alphabetical collection of questions on *patente*, April 20, 1792; Alison Patrick, "French Revolutionary Local Government, 1789–1792," in *The Political Culture of the French Revolution*, Colin Lucas, ed., (Oxford: Pergamon Press, 1988), p. 409.

[222] AN F¹² 761, dossier 9, letter of municipal officers of Granville to Central Office of Commerce, January 29, 1792.

[223] AM Marseille 4 D 43, fol. 85; *Patentes: Mésures générales pour l'exécution des loix relatives au droit de patentes* (N.p., n.d.) [Newberry Library Case folio FRC 10085].

[224] *L'Abeille politique et littéraire*, February 22, 1791. On discontent in Paris, AN T 51, *liasse* 9, letter of February 16, 1791; AN W 363, dossier 793/2, document 89bis.

[225] On early efforts, [Duplaine de Saint-Albine], *Lettres à M. le Comte de B*** sur la révolution arrivée en 1789*, VI: 364–365. On efforts after the abolition of guilds, AM Bordeaux D 90, fols. 31–31v°; D 91, fol. 178.

[226] BN Mss. Nouv. acq. fr. 1777, fol. 232.

[227] AN F¹² 781^A, dossier 3.

[228] AN D III 363, dossier 107.

[229] AM Bordeaux D 92, fol. 22.

The National Assembly undoubtedly believed that the d'Allarde law repre-sented some degree of resolution to the uncertain situation that had prevailed throughout much of France until this time. The abolition of guilds and the suppression of their right to police trades held out the hope of greater order in the workplace. It was, however, only a partial solution because the d'Allarde law did not address organizations of journeymen, particularly the *compa-gnonnage*, which had no formal legal standing but were highly organized, having often been a source of public disorder through their rivalries.[230]

As a result, after the passage of the d'Allarde law, and against a backdrop of economic difficulty in Paris, journeymen were able to organize themselves to make various demands against former masters.[231] In April 1791 journey-men tailors in Bordeaux scheduled a meeting about wage rates, much to the consternation of the municipal council, which sought to discourage them.[232] A week later, the municipal council learned that journeymen bakers were planning to meet, but prohibited them from doing so, citing the decree of the National Assembly proscribing all meetings by corporation or trade.[233] It also sought guidance from the district administrators of Bordeaux as to what course it ought to follow.[234] The following week, because of religious tensions in Bordeaux arising from the Civil Constitution of the Clergy, the council prevented journeymen bakers from undertaking their traditional promenade around the city with flags, fifes, and drums, although they did allow it during May.[235]

In June 1791 four journeymen carpenters asked permission from the munic-ipal council of Bordeaux to meet for the customary holiday of Saint Peter, but by this time the council was less receptive to such activities. It sternly told the carpenters that one of the fundamental bases of the constitution was the aboli-tion of all corporations of citizens of the same profession and that the meeting was therefore prohibited. In order to preempt any future requests, the council planned to post its refusal to permit such meetings around the city.[236]

In Paris in April 1791 a meeting of carpenters became a matter of con-cern to municipal authorities because of tension between former masters and journeymen.[237] Similarly, in June 1791 journeymen shoemakers organized to

---

[230] See, for example, AN D IV 51, dossier 1488, document 20; AN C 127, dossier 428, document 42; AM Marseille AA 7–7, fols. 61–62; 1 BB 3291; 1 BB 3329. For more on the *compagnon-nage*, Cynthia Maria Truant, *The Rites of Labor: Brotherhoods of Compagnonnage in Old and New Regime France* (Ithaca, NY: Cornell University Press, 1994); Abel Poitrineau, *Ils Travaillaient la France: métiers et mentalités du XVIe au XIXe siècle* (Paris: Armand Colin, 1992), pp. 62–77.

[231] On the economic climate, David Andress, "Economic Dislocation and Social Discontent in the French Revolution: Survival in Paris in the Era of the Flight to Varennes," *French History* 10 (1996): 30–55.

[232] AM Bordeaux D 90, fol. 125v°.

[233] AM Bordeaux D 90, fols. 142v°–143.

[234] AM Bordeaux D 139, fol. 49v°.

[235] AM Bordeaux D 90, fols. 167v°–168; AM Bordeaux D 91, fol. 31.

[236] AM Bordeaux D 91, fols. 142–143.

[237] BN Mss. Fonds Français 11697, fols. 146–147.

seek a wage increase, and when it was refused they staged a work stoppage.[238] Some deputies viewed such concerted efforts by workers of the same trade as a reversion to the corporate paradigm that the National Assembly was striving to efface. As a result, amidst a current of labor unrest, both in Paris and in the departments,[239] the deputy Isaac-René-Guy Le Chapelier came forward in the National Assembly to offer an additional measure.[240]

Noting that unrest and disorder were present in Paris as well as the provinces, Le Chapelier sought, he claimed, to curtail the possibility of disorder at its origin. Following the example of clubs, workers were coming together in towns to form assemblies, to elect a president, to name secretaries, and to arrogate to themselves a kind of legislative power, through which, he asserted, they extorted proprietors and arbitrarily established wage rates. Le Chapelier argued that municipal authorities had misinterpreted a decree allowing peaceful citizens to assemble, stating that this was a right generally applicable to unarmed individuals, but not to men of the same occupation. To allow such a development would represent a return to the society of corporations, the abolition of which was the basis of the constitution, and it was important to issue promptly a decree sanctifying the principles of the Assembly. The deputies, to whom "these principles seemed incontestable," as one newspaper observed, then approved a series of measures proposed by Le Chapelier.[241]

The first article proscribed the renewal of any type of corporation comprised of persons of the same occupation because the abolition of such corporations was a fundamental tenet of the constitution. The second article prohibited workers, journeymen, day-laborers or other persons of the same occupation from coming together in assembly and from naming presidents, secretaries or officers under the pretext of making regulations or of taking deliberations on their claimed common interests. The remaining articles forbade administrative or municipal bodies from receiving or answering petitions from such groups, declaring them unconstitutional.[242]

The provisions of the law, as well as the fact that they were presented by Le Chapelier in his capacity as a member of the Committee on the

---

[238] *Journal de la cour et de la ville*, June 13, 1791. See also *Le Spectateur national et le modérateur*, April 29, 1791, May 23, 1791.

[239] *Le Spectateur national et le modérateur*, April 28, 1791, May 3, 1791, May 23, 1791; *Assemblée nationale, corps administratifs, et nouvelles politiques et littéraires de l'Europe, réunis au Journal de Versailles, des départemens de Paris, de Seine et d'Oise*, May 17, 1791.

[240] Pilastre de la Brardière and Leclerc, *Correspondance de MM. les députés du Département de Maine-et-Loire*, IX: 357.

[241] *Procès-verbal de l'Assemblée nationale*, No. 680 (June 14, 1791), pp. 7–12. The observation is from *Le Spectateur national et le modérateur*, June 15, 1791. For additional consideration of the Le Chapelier law, Grace Jaffé, *Le Mouvement ouvrier à Paris pendant la Révolution française* (Paris: Librairie Felix Alcan, 1924), pp. 101–207; Sonenscher, "Journeymen, the Courts and the French Trades 1781–1791," pp. 105–106.

[242] *Procès-verbal de l'Assemblée nationale*, No. 680 (June 14, 1791). See also AN C 71¹, dossier 693, document 17; *Journal de la cour et de la ville*, June 15, 1791. For an illustration of the ideal envisioned by the Assembly, AN D IV 35, dossier 868, document 14.

Constitution – which acted as a kind of steering committee for the Assembly in drafting the constitution – indicates again how central the abolition of corporations was to the new ideal of the polity. Indeed, the primacy of political and constitutional principles is evident in the comment of an unnamed deputy who, after Le Chapelier read his proposed decree, stated that the decree was more necessary than ever because the ghost of corporatism and exclusive privileges was beginning to reappear.[243]

The Le Chapelier law completed the suppression of the guild structure in France, making the marketplace and the world of work more free than it had been for centuries.[244] Guilds had been a key feature of urban life since the medieval era, and their abolition was an action that many – members of corporations and the public alike – found deeply unsettling.

Neither the d'Allarde law nor the Le Chapelier law, however, addressed the issue of regulation. Few believed that the suppression of guilds meant the elimination of all regulations – indeed, the article of the d'Allarde law that granted an individual the right to exercise whatever trade or occupation he wished contained a provision stipulating that he must adhere to existing regulations or to whatever regulations might be made.[245] The d'Allarde law was perceived as fulfilling the promise of the night of August 4 and the Declaration of Rights, and the Le Chapelier law was viewed primarily as an effort to complete the eradication of the particularistic corporate spirit, which was perceived as antithetical to the common good. At the same time, no one was certain how the world of work would be governed, and hesitation and tentativeness prevailed.[246]

THE UNEXPECTED END OF REGULATION

Rather than providing a foundational base or merely some clarity, particularly with respect to the issue of regulation, the National Assembly enacted a measure that surprised even some of its own members and introduced greater

---

[243] *Procès-verbal de l'Assemblée nationale*, No. 680 (June 14, 1791), p. 8. See also *Journal de la cour et de la ville*, June 15, 1791, for an indication of the way in which the law was interpreted primarily as a measure against corporate bodies. In this argument I disagree with Michael Sonenscher, *Work and Wages: Natural Law, Politics and the Eighteenth-Century French Trades* (Cambridge: Cambridge University Press, 1989), pp. 351–352, that the law was tied to the Assembly's effort to limit the right of petition. Sonenscher admits the narrow scope of the Le Chapelier law and his linkage of it to the law of May 10, 1791, is largely by inference. Indeed, it could equally be argued that the law of May 10, 1791, reinforced the provision that meetings with political goals should convene by section rather than by trade, profession or corporation. For more on the primacy of constitutional ideals, Jean-Joseph Regnault, *La Constitution française, mise à la portée de tout le monde*, 2 vols. (Bar-le-Duc: Société Typographique, 1792), I: 85–86.

[244] Sewell, *Work and Revolution in France*, pp. 87–91.

[245] Jean-Pierre Hirsch, "Revolutionary France, Cradle of Free Enterprise," *The American Historical Review* 94 (1989), pp. 1286–1287; Hirsch, *Les Deux rêves du commerce*, pp. 241–242; Bossenga, "*La Révolution française et les corporations*," p. 412.

[246] AM Bordeaux D 227, no. 27, letter of representatives of municipal officers of Bordeaux to municipal officers of Paris, August 15, 1791.

disquiet into the workplace and the market. On September 27, 1791, just three days before the Assembly disbanded, the deputy Pierre-Louis Goudard put forward a project from the Committee on Agriculture and Commerce that proposed suppressing chambers of commerce, inspectors of manufacture and all other current bodies related to the administration of commerce and vesting all responsibility for the oversight of commerce with the Ministry of the Interior.

The opening line of Goudard's speech once again reflected the Assembly's overriding priority – he told his colleagues that they had directed their attention to commerce and proscribed the privileges that had oppressed it. After enumerating measures the Assembly had enacted, he asserted that it was now a question of dissolving all of the former institutions that comprised the administration of commerce and ascertaining the means by which the Assembly could sustain its principles and ensure that its decrees were carried out. He maintained that the National Assembly should also lay the foundations needed for its successor body to put a new system in place.

Goudard proposed the abolition of chambers of commerce because, as corporate bodies, they violated the principles of the constitution. It was necessary, he argued, to eradicate particular administrations and allow a general administration to replace them.

The chambers of commerce represented the interests of the business classes of commercial cities, which accounts for Goudard's characterization of them as corporate bodies – they stood for particular concerns. In Marseille, which possessed one of the most significant chambers, the Chamber of Commerce not only controlled trade with the Near East, it also oversaw quality control on products produced in the city, especially soap. During the eighteenth century the powers of the Marseille Chamber of Commerce grew to such an extent that they rivaled those of the municipal government.[247] Although Marseille is somewhat atypical, such far-reaching influence served as the basis for Goudard's contention that it was necessary to eradicate particular administrations.

Goudard also recommended the suppression of the inspectors of manufactures as relics of a bygone era. Inspectors of manufactures enforced production regulations laid down by the Crown, especially in the textile industries. They were above guilds but complemented guild efforts at quality control.[248] They had the power to make domiciliary visits to merchants' shops to ensure that production rules were followed. There were more than fifty inspectors and sub-inspectors posted in various locales throughout the kingdom, as well as itinerant inspectors based in Paris.[249]

---

[247] *Histoire du commerce de Marseille*, Gaston Rambert, ed., 4 vols. (Paris: Plon, 1949–1954), IV: 82–83, 303–308.

[248] Philippe Minard, "Colbertism Continued? The Inspectorate of Manufactures and Strategies of Exchange in Eighteenth-Century France," *French Historical Studies* 23 (2000): 477–496, especially 479–480.

[249] *Almanach Royal 1790*, pp. 146–148.

Whereas the institution may have been appropriate at a time when only a small number of people had been taught the useful arts, Goudard argued, the current structure of work was vastly different and the spirit of inventive genius was much more widespread. In fact, he stated, the efforts or discoveries of practitioners might be shackled by the "inquisitorial surveillance" of inspectors of manufactures. He also proposed doing away with the Bureau of Commerce, the intendant of commerce, and the director-general of commerce and manufactures.

In order to enable agriculture and commerce to make their wishes known, and to facilitate their ability to share knowledge or defend themselves against foreign competition, Goudard sought to vest responsibility for all commerce of the kingdom with the Ministry of the Interior.[250] He concluded his report by presenting twelve articles to the Assembly for approval.

As soon as Goudard had completed his presentation, a deputy asked that the entire project be tabled. He claimed that the proposal raised important matters and that it would be wrong to suppress such useful institutions and simply allow the Minister of the Interior to reshape them unilaterally. Many other deputies supported postponing the measures, leading Charles Regnault, a deputy for Nancy, to observe that the Assembly could adjourn the report, but that one important provision needed to be decided immediately – the suppression of all chambers of commerce. It would be unconscionable, he asserted, for the Assembly, after having abolished corporate bodies, to disband while allowing one to exist. Goudard responded that if the Assembly abolished chambers of commerce, the remainder of the decree could not be deferred without also doing away with inspectors.

After additional discussion, the Assembly voted to enact only four of the twelve articles in the project and to leave all other aspects to the next legislature, which never considered them.[251] The provisions that the Assembly adopted suppressed the chambers of commerce as well as all bodies involved in the oversight of commerce – inspectors and directors-general of commerce and manufactures. Deputies also abolished all trademarks in textiles and the offices of those who visited textile production sites to ensure conformity with production regulations, as well as some other lesser offices.[252]

Much like the masters of guilds, the inspectors of manufactures had been in a state of uncertainty throughout the duration of the National Assembly. In fact, in January 1790 they had met with the deputy Pierre-Augustin Rousillou, a member of the Committee on Agriculture and Commerce who had a particular interest in both the regulation of industry and the organization of labor, to try to ascertain the Assembly's intentions.[253] The unexpected

---

[250] It should be recalled that the ministry itself was only about a year old and still seeking to define itself.

[251] Hirsch, *Les Deux rêves du Commerce*, p. 243.

[252] *Archives parlementaires*, 31: 396–399. See also Hirsch, *Les Deux rêves du commerce*, pp. 240–242.

[253] International Institute of Social History (hereafter IISH), Pierre Bruyard Papers, *liasse* 187. On the characterization of Rousillou, Lemay, *Dictionnaire des Constituants*, II: 831–832.

abolition of their posts caught them unaware and, again much like guilds-men, left them adrift.[254]

According to Charles-Jean-Baptiste Bruyard, a Paris-based itinerant inspec-tor, the abrupt nature of the legislation, enacted with virtually no discus-sion and without a reading of the report, was, as had been the case with the abolition of guilds, a result of inaction on the part of the Committee on Agriculture and Commerce, which again had to be prodded by another com-mittee. According to Bruyard, there had been a reading of a project within the Committee on Agriculture and Commerce, to which the Committee on Finances and the Committee on the Constitution had been invited. The Committee on Finances had believed that the proposed suppressions would be fiscally beneficial and had adopted the project. For its part, however, according to Bruyard, the Committee on the Constitution had concluded that the exist-ing system of administration of commerce was incompatible with the consti-tution – the chambers of commerce were corporate bodies and the inspectors of manufactures, as well as other institutions, limited the freedom of produc-ers and manufacturers, making it necessary to suppress them. As a result, an abbreviated set of decrees was hurriedly compiled and put forward in the Assembly without a report, to the surprise of many deputies, which accounted for their reluctance to consider them.[255]

Bruyard also believed that the eradication of inspectors of manufactures and other bodies that had overseen commerce was an extension of the legislation that had abolished corporations. He asserted that the suppression of guilds had entailed the destruction of all regulations, even though, he acknowledged, the end of regulation had not been stipulated. Because the inspectors of manu-factures were responsible for enforcing production regulations, he contended, they had become superfluous.[256]

In any case, the effect of the legislation was to throw both the world of work and commerce into utter disarray. Even a provision conferring oversight of manufacturing to municipal authorities – "to maintain, as in the past, good order and good faith" – was not adopted.[257]

As had been the case with guilds, chambers of commerce and inspectors of manufactures had been suppressed not on the basis of liberal economic critiques but because their duties were perceived to be incompatible with the principles of the Revolution. At the same time, however, the National Assembly, exhausted and anticipating the end of its term of office, had created an extraordinary vacuum. All of the bodies that had formerly overseen labor and industry had been eradicated, and not only had no new institutions been created to replace them, but no clear responsibility for oversight of any sort had been fixed. The Ministry of the Interior had been given a vague mandate, which it interpreted narrowly, initially confining itself largely to enforcement

[254] IISH, Pierre Bruyard Papers, *liasse* 12.
[255] IISH, Pierre Bruyard Papers, *liasse* 250.
[256] IISH, Pierre Bruyard Papers, *liasse* 262.
[257] *Archives parlementaires* 31: 399.

of the occupational license payment. In addition, the dispersal of duties related to manufacturing to separate bureaus within the newly established ministry never allowed such issues to become a priority.[258] Ultimately, it would be only during the Napoleonic era that the ministry would achieve any significant role in the spheres of labor and industry.

By September 1791 then, there were no longer any guilds, any journeymen organizations, or any regulations governing labor, industry or commerce, which led to the apposite observation of Jean-Pierre Hirsch that "the French Revolution introduced free enterprise abruptly."[259] The enormous void created by the Assembly soon led to confusion both in the workplace and the market and a decline in the quality of goods and services. These developments, in turn, ultimately led to a desire for a reimposition of regulation, one component of which was a restoration of guilds, albeit in modified form.

*   *   *   *   *   *   *

Although d'Allarde acknowledged that the abolition of corporations would benefit industry and commerce, and Goudard made an allusion to Adam Smith's *The Wealth of Nations* in his presentation on September 27, it is clear from the debates that the abolition of guilds by the National Assembly, as well as its other actions in the realms of production and commerce, were primarily an attack on privilege and corporate bodies stemming from the meeting of August 4, 1789, rather than an effort to enact liberal economic doctrine. As part of its remaking of France, the National Assembly abolished corporations and they were never again reorganized.

The relationship of the elimination of guilds with the past, however, is less important than its implications for the future: The abolition of guilds had momentous consequences. Historians have noted that one factor that inhibited France in comparison to England during the eighteenth century was the survival in France of a guild system that discouraged both innovation in production and the formation of large-scale enterprises.[260] Although it has been argued that guilds were less of an impediment than had previously been believed, the artisanal method – whether inside or outside of the corporate structure – had been the dominant form of production,[261] and there can be little doubt that the eradication of corporations opened new possibilities.

---

[258] On the dispersal of responsibilities, Edith Bernardin, *Jean-Marie Roland et le Ministère de l'Intérieur (1792–1793)* (Paris: Société des Etudes Robespierristes, 1964), pp. 204–206.

[259] Hirsch, "Revolutionary France, Cradle of Free Enterprise," p. 1284.

[260] François Crouzet, "*Angleterre et France au XVIIIᵉ siècle: Analyse comparée de deux croissances économiques,*" in François Crouzet, *De la superiorité de l'Angleterre sur la France: l'économique et l'imaginaire, XVIIᵉ-XXᵉ siècles* (Paris: Librairie académique Perrin, 1985), p. 36.

[261] On the argument that guilds were less of an impediment than had been believed, *ibid.*; on guilds as having been the dominant form of production, Sewell, *Work and Revolution in France*, pp. 20–21; Heimmermann, "Work and Corporate Life in Old Regime France," p. 25.

The destruction of Réveillon's establishment in the spring of 1789 demonstrated the ability of guilds to thwart innovation, even if extralegally, and the memory of that event lingered for decades. Indeed, one of the chief arguments against the reestablishment of guilds under the Napoleonic regime and the restored Bourbon monarchy was that guilds could offer a platform for workers to coordinate action – legal or illegal – to obstruct mechanization or other transformations in manufacturing or in the workplace.

Moreover, the efforts of the Committee of Public Safety during the Terror brought out the possibilities of industrial-scale production and technical innovation. After the Terror, as a desire to restore guilds began to crystallize and then to strengthen, an argument against their restoration was that they would stifle innovation and industry. Indeed, for more than two decades, advocacy of the reestablishment of guilds and support of mechanization and industry were, for all practical purposes, mutually exclusive positions, despite efforts by some proponents of guilds to acknowledge and accommodate the needs of industry.

The d'Allarde and Le Chapelier laws resulted in what Steven Kaplan aptly termed *la fin des corporations*, but the focus on their definitive suppression has masked the vigorous debate on their reestablishment that developed in the absence of any regulation. The abolition of guilds brought about major changes in the world of work, and the regimentation of labor and the inauguration of mass production that took place under the Committee of Public Safety transformed it altogether.

The conditions to which the elimination of corporations and oversight gave rise, however – from a steep decline in the quality of goods and workmanship to theft, incompetence and restiveness among workers – fueled a sentiment to reestablish guilds. At the same time, the promise of mechanized production, which guilds could have impeded, became the leading counterargument. Because of these antithetical conditions, the abolition of guilds would not be irreversibly affirmed until thirty years after it had legally occurred.

The New Regime Begins, 1792–1799

> It is a prejudice of the old regime, which has found partisans even under the new, that the perfection of mechanization and the simplification of hand work are dangerous in that they deprive many workers of a means of existence.
>
> *La Décade philosophique, littéraire et politique, par une société de républicains*, 10 brumaire an III

As David Andress observed, "unlicensed, free-for-all competition was the terror of the economic Old Regime, and the whole guild system functioned to keep it at bay."[1] The measures enacted by the National Assembly meant that the well-ordered, hierarchical world of corporations and commerce had been recast into an unregulated, egalitarian system based on occupational licenses.

More broadly, guilds had performed numerous functions, from guaranteeing the quality of bread and meat to assuring the technical competence of workers. It had not been the intention of the National Assembly to end oversight altogether and the d'Allarde law had not sought to do away with regulation of trades – its objective had been only to end guild administration. The subsequent abolition of all inspectorates, only days before the Assembly disbanded, inadvertently created confusion and disorder.

The Assembly had proceeded along a path of debate and experiment and acted on the basis of political and constitutional objectives rather than economic ones. This contingent, discrete approach meant that the Assembly did not implement, or even consider, a comprehensive alternative program when it abolished guilds, which induced the disarray that followed. As conditions worsened, it seemed to many that in order to reestablish order, competence, and quality in the workplace, it was necessary to restore corporations in some fashion, but constitutional factors precluded such an action.

As this disorienting situation developed, France went to war with much of Europe during 1792–1793. A labor shortage brought about by conscription,

---

[1] David Andress, *The French Revolution and the People* (London: Hambledon and London, 2004), p. 41.

and the need to furnish the armies thereby raised, led to a major effort by the government to increase production, which spurred a larger movement toward mechanization. Ultimately, mechanization of production became the opposing model to any consideration of restoring the former guild system.

THE SYSTEM OF LICENSES

The National Assembly had established the occupational license to replace revenue lost by the abolition of municipal customs duties. The government sought strict enforcement of the *patente*, which it expected to generate substantial income, and at first it appeared that the transition had gone relatively smoothly.

By early 1792, however, the shift to the occupational license had produced confusion, both in Paris and in outlying departments, particularly in determining those who might be subjected to it. There was uncertainty, for example, as to whether surgeons had to purchase a *patente*, and the decision was that they would. Initially, members of the legal profession in Paris – men of law and official defenders – were required to purchase an occupational license, as were physicians.[2] Pierre-Nicolas Berryer, a former barrister to the *parlement* of Paris, contested the payment, arguing that there was no fixed charge for legal services. Any recompense, he asserted, was an honorarium, which meant that the practice of law was not a commercial enterprise. Berryer's arguments prevailed and he proudly noted in his memoirs that he saw his profession freed from taxation "incompatible with its dignity."[3] A question arose as to whether farmers were subject to it, but they were ruled exempt.[4]

Compounding the confusion was the fact that there were two categories of occupational license – the *patente simple* and the *patente supérieure*. The former applied to those practicing a single trade or profession, whereas those whose trade had a double component, such as producing and selling, or those who sold items that they had not manufactured, had to purchase a *patente supérieure*. The wording of the license itself, which authorized its holder to practice "whatever profession he pleases with the sole exception of those listed in article XIV of the law of March 17, 1791," appeared to presume a single trade or craft, but it was not explicit.[5]

In some respects, the system of occupational licenses resembled the former guild structure. Corporations had, of course, disappeared, but one still declared a trade, skill, or line of work when purchasing an occupational

---

[2] AN H² 2103, supplement to alphabetical collection of questions on *patentes*. Indeed, according to this document, the position of the government was that no profession or occupation was exempt from the *patente*.

[3] Pierre-Nicolas Berryer, *Souvenirs de M. Berryer, doyen des avocats à Paris, de 1774 à 1838*, 2 vols. (Paris: Ambroise Dupont, 1839), I: 155–156. He also noted that the physicians were unsuccessful in their appeal and remained subject to the *patente*.

[4] AN H² 2103, supplement to alphabetical collection of questions on *patentes*.

[5] AN H² 2103, *patente simple* for Charles Courtaud, March 8, 1792.

license. In addition, the system of occupational licenses distinguished between skilled and unskilled labor. Just as unskilled labor had been excluded from the guild structure, so, too, were unskilled and seasonal laborers exempted from the *patente*.[6] Grocers and wine merchants had to possess a *patente supérieure*, but flower, fruit, and vegetable sellers who sold from their residence were not subject to the occupational license.[7]

Moreover, against the backdrop of confusion with respect to occupational licenses, an even larger transformation was under way. Although it would be an over-idealization of the guild system to assert that the attainment of a mastership reflected a high level of skill that culminated in the achievement of the masterpiece – marriage and family connections provided advantages in securing masterships and occasionally the requirement of a masterpiece was waived altogether – it is also true that some degree of skill generally had to be demonstrated.[8] With the suppression of corporations and the introduction of the occupational license, as Marat noted, any attestation of skill was eradicated and became subject only to the market. Similarly, the inspectors of manufactures had ensured quality of production, but their dissolution had also made quality purely a function of the market. Within a relatively short time, both skill and quality went into sharp decline.

As a result, more than anything else, the introduction of the system of occupational licenses became inextricably associated with shoddiness and an abrupt deterioration in quality of workmanship and service. The association between fraud, charlatanry, and deceit and the implementation of occupational licenses was long lasting,[9] and lamentation of that erosion became a major element of efforts to reestablish guilds. As this decline was beginning, during the spring of 1792, on April 20, in the most fateful decision of its relatively brief existence, the Legislative Assembly, with only seven dissenting votes, declared war on Austria. Although there were different considerations among the constituencies that supported war, a common belief was that it would be brief.[10] Instead, more than two decades of nearly continuous warfare ensued and profoundly affected nearly every aspect of French society, including the organization of labor. Conscription drew off thousands of young men who might otherwise have entered trades. More significantly, the imperative of war manufacture to support the armies led first to a reordering of trades and a regimentation of labor, and later to the development of a policy of mechanization of manufacture by the government in pursuit of mass production.

The war began well for France, but by March 1793 the republic was in desperate straits. Many actions taken during that month by the National

---

[6] AN H² 2103, supplement to alphabetical collection of questions on *patentes*.

[7] *Ibid.*

[8] Heimmermann, "Work and Corporate Life in Old Regime France," pp. 349–361.

[9] See AN AD XI 76, *Essai sur les patentes et le commerce*.

[10] On the war, J.H. Clapham, *The Causes of the War of 1792*, reprint edition (New York: Octagon, 1969); T.C.W. Blanning, *The French Revolutionary Wars 1787–1802* (London: Longman, 1996).

Convention, which had succeeded the Legislative Assembly in September 1792, have captured the attention of historians, from the creation of the Revolutionary Tribunal to the dispatching of representatives on mission from the Convention to oversee the armies and galvanize the war effort, so it is not surprising that the abolition of the occupational license by the Convention on March 21, 1793, has generally been overlooked. It was, however, a critical event in the transformation of labor in France.

In an effort to increase tax receipts, the tax subcommittee of the Committee on Finances of the National Convention presented a report on March 21. One of the revenue sources the subcommittee had examined was the occupational license, and it asserted that the *patente* was not producing the amount of revenue expected. The calculation had been that the system would produce 23 million livres, but it had yielded only 6 million to 7 million, and recovery costs for even that amount had been 800,700 livres. Moreover, the *patente* had been the object of protests all over France, and when the possibility of its suppression had been announced, the news had been "avidly welcomed." One of the major deficiencies of the license was that it cost the same everywhere, from large cities to small villages.

Furthermore, the administration of the occupational license was riddled with exceptions and inequities, making it an object of resentment – in fact, the report cited the effort by physicians and men of law to escape subjection to it. Many individuals, the report claimed, sought to disguise their true occupation with false declarations, leading to a large number of disputes and impeding execution of the law.

For these and other reasons, the subcommittee recommended the abolition of the *patente*. With almost no discussion or debate, and acknowledging that the recommendations were "urgent and indispensable," the Convention voted to do away with the *patente*, making the abolition retroactive to January 1, 1793.[11]

The Convention suppressed the occupational license in order to gain the support of workers by removing one of their major grievances. Although its purpose was, in essence, tactical, the abolition of the *patente* had a profound effect on the structure of French labor by ending all distinctions within it and regulation of it.

The Old Regime nightmare of "unlicensed, free-for-all competition" had now been realized, and it served to transform labor into a more fungible commodity. If the abolition of guilds and the establishment of the *patente* marked the beginning of the formation of a largely undifferentiated mass of workers, the quashing of the *patente* advanced the process.

Moreover, the continuity and renewal of trades were adversely affected by the entry of young men into the revolutionary armies beginning in 1792,

---

[11] *Archives parlementaires*, 60: 379–380, 386. The repeal was apparently not well-publicized, however. During late April, more than a month after the suppression of the *patente*, the municipality of Paris inquired of its printer why his firm had not completed an order of 8,000 forms for the *patente*. The action may have been partly reflexive, because the municipality had been having difficulty with the printing firm. AN H^2 2121, liasse 3, documents 33, 36.

particularly in Paris. Indeed, artisans were the prevalent group among soldiers, and this was especially true for Paris.[12] The diversion of thousands of young men into the army depleted the artisanal pool and meant that other young men were lost to trades that they might otherwise have entered. As a result, the number of tradesmen was reduced, and trades were not able to renew themselves as they had in the past – the printer for the municipality of Paris, Patris, claimed that he was encountering difficulties because many of his workers had answered the call to defend the fatherland.[13] This also attenuated what might have served as a basis for reconstituting corporations had such a measure been decreed.

Indeed, by early 1793, less than two years after the abolition of guilds, there was disaffection with unregulated commerce – a police report of February 27, 1793, mentioned "hatred against grocers," who were accused of abusively taking advantage of the freedom of commerce. Considerable ire was also directed toward wine merchants for allegedly adulterating wine and toward butchers for including bones and feet while weighing meat and for excessive prices – all matters that would formerly have been dealt with by the respective guilds.

At the same time, however, there was not as yet any sense of wistfulness or regret for the loss of the guild system. During March 1793, the Lombard section of Paris discussed reestablishing two military corporations, but after a long, spirited debate the section decided against doing so. The deciding factor was that the section did not want to tolerate any corporation whatsoever, viewing such bodies as "contrary to equality and, sooner or later, a seed of discord."[14]

Another element that began to attract greater attention in early 1793 was the leverage that workers had over their employers. The master–journeymen relationship that had been at the core of guilds had largely precluded such influence, but the abolition of corporations had freed journeymen from whatever control masters might formerly have exercised. The Le Chapelier law had attempted to address the issue of journeymen working in concert, but by the spring of 1793 there was a growing sense among authorities that the world of labor was in disorder.

In April 1793 police reports noted collective action by journeymen bakers, and in the following month they reported that journeymen stonecutters, carpenters, and other workers "were laying down the law to those who

[12] Samuel F. Scott, *The Response of the Royal Army to the French Revolution: The Role and Development of the Line Army 1787–1793* (Oxford: Clarendon Press, 1978), p. 188; Alan Forrest, *Conscripts and Deserters: The Army and French Society during the Revolution and Empire* (Oxford: Oxford University Press, 1989), p. 22.

[13] AN H² 2121, liasse 3, document 36. Because the municipality was considering a switch to another printer, however, this document must be treated with considerable caution. AN H² 2121, liasse 3, document 30.

[14] AN AF IV 1470, extract of reports and declarations made in office of surveillance of the police, February 27, 1793 (grocers); list of reports and declarations made in office of surveillance of the police, March 2, 1793 (wine merchants); April 30, 1793 (butchers); March 4, 1793 (Lombards section meeting).

employed them."[15] Increasing awareness of worker unrest – or "insubordination" as authorities often termed it – would ultimately become an additional impetus for those seeking to restore guilds.[16]

THE DEMANDS OF WAR

Without question, however, the critical factor in the transformation of labor during the French Revolution was less the abolition of guilds than the establishment of an enormous war industry, particularly in Paris, to support the revolutionary armies in the field.[17] The scale of manufacture required to support hundreds of thousands of soldiers far exceeded the capacity of the traditional artisanal system that had heretofore predominated and dictated new modes of labor organization and production.

Under the influence of the revolutionary fervor that had propelled the declaration of war, few logistical preparations had been made, and by early 1793 shortcomings in a number of areas, including weapons and supplies, were apparent.[18] After mandating the raising of 300,000 men on February 24, 1793, the Convention undertook an enormous expansion of the manufacture of a number of products, one aspect of which – the production of muskets – has been analyzed in an admirable study by Ken Alder.[19]

Under the Old Regime, the Crown had procured muskets from three primary armories, in Charleville, Maubeuge, and Saint-Etienne. By early 1793, however, Charleville and Maubeuge had been captured and the armory at Saint-Etienne was in conflict with the central government over the price to be paid for each musket produced.[20] During June 1793 the situation became even more critical as Saint-Etienne came under the control of federalist troops from Lyon, and the central government lost its last source of muskets.

Desperate for weapons and needing to retain the support of the Parisian sections, which were demanding the establishment of national workshops to produce weapons, during the fall of 1793 the Committee of Public Safety spearheaded a massive state-sponsored program of arms production in Paris. The

[15] AN AF IV 1470, list of reports and declarations made in the office of surveillance of the police, April 6, 1793 (bakers); May 9, 1793 (stonecutters, carpenters and other workers).

[16] Hirsch, *Les Deux rêves du commerce*, p. 247.

[17] This process is treated at a bureaucratic level by Howard G. Brown, *War, Revolution and the Bureaucratic State: Politics and Army Administration in France, 1791–1799* (Oxford: Clarendon Press, 1995), especially Chapter 4.

[18] Scott, *The Response of the Royal Army*, p. 175. Indeed, in one instance, prior to the declaration of war, an effort undertaken was to forestall rather than to prepare – as war approached during the winter of 1792, officers of one Parisian section surveyed the workshops of toolmakers, furbishers, blacksmiths and other metal-working trades that could manufacture pikes. Their intention was not to prepare for war but to ascertain that no adversaries of the Revolution had placed an order for pikes. BHVP Ms. 749, fols. 157–158.

[19] Ken Alder, *Engineering the Revolution: Arms and Enlightenment in France, 1763–1815* (Princeton: Princeton University Press, 1997).

[20] *Ibid.*, pp. 218–220.

effort had enormous repercussions, particularly on members of what had been Old Regime guild trades – locksmiths, goldsmiths, key-makers, and others.[21]

On August 23, 1793, the Convention decreed the *levée-en-masse*, which, as R. R. Palmer noted, marked "the first time the world saw a nation in arms."[22] The Committee of Public Safety mobilized the human and material resources of France on a scale heretofore unknown – by the end of the summer of 1793 the armies of the republic numbered 500,000 men, all of whom had to be equipped with uniforms, footwear, and weapons.

Just as the republic introduced a scale of warfare unknown under the Old Regime, so, too, it had to devise a new standard of production – the artisanal economy of the Old Regime could never have achieved or sustained such levels of manufacture. In this context, as Alder noted, "work became (temporarily) associated with patriotism" so that "the meaning of work had to be continuously renegotiated during this period as the political equation changed."[23]

The Committee of Public Safety made clear from the outset the magnitude of the task to be undertaken. In a message to the general assembly of the Beaurepaire section of Paris on August 24, 1793, it stated:

The general conscription taking place at this time in order to expel all enemies of the Republic imperiously demands a considerable quantity of weapons.

It is necessary at the present time; it is necessary for the needs to come.

All Frenchmen must have weapons to oppose foreign enemies as well as the liberticide schemes of internal enemies.

It is imperative that a very great number of workers be devoted entirely and exclusively to the manufacture of weapons.

The committee mandated a census of all metal workers in the section, including the age of each worker, the nature of what it called his "ordinary work," the purpose to which he could be redirected, whether he was the father of a family, whether he had a workshop and workers, the number of workers he employed, and any other information necessary to determine the task he could be given to meet the goal of arms manufacture.[24]

The census was a reactive, improvised measure to address the crisis of production, but the committee also had a larger endeavor in mind. Indeed, the records of the Committee of Public Safety for late September 1793 reveal that it intended a total reordering of labor.

The shortage of muskets, the committee stated, meant that the greatest number of workers should be employed in their manufacture. Because Paris

[21] *Ibid.*, p. 262. See also Monnier, *Le Faubourg Saint-Antoine*, p. 67.

[22] R.R. Palmer, *Twelve Who Ruled: The Year of the Terror in the French Revolution* (Princeton: Princeton University Press, 1941), p. 60.

[23] Alder, *Engineering the Enlightenment,*" pp. 259–260, a point also made by Haim Burstin, "Problems of Work during the Terror," in *The French Revolution and the Creation of Modern Culture* 4 vols., Keith Baker, ed., (Oxford: Pergamon Press, 1987–1994), 4: 283–284, 287.

[24] BHVP Ms. 749, fol. 143. There were, for example, 323 metal workers in the Quinze-Vingts section. Monnier, *Le Faubourg Saint-Antoine*, p. 75.

had never had an arms manufacturing industry, however, it had to be assumed that none of the workers in the city had experience in this task. It was therefore necessary that workers engaged in arms manufacture "make almost a new apprenticeship, that they change their manner of working." To this end, the committee observed that the change of work methods could be more easily achieved by utilizing young workers "who are less devoted to the routine of a single type of work." The committee ordered that all workers in Paris be requisitioned for the manufacture of muskets and that they report to the central administration in order to indicate the component of the manufacturing process they could carry out.[25]

The transformation sought by the Committee of Public Safety was a movement from skill in a particular trade – "a single type of work," the artisanal model – to an emphasis on volume of production, a change of extraordinary magnitude.[26] The abolition of corporations had changed the structure of labor by doing away with the hierarchical system of masters and journeymen, but the trades around which guilds had formerly been organized had continued – in short, the structure of work had been altered, but, for the most part, not its nature. Again, in the parlance of the Committee of Public Safety, most men had continued with "a single type of work." The reorganization of labor carried out by the Convention in pursuit of war-related production, however, all but eliminated a host of formerly guild-based Old Regime metal trades – cutlery, locksmiths, edge-tool makers, farriers, coppersmiths, and many others – and would change the nature of work as well.[27]

Indeed, the Convention melded Parisian skilled workers with more casual laborers, and most were paid on either a piece rate or a fixed daily wage.[28] The blending of different levels of skill, and the emphasis on quantity rather than quality, served to homogenize and standardize work in a manner that would have been inconceivable under the guild system and improbable even during the period of occupational licenses. Not surprisingly, tension developed among workers – one police report stated that, other than matters pertaining to wages, a major source of discontent for workers at the troubled Capucins workshop was that many of them "knew nothing."[29] This marked yet another step in the progression of labor to something more fungible – from a skill to be developed to a commodity to be sold.

---

[25] BHVP Ms. N.A. 22, fol. 15.

[26] Alan Forrest, *The Soldiers of the French Revolution* (Durham: Duke University Press, 1990), pp. 137–138.

[27] Alder, *Engineering the Revolution*, p. 266. Similarly, at an earlier time, during late 1792, workers in wood and iron had been sought out to manufacture pikes. BHVP Ms. N.A. 152, fol. 161.

[28] Alder, *Engineering the Revolution*, pp. 267–269; Burstin, "Problems of Work during the Terror," p. 280.

[29] AN F⁷ 3688³, dossier 1–10 nivôse, document 233. On the problems in the Capuchins workshop, Alder, *Engineering the Enlightenment*, p. 271.

Expectations were high – one newspaper reported that the powers of Europe combined could manufacture barely 200,000 muskets per year, and that they would be disconcerted to learn that Paris alone could produce, during the same period of time, 360,000 muskets. The article also noted that under the Old Regime France had produced only 50,000 weapons per year.[30] The Committee of Public Safety and the Commune sent commissioners to the workshops to ascertain the measures necessary to accelerate arms production.[31]

The transformation of the nature of labor was reinforced by the incessant schedule of work – the foundries that manufactured muskets were in continuous operation, seeking to produce 1,000 weapons a day.[32] As earning power eroded during the winter of 1793–1794, unrest grew in the workshops, and the government responded by banning all assemblies of workers and imposing sentences of two years in irons for organizers of actions. Despite such threats, the strife continued.[33]

By the late winter of 1794, the Committee of Public Safety decreed that no worker engaged in the manufacture of arms could leave his workshop, even to move to another arms workshop, without authorization from the general administration for small arms manufacture. The decree vested enforcement of the measure with the Commission on Arms and Powder and the Commune. Revolutionary committees were to be responsible for forcing workers who had gone to work elsewhere to return to their original workshop.[34]

Much of the unrest was due to a labor shortage driven by the size of the revolutionary armies, and the shortfall grew worse over time. Indeed, in an effort to address the labor shortage, on 22 nivôse year III (January 11, 1795) the Convention eased anti-emigration laws against workers who were not ex-nobles or priests, who had left France since May 1, 1793.[35] The labor shortage became so severe that the Committee of Public Safety also extended an amnesty to navy deserters who were workers.[36] Both the unrest and the worker shortfall were factors that led republican governments to push for mechanization of production, and a major step in pursuing this objective was the founding of the Atelier de Perfectionnement.[37]

THE DAWN OF THE FACTORY SYSTEM IN FRANCE: THE ATELIER DE PERFECTIONNEMENT

The purpose of the institution was "to reduce the amount of work that the manufacture of muskets requires and to simplify it in such a way that all

[30] *Courier républicain*, 15 brumaire year II (November 5, 1793).
[31] *Suite du Journal de Perlet*, 20 frimaire year II (December 10, 1793).
[32] AN F⁷ 3688³, dossier 2, document 178; dossier 1–10 nivôse, document 233.
[33] Alder, *Engineering the Revolution*, p. 271; R.R. Palmer, *Twelve Who Ruled*, pp. 237–238, 240–241.
[34] *Suite du journal de Perlet*, 17 ventôse year II (March 7, 1794).
[35] BHVP Ms. 746, fol. 217; BHVP Ms. 745, fol. 138.
[36] BHVP Ms. 749, fol. 211.
[37] The best treatment of the Atelier de Perfectionnement is Alder, *Engineering the Revolution*, pp. 272–288.

kinds of citizens would be able to manufacture perfectly the separate pieces of a musket."[38] Of the pieces of the musket, the gunlock was the most difficult to produce, requiring nine separate components. The *atelier* created five machines to manufacture the pieces so that the gunlock could be produced more easily.[39]

In the end, despite the production of some gunlocks, the authorities judged the effort to be unsuccessful.[40] As Alder noted, however, "the French state had aspired to interchangeable parts manufacturing at a time of worker unrest and rising wages."[41] Without question, the first major effort at standardization and mechanization of production had been taken by the government, and even after the crisis of 1793–1794, the government would continue to take the lead in pursuing mechanization.

After Thermidor, the government regarded the massing of large numbers of workers in manufactories as undesirable and, believing that the exigencies of 1793–1794 no longer held, the Convention decided to shut down large-scale manufacture in Paris. During December 1794, members of the Convention became concerned that, amidst unrest in the arms workshops during the extraordinarily harsh winter of 1794–1795, workers were preparing to converge *en masse* on the Convention. In order to preempt such an action, the Convention sent three representatives to the workshops to invite them to send a delegation of twenty men to address the Convention. The deputation appeared and conveyed the workers' apprehension that production in the manufactories would be suspended as the most difficult part of winter approached.

The perception of the workers was correct – the deputy François-Antoine Boissy d'Anglas[42] delivered a report to the Convention on behalf of the Committees of Public Safety, General Security, Legislation, Military, and Finances that opened by observing that the meetings that had taken place in the workshops were malevolent in nature. As a result, he put forward a decree on behalf of the Committee of Public Safety mandating that, effective 1 pluviôse (January 20, 1795), the manufacture and repair of arms was to be transferred to private enterprise. The Convention approved the measure.[43] The decision provoked unrest, but the Convention persisted and by the spring of 1795 the state enterprise was no longer functioning.[44]

Nevertheless, production figures cited by Alder demonstrate the transformation brought about by the mandates of war production. Prior to September 1793, Paris had produced 9,000 muskets per year. During the

---

[38] AN F[12] 1310, Report on Atelier de Perfectionnement (undated).

[39] *Ibid.*

[40] Alder, *Engineering the Revolution*, p. 277.

[41] *Ibid.*, p. 280.

[42] On Boissy d'Anglas, John R. Ballard, *Continuity during the Storm: Boissy d'Anglas and the Era of the French Revolution* (Westport, CT: Greenwood Press, 2000).

[43] *La Décade philosophique*, 30 frimaire year III (December 20, 1794). Other national workshops were privatized as well. Monnier, *Le Faubourg Saint-Antoine*, p. 65.

[44] *Journal des débats et des décrets*, messidor year III (No. 1024); Alder, *Engineering the Revolution*, pp. 285–288.

following thirteen months, however, under the innovations imposed by the government, the city produced 145,600 muskets, which was twice the output of all of the armories of the Old Regime.[45] By December 1794, one million Frenchmen were under arms and Paris was the largest arms-producing site in the world.[46]

The achievement of such a level of production had been possible only with a fundamental reorganization of labor that proved transformative. In fact, the imperative of war production was a critical transitional phase between the guild system of the eighteenth century and the factory system of the nineteenth century. This was evident not only in the scale of production, but also in the virtual extinction of several former Old Regime trades and the regimentation of labor as a result of the manufacturing effort.

The transformation of production brought about by the republican government spawned a debate about whether the workers employed in the new enterprises were "artisans" or "proletariat." Alder has argued that the situation in the workshops was too fluid for either characterization to be apposite.[47] Indeed, in French phraseology, the issue appears to be *une question mal posée* – a badly posed question.

To the degree that the term "artisan" accords primacy to the ideals of skill and pride of craftsmanship over speed and volume of production, it is inappropriate to apply it to arms production under the Convention. To the degree that "proletariat" encompasses the concept of an undifferentiated mass of wage earners, it, too, is inapt. Although workers were often paid on a piece-rate basis, there were pay differentials based on skill within that arrangement, and differences were evident.[48]

The exigencies of war demanded new methods of production, and the effort carried out by the Convention was a period of change. The artisanal mode of production was in decline, to be sure, but what would become the factory system was by no means fully formed, nor would it be for decades to come. The transitional state of both labor and production should be recognized, and not cast in reductionist terms.

Indeed, the arms production project may be viewed in another manner, because it put into relief two issues upon which both opponents and proponents of the reestablishment of guilds drew. On the one hand, it revealed the possibilities of mass production, which would subsequently become attached to mechanization of production. In the view of advocates of mechanization, any restoration of guilds could offer workers a platform that might enable them to impede mechanization. On the other hand, proponents of the reorganization of corporations could point to the fact that it was agitation on the

[45] Alder, *Engineering the Revolution*, p. 288.
[46] Larry H. Addington, *The Patterns of War since the Eighteenth Century* (Bloomington, IN: Indiana University Press, 1981), pp. 21–22.
[47] Alder, *Engineering the Revolution*, p. 269.
[48] *Ibid.*, pp. 267–269.

part of labor that had led to the shutdown of the program and that a reestablishment of guilds could reimpose order on workers.

Alder's study is insightful, and scholars of the French Revolution, labor history, and the history of technology will unquestionably benefit from reading it. At the same time, however, the study of armaments is atypical in one critical respect: armaments production had been outside of the guild system under the Old Regime. In order to understand more fully the manner in which the demands of war led to the extirpation of many remnants of the former guild system and the movement toward wage labor, one must look elsewhere. In order to perceive the direct impact of war on a former guild trade, a consideration of shoemaking is particularly illustrative.

A FORMER GUILD TRADE TRANSFORMED

Under the Old Regime, the guild of shoemakers (*cordonniers*) had been the largest corporation in most cities. In Lyon, for example, there were nearly 1,000 masters or men received as masters, a number 33 percent greater than the next largest corporation, that of carpenters and other woodworkers, which had 750 masters or men received as masters.[49] Furthermore, the guild of shoemakers had a large number of journeymen, so many that they were not tabulated.[50] Although figures are not available, it was also the largest guild in Paris.[51]

Under the Old Regime, the production of leather shoes or boots was a careful and deliberate process.[52] The *levée-en-masse*, however, led to an unprecedented need for boots for soldiers – tens of thousands of pairs, although, not surprisingly, the effort at mass production of boots began later than that for weapons. On 18 frimaire year II (December 8, 1793) the deputy Bertrand Barère, a member of the Committee of Public Safety, informed the Convention that an earlier decree requiring shoemakers to give five pairs of boots for the use of the armies every ten days – a *décade* on the revolutionary calendar – was being ignored. Supply depots were empty and soldiers lacked boots as they marched to war – Barère claimed that even in the current difficult weather some troops went into battle with bare feet. In order to correct the situation, the National Convention decreed that on 1 nivôse (December 21, 1793) all shoemakers would be requisitioned until the end of the second *décade* of pluviôse (February 8, 1794) to work exclusively to produce boots for the military. Any shoemakers who made footwear for any other purpose would have those items confiscated and would have to pay a fine of 100 livres, which would be awarded to the individual who reported him.

[49] AN F¹² 763, table of communities of *arts et métiers* of Lyon, a document compiled in 1777.
[50] *Ibid.* In the document, however, in those few instances in which the number of journeymen is recorded, it is generally a substantial multiple. There were 14 master forgers, for example, and nearly 180 journeymen, and there were 300 master hatmakers and 1500 journeymen.
[51] *Guide des corps des marchands et les communautés des arts et metiers, tant de la ville et faubourgs de Paris, que du royaume*, p. 217.
[52] Heimmermann, "Work and Corporate Life in Old Regime Bordeaux," pp. 177–190.

The decree delineated the style for boots, which was to be unique to the military. The boots were to be produced in specified proportions of graduated sizes for each one hundred pairs, and the shoemakers would be paid the price decreed by the Maximum, the system of price controls imposed on items deemed "necessities," as well as on labor, by the Convention. If raw materials were supplied to the shoemaker, their cost would be deducted, again at prices specified by the Maximum. Army boots that were rejected would be confiscated for the benefit of the Republic.[53]

On 14 ventôse year II (March 4, 1794) the Convention mandated that all shoemakers were to furnish two pairs of boots, for which they would be paid, each *décade*.[54] In less than a year, however, it became clear that the voluntary effort had failed – on 16 nivôse year III (January 5, 1795) the Committee of Public Safety notified sections that they should exercise the "right of preemption" on shoemakers in their section. All boots in the shops of shoemakers were to be seized and turned in to government officials. The committee also indicated that shoemakers should prove by their list that they had made their deposit.[55]

Even this more severe undertaking was unsuccessful, because on 29 pluviôse year III (February 17, 1795) a municipal administrator wrote to the Lombard section of Paris that he had written many times previously to the civil committees seeking to stoke their zeal and to invite them to renew their efforts to persuade shoemakers to meet the provisions of the law. But these efforts, he noted, had not had the success that he expected. Even though Paris was home to a large number of shoemakers, and although the city had been carefully supplied with leather,[56] many shoemakers had not met the requirement of the law. As a result, the city of Paris was more than 150,000 pairs of boots in arrears. He urged sectional officers to renew the zeal of shoemakers and to have them comply with the law of 14 ventôse, both with respect to the boots that they owed and thereafter to deposit two pairs every ten days as the law mandated. If this was not done, shoemakers would be subject to heavy fines.[57]

Such patriotic exhortations clearly failed, however, because on 13 messidor year III (July 1, 1795) the Committee of Public Safety requisitioned shoemakers for an enterprise known as the Shoemaking Workshop (*Atelier cordonnerie*),

---

[53] *Archives parlementaires*, 81: 121–122.

[54] *Archives parlementaires*, 86: 78.

[55] BHVP Ms. 748, fol. 62.

[56] Indeed, the production of leather was regarded as so important that during September, 1794, the Commission on Commerce and Provisioning wrote to Lazare Carnot of the Committee of Public Safety to seek the recall from military service of thirteen tanners from the commune of St. Saen (Seine-Inférieure) to rejoin fellow tanners in the production of leather. AN F[12] 1556, report of Commission and Commerce and Provisioning to Carnot, 1 vendémiaire year III (September 22, 1794). Earlier the shortage of leather had hindered the effort. *Bulletin républicain, ou papier-nouvelles de tous les pays et de tous les jours*, 15 nivôse year II (January 4, 1794).

[57] BHVP Ms. 739, fols. 111–112.

a subsidiary of the Office for Uniforms (*Agence de l'habillement*).[58] The requisitioning of shoemakers was to be undertaken by the civil committees of the sections of Paris, working on behalf of the Office for Uniforms.

For the city of Paris, 500 shoemakers were to be requisitioned. Those requisitioned could not excuse themselves for any reason and would be paid according to a scale set by the Office for Uniforms. They were "entirely subject to the rules of the workshop" and could be disciplined for absence or negligence.[59]

Although the Office for Uniforms preferred to distribute the burden equally, by requisitioning approximately ten shoemakers per section, it recognized that shoemakers were not equally distributed throughout the city, with some sections having many more than others. As a result, administrators from the Office for Uniforms undertook a survey of workers subject to requisition in each section. Emphasizing that there was no time to lose if support of the armies was not to be compromised, the administrators asked sections to compile a list of shoemakers available for requisition and to designate ten for immediate compliance with the requisition.[60]

The administrators for the Office for Uniforms emphasized that those workers requisitioned should not and would not be deprived of the wages that they could otherwise claim, and even asserted that particularly industrious workers could find themselves in an advantageous situation. The office admitted, however, that it did not know how long the period of requisition would last.[61]

In response to its request for information, the Office for Uniforms did not receive the results that it expected. The Pont Neuf section, for example, replied that it had been unable to locate any shoemakers who might be eligible for requisition and that the section officers could not carry out the terms of the law.[62] The administrators of the Office for Uniforms responded that it seemed unlikely that there were no shoemakers in the section eligible to be summoned and ordered the officials to undertake a new search. Once again, however, the section asserted that there were no eligible shoemakers to be found.[63]

In the face of resistance from the sections, the Committee of Public Safety declared on 4 thermidor year III (July 22, 1795) that workers in the Shoemaking Workshop were to be guaranteed a pound of bread per day, and the Office for Uniforms noted that it hoped that this measure would reassure the sections during their requisition of shoemakers.[64] Nevertheless, only days later a section still claimed that it could not find any shoemakers within its jurisdiction.[65]

A few weeks later, the head of the Shoemaking Workshop wrote to the members of the Thermes section commending them for their work on

[58] BHVP Ms. 769, fol. 1; see also Monnier, *Le Faubourg Saint-Antoine*, pp. 66–67.
[59] BHVP Ms. 745, fol. 239.
[60] BHVP Ms. 745, fol. 237.
[61] *Ibid.*, fols. 237–238.
[62] BHVP Ms. 745, fol. 240.
[63] BHVP Ms. 745, fols. 244–245; Burstin, "Problems of Work during the Terror," p. 277.
[64] BHVP Ms. 745, fol. 246.
[65] BHVP Ms. 745, fol. 247.

requisitioning shoemakers, but noted that, despite such efforts, the workshop and the sections had not always achieved satisfactory results. He stated that it was critical to begin the production of boots for the army "by all means possible." For various reasons, the head noted, in the different sections there were a number of shoemakers who were unable to work at the *Atelier cordonnerie*, but in order to meet the terms of the decree it was in their interest to furnish at least ten pairs of boots to the workshop each *décade*. He closed his letter by asking the section officers to select only "sure and capable" persons for the Shoemaking Workshop.[66] The Thermes section submitted a list of shoemakers and on 3 vendémiaire year IV (September 25, 1795) the *atelier* asked the section officers to select ten for requisition.[67]

Subsequently, the workshop, in a tacit acknowledgement that its patriotic exhortations had been less than successful, raised the price it would pay for boots. On 27 vendémiaire year IV (October 19, 1795), the *atelier* decreed that the price for those produced in the workshop would be set at twenty-five livres per pair, and those produced outside of it would be purchased at thirty livres per pair. The director stated that he hoped this increase in price would "produce the result that one has the right to expect."[68]

The degree of success or rates of production of the *Atelier cordonnerie* are not known, but there can be little doubt that the effort by the Committee of Public Safety substantially transformed the trade of shoemaker as it had been practiced by masters, journeymen, and apprentices during the Old Regime. As R.R. Palmer observed, the Committee of Public Safety "was on the side of production" and its labor policies had a great deal in common with those of the early industrial capitalists.[69]

In fact, the emphasis on quantity rendered the Old Regime mode of manufacture obsolete and anticipated the factory system of the nineteenth century – as did the regimentation of labor – with production quotas and strict discipline of workers. Much like the woolen center of Lodève on the eve of the Revolution studied by Christopher H. Johnson, the Shoemaking Workshop, which had no machine technology, was moving toward the factory system.[70] Shoemakers were now confronted with an impersonal authority that had an overriding concern with the level of production.[71] Indeed, during May 1796, a

---

[66] BHVP Ms. 749, fol. 203.

[67] BHVP Ms. 749, fol. 204.

[68] BHVP Ms. 746, fol. 95. The need during the autumn of 1795 was critical, with troops complaining about being barefoot. McPhee, *Living the French Revolution*, p. 197.

[69] Palmer, *Twelve Who Ruled*, p. 242.

[70] Christopher Johnson, "Capitalism and the State: Capital Accumulation and Proletarianization in the Languedocian Woolens Industry, 1700–1789," in *The Workplace before the Factory*, p. 60.

[71] In a similar undertaking, a workshop for the manufacture of boots for the Army of the West, fighting the counterrevolutionary guerilla movement in Brittany, had been established in Nantes and had at one time produced 700 pairs of boots per day. It closed during December, 1795, because of a lack of funds. *Journal du Bon-Homme Richard*, 25 frimaire year IV (December 16, 1795). In the town of Bourg the requisition of shoemakers was more

rumor arose in Paris that shoemakers near Calais were planning an uprising, but this produced little more than a shrug of the shoulders, suggesting that the difficult lot of shoemakers was well known.[72]

Apart from the direct impact upon the Old Regime mode of manufacture of boots and shoes in terms of production and discipline, there was an indirect impact that is more difficult to document and must be inferred. The recalcitrance of section officials such as those of Pont Neuf, and the clear reluctance of shoemakers to be included on the list for possible summons, would suggest that many men must have left the trade to avoid requisition.

THE PUBLIC EXPERIENCE WITH THE END
OF GUILDS: BAKERS

The metamorphosis of former guild-based trades was not a process exclusively tied to war production. To understand more fully the disaffection that resulted from the abolition of guilds and the manner in which that abolition was experienced by ordinary French men and women, an examination of bakers in Paris is appropriate.[73]

The guild of bakers of Paris had been one of the oldest in the city, with origins that extended back to the medieval era and perhaps even earlier.[74] It had been governed by six officers, known as *jurés*, who were elected each year. These officials had as their primary task the protection of the privileges of their corporation, but there was a perceived public dimension to their duties as well. To be sure, the guild had strongly enforced its near monopoly on the baking and sale of various breads, as well as the right of the guild to discipline its members for infractions and to defend a host of other privileges and immunities. At the same time, however, the *jurés* had worked closely with the Lieutenant-General of Police and performed what today would be considered public functions – tasks that went beyond conditions of work. A principal obligation of the corporation, especially from the perspective of the police, was regulating the quality and weight of bread, responsibilities that were particularly critical during times of dearth.[75]

When guilds were suppressed in 1791, not only had the privileges of bakers disappeared, but so too had the ancillary functions that the corporation had carried out, particularly those dealing with the quality of bread or the

---

successful, but the program was hindered by a shortage of leather suitable for boots. *Arrêté du directoire du district de Bourg, concernant la suspension de la fabrication des souliers et bottes pour l'armée, jusqu'à l'approvisionnement de cuirs forts, du 18 vendémiaire an III* (N.p., n.d.).

[72] AN AF IV 1473, report of 30 floréal year IV.

[73] For a larger overview of the decline of professional standards in commerce, see James Robert Munson, "Businessmen, Business Conduct and the Civic Organization of Commercial Life under the Directory and Napoleon," Ph.D. dissertation, Columbia University, 1992, pp. 1–55.

[74] Kaplan, *The Bakers of Paris*, p. 155.

[75] *Ibid.*, pp. 164–165.

assistance provided during provisioning crises. Indeed, during a minor provisioning crisis in July 1791, municipal officials in Bordeaux had taken the
unusual step of summoning the former officers of the dissolved guild of bakers to assist with the problem.[76] In addition, the number of bakers proliferated substantially – in the faubourg Saint-Antoine the number of bakeries
increased by nearly 50 percent after the abolition of guilds[77] – making it more
difficult to monitor abuses.

The outbreak of war made the already formidable task of provisioning Paris
and other cities more difficult, and the guild, which the police, prior to the
Revolution, had firmly believed to be pivotal in supplying the city,[78] obviously
could not serve any kind of function in terms of supply or scrutinizing defects
in the production and sale of bread. By early 1793, police reports indicated
that elements of the Parisian populace were becoming disillusioned with freedom of trade and commerce, particularly with respect to the food supply.

At this time, the police perceived bakers as playing a useful role in preventing
discord in the selling of bread by weight. In fact, a police agent even suggested a
measure that recalled the former system of guilds – compelling bakers to place
a mark on their bread.[79] By April 1793, journeymen bakers, free of any threat of
action by the guild, were coming together to make demands by threatening to
stop work. The police were again alarmed and recognized the need to act.[80]

During February 1793, the National Convention made all unmarried or
widowed males between the ages of eighteen and forty liable for military service, but during the following month, on March 11, 1793, concerned about
provisioning the city, the Convention passed a law exempting those who
worked in bakeries in Paris from being called up.[81] Although the decree specified that only those who were already in the trade were eligible for exemption, within a few months there were major complaints against bakers and the
quality of bread, suggesting that unscrupulous men or men who knew little
about the production of bread – many undoubtedly seeking to avoid military
service – had made their way into the trade.

During September 1793, the police reported that the quality of bread at
several shops was "detestable" and at some gatherings individuals asked why
the bread was whiter at some bakeries – the suspicion arose that bakers in
some neighborhoods were putting ashes in bread in order to make the loaves
heavier.[82] By December 1793, there were complaints that bread in some parts

---

[76] AM Bordeaux D 92, fol. 22. The action was somewhat ironic because just a few months earlier, during April, 1791, district administrators had sought to prevent a meeting of journeymen bakers by invoking laws against assemblies of citizens meeting by corporation or trade.
AM Bordeaux D 139, fol. 49v°.

[77] Monnier, *Le Faubourg Saint-Antoine*, p. 73.

[78] Kaplan, *Bakers of Paris*, p. 189.

[79] AN AF IV 1470, report of March 2, 1793.

[80] *Ibid.*, report of April 6, 1793.

[81] AN AD XI 65, decree of National Convention, March 11, 1793. Bakers had earlier been
exempted from requisitioning to manufacture pikes. See BHVP Ms. N.A. 152, fol. 161.

[82] AN F⁷ 3688³, dossier 2, documents 69, 97, 120.

of the city was of such poor quality that many people were becoming sick. Citizens, the police noted, no longer complained about the scarcity of bread, but about its quality.[83] One report stated that bread had caused people to have stomach pains and a fever.[84] During December 1793, the revolutionary society of the Indivisibility section of Paris arrested a baker and took him to the police for using a poor-quality leavening agent and insufficiently cooking the bread.[85]

In fact, during January 1793, just a few weeks before the decree of the Convention exempting bakers from military service, the revolutionary committee of the Observatory section of Paris asserted that the spirit of liberty was little seen among bakers – the committee observed that bakers had maintained a corporate spirit since the Revolution. The committee argued that it was the manner in which bakers conducted themselves that threatened the populace with a scarcity of bread, and bakers arrogantly stated that if freedom of buying and selling was not restored, matters would go from bad to worse. The committee acknowledged that before the Revolution, when the guild of bakers had had the right to store supplies, there had been no "artificial" shortages and the price of bread had been stable and moderate. The bakers were almost all the same men as in 1789, the committee asserted, and its members wanted to make it easier for new bakers to establish themselves in the section because it believed that former guild members dominated the trade and discouraged competition despite the dissolution of the corporation.

Indeed, the Commune had considered establishing public baking ovens in Paris to introduce competition for bakers. The committee disagreed with this approach, and instead proposed subsidizing individual bakers to allow them to open their own shops. The new bakers, all of whom would be "good *sans-culottes*," would compete with existing bakers and help diminish lines at bread shops. The committee suggested to those who opposed the project – in the belief that it was not bakers who were lacking, but flour – that its intent was to destroy the *esprit de corps* that it believed still prevailed among bakers and was one of the primary causes of the current difficulties. The committee asserted that the corporation of bakers should have been totally destroyed and ought not to be allowed to exist, and that the only way to eradicate it was to put new bakers in place.[86]

---

[83] AN F⁷ 3688³, dossier 1–10 nivôse, documents 276, 310.

[84] AN F⁷ 3688³, dossier 11–20 nivôse, document 340.

[85] *Annales patriotiques et littéraires de la France, et affaires politiques de l'Europe; journal libre, par une société d'écrivains patriotes*, 25 frimaire year II (December 15, 1793).

[86] *Compte rendu par le Comité révolutionnaire de la section de l'Observatoire, sur les mesures à prendre pour détruire l'esprit de corps qui règne parmi les boulangers* (N.p., 1793). Similarly, during 1794, coal carriers in Paris felt compelled to defend themselves against the accusation that they were forming a corporation by refusing to admit new carriers. The coal carriers suggested measures that could be taken to dispel the notion that they were forming a corporation. The vehemence with which they denied maintaining a closed corporate structure suggests how opposed much of the Parisian populace was to that ideal. *Les Charbonniers de Paris à leurs concitoyens* (Paris, 1794) [BHVP 136437].

By 1795, however, against the backdrop of bread lines and other difficulties, such anti-Old Regime sentiments began to abate. During the latter portion of the winter of 1794–1795, as bread rationing set in, Parisians became restive, and a deep resentment toward bakers took root as residents stood in line before their shops.[87] Municipal authorities sought to appease public anger by prosecuting some bakers for cheating customers, but such actions did little to ameliorate shortages.[88]

Indeed, a police report of 13 germinal year III (April 2, 1795) from the Unity section of Paris noted that individuals waiting in line to buy bread were saying that the situation had been better during the Old Regime. As scarcity continued, such sentiments became more widespread.[89] Another report indicated that workers, although peaceful, were vocal in their complaints about the lack of bread in the section, and asserted that their ability to work was impaired by a lack of nourishment. In fact, some quit work altogether, announcing that they would return only when they received bread.[90]

Rumors of a reduction in bread allotments during the severe winter of 1794–1795 increased unease and led to complaints in which some spoke favorably of the Old Regime, and inhabitants expected action from the National Convention to address their plight.[91] By late March 1795, their disaffection was apparent – and workers spoke of taking cannons to the Convention.[92]

The prairial rising a few months later reflected alienation from the post-Thermidorian Convention, and the Convention passed unlamented among workers. A police report from Paris, only days after the Convention disbanded, observed that the populace was against the Convention, believing that it had concluded its work without addressing the welfare of the people.[93] The Convention also bequeathed to its successor, the Directory, a still-dire economic situation.

THE NATIONAL CONVENTION AND THE BEGINNING OF THE DRIVE FOR MECHANIZATION: THE INSTITUTIONAL FRAMEWORK

Although it had abandoned a direct role in the production of muskets, the government sought to establish an institutional framework for the pursuit of mechanization of production in the private sector. As Margaret Jacob noted,

[87] AN AF IV 1471, reports of 7 ventôse year III (February 25, 1795), 10 ventôse year III (February 28, 1795).

[88] *Jugement du Tribunal de police correctionelle*, 23 prairial year III [BHVP 136018 4°; BHVP 136019 4°].

[89] AN AF IV 1471, report of 13 germinal year III (April 2, 1795). On the scarcity of bread, see AN AF IV 1471, report of 28 germinal year III (April 17, 1795); on yearning for the Old Regime, AN AF IV 1471, report of 10 ventôse year III (February 28, 1795).

[90] AN AF IV 1471, reports of 12 germinal year III (April 1, 1795); 28 germinal year III (April 17, 1795).

[91] AN AF IV 1471, reports of 1 ventôse year III (February 20, 1795), 7 ventôse year III (February 25, 1795), 10 ventôse year III (February 28, 1795).

[92] AN AF IV 1471, report of 27 ventôse year III (March 17, 1795).

[93] AN AF IV 1472, report of 6 brumaire year IV (October 28, 1795).

"the application of mechanical and chemical knowledge to manufacturing of everything from fabrics to engines became a doctrine built into the ideological framework of French republicanism both at home and abroad."[94] An initial step, and eventual cornerstone, of this effort was the establishment of the Conservatoire des Arts et Métiers by the National Convention on 8 vendémiaire year III (September 29, 1794) after the presentation of a report by abbé Henri-Baptiste Grégoire.

Speaking on behalf of the Committee on Agriculture and Arts and the Committee on Instruction, Grégoire opened his report by noting that if, by using machines, one man could do the work of two or three men, then one had, in that sphere, effectively doubled or tripled the number of citizens. He extolled the virtues of machines and industry and scoffed at those who continued to claim that the improvement of industry and the simplification of handwork would deprive many workers of their means of existence. It did not take a genius, he stated, to realize that there was a greater amount of work than there were workers, and that simplifying handwork and lowering its cost would be a sure path to establishing profitable trade that would overwhelm foreign industry.

Grégoire claimed that France possessed a "prodigious quantity" of machines, especially those from the suppressed Academy of Sciences and those of Jacques de Vaucanson. More importantly, Grégoire noted, Vaucanson's tools for constructing machines had been preserved as well. The best means of utilizing the disparate collections of machines was to combine them at a single site – a *conservatoire* – that would facilitate their use and encourage additional development. Foreshadowing in some respects the idea of the industrial exhibition begun by the Directory a few years later, Grégoire said that the proposed *conservatoire* should include a space in which all new inventions could be displayed.

A critical element of Grégoire's argument was that, during the past few years, imports in France came to more than 300 million livres, and a large portion of them consisted of manufactured goods. He asserted that French manufacturers had great potential and that greater economic independence would be possible.

Grégoire stated that a large building was necessary for the proposed *conservatoire*, and indicated that priority should be given to textile machinery. Along with the machines, the *conservatoire* would retain samples of the products created by them for purposes of comparison, and would maintain designs of all machines.

Grégoire told the Convention that the proposed *conservatoire* could operate on an annual budget of 16,000 livres. He asserted that if the aim was to advance industry and carry its flame everywhere, then the urgency of making it a priority would be clear. The *conservatoire*, he opined, would become a

[94] Margaret Jacob, *Scientific Culture and the Making of the Industrial West* (Oxford: Oxford University Press, 1997), p. 183.

reservoir from which canals would emanate to fertilize every area of France by disseminating drawings, descriptions, and even models of machines. The report was heavily applauded, and the Convention approved the project.[95]

The Atelier de Perfectionnement had been dedicated primarily to systematizing the production of muskets, but it also had had a larger goal, which was to build and perfect machines for the manufacture of other objects the republic might need.[96] The Committee of Public Safety observed that the *atelier* was "a valuable resource to advance the perfection of instruments for the greater part of the mechanical arts" and on 13 nivôse year III (January 2, 1795) it ordered that it be placed under the jurisdiction of the Commission on Agriculture and Arts, with its collection of machines to be placed at the disposition of the Conservatoire des Arts et Métiers, which was overseen by the commission.[97]

The measure reflected the Convention's continuing change of course. The Conservatoire des Arts et Métiers was founded to give the French state a means to promote technology, but without owning the means of production, as had been the case during the Terror, particularly with the Atelier de Perfectionnement.[98]

The Commission on Agriculture and Arts wrote to the *conservatoire* to ask how many workers should be assigned to the *atelier*. The *conservatoire* replied on 25 germinal year III (April 14, 1795) that it believed that the commission should stock the *atelier* not only with machines that it might judge essential for the defense of the nation, but for industry in general. It recommended thirty workers as the proper level for staffing.[99]

The decree of 13 nivôse had created an "interesting subordination" of the Atelier de Perfectionnement to the *conservatoire* in the view of the new overseer of the *atelier*, the Committee on Agriculture and Arts. The committee believed that the *atelier* should continue to work on methods of manufacturing firearms but also pursue instruments pertinent to "mechanical arts," and to construct models and machines destined for the *conservatoire* and to do the same for machines currently in its collection that might be sent to outlying departments.[100]

The consolidation of the Atelier de Perfectionnement with the *conservatoire* did not occur until the *conservatoire* took possession of the former monastery

95 [Henri-Baptiste Grégoire] *Rapport sur l'établissement d'un Conservatoire des Arts et Métiers par Grégoire* (Paris: Imprimerie Nationale, 1794). On the warm reception given to the report, *Annales de la république française, et journal historique et politique de l'Europe*, 10 vendémiaire year III (October 1, 1794). It was also well-received outside of the Convention. *La Décade philosophique, littéraire et politique*, 10 brumaire year III (October 31, 1794).

96 AN F¹² 1310, report presented to Minister of the Interior by the Fourth Division [undated].

97 AN F¹² 1310, extract from register of decrees of Committee of Public Safety, 13 nivôse year III (January 2, 1795).

98 Alder, *Engineering the Revolution*, p. 315.

99 AN F¹² 1310, letter of members of *Conservatoire des Arts et Métiers* to Commission on Agriculture and Arts, 25 germinal year III (April 14, 1795).

100 AN F¹² 1556, report to Committee on Agriculture and Arts, (undated, but attached to proposed decree with date of 17 floréal year III, (May 6, 1795). See also AN F¹² 1310, report presented to Minister of the Interior by Fourth Division (undated).

of Saint-Martin des Champs during the year VI.[101] Until the merger the *atelier* did not develop as an innovative or dynamic institution, undoubtedly because of financial constraints on the government. Indeed, on 24 brumaire year IV (November 15, 1795) an official in the Ministry of the Interior lamented the fact that the *atelier*, which was "very costly to the Republic," was languishing because of a lack of needed materials.[102]

Despite the goal of developing and facilitating the use of machines in departments and the recommendation by the *conservatoire* to the Commission on Agriculture and Arts that it receive thirty workers, the *atelier* remained a small operation. Its final budget revealed a staff of five and an annual budget of only 15,100 francs – clearly leaving it with little capacity to do more than preserve the machines and other items in its collection.[103]

The founding of the Conservatoire des Arts et Métiers represented a significant departure because, like their royal predecessors, the men of the republic had given priority to agriculture over industry – during thermidor year II, even with a labor shortage, workers from Paris were sent to the countryside to assist with the harvest.[104] Indeed, undoubtedly to gain acceptance of his proposal, Grégoire had assured the Convention that the establishment of the *conservatoire* would take nothing away from agriculture, which would continue to have first priority.[105]

Without question, the Committee of Public Safety only belatedly recognized the necessity of making the manufacturing sector the subject of policy, although even its initial efforts were tied to reviving agriculture. On 20 germinal year II (April 9, 1794) the committee responded to a request for a subsidy from François Richard, who would become a major figure in the cotton industry during the Napoleonic period, with the following observations:

The Committee of Public Safety considers that one of the efficacious means to restore abundance is to give manufacturing a special protection from which will necessarily emanate the improvement of agriculture.

At long last the time has come when national industry, assisted by the salutary aims of the representatives of the people, is going to recover all of its spirit [and] vigor and will soon serve as a model for Europe.[106]

An outline of a plan to build up the republic's industry and manufacture "without harming rural industry" is found in a memorandum drafted on 5 prairial year III (May 24, 1795). By July 1794, the survival of the republic was

---

[101] On its movement to this site, Barry Bergdoll, "Les Aménagements du prieuré <<nationalisé>> (1798–1819)," in *Le Conservatoire national des Arts et Métiers au coeur de Paris*, Michel Le Moël and Raymond Saint-Paul, eds. (Paris: Délégation a l'Action Artistique de la Ville de Paris, 1994), pp. 51–56; AN F¹² 2178, no. 133.

[102] AN F¹² 1310, letter of head of Division of Minister of the Interior to Minister of the Interior, 24 brumaire year IV (November 15, 1795).

[103] AN F¹ᵇ I 56–59, dossier Atelier de Perfectionnement year V; BHVP Ms. N.A. 192, fol. 354.

[104] BHVP Ms. 769, fols. 99, 108, 109; see also BHVP Ms. 796, fol. 273.

[105] [Grégoire], *Rapport*, pp. 11–12.

[106] AN AF II 78, dossier 574, document 3.

assured, and in April 1795, France and Prussia signed a peace treaty. No longer preoccupied with war and survival, the men of the republic were now freer to take a larger view, and a major effort to mechanize production in France was one of the principal outcomes of that opening.

Drafted by the Bureau on Commerce, which advised the Committee of Public Safety on economic matters after Thermidor, the proposed plan focused on textiles, especially cotton and wool, and sought not merely to bring about prosperity but, by perfecting manufacture, to achieve "preponderance in the markets of Europe." The memorandum also noted that mechanization would alleviate the labor shortage in France, allowing for greater development of industry and agriculture. It asserted that in many departments, especially throughout the Midi, which possessed a number of manufacturing facilities, rural industry suffered from a rivalry for workers – cities attracted people from the countryside who were thereby lost as agricultural laborers. The great virtue of mechanization, the authors of the memorandum argued, was that it would restore a balance between the two sectors.

The goal of mechanization was to reestablish the manufacturing sector without upheaval and with an economy of operation that would lower the costs of production and thus reduce the price of the cloth produced. There were, according to the memorandum, inventors waiting only for a signal from the government, and production facilities in the Midi desired machines. The Bureau on Commerce was convinced of their usefulness and asked the Committee of Public Safety to support inventors to enable them to devote themselves to this undertaking.

The memorandum pointed out that the former Hôtel de Mortagne possessed a valuable collection of models and machines that could be useful in developing French industry. The collection had belonged to Jacques de Vaucanson, whom the authors of the memorandum credited with leading inventors and engineers on the road to perfection.[107] The machines were in good condition, and the collection was already open to nonprofessionals and inventors who had the ability to make copies and to develop new inventions or perfect those already in existence.

The Bureau on Commerce sought to concentrate particularly on machines for the textile industry, and endeavored to found an institution – overseen by skillful, enthusiastic and honest inventors and mechanics – that could develop such machines. The cost of an institution of this type would not be onerous for the government, the memorandum asserted, because twenty to thirty workers known for their skill and devotion to work would suffice. If access to machines was established in this manner, then others could imitate, copy or perhaps even perfect or improve them. As a result, different manufacturers in France would visit the depot of machines more frequently

---

[107] Vaucanson had a much larger reputation during the eighteenth and nineteenth centuries than in the modern era. David M. Fryer and John C. Marshall, "The Motives of Jacques de Vaucanson," *Technology and Culture* 20 (1979): 257–269.

and would be inclined to seek machines from Parisian mechanics. The cumulative effect of all of this would be to develop new means of production and achieve greater prosperity, allowing France to achieve preponderance over foreign industry.[108] Ultimately, the Vaucanson collection was also transferred to the *conservatoire* after it took possession of the Saint-Martin des Champs site.[109]

In addition to the creation of the *conservatoire* and the merging of collections, the Convention considered subsidies and support to entrepreneurs in order to revive production. An individual from the Department of Jura sought a site and an advance of 25,000 francs to establish a soap factory. The Commission on Agriculture and Arts examined the proposal for the committee of the same name. It noted that the applicant claimed to have discovered an indigenous plant that contained so much soda that it could be substituted for lye, thereby facilitating domestic production of soap. The commission observed, however, that establishing the proposed manufactory in the locality requested would place it far from a supply of olive oil and present other disadvantages, which led it to recommend that the request be rejected. The commission also asserted that the factories in Marseille – "momentarily in decline through the course of events," a discreet reference to the federalist revolt – would better merit the assistance of the government. The Committee on Agriculture and Arts agreed with the opinion and turned down the request.[110]

The petition is of interest for two reasons. The report shows the seriousness and care with which the Committee on Agriculture and Arts treated requests for assistance in an effort to revive production in the nonagricultural sector. More important, however, was the introduction by the Convention of a policy of offering sites from the inventory of nationalized property and advancing subsidies to individuals to restore and increase manufacturing capacity. This policy would be continued by the Directory and the Napoleonic regime and would ultimately have an important influence in some areas of the economy, especially the textile sector.

Indeed, the Convention carried out a comprehensive survey during the summer of 1794 to ascertain "all the types of production and industry that existed in the Republic," and on 14 messidor year II (July 2, 1794) it sent a questionnaire to all districts that was made deliberately simple in order to facilitate responses. It asked administrators whether there existed in their jurisdiction "manufactories, factories, and industrial establishments" and, if the answer was in the affirmative, to list them. All but about fifty districts responded to the questionnaire, and the Commission on Agriculture and Arts hoped that its analysis of the documents would produce "a kind of industrial geography of

---

[108] AN F¹²* 111–112, no. 10, 5 prairial year III (May 24, 1795).
[109] Dominique de Place, "L'Hôtel de Mortagne et les dépôts de l'an II," in *Le Conservatoire National des Arts et Métiers au coeur de Paris*, p. 50.
[110] AN F¹² 1556, report of Commission on Agriculture and Arts to Committee of Agriculture and Arts, 9 germinal year III (March 29, 1795).

France." The commission intended to print the results and once again circulate them to the districts and even allow the public to examine them in order to correct any errors or omissions. The information would then be used to found, extend, perfect – or abandon to their own devices – the various sectors of production.

It was a sweeping project, and one gains an insight into the ambitions of the commission from its discussion of pottery in the report. It indicates that the commission sought to carry out what would, during the twentieth century, be called industrial policy – favoring some industries over others – and to use industrial espionage.[111]

The commission stated that it believed it was necessary to perfect French pottery, an effort that had initially been advocated by the Committee of Public Safety.[112] The commission claimed to be in contact with an entrepreneur who was familiar with pottery processes, especially those of Josiah Wedgwood.[113] Under certain conditions, the commission stated, the entrepreneur was willing to establish a large pottery factory in France and to train French pupils in these processes. The commission said it was engaged in discussions with him, although the project seems not to have come to fruition.

The commission ultimately accorded primacy to the textile sphere, especially the perfection of spinning of all types and weaving. In addition to textiles, pottery was the other area to be given priority – these were the areas, the commission asserted, in which France was inferior to its enemies.[114] Although it did not move forward, the concentration on pottery, especially in the Wedgwood style, was a shrewd calculation. Josiah Wedgwood had intended to conquer the French market in 1769 and had made inroads in Germany through an unusual marketing strategy that centered on sending unsolicited items of his wares to 1,000 members of the German nobility. The export market for Wedgwood expanded substantially – by 1783 nearly 80 percent of total production was exported.[115]

The entire enterprise of seeking to compile an "industrial geography" of France and to identify certain sectors for support was extraordinary. The Convention's efforts to mechanize production and advance the nonagricultural sector were a major departure from past policies and a significant undertaking. Amidst the demands of war, the Convention consistently communicated the importance that it attached to mechanization, and exhorted officials in the departments to undertake particular efforts to this end.

[111] There was already a long tradition of industrial espionage between the two countries. J.R. Harris, *Industrial Espionage and Technology Transfer: Britain and France in the Eighteenth Century* (Aldershot: Ashgate, 1998).

[112] AN F^{12} 1556, undated report.

[113] Indeed, Wedgwood had been apprehensive about French competition. Horn, *The Path Not Taken*, p. 62.

[114] AN F^{12} 1556, statement of what has been done by division of Arts and Manufactures of Commission on Agriculture and Arts (undated).

[115] Nancy F. Koehn, *Brand New: How Entrepreneurs Earned Consumers' Trust from Wedgwood to Dell* (Boston, MA: Harvard Business School Press, 2001), pp. 32–36.

THE NATIONAL CONVENTION AND THE DRIVE TOWARD MECHANIZATION: IN THE FIELD

Although the recommendation on pottery did not come to fruition, the government vigorously pursued the proposal on textiles. Late in the year II and early the following year the Committee of Public Safety undertook an inquiry to determine the current state of wool production compared to the past, the results of which were discouraging and underscored the need to increase output. In Sedan, a traditional center of wool manufacturing, the level of production was about half of what it had been before the Revolution. In Rethel, lack of raw materials and a shortage of workers had significantly lowered output. Likewise, in Pont-à-Mousson, Boulogne, Carpentras, Carcassonne and other towns, a lack of workers and raw materials depressed production.

Although one cannot ascribe great accuracy to the questionnaire, it does reveal the direction of production and the perception of administrators. The document showed that the level of production had gone from 2,606,977 units (unspecified except as *nombre des pièces*) before the war to 802,408 since the war, and the number of workers had fallen from 594,911 to 320,874 and the number of finishing facilities from 1,404 to 894 during the same period.[116] With fewer facilities, declining production and a shortage of workers, the logic of mechanization was inescapable.

To this end, officials in the departments vigorously pursued industrial espionage and diffusion of technology. The use of industrial espionage and technology transfer was well established between Britain and France, each of which had sought to steal technology from the other in many fields during the eighteenth century.[117] Most textile machinery had originated in Britain, and the Convention and its successor, the Directory, intensified efforts to disseminate such machinery.[118]

The length to which the Convention was prepared to go in its imperative to mechanize is apparent in an incident that occurred during January 1795. The district agent for Lille had submitted a report on the state of textile production facilities, and in it mentioned that during 1789 or 1790 the municipality had purchased a machine for the spinning of wool that allowed one man to do the work of twenty, but when the machine arrived production was in a depressed state and unemployment was high. Workers in Lille, realizing that the introduction of the machine would significantly reduce the need for labor, had made strong representations not to allow it to begin operation. The municipal authorities had acceded to their request and the machine had been sequestered.

---

[116] AN F¹² 1344, inquiry made by Committee of Public Safety on the former and current state of production of cloth and woolens, year II-year III; general results (undated). For an account of the decline of the woolen industry in Elbeuf, Jeffry Kaplow, *Elbeuf During the Revolutionary Period: History and Social Structure* (Baltimore, MD: Johns Hopkins University Press, 1964), pp. 111–119.

[117] Harris, *Industrial Espionage and Technology Transfer.*

[118] AN AF III 21 A, dossier 70 G, documents 30–31.

The Commission on Agriculture and Arts observed to the agent that the current situation was entirely the reverse – that a labor shortage kept the republic from meeting all of its needs in textile production, particularly for its troops.[119] It was now a question of whether one should put into operation immediately a machine that could increase production and contribute to the greater good. The commission sought to discover the location of the machine, the identity of its maker, to whom it belonged and how advantageous it would be, if located, in the production of woolen cloth. The commission pressed the district agent to procure this information and the services of a skilled mechanician if necessary.[120]

Similarly, after French troops had retaken Belgium, they found a British cotton-spinning machine in a town near Brussels. The machine had belonged to a textile firm in Brussels, and the care the authorities took with the machine reflects how successfully the central government had communicated the urgency of mechanization. Representatives of the firm had requested compensation, which had been paid, and the machine had been declared property of the republic and transported to Dunkirk. The municipality of Dunkirk had asked that it be allowed to retain control of the machine, the technology of which was "absolutely unknown," so that copies could be constructed for use throughout northern France. The municipality also desired to train indigent workers on the machines as a form of poor relief, particularly as their number had increased due to the abolition of the port's exclusive privileges by the Convention.[121] The request had been granted, and the Minister of War had consented to grant a site in Dunkirk where the machine could be studied for duplication.[122] Indeed, Belgium proved to be a treasure-trove of British machines and Dunkirk became the collection and storage point for them. They were to be set up in a former textile mill opened by an Englishman named Mather in 1787.[123]

The Commission on Agriculture and Arts argued, however, that rather than installing the machines in a particular establishment, a more advantageous policy would be to bring them to the Conservatoire des Arts et Métiers, where they could be duplicated and disseminated, thereby furthering the progress of French industry. The commission proposed sending a trained mechanician to Dunkirk to select the best model of each type of

---

[119] On the labor shortage, AN AF IV 1471, summary of political situation of republic, pluviôse-ventôse year III (January–March, 1795).

[120] AN F¹² 2195, letter of Commission on Agriculture and Arts to national agent of district of Lille, 18 nivôse year III (January 7, 1795).

[121] AN F¹² 2195, undated memorandum on English machines to spin cotton.

[122] AN F¹² 2195, letter of Commission on Agriculture and Arts to national agent of district of Lille, 18 nivôse year III (January 7, 1795).

[123] AN F¹² 1556, report to Committee on Agriculture and Arts, 18 pluviôse year III (February 6, 1795). Subsequently, however, the Minister of the Interior became concerned about the state of the machines that were left in Dunkirk. AN F¹² 2195, letter of Minister of the Interior to commission of departmental administration of Department of Ourthe, 8 prairial year IV (May 27, 1796).

machine to send to the *conservatoire*. In addition, it suggested sending a draftsman to make drawings of machines not chosen or of those too difficult to move.[124]

The commission also argued that, with its port, Dunkirk already had a major economic resource and that any textile center to be established should be set up in the interior of France.[125] It wrote a draft decree that not only mandated the transfer of the best machines to the Conservatoire des Arts et Métiers, but also ordered that the machines not sent to Paris be sold to the highest bidder, on the condition that they be set up in France.[126]

STEMMING SENTIMENT TO REESTABLISH GUILDS

Even as the Convention pushed its goal of mechanization of production, it was aware of underlying favorable sentiment toward guilds. Officials in the Bureau on Commerce were of course opposed to masterships and corporations as harmful to industry, but at the same time, in a memorandum written during the summer of 1795, recognized that their abolition had unleashed great disorder and that an "anarchic confusion" currently reigned in commerce. The memorandum acknowledging this situation also asserted that there was a "commercial rage" that led everyone to be a merchant and no one to be a worker, and urged the government to address the situation.[127]

The bureau suggested reviving the occupational license, but in a manner that would return order to the workplace – an individual would present himself to his municipality or section and declare an occupation he wished to pursue. The process would be overseen by a commercial court (*tribunal de commerce*) where such institutions existed and by the justice of the peace where they did not.[128]

Within just two weeks the Convention sought to eradicate speculation, abuses, and illicit commerce and to reestablish some semblance of order in commerce by bringing back a modified version of the occupational license. On 4 thermidor year III (July 22, 1795) the deputy Théodore Vernier presented a report on the *patente* in the name of the Committee of Public Safety and the Committee on Finances.

---

[124] AN F¹² 1556, undated report of Commission on Agriculture and Arts attached to report of Committee of Agriculture and Arts, 18 pluviôse year III (February 6, 1795).

[125] *Ibid.*

[126] AN F¹² 1556, undated draft decree of Committee on Agriculture and Arts.

[127] AN F¹²* 111–112, no. 15, 21 messidor year III (July 9, 1795). The observation of the bureau is supported by a commentator during the summer of 1795 who asserted that the current state of commerce was such that honest businessmen, legitimately concerned about being enveloped in the general antipathy that the brigandage present in commerce inspired, dared not allow themselves to undertake legitimate endeavors. Instead, they preferred to stand aside and to await the return of observed rules rather than expose themselves to becoming victims of chicanery. *Annales de la république française, et journal historique et politique de l'Europe*, 23 messidor year III (July 11, 1795).

[128] AN F¹²* 111–112, no. 15, 21 messidor year III (July 9, 1795).

In the plan Vernier offered, the occupational license would apply only to merchants and the focus would be on reducing the number of merchants engaged in multiple lines of commerce by requiring them to purchase a separate license for each element of commerce. Those who practiced arts or trades were exempt from the *patente*, as were street vendors of flowers, fruits, vegetables and the like.

Those who did not wish to procure a license had one month to sell their merchandise. Those who did secure one were required, within ten days, to post in a prominent place the exact nature of their commerce.

Vernier, who had been a deputy in the National Assembly when guilds were abolished, assured deputies that the revamped *patente* did not amount to a revival of corporations and masterships. He reiterated the fact that arts and trades were exempt from the *patente*; its main purpose, he asserted, was to curtail speculation and abuses, particularly in daily necessities such as bread and meat.[129] The Convention approved the measure, but within weeks the law was being evaded by unscrupulous merchants.[130] Furthermore, more than a year later, the license was quietly broadened to include producers as well as merchants.[131]

The characterization of the current state of affairs as "anarchic confusion" highlights the attraction for contemporaries of reestablishing guilds in some form – doing so would restore a sense of order and help ensure quality in both goods and services. A police report of 10 ventôse year III (February 28, 1795) noted that citizens lined up outside the doorways of bakers in Paris were extremely disgruntled over rumored reductions in the bread ration and the high cost of food and other necessities. The discontent had given rise to conversations in which some malcontents had attempted to inspire a sense of regret at the loss of the Old Regime. By early April the police reported that workers were walking off the job and stating that they would not return until they had bread, and the next day crowds in front of bakeries were, in fact, speaking favorably of the Old Regime. The day after that, most workers were on the job, but the situation remained a matter of concern for the police.[132]

Again, the police reports should not be interpreted as reflecting a sense of enthusiasm for the reestablishment of guilds. Rather, they demonstrate a nostalgia for some organization of the world of work as the government – once more

---

[129] *Annales de la république française*, 7 thermidor year III (July 25, 1795); *Journal du Perlet*, 5 thermidor year III (July 23, 1795); *La Décade philosophique, littéraire et politique*, 10 thermidor year III (July 28, 1795). On the conditions that led to the proposal, *Annales de la république française*, 5 thermidor year III (July 23, 1795). For more on the reestablishment of the *patente*, Munson, "Businessmen, Business Conduct and the Civic Organization of Commercial Life," pp. 72–90.

[130] *Journal du Bon-Homme Richard*, 14 fructidor year III (August 31, 1795).

[131] *La Décade philosophique, littéraire et politique*, 20 frimaire year V (December 10, 1796).

[132] AN AF IV 1471, general reports of 10 ventôse year III (February 28, 1795), 12 germinal year III (April 1, 1795), 13 germinal year III (April 2, 1795), 14 germinal year III (April 3, 1795), 15 germinal year III (April 4, 1795), 28 germinal year III (April 17, 1795). On the chaos faced by authorities in economic reconstruction, AN AB^XIX 3889, decree of Committee on Commerce, 19 prairial year III (June 7, 1795).

in a contingent fashion – sought to negotiate a path between order and liberty and to define the boundaries between the economy and the government.

That even the Atelier de Perfectionnement experienced turmoil during prairial year III (May–June 1795) indicates the depth of worker unrest. The government replaced the inspector of the *atelier* that month and authorized the new inspector to take any measure necessary to restore order among workers – indeed, it warned the new inspector that he was expected to follow all regulations for the *atelier*.[133] Although they regarded the abuses in the workplace as only a passing phase, officials in the bureaus nevertheless believed that it was critical to encourage workers to return to workshops and to have rules governing work and quality, but without compromising the revolutionary ideal of liberty.[134]

In fact, at almost the same time that the bureau was acknowledging the difficulties caused by the abolition of guilds, a group of textile manufacturers in Carcassonne wrote to it on this very topic. In a letter sent after the bureau had acknowledged receipt of a completed survey on the state of commerce in the district, the producers stated that they wanted to offer additional suggestions to the bureau as it sought to rehabilitate commerce. Major abuses had arisen in the textile trade, they noted, with most of them having occurred since the abolition of guilds, masterships, inspections, and regulations. There was no longer any "subordination" between manufacturers and their "co-operators," and there were no efforts being made to prevent theft, fraud, and bad faith. Although they explicitly stated that they were not advocating the restoration of corporations – they wished, they said, to preserve individual diligence and public freedom – they did ask the bureau to formulate some well-crafted laws applicable to the current circumstances in order to remedy the situation.[135]

The government was already aware of severe problems in textile production. The Provisioning Commission had written to the Commission on Agriculture and Arts during early 1795 to inform it of numerous complaints that the Provisioning Commission was receiving about the quality of the cloth used in military uniforms.

The Provisioning Commission informed the Commission on Agriculture and Arts that it was being informed about the poor quality of cloth on a daily basis. The Provisioning Commission also argued that the situation was so serious that it required inspectors to be posted at production centers to assure quality. The Provisioning Commission argued that the placement of such inspectors would be in the general interest as well as that of the troops.[136]

---

[133] AN F¹² 1310, extract from register of deliberations of Commission on Agriculture and Arts, prairial year III (no day given).

[134] *Ibid.* On the state of work, AN AF IV 1471, general reports of 11 ventôse year III (March 1, 1795), 20 ventôse year III (March 10, 1795).

[135] AN F¹² 1391, letter of correspondents of Carcassonne to members of Committee (*sic*) on Commerce at Paris, 20 messidor year III (July 8, 1795).

[136] AN F¹² 1391, letter of Provisioning Commission to Commission on Agriculture and Arts, 29 ventôse year III (March 19, 1795).

Almost certainly aware of the deep disaffection with the unregulated market and workplace established since the Revolution, and aware also that the favorable recollections of the guild era that had crystallized could lead to some form of restoration of guilds, the Commission of Eleven, a committee charged by the National Convention to draft a constitution, included, among a few general dispositions, the proscription of guilds in the draft it presented on 5 messidor year III (June 23, 1795).[137] There are no records of the internal deliberations of the Commission of Eleven, but five of its members had been deputies to the National Assembly and a sixth was the son of a deputy to the Assembly, suggesting that the commission may have been trying to preserve its legacy with the article.

The depth of concern about the ruinous effects of the abolition of guilds became evident in an apparent challenge to the proposed proscription of corporations that appeared weeks later as an anonymous article in the prestigious newspaper *Le Républicain français*, on 17 thermidor year III (August 4, 1795). Stating that freedom of commerce, like all other freedoms, required regulation so that that freedom would not degenerate into license, the article denounced speculators who sought to increase the price of the daily necessities they sold, thereby making dearth ubiquitous. Such was the current state of affairs in Paris and everywhere else in France, the writer claimed, and this had been the situation for some time.

The article also quoted an unnamed deputy as saying that freedom of commerce was undoubtedly good in itself, but abuses of it were well known and it was the responsibility of the Convention to correct the situation. What should be done, the anonymous deputy asked, about a man who passed himself off as a painter but who did not know how to pencil-sketch or mix colors, or the use to which a graving tool was put? We would, he wrote, call him a charlatan, but was not the freedom of commerce currently the palladium of rogues and ignoramuses, with the wigmaker selling sugar, the bookseller selling boots and the cobbler dealing in metal badges?

Undoubtedly, the writer asserted, a sense of equity would not admit ranks, but if society would not make them, nature was not as just – nature often established privileges, both physical and moral. The security and good order of the state demanded that the Convention follow the precepts of nature. The people had suffered enough to make it possible to amend the article, the writer declared, in reference to the article in the proposed constitution that banned corporations.

Deputies had long been asked to pass laws repressing quackery, but, the author stated, corrupters had slipped into all segments of society. He argued that a man with a *patente* – the law had been passed nearly two weeks earlier – should not be allowed to practice two occupations concurrently. If a baker wished to make boots, he undoubtedly had the right, but nature had

---

[137] *Projet de constitution, pour la république française; présenté par la commission des onze dans la séance de 5 messidor, l'an 3* (Paris: Imprimerie Nationale, an III).

not conferred upon man such a degree of self-sufficiency – it was necessary to depend on other citizens in order to bond with them.

Moreover, if a man could practice all occupations simultaneously, he would soon reduce the prosperity of all. Enact limits, the article implored, so as not to allow men to change occupations, or at least not to practice two occupations together.[138]

The next day in the Convention, the deputy Pierre-Joseph-Denis-Guillaume Faure took up the issue when he rose to offer a motion of order, a procedure to register an objection with the intent to gain reconsideration of a measure – in this instance, the law on *patentes*. He began by strongly attacking speculators and abuses in commerce and the deleterious effects that these activities had had on society and went on to assert that if the National Assembly had foreseen the current upheaval, it would not have abolished guilds. Corporations would have known how to stop such vampirism and, if guilds still existed, one would not see workers abandoning their work for such activities.

His comments provoked murmurs of disapproval in what was a lightly attended meeting, but Faure, undeterred, continued in a forceful fashion. He professed to favor freedom of commerce and to oppose limits on or intervention in it, but the current deplorable circumstances made it necessary to oversee strictly the conduct of businessmen or rather, he corrected himself, of speculators. The effects of speculation and abuses were catastrophic, and Faure averred that the Convention was aware of the dimensions of the problem, but remained silent – it was as if it were closing its eyes on the edge of an abyss that was about to engulf it.

Faure did not suggest the reestablishment of guilds, but he did propose strong oversight and sought to prevent individuals from engaging in two occupations concurrently. He proffered a plan under which each section of Paris would subdivide itself into smaller areas and name commissioners to police commerce in those areas. Although they were to be from the neighborhood, their authority would emanate from the Committee of General Security. In fact, they would be vested with the power to arrest those engaged in illicit commerce. They would also be authorized to make searches day and night and to verify the integrity and the merchandise of individuals. The Convention voted to send the proposal to the Committees on Legislation and General Security, but it was never acted upon.[139]

Faure, a deputy for Le Havre, was not a leading figure in the Convention. He was in fact one of its oldest and more moderate members – during the trial of Louis XVI he had sought to prevent the execution of the king. He subsequently signed a protest against the expulsion of the Brissotins from the Convention and was arrested during the late summer of 1793, but was

---

[138] *Le Républicain français*, 17 thermidor year III (August 4, 1795).

[139] *Annales de la république française*, 19 thermidor year III (August 6, 1795); *Annales patriotiques et littéraires*, 19 thermidor year III; *Le Républicain français*, 20 thermidor year III (August 7, 1795); *Affiches d'Angers ou Moniteur de département du Maine et Loire*, 25 thermidor year III (August 12, 1795).

not transferred before the Revolutionary Tribunal. Released after the fall of Robespierre, Faure retook his seat in the Convention on 18 frimaire year III (December 8, 1794). After his return, he spoke on a number of issues before retiring from politics when the Convention disbanded.[140]

While Faure represented the moderate wing of the Convention, the fact that doubts about the abolition of guilds spanned the spectrum of the Convention became evident a few weeks after his speech. On 30 fructidor year III (September 16, 1795), as debate on the new constitution reached its final stage, the article that prohibited guilds came up for consideration. Edmund-Louis-Alexis Dubois-Crancé spoke against it. In an indication that he may have been its author, Dubois-Crancé used exactly the same words that had appeared in the item in *Le Républicain français* a few weeks earlier, concluding with the observation that the people had suffered enough to make it possible to amend the article.

Dubois-Crancé's observation brought a response from Antoine-Claire Thibaudeau, a member of the Commission of Eleven that had prepared the constitution. Thibaudeau replied that he, in fact, believed it was necessary to take precautions in order to guarantee to society that anyone who practiced an occupation was able to do it in a beneficial manner and without posing a danger to anyone. As an example, Thibaudeau said that it was unacceptable to allow anyone to call himself a pharmacist and to sell drugs that could poison people. Indeed, such concerns appear to have formed the basis for article 356, which allowed for the surveillance of professions that affected public health or safety. Thibaudeau, however, asked that the article prohibiting corporations be enacted and that Dubois-Crancé's proposal be sent to the Commission of Eleven. The Convention agreed.[141]

Although the effort to amend the article that proscribed guilds failed, the identity of the deputy who sought it is telling. Dubois-Crancé was a committed republican who had pursued the execution of the king as assiduously as Faure had attempted to stop it – a near-contemporaneous biographical entry characterized Dubois-Crancé as "one of the most ardent persecutors" of the monarch.[142] It is testimony to the severity of the situation that developed after the abolition of guilds that deputies of such disparate outlooks as Faure and Dubois-Crancé were prepared to consider their reestablishment. And Dubois-Crancé's misgivings are all the more notable because he had been a deputy in the National Assembly when corporations had been abolished.

Indeed, during the following year a similar development occurred, but in a more explicit fashion. During the year IV (1795–1796) Pierre-Charles-Louis Baudin, a member of the Commission of Eleven, claimed authorship of the article proscribing guilds, particularly the second paragraph that effectively

---

[140] *Dictionnaire des parlementaires français*, 2: 608–609; *Dictionnaire de biographie française*, 13: 768–769.

[141] *Le Républicain français*, 2nd complementary day year III (September 18, 1795); AN C 232, dossier 183bis, document 15^a.

[142] *Biographie universelle (Michaud) ancienne et moderne*, new edition, 11: 360.

guaranteed the permanence of freedom of commerce – any abridgement of it could only be temporary and could last no longer than one year. Although the article had been given careful consideration, Baudin asserted, the provision had opened the door to considerable abuse, which might become permanent. His regret was obvious.[143]

The discussion and resolution of the article prohibiting guilds reveals the provisory method of deputies that both precipitated and followed the abolition of guilds. Furthermore, to the degree that the committee appointed to draft a constitution – the Commission of Eleven – prevailed, it appears that once again constitutional considerations triumphed over economic ones.

With its approval by the Convention, the measure became article 355 of the new constitution. Its enactment meant that the prohibition of guilds had constitutional as well as legislative status, making it more difficult to overturn. Prior to the inclusion of article 355 in the Constitution of the Year III, the d'Allarde or Le Chapelier laws could have been repealed or superseded by legislative action. With the proscription of corporations inserted into the constitution, however, any reversal became much more arduous. In an effort to impart stability, the Constitution of the Year III was made difficult to amend – any revision would require a minimum period of nine years.

THE TRANSITION TO THE DIRECTORY

The National Convention disbanded on October 26, 1795, yielding to the Directory, but it was much more a transition than a change because, by the Two-Thirds Decree, the Convention had mandated that at least two-thirds of its members had to comprise the initial composition of the Directory. There was already residual antipathy toward the new body because of the Two-Thirds Decree – it had been the catalyst for an uprising against the Convention during the month of prairial – and that antagonism was compounded by a poor harvest in 1795 and a harsh winter that began as the Directory took office. Rampant inflation and the collapse of the paper currency stifled commerce and adversely affected the poor. Moreover, France was now in its sixth year of continuous revolution and French society remained in a state of flux and turmoil – indeed, the Directory was the fourth government in six years.[144]

Under such circumstances, it is not surprising that what had been, under the Convention, a favorable recollection of the Old Regime era of corporations began to crystallize during the Directory into a yearning to reinstate the guild system. The causes of such longing are not difficult to discern because the French populace regularly encountered abuses that would have been virtually inconceivable before the abolition of corporations.

[143] P.C.L. Baudin (des Ardennes), *Eclaircissemens sur l'article 355 de la constitution, et sur la liberté de la presse* (Paris: Imprimerie nationale, year IV).

[144] For useful general overviews of the Directory, M.J. Sydenham, *The First French Republic 1792–1804* (Berkeley, CA: University of California Press, 1973); Martyn Lyons, *France Under the Directory* (Cambridge: Cambridge University Press, 1975).

Chief among them was the appalling quality of bread. Shortly before the Directory took office, on 24 vendémiaire year IV (October 16, 1795), the police had written a letter to civil and charitable committees of the sections of Paris to acknowledge the "general cry" that had arisen against the poor quality of bread. The police admitted that they had received many complaints of underbaking and manipulation of ingredients, which produced substandard bread. The police invited the committees to visit all of the bread shops of their section in order to ascertain whether the complaints were true. The police asserted that vigilance on the part of authorities would lead to a return of bread that was properly baked and of the full, legal weight.[145]

A few weeks later, however, shortly after the Directory had taken office, a police report of 12 brumaire year IV (November 3, 1795) noted that the majority of bakers in Paris were consistently reproached for the bad smell and poor quality of their bread, but the bakers blamed it on the poor quality of the flour they received. Two days later the police observed that the bread was again of poor quality, having been underbaked because of a shortage of wood. A few months later, the bread of the baker Beaufils in the Quinze-Vingts section was described as "only paste" and there were a large number of complaints against him.[146] The terrible winter of 1795–1796 and the hardships and suffering it caused led to rapid disaffection with the political class, and the unacceptable quality of bread played a role in this.[147]

It was not only bread shops that left inhabitants alienated from the new economic system.[148] Butchers were also a source of great resentment. During the Terror, butchers had flouted the Maximum in Paris by selling meat above the set price and by selling better cuts of meat to those willing to pay more, as a consequence of which the Commune had devoted special attention to them.[149] During April, 1794, the municipal government of Paris enacted a measure that only butchers could buy meat animals for slaughter – ordinary citizens were prohibited from making such purchases.[150] Two years later, the police of Paris forbade the sale of meat on the streets, in alleys, at the entry to public buildings or on tray baskets.[151]

---

[145] BHVP Ms. 746, fol. 87.

[146] AN AF IV 1472, general report of 12 brumaire year IV (November 3, 1795); extract from police reports, 15 brumaire year IV (November 6, 1795); central bureau report of 19 pluviôse year IV (February 5, 1796).

[147] AN AF IV 1473, general report of 15 ventôse year IV (March 5, 1796).

[148] Early during the Directory there were major complaints against grocers as well, a number of whom were of doubtful reputation. The police noted that the "cries of despair" emanating from Paris were alarming and argued that only prompt action by the Directory could repress the threat that such misery represented. AN AF IV 1472, general report of 13 brumaire year IV (November 4, 1795). Also, *Journal du Bon Homme Richard*, 3 brumaire year IV (October 25, 1795).

[149] APP DB 402, extract from registers of deliberations of Department of Paris, 15 pluviôse year II (February 3, 1794); Department of Subsistence and Provisioning, 15 messidor year II (July 3, 1794).

[150] *Le Républicain français*, 14 germinal year II (April 3, 1794). The implication of the decree, of course, was that ordinary citizens were slaughtering animals in the city.

[151] APP DB 402, decree concerning commerce of butchers, 24 floréal year IV (May 13, 1796).

The degree of decline in the trade of butcher was particularly apparent in regulations issued during 1796 as a result of major public health concerns. In a decree issued in October 1796, the police of Paris noted that the multiplication of butcher stalls throughout the city had led to slaughterhouses and boiling vats appearing on city streets in contravention of former regulations and ordinances. Some butchers were even allowing the blood of animals to flow into the streets and were throwing offal on public passageways, creating fetid smells as well as a health hazard.

Among other measures, the police mandated that no new vat or stall could be opened without authorization from the police and butchers could only slaughter animals in stalls that were not open to the street. They were no longer permitted to allow blood to flow in the streets or in other dirt, and had to have a sump in their slaughterhouse to collect the blood of animals and drains with closed grills for the disposal of water containing blood. It ordered that the sump be emptied daily and all offal be transported outside of Paris. The regulation also required butchers to throw clean water in the streets in a quantity sufficient to wash them and to sweep away anything that could foul the air.[152] In addition, later in the year V the police issued another decree prohibiting the sale of meat of animals that had died or not reached a proper age.[153]

Prior to the Revolution, of course, all of these matters would have been addressed by the guild of butchers, and it is difficult to imagine that such situations would have developed under the former system. Since the Revolution, these issues had become the responsibility of the police, but the police were viewed as utterly ineffective, even at enforcing their own decrees.[154] As a result, a yearning for the old order began to form. The draconian penalties decreed for violations of the Maximum had not been able to prevent abuses or declines in quality that would have seemed inconceivable under the regime of guilds, and many citizens had to confront unhealthy conditions that would not have been present when corporations had been in existence.

Indeed, by the winter of the year IV at least two-thirds of Parisians were receiving some form of government assistance and some were scouring through garbage heaps seeking to satisfy their hunger.[155] Under such circumstances, it is not surprising that police reports document the formation of a favorable recollection of the guild system. A report from 11 nivôse year IV (January 1, 1796), in the midst of the particularly severe winter of 1795–1796, noted that public opinion expressed itself strongly, especially at the doors of bread shops. There was a desire for peace, a larger bread ration, greater control over bakers

---

[152] APP DB 402, decree concerning butcher establishments, 15 vendémiaire year V (October 6, 1796).

[153] APP DB 402, decree of 5 thermidor year V (July 23, 1797). Similarly, during the year VII (November, 1798) municipal authorities in Amiens reestablished regulations for butchers, particularly with respect to slaughtering animals. AN F² I 106²⁴, dossier Somme, ordinance of February 4, 1808.

[154] *La Décade philosophique, littéraire et politique*, 20 vendémiaire year V (October 11, 1796).

[155] Monnier, *Le Faubourg Saint-Antoine*, pp. 81–82.

and butchers and strict enforcement of laws. The police agent added that the
people were groaning under the weight of misery and strongly regretted the
old order of things because then, they said, they did not lack the basic necessities of life. The only question in the agent's mind was which old order the
people so regretted – was it the "royal regime" or the "decemviral regime," as
he termed it – a reference to revolutionary committees.[156]

A few weeks later the answer to that question became clear when the police
observed that in cafés and other public places conversations generally revolved
around the misery people were experiencing, in contrast to the pleasantness
of the Old Regime when they had everything in abundance. Under the current
government, people complained, there was substantial privation and the cost
of everything was excessively high. Workers complained of the lack of work
and claimed they did not earn enough to live.[157]

Two days later a police agent again observed that public misery was the
chief topic of conversation and that the government was the target of severe
criticism. In conversations, he noted, people established a parallel between the
Old Regime and the new one in a manner that was not complimentary to the
latter. During the summer of 1796, after the worst suffering had passed, citizens continued to make invidious comparisons between the current regime and
the old one, although again the police agent professed not to know whether it
was the Old Regime or the Terror that the people regretted.[158]

Under the Directory, the Minister of the Interior forwarded a *mémoire*
he had received to the Council on Commerce, an advisory body within the
ministry, and asked for its opinion. The *mémoire* dealt with various aspects
of administration, and, although the *mémoire* itself has apparently not been
preserved, the reply of the council makes clear that it advocated a restoration
of guilds, albeit using terminology different from that of the Old Regime. The
council noted that the *mémoire* did not use such words as privileges and masterships, but that these were disguised under new denominations – although
avoiding certain words, the concept of guilds had been maintained and even
glorified. The "new and arbitrary nomenclature" used in the *mémoire* would
abolish both the letter and the spirit of article 355, which the council characterized as one of "the clearest of the entire constitution." Citing article 355 as

---

[156] AN AF IV 1472, central bureau of canton, report of 11 nivôse year IV (January 1, 1796).
[157] AN AF IV 1473, general bureau of canton, report of 14 ventôse year IV (March 4, 1796).
[158] AN AF IV 1473, general report of 16 ventôse year IV (March 6, 1796); AN AF IV 1474,
central bureau, report of 18 prairial year IV (June 6, 1796). Again, the answer should have
become clear a few weeks later, when it became evident that even patriotic festivals could
not prevent the populace from yearning for the Old Regime. After a festival to celebrate
the overthrow of the monarchy, the pomp and illumination gave rise to only a single idea,
according to the police agent – that of peace. Peace would provoke widespread joy and lead
to a universal festival. With peace would come greater abundance, fewer expenses and the
government would be able to put on festivals that would not evoke comparisons with those
that took place under the monarchy, which were regarded more highly because of the distribution of wine and bread to celebrate royal marriages or other occasions. AN AF IV 1475,
central bureau, report of 24 thermidor year IV (August 11, 1796).

an "impregnable rampart" against the project, the council recommended the rejection of all the proposals contained in the *mémoire.*

In view of the clear constitutional stricture against corporations, it is not clear why the minister requested the council's opinion. At the same time, however, it is a reflection of the shift of opinion since the abolition of guilds that a proposal that would have effectively reestablished them received respectful consideration by the Ministry of the Interior rather than summary rejection or condemnation as a counterrevolutionary work.[159]

To whatever degree there was a longing for the Old Regime, much of it was grounded in dearth, because sentiment against the idea of corporations existed, rooted in the perception of the possession of exclusive privilege. During the summer of 1797 (thermidor year V), a deputy to the Council of Five Hundred, Jacques Garnier de Saintes, a notoriously volatile left-wing deputy, called the council's attention to the decree by the Parisian police that banned the sale of meat in public places. Garnier de Saintes asserted that the decree was unconstitutional and was tantamount to the reestablishment of guilds and proposed sending a measure to the Directory. Other deputies pointed out that it was a health and safety issue – diseased meat could be made to appear good – and therefore a police matter. Their argument prevailed, and Garnier de Saintes's proposal was defeated.[160] Nevertheless, the incident reveals the continuing hostility toward corporations – no one offered a defense of the former guild system.

To cite another example, during the Directory, a group of bonded weighers had to defend themselves against the charge of forming a guild-like structure. They argued that their weigh stations in ports, food markets, and other settings did not represent an exclusive privilege, which they claimed would be "subversive of the principles of liberty." Indeed, they asserted that any establishment that held an exclusive privilege ought to be prohibited. They argued that their occupation was a "social guarantee" of the fairness of merchants and could exist without the "feudal creation" of public weights. The weighers cited article 356 of the Constitution of the Year III, which stipulated that the law would monitor particularly those professions that involved public matters and the safety and health of citizens, and stated that in order to monitor, one did not have to create exclusive privileges – police regulations and "paternal inspection" would suffice.[161]

Clearly, one should not misinterpret the yearning for the old order reported by the police as a desire to restore guilds – what was sought was a return to the supply situation and lower level of abuses that citizens recalled when corporations were in existence. Hostility to privilege remained strong, and would have

[159] AN F¹² 750, dossier 5/1, undated report of Council on Commerce.

[160] *Annales politiques et littéraires*, 30 thermidor year V (August 17, 1797); *Journal des débats et lois du Corps Législatif*, no. 99. The response by deputies citing the health and safety aspects was intended to demonstrate that the measure was in compliance with article 356 of the constitution.

[161] *Mémoire au Corps Législatif* (N.p., n.d.) [BHVP 968462].

posed a major obstacle to a restoration of guilds had there been a willingness to undertake the task.

At the same time, however, there was a sense of loss. Asserting that all social bonds among citizens had been broken, an anonymous pamphleteer decried the fact that speculation had replaced commerce, swindling had replaced hard work, coarseness had replaced courtesy, and usurpation had established a disastrous mistrust. The author acknowledged that corporations had originated in fiscal needs and that they had evolved into privileged institutions, but they had, he argued, also performed useful functions – developing talent and enabling skill, industry, and commerce to flourish. In addition, each corporation had held its members to a standard of knowledge and conduct.

The author carefully noted that he was not advocating the reestablishment of masterships, privileges or guilds, nor did he believe that it was necessary to limit the freedom of commerce, industry or the arts. The constitution, he observed, prohibited all of these, and the fairness of those principles was incontestable. Nevertheless, he exhorted readers to remember the advantages of corporations, without creating their abuses once again.[162]

The pamphlet demonstrates that the favorable sentiment toward guilds was not the preserve of reactionaries or those hostile to the Revolution. The author respected the principles of the Revolution and the constitution – indeed, he lauded them – but he clearly believed that the abolition of corporations had had unfortunate consequences.

Public officials under the Directory maintained a strong stand against guild-like structures. During the Year IV the administrators of the Department of Haute-Saône moved against a body of men who unloaded ships and barges in the towns of Gray and Arc whom they believed had formed "a society or corporation." The group had met to deliberate in common, defying both constitutional law and police regulations. In moving against the body – the administrators ordered police of the two towns to dissolve them – the officials cited the Declaration of the Rights of Man, which, they stated, in granting rights to all citizens, had sanctioned the abolition of all types of corporations of citizens of the same occupation or profession. This fundamental base of the constitution, they asserted, had been reinforced on June 14, 1791 – a reference to the Le Chapelier law – and, as a consequence, the central administration ordered the body dissolved.[163]

The economic climate was extraordinarily bleak when the Directory took office, so it is easy to understand why the restoration of guilds might have held

---

[162] *Rendez-nous ce que nous avons perdu, c'est ce que nous avions le plus cher* (Paris: Lerouge, year V).

[163] AN F¹² 1560, decree of central administration of Department of Haute-Saône, 19 pluviôse year IV (February 8, 1796). It is clear that the group was virtually extorting merchants and that the police had ignored it because of some fear of the men involved. Nevertheless, the administration chose to interpret the matter in constitutional rather than criminal terms. The evocation of the Le Chapelier law rather than the d'Allarde law appears to be a result of the fact that these men had not formed a guild during the Old Regime, and the Le Chapelier law had banned meetings of men of the same occupation or profession for common aims.

such attraction. The relaxation of the Maximum by the Thermidorean regime unleashed an inflationary spiral, and the depreciation of the *assignat* hit workers and the poor particularly hard. As the Directory began, the *assignat* was worth approximately 5 percent of its face value.[164] A sack of firewood that cost 20 livres in 1790 cost 500 livres in 1795, and the price of candle wax had gone from 18 sous in 1790 to 41 livres in 1795. A one-pound loaf of bread in brumaire year IV rose to forty-five francs.[165] From the vantage point of 1795, it is easy to see why the Old Regime system of corporations may have seemed like a halcyon era.

Inflation, however, was only one dimension of the catastrophic economic situation. Production was well below 1790 levels for a variety of reasons, including lack of raw materials, conversion to war production, and damage to the economic infrastructure as a result of foreign and civil war.

As a result, in addition to the inflation and abuses the populace encountered, the level of work and commerce in daily life during the Directory was far below Old Regime norms, causing particular hardship among workers.[166] During brumaire year IV a police report in Paris that noted the poor quality and questionable weight of bread also observed that merchants closed their shops at sunset due to a lack of candles. Furthermore, merchants were reluctant to sell items because of suspicion of *assignats*.[167] Other reports highlighted the fact that commerce was in an alarming state of stagnation, leading to substantial unemployment. The severe situation during the winter of 1795–1796 also led to hostility toward the Directory early in its existence. One report claimed that in the faubourg Saint-Antoine alone there were 6,000 unemployed workers.[168] After the harsh winter, commerce continued to languish during the summer of 1796.[169] The economic situation remained exceedingly difficult for workers, who remained hostile toward the government.[170]

THE DIRECTORY AND THE PURSUIT OF MECHANIZATION

Because of the continuity of personnel between the Convention and the Directory, there was also a continuation of policy, and this was particularly true regarding the pursuit of mechanization of production. In the first budget

---

[164] Lyons, *France Under the Directory*, p. 72.

[165] *Ibid.*, pp. 72–73. During November, 1795, at the beginning of the Directory, a newspaper had observed that merchandise was selling for 100, 150, or even 200 times the amount that it had cost before the Revolution. *Journal du Bon Homme Richard*, 18 brumaire year IV (November 9, 1795).

[166] Monnier, *Le Faubourg Saint-Antoine*, pp. 82–83.

[167] AN AF IV 1472, reports of 15 brumaire year IV (November 6, 1795), 25 brumaire year IV (November 16, 1795).

[168] AN AF IV 1472, reports of 5 pluviôse year IV (January 25, 1796); 8 pluviôse year IV (January 28, 1796) and 13 pluviôse year IV (February 2, 1796).

[169] AN AF IV 1475, report of 17 thermidor year IV (August 4, 1796).

[170] AN AF IV 1475, report of 9 fructidor year IV (August 26, 1796). The government continued to monitor the attitude of workers toward it. AN AF III 47, dossier 169, document 120.

for the Ministry of the Interior under the Directory, 200,000 livres were allotted for subsidies for manufacturing, but this was utterly inadequate.[171] The Ministry of the Interior had an ambitious agenda under which it wanted the government to provide both leadership and subsidies, and argued that the government should spare nothing in order to restore industry and the arts.[172] There had been major advances since the Revolution, the ministry argued, but it was necessary to perfect, encourage, sustain, and enlighten those who were achieving them.

The ministry cited a particular need to rebuild the commerce of Lyon and to build up the "useful arts" in departments in which they were almost unknown or neglected. Laws should support innovation among inventors, the ministry asserted, and a law dealing with apprenticeships was indispensable. The Conservatoire des Arts et Métiers, which the ministry characterized as "perhaps the most beautiful monument that the Convention had raised to the arts," had not yet reached its full potential because, the document asserted without elaborating, the interpretation of the law that had established it fifteen months earlier had been misguided.

A host of production facilities had disappeared and others were on the verge of ruin, and even those that were able to maintain themselves were far below the level of prosperity they had previously enjoyed. The ministry exhorted the government to support "the arts" through all of the avenues at its disposal.[173]

A few months later, on 3 messidor year IV (June 21, 1796), the Council of Ancients issued a "declaration of urgency" in which it asserted that "the interest of commerce," as well as that of "public prosperity," necessitated the granting of immediate subsidies to producers and manufacturers in France. On 6 messidor the Council authorized 4 million livres "fixed value," a clear reference to the difficult situation with the currency, to be spent with a special focus on wool, linen, and silk. The Council also stipulated that one quarter of the amount appropriated be directed to the establishment of a loan fund to rebuild production in Lyon.[174]

In addition, representatives of the French government in foreign countries sought to convince manufacturers to relocate their production facilities to France. A French official persuaded John Ford of Philadelphia to move his enterprise to France, but after doing so he encountered months of delay and considerable frustration when he became enmeshed in bureaucratic delays and

[171] AN AF III 93, dossier 397, abridged statement ... of annual expenses ... for the administration of Department (*sic*) of the Interior, pluviôse year IV.

[172] The demand was being made in the press. *Journal du Bon Homme Richard*, 14 frimaire year IV (December 5, 1795).

[173] AN AF III 93, dossier 397, report presented to Executive Directory by Ministry of the Interior, 20 pluviôse year IV (February 9, 1796).

[174] The proposal attracted attention and generated some controversy. See *La Décade philosophique, littéraire et politique*, 30 germinal year IV (April 19, 1796). On the provision with respect to Lyon, AN AD XI 72, law of 6 messidor year IV (June 24, 1796).

the fiscal difficulties of the Directory during the years IV and V. Ultimately, however, his factory was successful.[175]

The Ministry of the Interior made economic recovery a priority. During the year V, after the preliminaries for the Treaty of Basle had been concluded, the newly named Minister of the Interior, Nicolas-Louis François de Neufchâteau, wrote a circular to the central administration of each department in which he stated that now that peace was imminent the government would address economic recovery. Acknowledging that "disasters" had struck major producers, he praised merchants for their perseverance. He asserted that one of the tasks of the Ministry of the Interior was to revive trade and commerce, and further that he regarded the support of national commerce as the principal concern of the state.

He proclaimed that because there were no longer privileges, corporations or days of work taken away, France was about to ascend to an unprecedented level of prosperity. He asked departmental administrators to join the ministry in the effort to achieve it by furnishing information on trades and commerce in each department.[176]

The city of Lille illustrates the dire situation that the Directory confronted in the economic sphere. Before the war, the textile industry – woolens, cotton, silk – had flourished and employed approximately a third of the populace in the Lille region. During the war, the city had been heavily shelled by Austrian forces, and the bombardment had destroyed and burned the area in which many production sites had been located, along with tools and raw materials. This had prevented workers from reopening their workshops, and the Maximum and the depreciation of the *assignat* had also served to ruin their livelihood. The workers sought financial assistance from the government to reopen their workshops, which was approved.[177]

The magnitude of the task in Lille during the year V is evident in a report indicating that the economy of the city remained at a fraction of its pre-Revolution level. Whereas before the Revolution there had been 900 workers in weaving, in 1797 there were 196. In textile manufacturing there had been 366 workers in 1788, but there were only 60 in 1797. In spinning, there had been 10,000 workers in 1788, but that number had been reduced to 1,100 by 1797.[178]

During June 1798, the Minister of the Interior wrote to the commissioner of the Directory at Lille to inquire about a cotton-spinning machine in Lille

[175] AN F[12] 2202[A], dossier Regnaud, John Fort (*sic*) and other Americans ... years 4, 5, *liasse* Fort, year 7, letter of Minister of the Interior to Minister of Finances, 9 germinal year VII (March 29, 1799). Also on Ford, Serge Chassagne, *Le Coton et ses patrons: France, 1760–1840* (Paris: Editions de l'Ecole des Hautes Etudes en Sciences Sociales, 1991), pp. 246–247.

[176] AN F[12] 1557, circular of Ministry of Interior to central administration of departments, 9 fructidor year V (August 26, 1796).

[177] AN F[12] 679, undated report to Minister of the Interior, (but approval of minister dated 6 messidor year V (June 24, 1797).

[178] AN F[12] 1557, state of manufacturing in Lille, 13 nivôse year VI (January 2, 1798). See also Lyons, *France Under the Directory*, p. 182.

that had been brought to the attention of the minister. The machine, built by an Englishman at the beginning of the Revolution, was reputed to be superior to that of any other currently in use. The Englishman had since disappeared, and the machine had never been put into operation, but was supposed to be in storage in Lille. The minister asked the commissioner to investigate the machine and to provide blueprints of it, as well as samples of its output.

Of greater interest, however, is the fact that in the course of the letter the Minister of the Interior referred to the government's overall program in the economic sector. The government, he stated, had made "numerous sacrifices in order to introduce into France the knowledge of machines that the English employ with so much advantage" for cotton-spinning. The minister asserted that the undertaking was at last beginning to achieve success, and that the government was constructing and placing machines to such a degree that cotton-spinning facilities were found throughout the republic. It was because the machine in question could lend itself to improving this effort, the minister wrote to the commissioner, that he had such an interest.[179]

However committed the government may have been to economic recovery and advancement, it was constrained by a number of factors. The primary constraint, of course, was war. Even as the armies were becoming smaller and living off the occupied territories, war-related output continued to absorb raw materials and occupy a large portion of production. Although the most dangerous moment had passed, the Directory was still fighting for the survival of the Revolution.

Furthermore, the Directory was hindered by economic circumstances and its own *laissez-faire* economic ideology. Although war-related manufacture became increasingly systematized through war contractors, thereby permitting a redirection of production, the depreciation of the *assignat* precluded capital investment. In addition, until the eve of its overthrow, the Directory, in most instances, refused to make direct loans to individuals to reestablish manufacture. When one businessman wrote to the Ministry of the Interior for assistance, citing the effects of requisitions and the Maximum, the minister replied that he could assure him that such measures would not be repeated in the future. At the same time, however, the minister stated that all that the government could do was to provide this guarantee and to begin to repair "all the wrongs inseparable from a revolution."[180] Indeed, the ministry routinely sent out letters to those seeking assistance stating that "the state of distress" of government finances did not permit it to grant any assistance.[181]

[179] AN F¹² 2195, dossier Nord, letter of Minister of the Interior to commissioner of Executive Directory at Lille, 30 prairial year VI (June 18, 1798).

[180] AN F¹² 1559, letter of Minister of Interior to Bouin, 19 fructidor year V (September 5, 1797).

[181] AN F¹² 1559, letter of Minister of Interior to Desmagny, 13 brumaire year V (November 3, 1796); AN F¹² 2178, no. 145. See also AN F¹² 2178, no. 95, no. 96, no. 103, no. 115, no. 150.

The Ministry of the Interior sought to revive the economy, but, with little direct financial support to offer, its efforts were well intended but largely ineffectual. As an example, it commissioned a former inspector of manufactures at Tours to report on how to revive industry and commerce in the former provinces of Maine and Anjou.[182] Similarly, during the year IV, it sent a member of the Council on Arts and Manufactures to investigate the merits of a machine for the processing of silk.[183] Not surprisingly, given such limited efforts and a lack of funds, the economy remained virtually inert.

In a report on the state of commerce at Bordeaux, the Consultative Bureau on Commerce of Bordeaux had alluded to a labor shortage in the region, and this became a major issue for the Directory, even as unemployment in Paris and elsewhere remained high.[184] Like the Committee of Public Safety before it, the Ministry of the Interior during the Directory became totally committed to mechanization of production – in his circular to the departments, the Minister of the Interior had solicited suggestions on how to save labor through mechanization.[185] With mechanization widely perceived as the antithesis of the formerly guild-based, artisanal mode of production, the policy of the Ministry of the Interior represented an administrative reinforcement of the constitutional proscription of corporations.

The government also pursued other efforts. It was the Directory that completed the merger of the Atelier de Perfectionnement with the Conservatoire des Arts et Métiers, confirming the high priority accorded to mechanization of production. In founding the *conservatoire*, the National Convention had given precedence to mechanization – the first three articles of the decree that founded it related to machines and mechanized manufacture.[186] In consolidating the Atelier de Perfectionnement with the *conservatoire*, the Directory reinforced this mandate.[187]

At the same time, however, a backlash developed against mechanization of production. Doubts had begun to crystallize after the approval of Grégoire's project for founding the Conservatoire des Arts et Métiers in 1794, but these strengthened in the aftermath of the severe dearth of 1795–1796 and were rooted in the belief that mechanization deprived workers of their means of sustenance.[188] Indeed, as the *conservatoire* prepared to take possession of its site – the former monastery of Saint Martin des Champs – the Council of Five

---

[182] AN F[12] 2178, no. 74, no. 138.

[183] AN F[12] 2178, no. 37.

[184] AN AF III 47, dossier 169, document 120; AN F[12] 1557, letter of members of Consultative Bureau of Commerce of Bordeaux, 29 fructidor year V (September 15, 1797). On problems with investment and credit, see Lyons, *France Under the Directory*, p. 183.

[185] AN F[12] 1557, circular of Ministry of Interior to central administration of departments, 9 fructidor year V (August 26, 1797).

[186] BHVP Ms. N.A. 192, fol. 350.

[187] BHVP Ms. N.A. 192, fol. 354; AN F[12] 2178, no. 133; *La Décade philosophique, littéraire et politique*, 30 floréal year VI (May 19, 1798).

[188] *La Décade philosophique, littéraire et politique* 10 brumaire year III (October 31, 1794); *Journal d'économie politique*, 10 vendémiaire year V (October 1, 1796).

Hundred defeated a motion that would have prevented the establishment of the Conservatoire des Arts et Métiers.[189]

To be sure, doubt or hostility toward mechanization of production did not necessarily translate into support for the reestablishment of guilds. Moreover, although it would be excessive to characterize this period as a crossroads, it is equally apparent that, with republican deputies calling for a reconsideration of the dissolution of guilds and with misgivings about mechanization extant, the future with respect to both guilds and mechanization was by no means clear.

As one scholar of the Directory noted, industry remained overwhelmingly rural and artisanal in nature – large concentrations of manufacture remained rare. Furthermore, little progress was possible until financial stability was reestablished.[190]

THE INDUSTRIAL EXHIBITION OF THE YEAR VI

An innovative project undertaken by the Ministry of the Interior during the fall of 1798 to advance mechanization met with great success, particularly in influencing the public to become better disposed to the pursuit of mechanized production and to stem the favorable sentiment toward the former system of corporations. The undertaking was an industrial exhibition held at the end of the year VI, in conjunction with the Festival of the Founding of the Republic – the first industrial exhibition ever held in the Western world.[191]

The origins of the exhibition were remarkably casual. There had been criticism of the previous festival, with a sense that national festivals were becoming stale, so the ministry began searching for some sort of innovation.[192] The Minister of the Interior, François de Neufchâteau, convened a meeting of many distinguished men to consider different ideas to make the festival more striking. The group weighed various suggestions, ranging from mounting a larger version of a village fair to staging chariot and horse races, before François de Neufchâteau observed that the mechanical arts could be treated with a seriousness comparable to the suggestions just advanced. His idea met with quick and unanimous consent.[193]

It was not surprising that François de Neufchâteau would make such a suggestion – from the outset of his time as minister, he had made clear his

---

[189] *La Décade philosophique, littéraire et politique*, 10 pluviôse year VI (January 29, 1798).

[190] Lyons, *France Under the Directory*, pp. 179–180.

[191] This exhibition remains understudied, but see James Livesey, *Making Democracy in the French Revolution* (Cambridge: Harvard University Press, 2003), pp. 219–222; Horn, *The Path Not Taken*, pp. 186–194; Pieter van Wesemall, *Architecture of Instruction and Delight: A Socio-Historical Analysis of World Exhibitions as a Didactic Phenomenon (1798–1851–1970)* (Rotterdam: OIO Publishers, 2001).

[192] On the criticism, *Bulletin de Paris*, 3 vendémiaire year VI (September 24, 1797); *La Décade philosophique, littéraire et politique*, 10 vendémiaire year VI (October 1, 1797).

[193] Claude-Anthelme Costaz, *Histoire de l'administration en France de l'agriculture, des arts utiles, du commerce, des manufactures, des subsistances, des mines et des usines*, 2 vols. (Paris: Huzard, 1832), 2: 315–316.

intention to revive manufacturing and advance mechanization of production. In a circular sent to administrators of departments soon after he became Minister of the Interior, he noted that France was now free from, among other things, privileges and odious guilds, and that he believed the country was being called to a degree of glory and prosperity heretofore unknown.[194]

The head of a division in the Ministry of the Interior wrote to the Executive Directory to seek permission to stage an exhibition of products of industry in conjunction with the Festival of the Founding of the Republic on 1 vendémiaire (September 22). The Executive Directory approved the idea on 7 fructidor (August 24), less than a month before the festival was to be held, but the margin of time was even narrower than that because the exhibition was scheduled for the complementary days at the end of the year VI, just prior to 1 vendémiaire year VII.

Not surprisingly, the Executive Directory was concerned about the limited amount of time available – the Directory did not want the exhibit to appear mediocre and worried that too small a number of objects would not convey a positive image of French resources. There was no time to lose, the Directors stated, in putting out a call to all parts of France for the most beautiful objects or items from factories of every kind. It was imperative, they stated, to publish the circular immediately.[195] It was sent on 9 fructidor, so hastily that the site was not yet known, and the exhibition was described as "a new kind of spectacle."[196]

The extraordinarily limited amount of time in which the exhibition was planned is apparent in the fact that the announcement reached Angers only on 13 fructidor and was published on 16 fructidor – approximately two weeks before the scheduled opening.[197] Indeed, the Ministry of the Interior quickly realized that there was insufficient time for exhibitors beyond the surrounding region to participate, and therefore published a notice stating that the void would have to be filled by departments that adjoined Paris. The ministry extended the deadline for application by three days and invited exhibitors from any industry whatsoever to participate.[198]

As a result, when the exhibition opened – with some arcades still unfinished[199] – the vast majority of participants were from Paris and the Paris region. Of the 106 exhibitors for whom a place of origin is listed, sixty-seven

[194] AN F¹² 1557, circular of Minister of Interior to central administration of departments, 9 fructidor year V (August 26, 1797).

[195] AN F¹c I 91, dossier Festival of Founding of the Republic, *liasse* non-dated items, letter to Jaquemont, 7 fructidor.

[196] AN F¹² 985, dossier 1, document 1; *Gazette nationale ou le Moniteur universel*, 11 fructidor year VI (August 28, 1798); *Affiches d'Angers*, 16 fructidor year VI (September 2, 1798).

[197] *Affiches d'Angers*, 16 fructidor year V (September 2, 1798); *Gazette nationale ou le Moniteur universel*, 11 fructidor year VI (August 28, 1798).

[198] *Journal des débats et lois du corps législatif*, fructidor year VI, no. 119, 26 fructidor year VI (September 12, 1798).

[199] AN F¹² 985, dossier 1, document 1; *Bulletin décadaire de la république française*, 2ᵉ décade de vendémiaire an VII.

were from Paris and another eight were from the surrounding region, including four from the Department of Seine-et-Oise.²⁰⁰ The need to occupy exhibition space may also account for the presence of products that one would not necessarily associate with an industrial exhibition – false teeth made from minerals by a dentist from Paris, for example, or representations of exotic birds made from colored feathers by an artist from Paris.²⁰¹ Although the program noted that invitations had gone out too late to benefit manufacturers in departments far from Paris, manufacturers from Toulouse, Sedan, Besançon, Troyes, Rouen, and other cities and towns outside of the Paris region were present.²⁰² The products deemed worthy of special recognition were displayed in the "Temple of Industry."²⁰³

The exhibition opened with great fanfare at the Champ de Mars at 10:00 a.m. on the third complementary day of the year VI (September 19, 1798) – three days in advance of the Festival of the Founding of the Republic. Preceded by trumpeters, heralds, a cavalry detachment, an infantry unit, a marching military band, the exhibitors and the jury, the Minister of the Interior, François de Neufchâteau, entered and toured the exhibit before delivering a speech.²⁰⁴

In the center of the arcades in which the exhibitors were located was the Temple of Industry, and the jury judging the products proclaimed that it hoped that the exhibition would mark the beginning of a new era for French industry. The exhibition was intended to be an annual event to assist the progress of industry by inspiring emulation.²⁰⁵

François de Neufchâteau delivered his lengthy speech from the Temple of Industry. It is indicative of the perception by contemporaries of an antithesis between the guild system and industry that he noted at the outset that, among other reforms of the Revolution, the "disastrous regulations of privileged corporations" had been swept away. He mentioned that the Executive Directory regretted that it had not been possible for the current exhibition to include products from a number of departments because they had had so little time after receiving the announcement of it. After speaking at length on the link between the progress of the arts and freedom – another rebuke of corporations that would have been well understood by his audience – François de

---

²⁰⁰ AN AD XI 67, *Exposition publique des produits de l'industrie française. Catalogue des produits industriels qui ont été exposés au Champ-de-Mars pendant les trois derniers jours complémentaires de l'an VI...*

²⁰¹ *Catalogue détaillé des produits industriels, exposés au Champ-de-Mars* (Paris: Guillemat, n.d.); *Annales de la république française*, 4 vendémiaire year VII (September 25, 1797).

²⁰² AN AD XI 67, *Exposition publique des produits de l'industrie française.*

²⁰³ *Directoire Exécutif. Procès-verbal de la fête de la fondation de la république, célebrée à Paris le 1ᵉʳ vendémiaire l'an 7* (Paris: J. Gratiot, n.d.); *Catalogue détaillé des produits industriels*; *Nouvelles de Paris*, 5 vendémiaire year VII (September 26, 1798).

²⁰⁴ AN F¹² 985, dossier 1, document 2.

²⁰⁵ AN AD XI 67, *Exposition publique des produits de l'industrie française.* The idea of the exhibition as an annual event had also been enunciated in the circular announcing it. AN F¹² 985, dossier 1, document 1.

Neufchâteau concluded by stating that if he had succeeded in deepening love of the arts among the populace and increasing love of the Republic, then this day would be the greatest of his life.[206]

James Livesey analyzed this same speech and placed a particular focus on François de Neufchâteau in support of his argument that the Directory – especially during the time when François de Neufchâteau was Minister of the Interior – sought to create the idea of a "commercial republic," which he defined as "a developmental theory that harnessed aspirations to equality of dignity to economic development." Seeking to transcend the association between republicanism and political violence after the Terror, the commercial republic sought to marry republicanism with commerce in the belief that "a prosperous country would be a free one."[207] Moreover, it was also the answer to a question posed by Haim Burstin about whether the revolutionary government would form a welfare state or an entrepreneurial state[208] – it would be the latter, which was another way for the Directory to separate itself from the legacy of the Terror.

Livesey concentrated on the agricultural sector, which was of course the dominant sphere of the economy, but in the industrial domain prosperity would come from production, and production would be enhanced through mechanization. The industrial exhibition, held in tandem with the Festival of the Founding of the Republic, was a compelling display of the link between commerce and republicanism and a brilliant means of engaging the public with that vision.

Indeed, the exhibition was extraordinarily popular with the public – a major newspaper account of the Festival of the Founding of the Republic, which characterized it as the most moving since the Festival of the Federation of 1790, included a particular mention of the exhibition.[209] Another singled out the industrial exhibition and the juried competition of products as having produced "the most agreeable sensation among the public and manufacturers."[210]

A more telling indicator of public interest in the exhibition, however, was the fact that it was extended by ten days, until 10 vendémiaire.[211] Attendance had been kept down initially by inclement weather that had limited the event to one day instead of the scheduled three, so after receiving the result of a vote taken among the exhibitors in favor of an extension, the Minister of the Interior authorized not only the prolongation of the exhibition, but also its

---

[206] *Gazette nationale, ou le Moniteur universel,* 1 vendémiaire year VII.

[207] Livesey, *Making Democracy in the French Revolution,* with the quotations from p. 164 and p. 104 respectively.

[208] Burstin, "Problems of Work during the Terror," p. 290.

[209] *Gazette nationale, ou le Moniteur universel,* 3 vendémiaire year VII (September 24, 1798).

[210] *La Décade philosophique, littéraire et politique,* 10 vendémiaire year VII (October 1, 1798). See also *Bulletin décadaire de la république française,* 2nd *décade* of vendémiaire year VII; *Annales de la république française,* 3 vendémiaire year VII (September 24, 1798).

[211] AN F[12] 985, dossier 1, document 6.

illumination at night.[212] He also extended a special invitation to the members of the Executive Directory to attend and encouraged them to view the exhibits.[213] Ultimately, however, continuing bad weather blew over some arcades and led the government to close the exhibition before the ten days had passed.[214]

A newspaper report on the awards ceremony for exhibitors included a comment that one would not have seen such an exhibition under the monarchy, in another allusion to the system of guilds.[215] In fact, although other factors, especially a lessening of hardship and scarcity, played a more significant role, after the industrial exhibition there was almost no further mention in police reports of a preference for past systems, whether that of the Old Regime or the Terror.

The exhibition offered something that had been lacking since the dissolution of guilds – an alternate vision of production. It was not, to be sure, a comprehensive, alternative economic program because it did not address unresolved problems created by the abolition of corporations, such as apprenticeship or quality control. At the same time, however, to the extent that the guild system had been idealized during a time of dearth, the passing of hardship had still not led to the perception of a means to return to quality, trust and good order other than reestablishing corporations. The exhibition held out another perspective, one that looked forward rather than backward.

The broader impact of the industrial exhibition on public opinion was notable and significant. Even among those not favorably disposed toward the reestablishment of guilds, there was an underlying suspicion of mechanization of work as potentially damaging because it could deprive workers of their means of existence – commentators felt the need to endorse and promote the idea of mechanization to overcome resistance to this idea.[216]

Furthermore, until the industrial exhibition, mechanization and the pursuit of industry had in large measure been linked with the Jacobin military effort, particularly conscription and the regimentation of labor – as a result, the pursuit of mass production and mechanization were generally associated with coercion and intimidation. Against this backdrop, although corporations may have been resented before the Revolution, by the the year VI (1798) they represented a time of stability and plenty and seemed far less pernicious than would have been the case a decade earlier.[217] The industrial exhibition

---

[212] AN F¹² 985, dossier 1, documents 4, 5, 9, 11; AN AF III 93, dossier 401, letter of Minister of Interior to Executive Directory, 5 vendémiaire year VII; *Gazette nationale, ou le Moniteur universel*, 5 vendémiaire year VII.

[213] AN AF III 93, dossier 401, letter of Minister of the Interior to Executive Directory, 5 vendémiaire year VII.

[214] *Nouvelles de Paris*, 9 vendémiaire year VII (September 30, 1798); *Annales de la république française*, 10 vendémiaire year VII (October 1, 1798).

[215] *Gazette nationale, ou le Moniteur universel*, 12 vendémiaire year VII (October 3, 1798).

[216] *La Décade philosophique, littéraire et politique* 10 brumaire an III (October 31, 1794); *Bulletin décadaire de la république française*, 3ᵉ décade de brumaire an VII (November 1798).

[217] On the sense of dearth that persisted in some areas, *Bulletin de Paris*, 8 vendémiaire year VI (September 22, 1797), which provides a report on Le Havre.

offered a more benign view of mechanization, making it appear more promising than menacing. The exhibition gave mechanization of production a public following and conferred upon those who pursued it an aura of being progressive and modern.

The circular of the Minister of the Interior had urged local officials to stage similar events,[218] but there is no evidence that this occurred.[219] The exhibition, however, did inspire the planning of a similar effort for the following year by the administrators of the Department of Lot-et-Garonne – on 12 pluviôse year VII (January 31, 1799) administrators at Agen announced their intention to hold a departmental exhibition to augment the national one and to inspire other local exhibitions that would lead to innovations by producers and reinforce the goals of the government. It would offer a venue for manufacturers and businessmen "who would initially not dare show themselves at the Champ-de-Mars with the products of their industry" and aid them by holding a preliminary competition through which they could perfect their efforts. The administrators issued a decree authorizing the departmental exhibition and hoped it would serve as a model for other departments. Again, however, there is no evidence that the departmental exhibition was held, nor that it led to a similar effort by any other department.[220]

The first exhibition had been almost impulsive, but two weeks after its conclusion François de Neufchâteau was already planning the exhibition for the following year.[221] It did not take place, however – François de Neufchâteau was ousted from the Ministry of the Interior during the summer of 1799. Although his successor, Nicolas-Marie Quinette, was an enthusiastic supporter of revolutionary festivals, the unfavorable turn in the war during 1799, which Quinette euphemistically termed "the current circumstances," led to a scaling back of festivals, beginning with the Festival of Freedom scheduled for 9 and 10 thermidor. Indeed, justifying his decision, Quinette observed that if the ancient Athenians deserved any reproach, it was for not allowing funds allocated for the theater and the circus to be used for war. Although festivals would continue to be held, those aspects of them that demanded major preparations were to be suspended until peace had been achieved.[222] Citing a lack of funds because of the war, as well as an inadequate amount of time to prepare for it, Quinette cancelled the exhibition for the year VII less than a month before it was to open.[223]

A statue of industry was constructed for the Festival of the Founding of the Republic during the year VII, and a few machines recognized by the Institut

[218] *Affiches d'Angers*, 16 fructidor year VI (September 2, 1798).
[219] *Affiches d'Angers*, 2 vendémiaire year VII (September 23, 1798); *Journal de Toulouse, l'observateur républicain*, 5 vendémiaire year VII (September 26, 1798).
[220] *Bulletin décadaire de la république française*, 1st *décade* of floréal year VII.
[221] AN F¹² 985, dossier 1, document 15; *Bulletin décadaire de la république française*, 3ᵉ *décade* of brumaire an VII; AD Isère L 285, document 67.
[222] AN F¹ᵃ 23, dossier year 7, Festival of Freedom, fixed for 9 and 10 thermidor...
[223] AD Isère L 285, document 66.

National were put on display, but there was no exhibition. Winners from the previous year were again recognized in a ceremony, and the same pattern occurred the following year – indeed, the minutes of the ceremony for the year VIII were utterly unchanged from those for the year VII, not even correcting the phrase "last year" in reference to year VII .[224] The industrial exhibition fell into abeyance until the Consulate, when a member of the jury from the exhibition of the year VI, Jean-Antoine Chaptal, became Minister of the Interior and revived it.

THE FAILURE OF THE DIRECTORY TO REORDER THE WORKPLACE

The government also sought to bring greater order to the workplace. When the National Assembly had abolished guilds and regulation in 1791, it had not established procedures for apprenticeships or any other of the numerous functions formerly performed by corporations, and neither did its successor, the Legislative Assembly. The National Convention, with its emphasis on production, had brought about a greater homogenization and regimentation of labor, but it had disbanded without reorganizing the workplace in any fashion. The need for legislation was evident in the deterioration of such trades as baker and butcher, but the decline was mirrored in other trades as well.

On 19 frimaire year IV (December 10, 1795), only a few weeks after the Directory assumed power, the Ministry of the Interior wrote to a deputy in the Council of Ancients to notify him that a project on apprenticeships was soon to be submitted to the Executive Directory for consideration.[225] Some months later, the ministry informed an entrepreneur that it was working on a project to reestablish regulations for and order in manufactories.[226] It would appear that these efforts were not realized, however, because nearly a year later the ministry wrote to another businessman in Pau to inform him that the ministry had asked the Executive Directory to send a message to the Council of Five Hundred to invite it to ascertain the relationship that should exist between workers and the heads of manufactories.[227]

A letter written to the Ministry of the Interior in late 1796 from a master hired for a public workshop provides insight into why the need for legislation governing workshops was felt so keenly. The letter was concerned primarily

---

[224] *Bulletin décadaire de la république française*, 3ᵉ décade de fructidor an VII; *Bulletin décadaire de la république française*, 2ᵉ décade de vendémiaire an VIII, in which the description in the issue cited immediately above is repeated verbatim; *Procès-verbal de la fête anniversaire de la Fondation de la république, célébré à Paris le 1 vendémiaire an 8* (Paris: Imprimerie de la République, an VIII); AN F¹ᶜ I 91, program for Festival of Founding of the Republic, year VIII.

[225] AN F¹² 2178, no. 4.

[226] AN F¹² 2178, no. 120.

[227] AN F¹² 2178, no. 136.

with the fact that the salaries of the master and his son, who were from Aix-la-Chapelle and who had come to Paris to establish a needle manufactory, were significantly in arrears.[228] At the same time, however, the master, Langour, took the opportunity to complain about the atmosphere in the workshop. The shop had four students – the word "apprentice" was never used – but Langour stated that the administration of the shop was not what it should be. The cost of production was high, and little work was done because "each wants to be the master," and sometimes the students refused to take instruction. Langour asked the Minister of the Interior to take these matters into consideration and order that the strictest measures be taken for the prompt organization of "one of the best workshops of the Republic."[229]

Skill, however, was not the only matter at issue – as Langour's letter indicated, discipline was another. A group of entrepreneurs who owned cotton-spinning machines argued to the Executive Directory that, among other problems, "insubordination" among workers and the absence of any regulations were a major source of many of the economic problems confronting France. As one of two requests to the Directory – protection of the domestic market being the other – the entrepreneurs asked for regulations against "insubordination and greediness" by workers. They described what they were seeking as "a kind of industrial code that reconciles the rights that belong to them as French citizens with their duties to the state, to which they owe work, and to manufacturers ..."[230]

One should treat the word "insubordination," as used by the entrepreneurs, with caution. On the one hand, there were certainly abuses by workers and no venue, other than the criminal court, in which to address them. On the other hand, entrepreneurs and others yearned for a degree of authority over workers analogous to that which had been enjoyed by masters under the Old Regime. As the communication of the cotton-spinning entrepreneurs acknowledged, however, the Revolution had inaugurated individual rights, including, for workers, making the control formerly wielded by the corporate system a vestige of the past. Nevertheless, the desire for authority over workers persisted, and led many employers to view the system inaugurated by the Revolution as riddled with "insubordination."

The request of the cotton-spinning entrepreneurs is of interest for an additional reason. It reflected a shift in vocabulary, with "industrial code" or a similar term superseding the mention of a possible restoration of guilds. Rather than a backward-looking reversion to the *status quo ante* through

---

[228] Indeed, salaries of employees in the Ministry of the Interior itself were in arrears. *Annales politiques et littéraires*, 10 messidor year V (June 28, 1797). A few weeks later, in the Council of Five Hundred, a proposal by a deputy for the council to formulate a new plan to restore the nation's finances was greeted with laughter. *Annales politiques et littéraires*, 29 thermidor year V (August 16, 1797).

[229] AN F¹² 1557, letter of head of division of arts and manufactures to Bergeron, 27 frimaire year V (December 17, 1796).

[230] *Au Directoire Exécutif. Les Entrepreneurs des filatures mécaniques de coton* (Paris, n.d.).

the reintroduction of guilds, the concept of an industrial code suggested a more forward-looking adaptation of worker rights with the needs of manufacturers.

Ultimately, however, despite its stated intention and despite the requests that it received to do so, the Directory failed to enact any laws to reimpose order or regulation in the workplace. No law on apprenticeships came into existence, nor did any on relations between employers and employees. The disarray into which the formerly structured world of work had been plunged by the legislation of 1791 remained unresolved.

The failure to establish procedures for apprenticeships or to reestablish rules to govern workshops, as well as the difficult and at times desperate economic circumstances during the Directory, deepened the dissolution of the corporate world of trades as workers struggled to survive. The degree to which the ordered, corporate world of work could be recalled, and also the degree to which it had become confused by the time of the Directory, is apparent in a report sent to the Bureau on Commerce from Saumur a few months before the National Convention disbanded.

According to the document, before the Revolution Saumur had been an entrepôt for more than eighty towns throughout Anjou and Upper and Lower Poitou. The Vendée uprising, the Maximum, the depreciation of the *assignat* and requisitions, however, had destroyed workshops and brought economic ruin. Taverns and cabarets were the sites of transactions, and commerce had become the object of "commonplace abuse." The ubiquity of bad faith had led to significant corruption and a deterioration of commerce. The report stated bluntly that the abolition of corporations had led to the disappearance of "fundamental obligations" and "the sacred duty of obligations." Indeed, the account asserted, a ruinous situation had come about in which a baker was selling *eau de vie* and wine, a shoemaker was selling coffee and sugar, a blacksmith was selling cloth, and a wigmaker was selling wood.[231] It was this sort of situation that the Directory failed to address in any meaningful manner, thus allowing a sentiment in favor of guilds to continue.

The dissolution of the corporate paradigm and the failure of the Directory to achieve any oversight of workers posed an additional problem for municipal authorities, especially in Paris. A police report from 30 messidor–1 thermidor year V (July 18–19, 1797) mentioned "meetings of workers of different professions" that lasted until nine o'clock in the evening. A meeting of men of different trades would have been unusual in the corporate world of trades during the Old Regime. Furthermore, under the Old Regime, guilds had served as an adjunct to the police, overseeing journeymen and apprentices.

After the abolition of corporations, however, only the police were available to oversee workers, and following the politicization of Parisian sections, particularly during 1793–1794, and the privation of 1795–1796, it is clear that the

---

[231] AN F12 1557, report on commerce and Saumur, messidor year III (June–July 1795). Years later, a similar state of affairs existed in Elbeuf. Becchia, *La Draperie d'Elbeuf*, p. 403.

combination of politicization and hardship led police increasingly to perceive workers as a potential threat. In a report of 20 prairial year V (June 20, 1797) the police noted that although there was social peace at the moment, cries of misery were acquiring a new force, and that everywhere the police had been able to observe, workers had seemed less content and more inclined to complain about the difficulty of living.[232]

Indeed, the issues of politicization of workers and workshop discipline were not purely abstract matters for the Directory. In year IV workers in the government printing office stopped work after the Directory ordered the arrest of seven workers allegedly plotting to sabotage the Constitution of the Year III by preventing the forwarding of laws and all other services. The Directory had ordered the workers to resume work, but unrest had continued, leading the Directory to charge the police of Paris to intervene. The police commissioner, however, had promised that the workers would not be arrested, and so released them. The Directory ordered the police commissioner to carry out its mandate, to which he agreed.

For their part, the workers claimed that the reason for the stoppage was to seek an increase in wages, which they insisted was necessary to live. In fact, the Minister of Justice acceded to their demand and raised the daily wage. He wrote to the director of the government printing office that he wished to treat the workers "as favorably as circumstances might permit" but at the same time it was his intention "to repress severely tumultuous movements by which they seek to support their demand for exaggerated wages." The minister stated that he would always regard work stoppages as one of the most serious of crimes.[233]

INDUSTRIAL POLICY DURING THE DIRECTORY

During the Directory there was a vigorous internal debate within the Ministry of the Interior on how to revive both the quality and level of production. Indeed, the lines of policy laid down by the Ministry of the Interior during the Directory, which were subsequently refined and codified under the Napoleonic regime, formed the basis for French economic and industrial policy during the early nineteenth century. In part, this was due to continuity among the civil servants in the Ministry of the Interior, which maintained stability despite changes of government and ministers.[234]

A division of the Ministry of the Interior prepared a document that argued for reviving the textile industry. A commission formed by the ministry to examine the textile sector asserted that of all the branches of industry that had developed in France, few had been as prosperous, particularly that of quality

---

[232] AN AF IV 1477, report of 20 prairial year V (June 8, 1797).

[233] AN AA 13, dossier 558.

[234] Harold T. Parker, "Two Administrative Bureaus under the Directory and Napoleon," *French Historical Studies* 4 (1965): 150–169.

wool. At the same time, however, few industries, the division argued, had experienced a quicker or more universal deterioration, a decline that would be extremely difficult to remedy.

After acknowledging the lack of resources available to revive the industry and other factors that constrained it, the commission observed that it had begun by compiling a table of all woolen mills still in operation and had had government agents inventory the production profile of each establishment. It had also sought to ascertain the state of raw materials for the industry.

The commission asserted that the primary causes of the decline of the woolen industry were the Maximum, the system of requisitions and the cessation of quality control among producers. The law of the Maximum, the commission argued, had had a catastrophic effect because it had led both to deterioration in the quality of wool produced and a shortage of raw material. Ultimately, the Maximum had produced "three incalculable difficulties" – interruption of all production, the export of raw materials to foreign lands and the development of foreign competition.

Requisitions had also choked off the supply of raw materials necessary for production. The raw materials had been confined to warehouses and could be released only after long and tedious bureaucratic procedures. Consequently, many established proprietors, unable to secure the material necessary for operation, closed their production facilities. They were in turn succeeded by new manufacturers who, with "no reputation to maintain" and little knowledge of the trade, had made "detestable use" of raw materials that they were able to procure and had flooded the domestic market with wool of inferior quality.[235]

Finally, the abolition of all regulations on production quality had favored the stratagems of inferior producers and significantly contributed to loss of quality and a decline in production. There had to be, the commission lamented, a happy medium between "the intolerable servitude of former regulations and the current anarchy." The consumer ought to have a bond of good faith with the producer, but if the latter could enrich himself through the selling of inferior goods, he would follow this route. The poor quality of goods had led to the virtual extinction of the Near Eastern trade for the former province of Languedoc and the loss of export markets for Elbeuf. These facts, the commission argued, demonstrated the necessity of establishing "simple regulations to stop arbitrariness in manufacture" in order to provide guarantees of the invariability of the method of production.

The commission noted that it was not within its power to destroy the vices that had damaged the manufacturing industry, but that it had tried to moderate their effects. It had adopted a system of encouragement that rested on

---

[235] In Elbeuf, such producers were pejoratively termed *"fabricants de la Révolution."* Becchia, *La Draperie d'Elbeuf*, p. 402. Chaptal, in fact, later made it a policy to weed out such manufacturers when he was Minister of the Interior. Christopher H. Johnson, *The Life and Death of Industrial Languedoc, 1700–1920* (New York: Oxford University Press, 1995), p. 16.

general principles that allowed few exceptions. The first priority, the commission argued, should be to assist individuals or manufacturers who, having made some discoveries useful to the art of fabrication, could not put them into operation because of a lack of means, or to assist those who wanted to establish a new industry and sought an advance to do so.

The second principle was to refuse to support entrepreneurs who had established themselves in areas in which similar enterprises had once existed. It was apparent, the commission asserted, that any grants or advances that might be made would transform these individuals into "privileged beings" and that they had brought about the ruin of former manufacturers who, using the same raw materials and the same workers, had not been been able to compete with the new entrepreneurs by maintaining quality workmanship or in the purchase of raw materials.

The commission proposed several sorts of grants, subsidies or loans that could be offered by the Directory – advances in *assignats* or specie to be repaid on a fixed schedule or, in some cases, even an outright grant. It recommended in particular making national buildings available for use by entrepreneurs for a number of years or the conveyance of buildings to entrepreneurs at a fair market price.

The last proposal, on national buildings, was contrary to laws on the sale of national lands, which required that they be auctioned, and the commission had advocated reform of the laws regulating the sale of national property. The commission, in fact, asserted that it had demonstrated often that a building given to an intelligent manufacturer produced far more for the state than the price it would gain from an individual buyer. It recommended additional consideration of the issue.[236]

The document had several implications, both explicit and implicit, for future economic development. The first was apparent in the concentration of the document on the textile industry. A major lesson that the French had drawn from the Eden-Vergennes Treaty of 1786, after the internal market had been overwhelmed by British cloth, had been that an economy could be built on a mechanized textile trade, and that belief would become a foundation for the policies of the Ministry of the Interior.[237]

Additional implications followed from the principles outlined in the document. The first guideline – providing assistance to those who had made discoveries useful to the art of fabrication – signified that support would be channeled overwhelmingly to individuals pursuing mechanized production.

---

[236] AN F¹² 1556, Fifth division, textile manufacture, linen trade, cotton fabric (undated).

[237] Indeed, a textile producer whose enterprise developed into one of the major producers in France under Napoleon, François Bauwens of Passy, wrote to François de Neufchâteau during November, 1798, calling his attention to the possibilities of developing a textile industry in France using British machinery. Bauwens proposed developing Paris and other cities as centers of production, in the fashion of Manchester and Birmingham. The program, he argued, could be accomplished in a short time and its goal would be to generalize industry in France, offering substantial advantages to the Republic. AN AF III 21ᴬ, dossier 70 G, document 30.

The second precept – not providing assistance to entrepreneurs who had established themselves in an area in which similar enterprises had once existed – clearly sought to address the issue of quality control. It indicated an assumption by the commission that most new manufacturers were dishonest or corrupt.

Finally, although not explicitly acknowledged, the desire to amend the law on national properties in order to allocate available buildings was intended to make them available for entrepreneurs with mechanized production capability – not as workshops for artisans.[238] Whereas the Old Regime had supported and sustained the artisanal guild system, revolutionary regimes had been unrelentingly hostile to it, and that antipathy, along with its corollary, support of mechanization of production, was codified in the commission's proposals.

The Directory was correct to concentrate on textiles, which held promise for mass production.[239] At the same time, however, proposals or efforts to improve quality repeatedly collided with a deep sense of caution concerning measures that could lay a foundation for a restoration of guilds. The problems confronting the Directory as it sought to rejuvenate the textile sector were particularly significant.

Beginning during the summer of 1796, Claude Reusse, a merchant from Gallet (Oise), sought to inform the government of abuses in the manufacture of cloth. The Executive Directory forwarded his letter to the Minister of the Interior, who expressed his concern about the information it contained. It was a goal of the government, the minister stated, to revive industry and to address the abuses outlined by Reusse. Reusse had proposed that the government appoint him as a commissioner to oversee production, but the minister observed that the law of September 27, 1791, had suppressed various offices that had overseen manufacture, and that law had not been repealed or undone. As a result, the minister asserted that he could not appoint Reusse to any such office without compromising his responsibilities.[240]

Reusse persisted, however, and the following month wrote to the Minister of the Interior again about abuses in the manufacture of cloth used for army uniforms. The manufacturers in question, located in the Department of Oise, had banded together to use adulterated wool that decreased the usable life of the fabric by half, and were also perpetrating other frauds.[241] Reusse again offered his services as a commissioner to oversee the production of cloth to assure its quality. In order to reduce the burden on the government, Reusse even proposed that his salary be paid in cloth from the producers in question.[242]

[238] During July, 1798, the ministry asked the Executive Directory for buildings to house British machines being brought to France. AN AF III 21ᴬ, dossier 70 G, document 31.
[239] Lyons, *France Under the Directory*, p. 178.
[240] AN F¹² 1391, letter of Minister of the Interior to Reusse, 28 thermidor year IV (August 15, 1796).
[241] On problems with uniforms, Forrest, *Soldiers of the French Revolution*, pp. 139–140.
[242] AN F¹² 1391, letter of Reusse to Minister of the Interior, 6 vendémiaire year V (September 27, 1796). It may be a validation of the arguments made by Reusse, however, that subsequently the

Indeed, the anger and dismay that such fraud caused within the army is abundantly evident in a letter from an inspector-general, General Schauenburg, to General Desaix during the year V. He sent Desaix a uniform that he had taken from a supply depot operated by new suppliers, the "entrepreneurs généraux," and, with clear exasperation, instructed Desaix to hold it up to light so that he would be able to see that it was only "transparent canvas." He enumerated many other deficiencies beyond the poor quality of the cloth, including the fact that the uniforms were ill-fitting and scraped the underarms of soldiers. He also sent Desaix a boot that was deficient and angrily denounced the entire system of outfitting the troops.[243]

Despite the clear importance of the matter in question – the military effort – there is no indication that the minister accepted Reusse's offer, undoubtedly for the reason he had stated in his earlier letter. Moreover, to have appointed an official to assure the quality of fabric would have breached the ideology of the Revolution, particularly its commitment to freedom, and would also have been perceived by many contemporaries as a reversion to what was frequently referred to as intolerable servitude to old regulations.[244]

Whether Reusse was, in fact, a concerned citizen or whether he was seeking to secure a position during an era of economic hardship cannot be determined, but it is clear that other contemporaries regarded the issue of restoring quality in production as the most critical factor in reviving industry in France. An anonymous pamphlet that appeared under the Directory noted that the legislature had reestablished oversight to guarantee the standard of gold and silver content in appropriate objects. The author proposed to extend such supervision of quality to other manufacturing sectors because he believed it was necessary in order for them to recover. The majority of manufactures, he asserted, had been brought to a level of great degradation by abuse of the unlimited freedom in production ushered in by the Revolution. It was critical, he argued, to correct the problem.[245]

The conflict between restoring quality and preventing the establishment of any foundation that could potentially serve as a platform for the restoration

Executive Directory vested the outfitting of troops with a single supplier, which would have assured greater accountability. AN F^{12} 1391, letter of Minister of the Interior to the Central Administration of the Department of Loir-et-Cher, 29 ventôse year VII (March 19, 1799).

[243] Bibliothèque nationale et universitaire de Strasbourg (hereafter BNU Strasbourg), Schauenburg Papers, Ms. 452, letter of Schauenburg to Desaix, 28 pluviôse year V (February 16, 1797). I am grateful to Rafe Blaufarb for providing me with this reference.

[244] On the commitment to commercial freedom and lack of regulation during the Directory, Bossenga, "La Révolution française et les corporations," pp. 412, 416–417; and Bossenga, "Economic Privilege and Government Regulation: Guilds, Public Officials, and the Bourgeoisie in Lille, 1700–1820," *Proceedings of the ... Annual Meeting of the Western Society for French History* 11 (1993): 224–225, 226.

[245] AN AD XI 72, *Projet pour la restauration des manufactures en France*. The pamphlet alludes to the date of 19 brumaire for the action regarding the oversight of gold and silver, and such an action did occur on 19 brumaire year VI (November 9, 1797). It was also carried out in Lille. Hirsch, *Les Deux rêves du commerce*, p. 249.

of guilds is even more apparent in a similar issue that arose during the year
VI. In an effort to correct abuses in the textile trade, an inhabitant of Rouen
named Renault proposed a revival of the system of visits and trademarks
that had been abolished in September 1791. The suppression had, however
unintentionally, led to a decline of quality, he argued, and broken confidence
with consumers. To restore the textiles produced in the Department of Seine-
Inférieure to their former quality, he proposed reviving visits by the suppressed Office of Inspections. In this manner, he asserted, it would be easy to
eradicate in a short time the abuses that had destroyed commerce and to win
back markets that had, since the Revolution, been lost to Silesian textiles.[246]

A division of the Ministry of the Interior prepared a report in response to
the suggestion of reestablishing visits and trademarks in the textile industry.
It began by lamenting the decline into which commerce and manufacture had
fallen, a decline attributable to many causes. One aspect that had attracted
particular attention, the report noted, was the former system of visits and
production trademarks, because many believed that reinstating them would
correct many of the deficiencies in the quality of cloth produced. Indeed, the
report stated, a resolution to this end had been prepared for submission to
the Council of Five Hundred. It had already been submitted to the Council of
Ancients, but the subcommittee charged with consideration of it, headed by
Charles-François Lebrun, had recommended rejection.

Lebrun acknowledged the "decadence and fragmentation" of French production, but argued that it was the result of a number of factors, including the
assignats, the law of the Maximum, the ravages of war, labor shortages, lack
of capital, high interest rates, and reduced consumption. It was an oversimpli-
fication, the report argued, to focus simply on the regulatory system that had
been abolished in 1791.

Asserting that the question of visits and trademarks was one of the most
significant that had arisen in the administration of commerce, the division
observed that the question had produced disagreement. Without claiming a
full consideration of the issue, however, the document argued against the proposal to revive visits and trademarks.

The division acknowledged the reasons put forward for reestablishing visits
and trademarks – defective textiles that had ruined commerce – but asserted
that the revival of the old system was misguided. The report claimed that strict
regulations on production would be "an invincible obstacle to the progress of
industry" because such regulations would not allow for technical improvement, new processes for production or changes in the preferences of consumers. The foreign competition that had driven French textiles out of traditional
foreign markets were not subject to visits, the division argued, and it criticized
the "blind confidence" that trademarks allegedly inspired.

[246] AN F[12] 1556, Observations on inspections and trademarks of textiles..., 1 germinal year VI
(March 21, 1798). Rouen was a site of particularly strong calls for a reimposition of regula-
tions to ensure quality. *La Décade philosophique, littéraire et politique*, 10 thermidor year
VI (July 28, 1798).

The report maintained that any decision must also take account of article 355 of the Constitution of the Year III, which, among other provisions, proclaimed that there would be no limitation of any kind on trade or industry. In view of such a formal disposition, the division argued that one could not possibly envisage reestablishing visits or trademarks as they had formerly existed. Furthermore, article 355 precluded the formulation of any rules for policing relations between producers and workers by the Directory. In any case, the document asserted, good faith and probity should inspire confidence more than a trademark, and it was this ideal that the government should pursue rather than implementing "coercive regulations."[247]

Like the document prepared earlier by another division that argued for concentration on development of the textile sector, the report of this division represented yet another effort by the Ministry of the Interior to serve as a bulwark against any measure that might lead to a reestablishment of corporations. The issue of trademarks on textiles had been debated since 1789, but revolutionary bodies had resisted allowing them, viewing such marks as corporate vestiges and antithetical to the principle of laws applicable to all.[248] Through its participation in the debate on issues of quality and production, the ministry sought to prevent any action that could serve as a base to reconstitute guilds.

As the idea of restoring visits and trademarks suggests, however, traditional outlooks persisted throughout the Revolution. During the year VI a producer of braided rope in Toulouse, Flages, had entered his product into the competition for the exhibition of products of French industry. Pressed by the brief period of time available, however, he had sent a flawed sample to Paris, but it had nevertheless been favorably reviewed by the jury, although it had not been admitted for exhibition. Shortly after the exhibition closed, Flages wrote to the Minister of the Interior and, although he claimed not to be seeking an exclusive privilege, he asked that in lieu of a patent on his rope that he instead be awarded the title of "premier rope-maker of the Republic."[249]

A division of the Ministry of the Interior prepared a report on the matter for the Minister of the Interior. The document praised the utility of the rope and the progress it enabled, especially in the perfection of spinning and by providing a real economy in the use of raw materials. Indeed, the report asserted that the rope was comparable to the best-known quality ropes and placed Flages among those in the front rank of producers.

The title he was seeking, however, which the division noted the Minister could not confer, would not only discourage emulation but could also represent an injustice to other rope-makers – it was important not to hinder their

[247] AN F¹² 1556, Reflections on project for reestablishing visitation offices and trademarks on textiles, fourth division (undated).

[248] AN F¹² 652, memoir to National Assembly from textile producers of Bédarieux, December 5, 1789, and undated report by Rousillou on memoir.

[249] AN F¹² 2202ᴬ, dossier Haute-Garonne, letter of Flages to Minister of the Interior, 13 vendémiaire year VII (October 4, 1798).

efforts at improving the quality of their product. The authors of the report believed that the request to be named "premier rope-maker of the Republic" was a maneuver to gain greater attention and suggested that he instead send a sample to the Conservatoire des Arts et Métiers, where it might contribute to the progress of industry.[250]

Even allowing for the probably correct belief that the request was motivated by a desire for greater publicity for his product, it is nonetheless of interest. Flages was sufficiently forward-looking to seek to compete in the industrial exhibition, yet he also sought a distinction clearly associated with the Old Regime, albeit in a modified form. Once again, acknowledging that in all probability there were ulterior motives involved, the incident nevertheless provides insight into how the propensity to reestablish guilds, also in a modified form, was able to continue to exist – during a time of commercial disorder, reformed former institutions appeared to offer a solution. As James Munson noted, "the agonies of commerce under the Revolution were presented as the degeneration of a once honorable and productive enterprise into a sterile nexus of short-sighted and unethical practices,"[251] so it is little surprise that a focus on the past remained.

* * * * * * *

The abolition of guilds and oversight in 1791 had been dictated by the hostility of the National Assembly toward privileged corporatism, and the years that followed their destruction had shown both the potential promise and pitfalls of the action. Although deputies had anticipated unrest arising from the eradication of corporations, which had led them to delay it, it is virtually certain that they had not envisaged the array of problems that arose from the act.

The abrupt, widespread and precipitous decline in the quality of goods and services that developed in the aftermath stunned contemporaries – for many years, the dominant memory associated with the suppression of corporations was degradation and decline.[252] Guilds had performed a number of functions and neither the National Assembly nor the Legislative Assembly, to which the National Assembly had delegated the responsibility, made any provision to fulfill the tasks formerly carried out by guilds.

The declaration of war compounded public frustration – substandard food, for example, became virtually commonplace. This was followed by dearth, and the years of hardship after the abolition of guilds encouraged sentiment in favor of their reestablishment. This sentiment did not represent an endorsement of corporations – rather, it was rooted in a yearning for adequate supply and good quality.

---

[250] AN F¹² 2202ᴬ, dossier Haute-Garonne, report of Bureau of Arts, fourth division, to Minister of the Interior, 19 brumaire year VII (November 9, 1798).
[251] Munson, "Businessmen, Business Conduct and the Civic Organization of Commercial Life," p. 11.
[252] AN AD XI 76, *Essai sur les patentes et le commerce*, which was written during the Napoleonic era.

Deputies of the National Convention were aware of public disaffection, and some challenged the inclusion of article 355, which continued and strengthened the proscription of corporations, in the Constitution of the Year III that established the Directory. As conditions worsened under the Directory, public disillusionment deepened.

The abolition of guilds significantly recast the world of work, and the outbreak of war transformed it further. The need to outfit large armies raised through conscription led to a reorganization and regimentation of labor that in some respects foreshadowed the factory system. In the production of muskets, for example, artisans from formerly guild-based trades were swept up and melded with unskilled laborers in a proto-assembly line process to manufacture the components of weaponry. The blending of skilled and unskilled labor in a common production process would have been inconceivable under the Old Regime. War production marked an early step in the metamorphosis of labor from a skill to be developed and certified to a commodity to be sold and a shift in emphasis from quality to quantity in manufacture.

Moreover, another aspect of the manufacturing program undertaken by the Convention was that it revealed the extraordinary potential of untrammeled production. The levels of manufacture achieved, far beyond the artisanal scale that had heretofore prevailed, suggested possibilities that previously had not seemed attainable or perhaps even imaginable. Up until the very end of the Old Regime, guilds had generally sought to prevent technical improvements or the implementation of any other development that they viewed as detrimental to their trade or guild – the Réveillon riot is an especially pertinent example and one that remained with contemporaries.[253]

As a citizen named Chaussier observed, in an analysis that appeared on the very day that the National Convention approved the article in the proposed constitution proscribing guilds, for a long time progress in the arts had been held back by "reflexive and servile attachment" by corporations to outdated and routine methods. Furthermore, members of guilds had been imbued with a malevolent particularistic outlook that led them to draw a kind of veil over their operations, leaving knowledge of the arts concentrated only in the hands of those who practiced them. Useful advances of any kind were not widely disseminated and were even concealed.

In the current situation, Chaussier argued, with the abolition of corporations, all efforts should be directed toward the same goal, focusing on the general welfare rather than any particular interest. Hidden secrets ought to be unveiled and means of improvement should not be confined to a single facility – if an innovation was beneficial, it should become common knowledge.[254] To many contemporaries, the absence of guilds offered a new model for economic development and progress. At the same time, however, the myriad problems associated with the dissolution of corporations remained, to the

[253] Rosenband, "Jean-Baptiste Réveillon," pp. 481–510.
[254] *La Décade philosophique, littéraire et politique*, 30 fructidor year III (September 16, 1795).

chagrin of most contemporaries – indeed, the exhortation of Chaussier to maintain their abolition must be read in this context.

The decline of quality and concern about workers without oversight, compounded by severe hardship, created a favorable recollection of guilds with which public officials had to contend. The dearth and abuses that formed the basis for a positive attitude toward corporations also contributed to the unpopularity of the Directory, but the Directory never seriously considered restoring the guild structure, which seemed more attractive retrospectively – it loomed as an alternative model during a time of scarcity and dissatisfaction. In any assessment of the Directory it should be recognized that by not permitting guilds to regain a foothold, at times despite marked public discontent, the Directory helped mechanization to take root, despite continuing war that sharply constrained the government's ability to support industry. Even as mechanization of production began to take hold, however, a residual sentiment to reestablish guilds, fueled by labor unrest and abuses encountered on a daily basis, persisted.

3

The Reemergence of Guilds as a Policy Issue, 1800–1811

> It was a first step toward the reestablishment of guilds; one could, however, justify this decision for valid regulatory reasons.
>
> Antoine-Claire Thibaudeau, *Mémoires sur le Consulat*,
> on the reorganization of butchers in Paris in 1802

If there was a moment during the Revolutionary and Napoleonic epoch when guilds might have been restored, it was during the reign of Napoleon Bonaparte.[1] To the degree that it sought to reconcile royalists and republicans, for example, the Consulate was nonideological. At the same time, it had definite objectives, and it clearly valued order over freedom.[2]

The Council of State debated the restoration of guilds during the early period of the Consulate, and apparently recommended their reestablishment, but this did not occur. Moreover, many disparate efforts, both governmental and nongovernmental, to reorganize guilds, individually and comprehensively, continued for a decade.

THE CONSULATE AND THE REEMERGENCE OF THE ISSUE OF GUILDS

The coup that toppled the Directory in November 1799 and ultimately brought Napoleon Bonaparte to power was undertaken by members of the political

---

[1] Michael Sibalis, "Corporatism after the Corporations: The Debate on Restoring the Guilds under Napoleon I and the Restoration," *French Historical Studies* 15 (1988): 718–730; Jean Tulard, "*Le Débat autour du rétablissement des corporations sous le Consulat et l'Empire,*" in *Histoire du droit social: Mélanges en hommage à Jean Imbert*, Jean-Louis Harouel, ed., (Paris: Presses Universitaires de France, 1989): pp. 537–541. See also the statement of Georges Lefebvre, *Napoleon*, 2 vols. (New York: Columbia University Press, 1969), I: 151, that "had it been left entirely to Bonaparte, one would surely have witnessed the rebirth of guilds." This assertion must be weighed against the comment of Chaptal that Bonaparte had little inclination to restore guilds. Chaptal, *Mes Souvenirs sur Napoléon* (Paris: Plon, 1893), p. 289.

[2] Indeed, a change of vocabulary that occurred under the Bonapartist regime reflected this priority – the inhabitants of France were often referred to not as "*citoyens*," but as "*administrés*."

elite to deal with a major political crisis that included stalemates in domestic and foreign relations, an unwillingness to accept political change and a weak executive authority. In the final analysis, however, although it has occasionally been overstated, much of the Directory's failure was economic. The general reaction to the coup was apathy,[3] due in large measure to the parlous state of the economy. The lack of interest was nearly total, encompassing indifference not only to the overthrow of the Directory, but also to the new regime itself – in fact, the conspirators felt compelled to send out representatives to facilitate acceptance of the new government.

During the following weeks, a commission of fifty-three men began to draft a constitution to give the new government both legality and definition. Many believed that Sieyes had a draft constitution prepared, but he did not, and this enabled Bonaparte to shape the document in a manner much more favorable to himself. The promulgation of the Constitution of the Year VIII during December 1799, reflected Bonaparte's outmaneuvering of Sieyes because it established Bonaparte's preeminent position in the new government – a role Sieyes had undoubtedly envisaged for himself.[4]

The new leader of France established through the Constitution of the Year VIII, Napoleon Bonaparte, was only thirty years old. In fact, because of his young age, in the government he had just overthrown he would not have been eligible to serve as a Director or as a member of the Council of Ancients, and he was barely of the minimum age to serve in the Council of Five Hundred. As First Consul under the new constitution, however, he was virtually omnipotent and was eager to reorganize France.

One of the key institutions Bonaparte established in the effort to refashion the French state was the Council of State. At its inception it consisted of 29 men and not only drafted all of the legislation submitted to the Legislative Body and the Tribunate, but also advised Bonaparte on various issues, particularly administrative ones. Its deliberations were closed, and it was in this body alone that Bonaparte allowed open discussion and overt disagreement, which he apparently enjoyed.[5] Furthermore, within the Council of State, the section of the Interior, which dealt with issues involving the organization of labor, was considered one of the most exciting and challenging assignments.[6] In addition, two of the six members of the section of the Interior were former members of the National Assembly, which had abolished guilds.[7]

[3] Monnier, *Le Faubourg Saint-Antoine*, p. 271.

[4] On Bonaparte's rise to power, Malcolm Crook, *Napoleon Comes to Power: Democracy and Dictatorship in France, 1795–1804* (Cardiff: University of Wales Press, 1998); Jean-Paul Bertaud, *1799: Bonaparte prend le pouvoir*, 2nd ed. (Brussels: Editions Complexe, 2000); Isser Woloch, *Napoleon and His Collaborators: The Making of a Dictatorship* (New York: Norton, 2001); Philip Dwyrer, *Napoleon: The Path to Power* (New Haven, CT: Yale University Press, 2008).

[5] Chaptal, *Mes Souvenirs sur Napoléon*, pp. 55–56; Charles de Lacretelle, *Histoire du Consulat et de l'Empire* (Paris: Amyot, 1846), p. 363; Crook, *Napoleon Comes to Power*, p. 80.

[6] Pierre-Louis Roederer, *Mémoires sur la Révolution, le Consulat et l'Empire*, Octave Aubry, ed., (Paris: Plon, 1942), p. 121.

[7] *Le Conseil d'Etat: son histoire à travers les documents d'époque 1799–1974* (Paris: Editions du CNRS, 1974), p. 30.

Aware of the economic difficulties that had led to disaffection with the Directory, and apprehensive about worker unrest, the situation of workers became a matter of concern to the new regime early on.[8] As the Constitution of the Year VIII was being drafted, the government sought to investigate a means to secure employment for workers during the winter.[9] Its motives were practical – the regime was concerned that counterrevolutionaries were seeking to exploit hardship among workers to challenge the new government, although police agents asserted that the Consulate was gaining acceptance among workers.[10] Indeed, by the spring of 1800 it was clear that workers were exhausted by politics and could not be raised to action by agitators despite the difficult economic conditions.[11]

Nevertheless, at a more fundamental level – beyond keeping workers from becoming restive as the regime consolidated – a key focal point was, as the prefect of the Department of Seine, Nicolas-Therèse-Benoît Frochot, characterized it, "the insubordination of workers."[12] Paris, as Michael Sibalis noted, had the largest agglomeration of artisans, workers and indigents in continental Europe, making "insubordination," which could have a wide variety of meanings for ruling authorities, from political insurrections to work stoppages or strikes, a critical issue.[13] Without question, its antithesis was discipline and order, which was what the new regime sought, and one means of achieving those goals was to restore guilds.

Indeed, an undated memorandum from within the government concerning arts and trades, which evidence suggests was written during the early period of the Consulate, indicates that a law proposing the re-creation of trade corporations was submitted to the Council of State. There was, however, considerable disagreement among those who drafted the law. On the one hand, proponents of the reestablishment of corporations asserted that the proposed law would correct former abuses because it would not permit any restrictions on industry, nor would it allow any fees to be charged for entry to a guild. In this manner, the advocates for reestablishment declared, the flaws of the former system would be corrected.

On the other hand, the memorandum noted that opponents of corporations had cited the principles of Turgot and the economic system of "absolute freedom." The document clearly implied that the view that had prevailed was

8 Chaptal, *Mes Souvenirs sur Napoléon*, pp. 284–285, 287, 291.
9 AN AF IV 925, dossier 1, document 63. Just prior to the coup that overthrew the Directory, the Council of Five Hundred had also addressed this concern. Joseph-Antoine Bostic d'Antic, *Rapport fait par Bosc (de l'Aude), sur les moyens d'assurer du travail aux ouvriers pendant cet hiver, et de raviver l'industrie, séance du 16 brumaire an 8* (Paris: Imprimerie Nationale, year VIII, 1799). See also, Monnier, *Le Faubourg Saint-Antoine*, p. 87.
10 AN AF IV 1329, reports of 15 frimaire, 19 nivôse, 11 pluviôse, 12 pluviôse year VIII (December 6, 1799, January 9, 1800, January 31, 1800, February 1, 1800).
11 AN AF IV 1329, reports of 15 pluviôse, 25 floréal and 27 floréal year VIII (February 4 and May 15 and 17, 1800).
12 Bertaud, *1799, Bonaparte prend le pouvoir*, p. 70.
13 Michael David Sibalis, "The Workers of Napoleonic Paris 1800–1815" (Ph.D. dissertation, Concordia University, 1979), p. 2.

that absolute freedom in political economy was injurious, isolating one individual from another and, in an apparent reference to problems with the quality of goods and services, also harmful to consumers, merchants and workers. Furthermore, the majority argued, in politics absolute freedom was "no longer advisable." These were the issues, the authors of the document stated, that the government should examine, and they urged the Council of State to determine its goals for society before opening discussion on what they stated was "this important matter."[14]

The debate on the reestablishment of guilds represented in microcosm the goals and tensions of the larger Napoleonic settlement. Since 1789 a major focal point of the Revolution had been freedom and individual rights, and the National Assembly had abolished corporations in 1791 because their privileges had constituted an infringement of both. From the vantage point of 1799, the "absolute freedom" enacted in the economic and political spheres had produced nearly a decade of worker activism that had contributed to the toppling of the monarchy and threatened revolutionary governments. Furthermore, such freedom had led to worker actions and a decline in the quality of goods in the marketplace. Although there had been disorder and violence under the former guild system, the unrest had not posed a particular threat to the ruling order. Against the backdrop of years of turmoil and deterioration in the quality of goods and services since their abolition, corporations were associated with good order and high standards of production.[15] As a result, men both inside and outside the government were willing to curtail political and economic freedom to achieve greater order and better quality, which accounts for the recommendation to the Council of State.

In his examination of the establishment of the Napoleonic regime, Isser Woloch observed that the revolutionary ideals that remained embedded in the Napoleonic dictatorship were largely due to the work of men whom he labels "ex-revolutionary collaborators."[16] The Council of State's decision not to reestablish guilds, despite the putative reforms that doing so might achieve, appears to be an instance of this phenomenon. The reestablishment of corporations in virtually any form would have represented an unacceptable reversion to the Old Regime and a fundamental betrayal of the Revolution – a stance evident in the processing of a petition within the Ministry of the Interior. A businessman had written to suggest that guilds be reestablished as a means of restoring quality in production and consumers' confidence in merchandise. A summary of the petition had raised a question of great pertinence for commerce.

The "observations" appended by the ministry to the summary noted that the reestablishment of guilds would reinstate bodies that were contrary to the

---

[14] AN AF IV 1060, dossier 1, document 31. The document begins with a heading "*Note pour les Consuls,*" suggesting that the primacy of the First Consul was not yet fully established, and it makes clear that "thought" and "intention" were not yet established.

[15] AN F[12] 2366–2367, *mémoire* of de Breval to Minister of the Interior, 22 ventôse year X (March 13, 1802); AN AD XI 76, *Essai sur les patentes et le commerce.*

[16] Woloch, *Napoleon and His Collaborators,* p. 243.

principles of freedom. At the same time, however, it was necessary to put in place some form of oversight to prevent fraud in the dimensions and quality of cloth and other merchandise.[17]

Consequently, although corporations were not restored at the beginning of the Consulate, neither was it decided to proscribe them in the manner of article 355 of the Constitution of the Year III, a fact not lost on contemporaries, as is evident in the many requests that the government continued to receive to restore them. The matter was simply left open, which produced something of an anomaly in the Napoleonic government. In a regime generally and correctly regarded as centrally directed and authoritarian, in the absence of a clear decision by Bonaparte himself, a struggle broke out within the government over the issue of guilds.

On one side were those who wished to reestablish corporations, primarily administrators and officials – the police in Paris, along with some prefects and ministers. It is clear that advocates of the restoration of guilds did not envision a simple reversion to their old form, but sought to include reforms and safeguards. There could be no privilege conferred on a restored body and it was imperative that an individual's right to freely exercise any trade be preserved.[18]

On the other side were those who opposed any reestablishment of guilds, and this resistance was concentrated in the Ministry of the Interior. The ministry believed strongly in the ability of market forces to correct deficiencies in production and quality and opposed efforts to resolve such issues through regulation.[19] The contest between these two positions and their constituencies continued throughout much of the Napoleonic regime.

In logistical terms, it would not have been difficult to restore guilds – production continued to be centered on small workshops with a master artisan and a few journeymen[20] – and there was clearly an expectation that some sort of reestablishment would be forthcoming. In the Ministry of the Interior, for example, a subdivision known as the General Council of Agriculture, Arts and Commerce, organized during the year IX, outlined its future responsibilities, among which were regulations for and governance of corporations – a reference to worker bodies.[21]

Furthermore, as members of the Council of State undertook missions or tours to various regions of France, some of them encountered a strong desire to restore guilds. During the year IX, the Counselor of State Jean-Girard

---

[17] AN F[12] 502, dossier 1[b], entry of 19 floréal (no year given).
[18] AN F[12] 4897, letter of Minister of the Interior to Bigot, October 24, 1806; AN F[7] 3024, report to Minister of the Interior, 28 ventôse year XII (March 19, 1804); draft letter to prefect of Department of Gers, March 28, 1807.
[19] AN F[12] 1391, opinion of Council of Agriculture, Arts and Commerce, Ministry of the Interior, 4 frimaire year X (November 25, 1801).
[20] Sibalis, "The Workers of Napoleonic Paris," p. 10.
[21] AN F[12] 501[A], undated list of matters relative to commerce. On the overall organization of the General Council, *Almanach National de France An X* (Paris, n.d.), p. 101.

Lacuée de Cessac wrote in a report that, among other actions, the reestablishment of guilds would help to meet the needs of "manufacture."[22] Similarly, in the Department of Oise, in response to a government questionnaire asking what measures might return manufacturing to its highest degree of prosperity, one of the suggestions was to reestablish guilds.[23] Even in Paris, which at this time was a site of mechanized production, there was a sentiment to restore oversight. One report advocated that the government reestablish surveillance of the quality of merchandise, a responsibility formerly carried out by guilds and inspectors of manufacture.[24]

Indeed, rumors were rife in Paris during the early years of the Consulate that guilds would be restored. On 21 thermidor year IX (August 9, 1801) a police report noted that the reestablishment of corporations was the subject of many conversations and that, in general, this was desired.[25] Two weeks later, the police reported that in the *faubourg* Saint-Antoine a rumor had arisen that the former syndics of the Six Corps and of guilds had been summoned to advise the government on the best means to reestablish guilds.[26]

By the winter of 1801, it was rumored not only that corporations would be restored in the same fashion as they had existed under the Old Regime, but also that the Farmers-General, venality of office and other Old Regime features would be reinstated as well – it was said that the Council of State was acting on these projects.[27] The following summer a rumor circulated that the pressing need of the treasury for revenues would lead to a reestablishment of corporations.[28] During the fall of 1802 a rumor again arose that guilds would be restored and that there was general approval for this.[29]

Moreover, ancillary issues implicitly militated toward the restoration of guilds. In a survey taken by the government of councils of commerce across France, the single greatest concern, cited by fifty-seven councils, was the need to reestablish apprenticeships, a responsibility that had been overseen by guilds.[30] Indeed, in the year X, when the government solicited advice regarding

---

[22] AN AF IV 1012, mission of the year IX, chapter 8.

[23] AN AF IV 1012, dossier chapter 8.

[24] AN AF IV 1012, dossier Manufactures (Seine), part 43. For another request to reestablish oversight, Becchia, *La Draperie d'Elbeuf*, pp. 408–411.

[25] AN F⁷3829, dossier thermidor year IX, report of 21 thermidor year IX (August 9, 1801).

[26] AN F⁷ 3829, dossier fructidor year IX, report of 5 fructidor year IX (August 23, 1801). Louis-Sébastien Mercier traced the trajectory of rumors in the streets of Paris through the embellishments of criers and newspaper sellers. Louis-Sébastien Mercier, *Le Nouveau Paris*, 6 vols. (Paris: Fuchs, n.d.), 2: 67–69. Indeed, during the year IV authorities in Paris prohibited criers and newspaper sellers from adding anything to the summaries stated in the newspapers or adding anything not stated therein. *Bulletin national, ou papier-nouvelles*, 19 messidor year IV (July 7, 1796).

[27] AN F⁷ 3830, dossier nivôse year X, report of 8 nivôse year X (December 29, 1801).

[28] AN F⁷ 3830, dossier messidor year X, report of 28 messidor year X (July 17, 1802). See also AN F⁷ 3830, dossier fructidor year 10, no. 13, report of 15 fructidor year X (September 2, 1802).

[29] AN F⁷ 3831, report of 20 vendémiaire year XI (October 12, 1802).

[30] AN F¹² 2366–2367, note of councils of commerce who have sent their observations on the project of law…

a law on manufacturing, a group of manufacturers in Louviers joined with those of Elbeuf to request the reestablishment of guilds and to ask that they oversee mandatory apprenticeships.[31] The Council of Agriculture, Arts and Commerce of the Department of Meurthe cited guilds' ability to resolve disputes in the workplace, which it regarded as superior to the current system of justices of the peace.[32] At the same time, however, in a separate request from Paris to put in place laws concerning apprenticeships, it was explicitly noted that this should be done in a manner that would reconcile apprenticeships to the principles of "freedom and the republican regime" – a clear stricture that if responsibility for apprenticeships were vested with reestablished corporations, this could not be a simple reversion to the *status quo ante*.[33]

In a consideration of Paris undertaken by a member of the Council of State, it was noted that a "new industry" centered on cotton had arisen in that city, and it was this development that formed the basis of one of the chief countervailing forces to the restoration of guilds.[34] The report attributed the progress in commerce since the start of the Revolution to, among other factors, the "genius of liberty" – a reference, at least in part, to the absence of guilds.[35] The overriding concern of those opposed to the reestablishment of guilds was that any such reestablishment could impede the modernization of production, especially mechanization, and the sacking of the Réveillon manufactory in 1789 was a primary argument in support of this view, especially in Paris.

The terms of the debate also served to shape its vocabulary, with each side seeking a linguistic advantage. Proponents of guilds emphasized the current situation of "unlimited freedom" or some variant of the term in a pejorative fashion. Those opposed to guilds employed phrases such as "inquisitorial regime" or "routine" to characterize the guild and inspectorate systems as ossified, oppressive and opposed to progress.

Just as there was a debate within the government on the reestablishment of guilds, there was public discussion of the issue. Soon after Bonaparte took power, Joseph-Antoine Bosc, a member of the Tribunate, published a pamphlet on means to improve agriculture, manufacturing and commerce in France. As a member of the Tribunate and a former deputy in the Council of Five Hundred, Bosc was in all likelihood politically attuned, but it is not clear whether his pamphlet appeared in reaction to discussions within the government.

---

[31] AN F¹² 2366–2367, entrepreneurs of manufactures of Louviers, meeting with those of the manufactures of Elbeuf, to ask the government to grant them the following dispositions (undated).

[32] AN F¹² 2366–2367, extract from register of deliberations of Council of Agriculture, Arts and Commerce of Department of Meurthe, 20 messidor year X (July 9, 1802). The council also regretted the loss of guilds with respect to the issue of workers quitting employment. See also AN F¹² 2366–2367, letter of Minister of the Interior to Breval, 14 floréal year X (May 4, 1802).

[33] AN AF IV 1012, dossier Commerce (Seine), number 58.

[34] For the comment on the "new industry," AN AF IV 1012, dossier Commerce (Seine), no. 48.

[35] AN AF IV 1012, dossier Commerce (Seine), no. 49.

Bosc acknowledged that the quality of various products had deteriorated since the "oppressive and regulatory regime" had been abolished and untrammeled freedom in production had begun. He listed many of the abuses that had arisen and lamented that it was through such corruption that cities once famous for the quality of their goods had lost their reputation. Nevertheless, he argued strongly against reestablishing guilds, claiming they were "injurious and dangerous" and would present "serious disadvantages."

Bosc did advocate the creation of regulations for apprenticeship, but as a discrete action rather than as a component of any restoration of corporations. Indeed, he described apprenticeships and *compagnonnage* as analogous to the military. Characterizing apprenticeships and *compagnonnages* as "paternal and salutary," he asserted that they united master and pupil in a double bond of comradeship and obedience, somewhat like the severe discipline that linked officer and soldier and contributed to their common success. Was it not then appropriate, he asked, that a man who dedicates himself to a profession offer to the society that protects it a guarantee of his morality and skill before gaining the right to exercise it? The current state of unlimited freedom had populated workshops with ignorant, immoral and greedy men who were pitted against each other, with no advantage for the perfection of their trade and no benefit to society.[36]

The fact that Bosc believed it necessary to argue against the reestablishment of guilds demonstrates that that proposal had a constituency and was at least perceived as being under consideration. Indeed, a counterargument appeared during the year IX, when Jacques Peuchet published a reference work in which he made favorable references to corporations. In the entry for "*jurande*" he criticized their abolition and asserted that their restoration could be useful. In addition, in an appendix Peuchet wrote that guilds were "useful corporations that, for some slight inconveniences, had a thousand advantages."[37]

One anonymous reviewer made that statement a focal point of his critique of the book. Citing the issue of guilds as "clearly a main question," the reviewer sought to invert Peuchet's equation, stating of corporations that "for some advantages, they have a thousand disadvantages." The reviewer acknowledged

[36] Joseph-Antoine Bosc, *Essai sur les moyens d'améliorer l'agriculture, les arts et le commerce en France* (Paris: Patris: an VIII), pp. 4–5. On Bosc, see Michaud, *Biographie universelle, ancienne et moderne*, 2nd ed., 5: 110–111; *Dictionnaire des parlementaires français*, 1: 402–403.

[37] [Jacques] Peuchet, *Vocabulaire des termes de commerce, banque, manufactures, navigation marchands, finance mercantile et statistique* (Paris: Testu, an IX), pp. 141, 549. Peuchet was a moderate, but not a reactionary – he had been an ardent partisan of the Revolution in 1789 and had become a municipal official in Paris with the police. He had, however, come under suspicion during the Terror and was briefly detained, so he left for the countryside and became an administrator at Gonesse. Under the Directory, he returned to police duties. *Nouvelle biographie générale*, 39: 770–771. Indeed, it is notable that several of the men who were sympathetic to the reestablishment of guilds had been municipal administrators – Dubois, Peuchet and, to a lesser extent, Frochot – where they had almost certainly seen personally the adverse effects of their abolition.

that manufacturing had generally deteriorated since the Revolution, but stated that the suppression of guilds was not the only reason for this and pointed out other contributing factors. The reviewer asserted that it would be a great error to believe that reverting to the constraints and regulations of the Old Regime would reestablish the kind of prosperity then enjoyed. That prosperity had existed, he claimed, not because of regulations, but in spite of them – it had been a result of such factors as rich soil and a favorable geographic position.[38]

Other than reactions to the d'Allarde law or to discussions of article 355 of the Constitution of the Year III, the debate that began under the Consulate was the first extended public discussion of guilds since the failure of Turgot's reforms nearly a quarter of a century earlier. Furthermore, because the question of corporations was never definitively resolved by the Bonapartist regime, it continued to reemerge well into the Empire.

Indeed, not only within France, but outside of it, the dissolution of guilds was viewed as questionable or even as a failure. In early 1802 a Parisian newspaper reported that the subject of the essay competition of the Society for Useful Arts of Hamburg was to determine the advantages and general inconveniences of guilds and to suggest modifications to their previous form. The winning entry, by M. Weiss, contended that "the great multiplication of workers in each profession" deprived them of the means to earn a living from their work and harmed the prosperity of industry. This prosperity, it was argued, rested upon having knowledgeable workers in a proportional number to consumers, so masterships should be accorded only to a limited number of sufficiently skilled individuals.

Weiss sought to debunk arguments favoring the abolition of corporations and to demonstrate the problems that would result if this occurred in Germany. Among reform measures, he proposed greater screening of candidates for apprenticeships, the establishment of a minimum age of sixteen to begin apprenticeships, setting a three-year limit on the duration of apprenticeships, reducing to the lowest possible level the cost of apprenticeships and prohibiting less skillful masters from taking on apprentices. Although Weiss also addressed other issues, the clear theme of his essay was that reforming guilds was preferable to abolishing them.[39] In the final analysis, as these writings demonstrate, the abolition of corporations was not universally regarded as an unqualified success; indeed, the wisdom and utility of the action remained open to question.

The debates both inside and outside of government indicated that the reestablishment of guilds was regarded as a possible solution to the problems that had arisen in French manufacturing since the Revolution. In fact, after its reorganization during the year XI, even some members of the Chamber of Commerce of Paris were open to the possibility of reestablishing corporations.[40] At the

[38] *La Décade philosophique, littéraire et politique*, 10 floréal an IX (April 30, 1801).

[39] *La Décade philosophique, littéraire et politique*, 20 nivôse year X (January 10, 1802).

[40] Archives de la Chambre de Commerce et d'Industrie de Paris 2 Mi 1, meeting of 10 thermidor year XI (July 29, 1802).

same time, however, the Ministry of the Interior undertook a concerted effort to advance mechanization and industry, particularly after Chaptal replaced Lucien Bonaparte as minister, and this effort temporarily countered the evolving sentiment in favor of reestablishing guilds.

CHAPTAL AND THE REVIVAL OF INDUSTRIAL EXHIBITIONS

Chaptal was a chemist by training and had become involved in developing the textile industry in Montpellier, particularly dyeing, before the Revolution – indeed, in his memoirs he claimed to be the first chemist to apply his knowledge directly to industry (*les arts*). After a brief involvement with federalism, from which he extricated himself during the Convention, he organized the production of saltpeter in lower Languedoc and Provence. Despite his federalist background, the Committee of Public Safety called him to Paris to expedite the production of saltpeter and gunpowder throughout France to enable the armies of the republic to go on the offensive. Chaptal remained in this post until the fall of Robespierre, after which he returned to Montpellier, but the remarkable levels of production he had attained left a deep impression on him.

Chaptal became a member of the Council of State in 1799 and worked on public instruction and administration before being named interim Minister of the Interior on 15 brumaire year IX (November 6, 1800). Bonaparte confirmed him in that position on 1 pluviôse year IX (January 21, 1801), and one of the priorities he set was the renewal of commerce and industry.[41]

One of the first efforts to rejuvenate commerce was the government's reactivation of an event that had been initiated by the Directory – the exhibition of products of French industry. The first industrial exhibition had been held in conjunction with the Festival of the Founding of the Republic, and the intent had been to make the exhibition an annual event, but because of the costs of war, subsequent festivals had not included an industrial exhibition.

Chaptal, who had been a judge in the first exhibition, sought to revive the original format of inviting producers and manufacturers from across France to showcase their work. On 13 ventôse year IX (March 4, 1801), the consuls approved a proposal on exhibitions by the Minister of the Interior. The exhibitions were envisaged as an annual event to be held during the five complementary days of the Revolutionary calendar, thereby remaining associated with the Festival of the Founding of the Republic. All manufacturers were eligible

---

[41] Chaptal, *Mes Souvenirs sur Napoléon*, pp. 31–59; Michaud, *Biographie universelle, ancienne et moderne*, 2nd ed., 7: 498–502. Indeed, just a few weeks after his confirmation in the position, Chaptal declared, in reply to a letter from Toulouse, that it was his intention to have the government aggressively promote machine production in France. AN F^{12} 4861, letter of Majorel to Minister of the Interior, 6 pluviôse year IX (January 26, 1801); letter of Chaptal to Majorel, 23 pluviôse year IX (February 12, 1801). For additional perspective, Jeff Horn and Margaret C. Jacob, "Jean-Antoine Chaptal and the Cultural Roots of French Industrialization," *Technology and Culture* 39 (1998): 671–698.

to compete and the winners would be presented "to the government" by the Minister of the Interior.[42]

After receiving approval for the exhibitions, Chaptal sent a circular to prefects in which he alluded to the importance of the exhibition of the year VI, but wrote that the government wanted to perfect the exhibitions to bring about even greater results. He observed that the first exhibition had shown mainly the products of Parisian exhibitors and that industry itself was not extensively developed at that time. It was up to the prefects, he asserted, to help make the upcoming exhibition a success. It would provide major benefits by inspiring emulation and, after what Chaptal characterized as ten years of difficulty, French industry would again rise to a high degree of prosperity. Undoubtedly to incite greater efforts on the part of prefects, he notified them that porticos at the exhibition were to be reserved for the products of each department and contended that it would be possible to follow the growth and progress of industry through successive exhibitions. He closed the circular by reminding prefects that the government was entrusting them with major tasks and that their renown and that of the state necessitated great efforts. They could not rest, he declared, until they could say to themselves that French arts were the most perfect in Europe.[43]

The exhibition was held during the complementary days of the year IX (September 18–22, 1801) and, in what was almost certainly an attempt to convey that the industrial arts had parity in prestige with the fine arts, the second exhibition was held in the courtyard of the Louvre rather than at the Champ de Mars. In addition, as if to underscore the parallelism, the annual salon was held simultaneously at the Louvre. Chaptal believed that the exhibition was eagerly anticipated by the public, leading him to write to the Minister of War to ask for a doubling of the guard for the event, a request to which the Minister of War acceded.[44] Chaptal's optimism was not misplaced. Police reports noted that the exhibition was a focus of public attention and that attendance was heavy. Even delayed openings did not affect the crowd's behavior, which was peaceable at all times.[45]

The sense of regional pride the exhibition generated is evident in a proclamation by the prefect of the Department of Nord in preparation for the exhibition of the year IX. After five manufacturers from the department were admitted to the exhibition, the prefect, alluding to the damage the department had suffered during 1793–1794, stated that its misfortunes had not stifled its industry – to him the acceptances represented the department's recovery.[46]

---

[42] AN F^{1a} 24, dossier year IX, undated (but after 13 ventôse) circular of Minister of the Interior to prefects of departments.

[43] *Ibid.* On the efforts of one prefect to encourage participation from his department, AD Nord M 557/5.

[44] AN F^{1c} I 91, report presented to Minister of the Interior, 14 fructidor year IX (September 1, 1801).

[45] AN F^7 3829, police reports of 2nd complementary day, year IX (September 19, 1801); 3rd complementary day, year IX (September 20, 1801).

[46] AD Nord M 557/5, proclamation of prefect of Department of Nord, 28 thermidor year IX (August 16, 1801).

Indeed, the prefect could not contain his disappointment after the entrants failed to receive a medal, which led him to write Chaptal to express his disillusionment with that outcome. Chaptal attempted to assuage the prefect's wounded feelings in his reply, but also sought to further his goal of advancing French industry by chiding the prefect for his response. He expressed appreciation for the prefect's efforts and assured him that the jury that awarded prizes at the exhibition had faced a difficult task, but had carried out that task with impartiality. Chaptal then told the prefect that a more appropriate reaction would have been to prompt greater efforts from the manufacturers in his department. He concluded by expressing the hope that they would redouble their efforts in order to earn distinction at the next exhibition.[47]

The items displayed had been chosen in a competition judged by a jury of five men named by the prefect of each department. The exhibition was to award twelve gold medals, twenty silver medals and thirty bronze medals. In the competition for the year IX, half of the gold medals went to entrants in textiles. In fact, citations for some of the medal winners clearly reveal the movement toward mechanized production and large-scale enterprise that was under way. One of the bronze medal winners, Joseph-Marie Jacquard, from Lyon, had invented a loom that eliminated the need for a worker during the production of cloth – within a decade thousands of them were operating in France.[48] The Ternaux brothers, who won a gold medal, were also in textile production, the citation noting that they had four establishments – in Louviers, Sedan, Reims and Ensival – that employed between 4,000 and 5,000 workers.

In another indication of the prestige that the government sought to attach to their efforts, the medal winners met with the three consuls who had visited the exhibition with the Minister of the Interior on 2 vendémiaire year X (September 24, 1801).[49] The ceremony with the consuls also demonstrated that the exhibition had been designed in part to provide a psychological boost to French industry. In his speech a member of the jury that selected the medal winners, Claude-Anthelme Costaz, stated that the exhibition should calm unease over the future of French commerce and silence those who proclaimed the decline of French industry. He told the consuls that an annual industrial exhibition would be an institution of the greatest interest and would serve to foster industrial development and consumer sophistication. Like its predecessor, the exhibition made a major impression on the French public.[50]

[47] AD Nord M 557/5, letter of Minister of the Interior to prefect of Department of Nord, 22 frimaire year X (December 13, 1801).

[48] The machine that Jacquard patented in 1804 has been characterized as "unquestionably the most complex mechanism in the world." James Essinger, *Jacquard's Web: How a Hand Loom led to the Birth of the Information Age* (Oxford: Oxford University Press, 2004), p. 37.

[49] *Gazette nationale ou le Moniteur universel*, 3 vendémiaire year X (September 25, 1801).

[50] AN AD XI 67, *Seconde exposition publique des produits de l'industrie française. Procès-verbal des opérations du jury nommé par le Ministre de l'Intérieur pour examiner les produits de l'industrie française mis à l'Exposition des jours complémentaires de la neuvième année de la République*. On the impression that it made upon the French public, BHVP 8° 106973, no. 63.

One lengthy commentary stated that the exhibition would be remembered as "a memorable epoch in the history of French industry" because it provided a preview of the results of improvements in manufacturing, as well as hope and encouragement for the future. Praising the exhibition for being better planned and more inclusive than its predecessor, it also extolled the architecture and layout of the exhibits. Visitors had been drawn both by curiosity about the various types of industry in France and national pride, which sought to make comparisons between French and foreign manufactures. The exhibition, the commentator wrote, was reassuring and satisfying, and demonstrated that French manufacturing had, in many areas, maintained its superiority.

The commentator singled out several products for particular praise, including cashmere produced by the Ternaux brothers, stating that it was the equal of British cashmere, a textile in which the British distinguished themselves. Similarly, although the British had an advantage in cotton spinning and cloth, their cottons were no better than those exhibited by Bawens [*sic*], Richard and Lenoir and others. The commentary praised other products and noted that in pottery, a field in which the British had supplied many of the needs of the continent, French producers had exhibited superior products.

The article also noted that French manufactories were generally newer than their British counterparts, but that France was struggling with factors brought about by the Revolution, including a lack of specie, high interest rates, labor shortages, disorder in workshops and the uncertainty and shock of revolution. The author argued that it was necessary for French consumers to overcome their blind prejudice that foreign products were superior to French ones, and hoped that the exhibition would overpower that sentiment. He lauded the exhibition and its organizers, hailed its benefits and concluded by expressing the hope that further improvement in French industry would be evident at the next exhibition.[51]

At a more elite level, the effect of the industrial exhibition was evident in a lecture given at the Institut National des Sciences et Arts, Littérature et Beaux-Arts by Armand-Gaston Camus. Camus, a former deputy to both the National Assembly and the National Convention, had been so impressed by the exhibitions of the Year VI and the Year IX that he had investigated whether there had been such events in the ancient world. His conclusion was that the exhibition was a "purely French" institution and that the ancients had never conceived of anything like it. He also noted proudly that the exhibitions had been the result of the work of two members of the Institute, François de Neufchâteau and Chaptal.[52]

In fact, the government staged another exhibition the following year, the year X. In the year IX the three consuls had visited, but in the year X Bonaparte, Josephine and the other two consuls not only attended, but remained for

---

[51] *La Décade philosophique, littéraire et politique*, 10 vendémiaire an X (October 2, 1801).
[52] *Mémoires de l'Institut National des Sciences et Arts, Littérature et Beaux-Arts*, 5 vols. (Paris: Baudouin, 1798–1804), 5: 485–495.

three hours – far beyond a purely ceremonial obligation.[53] Indeed, Bourrienne claimed that the First Consul was pleased by it, and the exhibition received extensive coverage in the press. His gratification was all the greater because, as a result of the Peace of Amiens, a large number of foreigners, especially British and Russians, visited Paris, and he believed that the exhibition presented a positive impression of the progress of French industry. According to Bourrienne, Bonaparte was sympathetic to the view that the promotion of industry required the protection of government.[54]

The exhibitions produced a favorable impression in the departments as well and generated local analogues – the Society of Agriculture and Commerce of Caen, seeking to augment the government's efforts and those of the prefect to encourage the industrial arts, sponsored an exhibition at the Hôtel de Ville of Caen during the spring of 1803 that featured over 100 exhibitors.[55] Within a few years, local exhibitions or fairs were being held regularly.[56]

Bourrienne recalled Bonaparte's satisfaction that the exhibition attracted British visitors because of the Peace of Amiens, but without question there was a crisis of confidence among the commercial classes in France, who were fearful of the prospect of a trade treaty with Great Britain after the signing of the peace treaty. As early as October 1801, as negotiations were concluding, the police of Paris reported that textile manufacturers in Rouen were voicing their fear that peace with Great Britain would lead to a precipitous decline in production and that they could be ruined by British imports. They sought a ban on British imports, claiming that they needed several years to regain momentum.[57]

During December 1801, the Minister of the Interior sent a circular to prefects asking that they calm fears among the commercial classes about the introduction of foreign products into France.[58] He asked the prefects to reassure them that the government's priority was "the prosperity of commerce

---

[53] *Gazette nationale, ou le Moniteur universel*, 1–2 vendémiaire year XI (September 23–24, 1801).

[54] Louis-Antoine Fauvelet de Bourrienne, *Mémoires de M. Bourrienne, Ministre d'Etat sur Napoléon, le Directoire, le Consulat, l'Empire et la Restauration*, 10 vols. (Paris: Ladvocat, 1829), V: 53–56. Bourrienne added, however, that Bonaparte compromised that protection by his unwillingness to allow complete freedom. On press coverage, *Gazette nationale, ou le Moniteur universel*, 3, 12, 13, 14, 15 vendémiaire year XI (September 25, October 4, 5, 6, 7, 1802). For more on the exposition of the year X, AN AD XI 67, *Exposition publique des produits de l'industrie française an X.*

[55] AD Seine-Maritime 8 M 34, Society of Agriculture and Commerce of Caen. Catalog of productions of arts to be exposed at *Hôtel de Ville*, from 25 germinal until 5 floréal. In addition, during the spring of 1803, as the First Consul passed through Lille on his way to Brussels, the prefect of the Department of Nord sought to arrange a local exhibition of products for him. AD Nord M 557/80, letter of prefect of Department of Nord to sub-prefect of Lille, 17 germinal year XI (April 7, 1803).

[56] AN F¹² 985, dossier 1, document 39; *Assemblée générale de la Société d'Agriculture, Commerce et Arts du Département de la Drôme, du 23 brumaire an IX de la République* (Valence: Viret, an XI), p. 19.

[57] AN F⁷ 3830, dossier vendémiaire year X, report of 27 vendémiaire year X (October 19, 1801).

[58] On such fears, Becchia, *La Draperie d'Elbeuf*, p. 412.

and national glory," and that the government was seeking to provide all the assistance it could in order to develop these. He asserted that the government wished to protect producers and that it would continue to stifle any competition that could harm them.[59]

The attempt to reassure does not appear to have succeeded because a few months later, during the summer of 1802, the Minister of the Interior wrote to prefects to inquire about reactions to false rumors of a trade treaty with Great Britain. The prefect of the Department of Seine-Inférieure replied that he had had to reassure members of the commercial establishment of Rouen that their worries were groundless because the government would not betray their interests.[60] The textile industry of Rouen, especially the cotton sector, had experienced a depression during 1787–1789, which the Chamber of Commerce of Normandy had attributed to the Eden-Vergennes Treaty of 1786, but that treaty had only come into effect during mid-1787, meaning that it had augmented rather than caused the depression. As Gavin Daly observed, however, "the Rouen commercial classes remained convinced of the evils wrought by the treaty."[61] Although some mechanization of production had begun in Rouen by 1799 "the traditional labour-intensive spinning wheel still remained the dominant mode of production in the region."[62]

From Amiens itself, the prefect of the Department of Somme wrote that new rumors of a trade treaty with Great Britain had caused alarm. He asked the minister to meet with a member of the Council on Commerce of Amiens who was currently visiting Paris so that he could reiterate the observations made on this issue at the end of the year IX.[63] The apprehension of businessmen and manufacturers illustrates why proponents of the industrial exhibitions attached such importance to their confidence-building aspect.

Indeed, on the basis of the enthusiasm generated by the exhibition of the year IX, and in the elation that followed the Peace of Amiens, the Society for the Encouragement of National Industry was founded during the year X (1801–1802) to promote mechanization in industry to enable France to compete with neighboring countries, especially Great Britain. The purpose of the society was to advance French manufacturing and to disseminate knowledge of improved processes or techniques in production. To this end, among other activities, the society published a journal and offered prizes and support for innovations in production.[64] The organization was not an official government body, but it

---

59 AN F¹ᵃ 24, circular of 15 frimaire year X (December 6, 1801).

60 AN F¹² 2471, letter of prefect of Department of Seine-Inférieure to Minister of Interior, 28 thermidor year X (August 16, 1802).

61 Gavin Daly, *Inside Napoleonic France: State and Society in Rouen, 1800–1815* (Aldershot: Ashgate, 2001), p. 33.

62 *Ibid.*

63 AN F¹² 2471, letter of prefect of Department of Somme to Minister of the Interior, 26 messidor year X (July 15, 1802). Also on unease at the prospect of a treaty with England, AN F¹² 2179, entry of 17 frimaire year X (December 8, 1801); AN F¹² 2471, letter of prefect of Department of Aube to Minister of Interior, 16 thermidor year X (August 4, 1802).

64 *Bulletin de la Société d'Encouragement pour l'industrie nationale* 1 (year XI), iii-iv; Costaz, *Histoire de l'administration en France*, II: 294–303.

enjoyed considerable support from the government, both logistically and financially. Indeed, Bonaparte had made a major financial contribution to help found it, and its membership included many ministers and public officials.[65]

After Chaptal left the Ministry of the Interior in 1804, the industrial exhibition fell into abeyance. In 1806, however, Chaptal's successor as Minister of the Interior, Jean-Baptiste Nompère de Champagny, revived it. Noting that much progress had been made since the last exhibition, Champagny asserted that the next would have an aura of novelty. In addition, by presenting products from all departments, many of which had been significantly underrepresented in earlier exhibitions, it would be more complete. The 1806 exhibition would be larger and, at fifteen days, longer than earlier ones, and all exhibitors would be admitted on the basis of juried competitions.

Unlike the earlier exhibitions, however, which had been designed almost exclusively to showcase French industry, the exhibition of 1806 had an additional underlying purpose – to ameliorate unemployment and an economic slowdown in Paris. During February 1806, Champagny had written to Bonaparte to report an economic slowdown and a rise in unemployment in the city. Champagny suggested that to increase employment the Emperor could order furniture and coaches for his palaces, but acknowledged that this would have only a limited effect and would do nothing to help other workers, such as hatmakers and textile workers. He therefore suggested reviving the industrial exhibition.

The exhibition would coincide with the return of the French army after its victory over Austria. The army's return would draw many visitors to Paris and increase consumption, and the minister also expressed hope that the accolades bestowed on the army would serve as a kind of encouragement to industry. In a sense, the minister argued, the exhibitions had become a victim of their own success – Paris had become, in his words, "a continual fair" with an extraordinary array of merchandise. The proposed exhibition would seek to bring together the best products, most of which would not customarily be found in the same marketplace. The exhibition would make a powerful impression on foreigners or visitors from the provinces – a much more powerful impression than the sight of shops spread throughout the city. The exhibition would be so spectacular that most in attendance would not leave "without yielding to the seduction of making a purchase," which in turn would help lift the economy out of its slump. In order to accommodate the larger crowds, the exhibition should not be held in the courtyards of the Louvre, as those of the years IX

---

[65] AN F¹² 502, dossier 12, Society for Encouragement of National Industry; AN F¹² 2333, notice on the Society for Encouragement of National Industry, by E.J. Guillard-Senainville; AN F¹² 2179, entry of 17 pluviôse year X (February 6, 1802); Costaz, *Histoire de l'administration en France*, II: 294–295. For more on the founding of the society, Andrew J. Butrica, "Creating a Past: The Founding of the Société d'Encouragement pour l'Industrie Nationale Yesterday and Today," *The Public Historian* 20 (1998): 21–42. There is no question that "the Société d'Encouragement originated within the state," if by "the state" one means employees of the state, but I do not agree that the evidence is conclusive that the society was not a private association.

and X had been. The minister suggested holding it at the Place de la Concorde, the Place Vendôme, the Place des Vosges or on the boulevards.[66]

He clearly received quick approval for the idea of the exhibition because only two days later the Minister of the Interior sent a circular to prefects of the departments soliciting the participation of exhibitors. Concerned that his original circular had been misunderstood, Champagny sent a second one on February 22. He stressed that the forthcoming exhibition was to differ from preceding ones. Rather than displaying the most striking products, it was to be instead "a kind of geographic industrial map of all of France," which was the reason the minister sought to contact the prefects. The exhibition was intended to offer a new, great and instructive spectacle.[67]

Planning for the exhibition expanded beyond the bureau of the Ministry of the Interior that had been responsible for the previous exhibition, leading to discord between the bureau and the minister.[68] The scale of the event became so large and generated such logistical difficulties that the exhibition, originally scheduled to open on May 25, had to be postponed twice and did not open until September.[69]

Although it did not delay the exhibition, during the planning phase there was a moment of embarrassment when the Minister of the Interior sought medals to be awarded to the winning exhibitors and the Director-General of the mint had to inform him that the medals he had requested, which were based on earlier exhibitions, were unsuitable because the principal figure on them was that of the republic. New medals would have to be recast, because although one could chisel off a medal whatever one wished, it would be impossible to replace it with a relief.[70]

Ultimately, the exhibition was held in the Esplanade of the Invalides and, with over 1,400 exhibitors, was much larger than the three preceding ones.[71] More importantly, the standard for judging was changed, with judges directed to give awards to machines that had already demonstrated some degree of commercial success rather than those that merely evinced commercial

---

[66] AN F¹² 513, dossier 2, letter of Minister of the Interior to Emperor, February 12, 1806; undated report to Emperor; undated memorandum on means of reviving activity in workshops of capital, with the quotation from the last. See also AN AF IV 942, report of Minister of the Interior to Emperor, February (no date), 1806; report of Minister of the Interior to Emperor, February 12, 1806.

[67] AN F¹² 985, dossier 2, document 35. Paris was still heavily represented, however, because the screening jury for Paris admitted 269 exhibitors. AN F¹² 985, dossier 2, document 66.

[68] AN F¹² 985, dossier 2, document 36.

[69] AN F¹² 985, dossier 1, document 54. One difficulty, for example, was who would bear the cost of transporting objects to the exposition – in at least one instance, the ministry subsidized the expense. AN F¹² 2180, dossier June 6, 1806, no. 12. The ministry received a grant of 60,000 francs from the government to defray costs of the exposition. AN F¹² 4791, decree of February 15, 1806.

[70] AN F¹² 985, dossier 5, document 27.

[71] On the 1806 exposition, Daryl M. Hafter, "The Business of Invention in the Paris Industrial Exposition of 1806," *Business History Review* 58 (1984): 317–335.

potential – in the words of Daryl Hafter, "the business formula fostered by the exposition was commercial viability through the use of new machines or processes."[72] In emphasizing that low cost along with quality would be factors in the competition, it is apparent that the government was seeking to foster mass production.[73] Moreover, to stimulate the economy, the exhibition was to be followed by a fair at which the products and samples from the exhibition would be sold.[74]

Indeed, Hafter notes that the jurors in the 1806 exhibition "took the over-simplified view that advances in mechanization would automatically give French goods a competitive edge" and that "they attempted to introduce and expand the use of machinery in industries that retained many features of their artisanal heritage."[75] French mechanization was hindered by cheap labor, and French manufacturers often oriented production to seasonal work patterns, including establishing factories in rural areas.[76] As a result, the impetus toward mechanization was not as sustained or as comprehensive as it was in Great Britain.

Nevertheless, Hafter argues that the 1806 exhibition "stimulated the beginnings of light industry in France," particularly because judges sought "to encourage the invention of machines that would enable a few to produce what had required the energy of many craftsmen during the Old Regime."[77] In this sense, the 1806 industrial exhibition clearly represented – and was designed to emphasize – the shift from artisanal to mechanized production during the Napoleonic era.[78]

The government regarded the exhibition, which concluded in October 1806, as a major success – the Minister of the Interior awarded special payments to those involved in its planning and execution.[79] The minister also arranged for a special closed visit by the student body of the Ecole Polytechnique.[80] Bonaparte was on military campaign and was therefore unable to attend, but the jury believed that the exhibition had brought to the public's attention the significant progress that had been made in several major branches of industry. This was especially the case in the field of textiles, which was accorded primacy of place at the exhibition.[81]

[72] *Ibid.*, pp. 322–325, with the quotation from p. 325. See also the speech of a member of the jury, Louis Costaz, in *Rapport du jury sur les produits de l'industrie française, présenté à S.E. M. de Champagny, Ministre de l'Intérieur, précédé du procès-verbal des opérations du jury* (Paris: Imprimerie Impériale, 1806), p. ix.
[73] AN F^{12} 985, dossier 2, document 40.
[74] AN F^{12} 4791, decree of February 15, 1806; APP DB 513, dossier National Fair of 1806 at Paris, notice of Prefect of Police, April 1, 1806. See also Wesemael, *Architecture of Instruction and Delight*, pp. 65–66, 69.
[75] Hafter, "The Business of Invention," pp. 330–331.
[76] *Ibid.*, p. 331.
[77] *Ibid.*, p. 334.
[78] Wesemael, *Architecture of Instruction and Delight*, p. 84.
[79] Forty-three individuals received bonuses ranging from 50 livres to 1200 livres, with a total of nearly 7,000 livres awarded. AN F^{12} 985, dossier 3, document 83.
[80] AN F^{12} 985, dossier 1, document 60.
[81] *Rapport du jury*, p. xi,

The government was also eager to publicize the exhibition. When a delay developed in the publication of the minutes, the Minister of the Interior pushed an official in the ministry to expedite the process.[82]

In 1808, as an economic crisis that would culminate in 1811 began to develop, the government found itself forced to make a painful decision – it cancelled the industrial exhibition that had been scheduled for May 1809.[83] Moreover, a week later, after apparently rescheduling the exhibition for 1811, the government also extended the interval at which exhibitions would be held to once every five years.[84]

The decision to cancel the exhibition was regarded as so significant that it was deferred until Bonaparte personally ratified it.[85] As a result, the decision became definitive only in late August.[86] The cancellation dealt a blow the government's prestige, which was undoubtedly the reason why the final determination was made by Bonaparte himself. Indeed, the Napoleonic government would not mount another industrial exhibition during the remainder of its existence.

DEVELOPMENTS IN PARIS

The Council of State debated the issue of guilds during the Consulate. The primary impetus for the discussion was a perception of disarray among the working classes, including violations of apprenticeship contracts, worker actions and the production of shoddy goods.[87] An underlying catalyst for the debate, however, was the reorganization of the butchers of Paris into a corporation by the Minister of the Interior, which appeared to presage a reestablishment of guilds.[88]

The reorganization of the butchers had been prompted by an earlier undertaking of Louis-Nicolas-Pierre-Joseph Dubois, the Prefect of Police in Paris. Dubois was born in Lille, the son of a sub-delegate of the intendancy of Mortagne. He had come to Paris during the 1780s and in 1789 had become one of the new administrators of the municipality. He had gone on to hold other judicial and administrative posts before being named Prefect of Police by Bonaparte on March 8, 1800. One of his major priorities was improving

---

[82] AN F¹² 985, dossier 3, document 80.
[83] AN F⁷ 2180, reports for July 15, 1808, no. 7.
[84] AN F¹² 2180, reports for July 22, 1808, no. 3.
[85] AN F¹² 2180, reports for July 29, 1808, no. 1.
[86] AN F¹² 2180, reports for August 26, 1808, no. 4.
[87] Indeed, the Ministry of the Interior had indirect experience with worker actions. During fructidor year IX (August–September, 1801), carpenters who were preparing the site for the industrial exhibition walked off the job, demanding an increase in their wage rate from the employer contracted by the ministry. The workers also prevented other carpenters who were willing to accept the wage rate offered from working. A clearly chagrined Minister of the Interior wrote to the Prefect of Police of Paris to ask him to arrest the instigators of the action. AN F¹³ 508, letter of Minister of the Interior to Prefect of Police, (no day) fructidor year IX (August–September, 1801).
[88] Thibaudeau, *Mémoires sur le Consulat*, p. 344.

the sanitary conditions of Paris, including those of its food markets and food supply.[89]

It was almost certainly this concern that led Dubois to favor the reestablishment of guilds, particularly in occupations connected to the food supply. Indeed, the decree of 12 messidor year VIII (July 1, 1800) that established the Prefect of Police in Paris charged that person with responsibility for the salubrity of the city, in particular the prevention of epidemics and contagious diseases, as well as the safety of commerce.[90] It was undoubtedly under the provisions of this decree that Dubois established various bodies of workers in Paris.

During the late summer of 1801 (fructidor year IX), as fluctuations in the price of bread upset the public and became a matter of concern to the police, a plan to shift oversight of the grain supply from the police to bakers themselves began to take shape. The critical element of the project was a requirement that each baker in Paris keep 150–200 sacks of flour in permanent reserve, an arrangement characterized by the police as better than all others because it would assure the availability of bread.[91]

The government enacted a scaled-down version of this concept on 19 vendémiaire year X (October 11, 1801), apparently at the instigation of Dubois, in a decree that was neither published nor printed and under which all bakers in Paris were ordered, as a guarantee, to deposit fifteen sacks of flour in a municipal warehouse. The decree authorized the bakers to name four syndics to supervise the deposits of flour. Any baker who quit the trade without permission or who was removed from it would forfeit his fifteen sacks.[92]

This furtive action represented the first reestablishment of a body structured in the manner of a corporation since the dissolution of guilds in 1791. Through this measure, however, the new Napoleonic regime enhanced the provisioning of the city, with the expense borne by its bakers rather than the government. The syndics established through the measure later succeeded in persuading the government to allow the bakers to organize themselves into a body.[93]

Whereas the reorganization of bakers into a body had been cloaked in secrecy, that of butchers was more overt. A group of former master butchers

[89] *Dictionnaire de biographie française*, 11: 956–957.

[90] *Collection officielle des ordonnances de police, imprimé par ordre de M. le Préfet de Police*, 3 vols. (Paris: Boucquin, 1880–1882), I: vi–vii.

[91] AN F⁷ 3829, dossier fructidor year IX, report of 29 fructidor year IX (September 16, 1801).

[92] AN F¹² 502, dossier 26, undated report to Minister of the Interior.

[93] AN F¹² 2471, dossier 26, report to the government, 11 vendémiaire (no year given). A draft of the regulations was completed on the 5th complementary day of the year XI (September 22, 1803), but it took months for the Minister of the Interior to approve it. AN F¹² 2471, dossier 26, Prefecture of Police, notice of matters sent to Minister of the Interior. For more insight on the concerns of the police, APP DB 305, meeting of extraordinary committee of the Interior, 6 frimaire year X (November 27, 1801). This meeting followed a minor provisioning problem in Paris. AN F⁷ 3830, dossier vendémiaire year X, reports of 11, 14, 15 vendémiaire year X (October 3, 6, 7, 1801).

wrote to the Prefect of Police, apparently after learning of what had happened with the bakers, to propose a reorganization of their trade. Prior to the Revolution, they noted, approximately 300 master butchers had controlled 450 stalls in different parts of the city, and the guild had undertaken inspections and enforced its own regulations to assure the safety of the meat supply. All of these arrangements had disappeared with the abolition of corporations and had, the butchers asserted, introduced "confusion" and "disorder" into the meat trade, which had been "entirely abandoned to itself."

Currently, the butchers claimed, there were nearly 700 stalls operating in Paris, with more opening daily, and that figure excluded those operating in the different markets of Paris or at les Halles. Some 2,000 men had designated themselves as butchers, and the smaller market for each contributed to higher meat prices.[94] Furthermore, the butchers asserted, many of the practitioners had little knowledge of the trade.

The butchers declared that there were no obvious solutions, and that any reform would entail substantial disadvantages. Nevertheless, they argued that by taking action the government could prevent even greater difficulties and strike at bad faith and greed. They proposed reducing the number of butchers in Paris, a measure they claimed would lead to greater safety of the meat supply and reduce the price of meat. They acknowledged that freedom was a benefit, but argued that it could be enjoyed only when it did not present a threat to society. They asserted that the commerce of meat should not have "unbridled freedom," but should instead be limited and the object of inspection and strict regulation. The butchers claimed that dog, donkey and horse meat had been sold in markets and stalls in Paris, as had meat from diseased or stillborn animals.

The butchers argued that the number of police assigned to monitor the safety of the meat supply was insufficient. They claimed that a reduction in the number of butchers in the city and the organization of 400 former master butchers, who would pay the *patente*, into a corporation, with internal policing of the trade, was the most advantageous solution. The butchers admitted that a reduction in the number of butchers could not be undertaken abruptly, so they suggested some more immediate measures, including having practitioners provide a domicile and an attestation of their skill. They also proposed having former master butchers inspect meat coming into Paris.

The butchers anticipated that their proposals would provoke protests, including that the curbs would serve only to restore butchers' privileges. Nevertheless, they asserted that the reestablishment of limits would be in the general interest. Indeed, in an indication of how sensitive an issue it was, the butchers returned at greater length to the argument that reorganizing them into a corporation was not a matter of privilege. They proposed creating 600

---

[94] This may have been an exaggeration, but during the 1820s a Prefect of Police estimated that in 1801 there had been up to 1,200 butchers or meat merchants in Paris. AN F⁷ 4219, report of Prefect of Police to Minister of Interior, October 7, 1828.

stalls for Paris, with each butcher posting a bond of 3,000 livres, and closed by arguing once again that their plan would serve the public interest.[95]

There can be little doubt that the meat supply was an object of concern for the police during the early months of the Consulate. On the eve of the coup of *brumaire* a police report stated that 1,437 pounds (652 kilograms) of unfit meat had been seized at les Halles, and a police report shortly after the coup referred to measures to be taken to stop the threat that the butcher trade presented to the public. The report of the following month revealed the dimensions of the problem, recounting the seizure at a market of meat that was clearly unfit for human consumption.[96] During the spring of 1800, Dubois wrote to police officials to denounce the "innumerable abuses" in the commerce in meat that, he claimed, posed such a serious threat that they had become a major source of complaints from all over the city.[97] During the late fall of 1800 Dubois ordered the police to begin to survey butchers to achieve oversight.[98]

With the Constitution of the Year III, particularly its article 355 prohibiting corporations, having been overthrown, the reorganization of butchers into a body was legally possible, and the government authorized it in Paris on 8 vendémiaire year XI (September 30, 1802) following a report by the Minister of the Interior. Under the provisions of the law, which was published in *Le Moniteur*, all individuals who were working as butchers had to register with the Prefect of Police.[99] The prefect would then name thirty butchers, one-third of whom had to be drawn from those paying the lowest level of the *patente*, and these thirty would elect a syndic and six deputies. In the future, no one could practice the trade of butcher without having received permission from the Prefect of Police, who would rely on the opinion of the syndic and deputies before granting such permission.

Those who exercised the occupation of butcher had to post a bond, and the funds collected would assist butchers injured on the job. Determination of those eligible for assistance was to be made by the syndic and his deputies, with the final approval of the Prefect of Police. No butcher could quit the trade without a notice of at least six months, and any butcher who did not observe this provision would forfeit his bond. In addition, any stall that did not offer meat for three consecutive days would be shut down for six months.

Finally, under the terms of the decree, the syndic and his deputies were to present a proposed set of statutes and regulations for the butcher trade to the Prefect of Police. They were to come into force only after they had been

[95] BHVP Ms. CP 4869. Two references in the *mémoire* to "twelve years" of disadvantageous situations suggest that the *mémoire* was written during 1801.
[96] AN AF IV 1329, account of operations of central office of Paris, vendémiaire year VIII; frimaire year VIII; nivôse year VIII.
[97] APP DB 402, Prefect of Police to commissars of police, 12 germinal year VIII (April 2, 1800).
[98] APP DB 402, Prefect of Police to commissars of police, 14 frimaire year IX (December 5, 1800).
[99] *Gazette nationale, ou le Moniteur universel*, 13 vendémiaire year XI (October 5, 1802); the police regulations were set forth in *Gazette nationale, ou le Moniteur universel*, 20 vendémiaire year XI (October 12, 1802).

confirmed by the Minister of the Interior "in the customary format for all regulations of public administration."[100]

The decree was careful to avoid the use of any vocabulary reminiscent of Old Regime guilds – such words as *corporation, jurande* and *maîtrise* are notably absent – and the regulations were characterized by the government as a matter of public administration. Despite such precautions, the perception arose that a guild had been reestablished and as Thibaudeau, a member of the Council of State, noted, it appeared to be the first step toward a general restoration of guilds.[101]

In fact, there was also a debate within the Ministry of the Interior when the prefect of the Department of Haute-Garonne established a bond to be paid by each butcher of the department, which, on the recommendation of a division in the ministry, the minister had approved. Another of the ministry's divisions sought to reverse the action, however, asserting that it was contrary to the d'Allarde law of March 17, 1791, and the law on *patentes*. The d'Allarde law had sought to assure complete freedom in occupations, and the imposition of a fine by the prefect on those butchers who failed to pay a bond would deprive them of "a natural right consecrated by this law."

The decree of 8 vendémiaire year XI had "derogated" this law for Paris, but the decree had come from the central government and was applicable only to Paris, the provisioning of which had always required special measures. No exception had been offered to other major cities of the republic, and the prefect of the Department of Haute-Garonne had, in fact, established one that weighed on both villages and cities in his department.[102]

The debate within the government, particularly with respect to butchers, illustrates the manner in which the boundaries of economy and government were being defined. The reorganization of butchers in Paris was justified in terms of public health rather than police of the trade. Public health was, in fact, becoming a valid criterion through which unease about the competing claims of order and liberty could be mediated and resolved.

In a larger sense, the reconstruction of bodies of both bakers and butchers in Paris reflects the provisional, contingent approach to points at issue taken by both the revolutionary and Napoleonic governments. There was no grand design, whether on parts manufacture or large enterprises during the Revolution or the organization of the grain trade under Bonaparte – most undertakings were an improvisation. One should not envision an internally coherent, emerging political economy evolving during the revolutionary and Napoleonic epoch; rather, a more makeshift set of structures were created and elaborated on a case-by-case basis. This is particularly true of the Napoleonic regime, which continuously thought of itself as evolving.[103]

---

[100] AN AD XI 65, decree of regulations for practice of the profession of butcher in Paris, 8 vendémiaire year XI (September 30, 1802).

[101] Thibaudeau, *Mémoires sur le Consulat*, p. 344.

[102] AN F⁷ 3024, report to Minister of the Interior, 28 ventôse year XII (March 19, 1804).

[103] M.J. Sydenham, *The First French Republic, 1792–1804* (Berkeley, CA: University of California Press, 1973), p. 297.

THE COUNCIL OF STATE WEIGHS THE REESTABLISHMENT
OF GUILDS

At the same time, however, the perceived attitude by contemporaries of uncertainty on the part of the regime toward corporations is apparent in an exchange between a group of cloth manufacturers in Bédarieux (Hérault) and the Minister of the Interior during the year X. On 2 floréal year X (April 22, 1802), a group of textile producers from Bédarieux wrote to the minister to complain about several manufacturers in the vicinity of the town who were turning out cloth of inferior quality under the Bédarieux label. Some of this material had surfaced in the wholesale market at Marseille, where it was selling at a price half that charged by the original Bédarieux producers. The latter had contacted the Chamber of Commerce of Marseille and had provided it with a list of those who were using the Bédarieux label legitimately.

In its letter to the minister, the group bemoaned the inadequacy of this course of action for "repression," a term reminiscent of the abolished guild regime. They asked the Minister of the Interior to take action and to post an official list in the wholesale market of Marseille of all of the "producers of different guilds (*jurandes*)," an even more explicit Old Regime term that the government had assiduously avoided."[104] Indeed, in his reply, the minister strongly reminded the producers that guilds no longer existed. With respect to the official list that they had requested, he noted that manufacturers increased or decreased in number on an almost daily basis so that producing an exact list would be impossible. Furthermore, he asserted, to post such a list only in the wholesale market of Marseille would be insufficient. Nevertheless, the minister reminded the producers that nothing prevented them from doing themselves what they proposed the ministry do. They could easily write to merchants who sold cloth and supply them with a precise list of manufacturers and a copy of the trademark of each. As a result, there would be much less to fear in the forgery of names or quality, and it would provide a more solid foundation for any prosecution.[105]

The minister's letter illustrates the unresolved attitude toward guilds or guild-like bodies during the early Consulate, and in many respects foreshadowed legislation of the following year. On the one hand, the government wished to restore confidence in the quality of goods, which had, before the Revolution, been overseen and assured mainly by guilds. On the other, it did not want to restore corporations, because they could impede innovation and mechanization of production.[106] In this instance, the regime equivocated. It

---

[104] AN F^{12} 1556, letter of textile producers of Bédarieux to Minister of the Interior, 2 floréal year X (April 22, 1802). Ironically, during December, 1789, a manufacturer from Bédarieux had written to the National Assembly arguing for the end of all regulations and the abolition of the inspections system, but subsequently resentment toward commercial upheaval increased. Johnson, *The Life and Death of Industrial Languedoc*, pp. 13, 15.

[105] AN F^{12} 1556, letter of Minister of the Interior to textile manufacturers of Bédarieux, 5 prairial year X (May 25, 1802).

[106] Becchia, *La Draperie d'Elbeuf*, p. 442, associates innovation by producers with the abolition of guilds during the Revolution, which suggests that the concern was not purely theoretical.

allowed a group of producers to define themselves as a virtual corporate entity and to affix production marks to assure quality, but refused to allow the group to reconstitute formally or legally as a guild.

One aspect of the safeguarding of industry was protection from the claims or interference of guilds, which could threaten the development of industry. At the same time, however, the lack of a viable system of apprenticeships and a decline in the quality of goods lent weight to those who argued for some form of restoration of corporations, and the reorganization of butchers provided a catalyst for discussion of the issue.

The Council of State took up the matter early in the year XI, along with that of privileged companies. On 27 nivôse year XI (January 17, 1803) the Council of State examined a fifteen-page document concerned solely with the issue of whether or not corporations should be reestablished. Unlike most reports treated by the Council of State, that of 27 nivôse gave no indication of who the reporter was nor the section in which it originated. A prefatory note stated that the document did not address the proposed law of the special commission of Regnaud de Saint-Jean d'Angély – the nucleus of the future law of 22 germinal year XI. Rather, it examined only one major question, the reestablishment of corporations; everything else was only a consequence.

The report opened by observing that on one side commercial interests had asked the government for a law to enforce apprenticeship contracts and relations between workers and employers, and to guarantee to manufacturers the ownership of trademarks that they impressed on their products. On the other side, others had proposed the reestablishment of guilds. The question for the Council of State to determine, the report stated, was whether the regulatory system would prevail over freedom of industry.

To set the stage for the discussion, the document examined legislation going back to Turgot's edict of 1776 and asserted that, after their reorganization, guilds believed it their right to place limits on industry. The report put forward arguments both for and against the restoration of guilds, acknowledging the decline in quality that had occurred since their abolition. It stated that the cause of the difficulties that had generated so many complaints was "the circumstances of the Revolution."

At the same time, however, the document asserted that it would be a mistake to argue that the difficulties of the preceding years would not have occurred if guilds had not been abolished – the regime of freedom was not to blame. It was only since the regime of freedom had emerged that France had seen the rise of large factories that joined the various types of workers needed to perfect the items manufactured. If guilds were restored, manufacturing could once again fragment, as during the time of corporations, to the practice of only one principal occupation. If an array of corporations were combined in a production facility, it would be subject to a multitude of rules and multiple guild officers. Corporations tended to separate occupations, whereas the system of freedom allowed individuals to combine them. No one wished to go back to the pre-1789 structure of guilds because it was disadvantageous to industry, but the report concluded with the prediction that a reestablishment of corporations in a modified form would soon occur.[107]

As described by Thibaudeau, the discussion was condensed to a demarcation between the reestablishment of masterships and guilds versus the freedom of industry. Members of the Council of State discussed the issue extensively, with speakers presenting arguments both for and against the restoration of corporations. It was a reflection of the strength of the arguments on each side of the question that Thibaudeau himself admitted he could not decide definitively, but that he leaned toward freedom of industry. In fact, when the question came to a vote, the Council of State voted by a large margin not to reestablish guilds.[108]

The result was not surprising – according to Chaptal, Bonaparte valued industry and in the area of manufacture allowed himself to be dissuaded from his propensity for regulation. Furthermore, Chaptal claimed, Bonaparte had little inclination to reestablish corporations because he believed them to be inimical to public order and to the strengthening of his authority.[109]

LEGISLATING THE WORKPLACE: THE LAW OF 22 GERMINAL YEAR XI

Although the Council of State did not restore guilds, it did address other labor issues, including apprenticeships and worker discipline. Such regulations had long been sought by both public officials and private individuals; the mayor of Sedan, for example, had written to the Minister of the Interior with some observations on these issues. Furthermore, in reply to a letter inquiring about the same from an individual in Regny, the Ministry of the Interior stated that a set of regulations aimed at resolving the issues had been drafted.[110]

Indeed, on 13 ventôse year X (March 4, 1802) Chaptal submitted to the consuls a proposed law to correct various abuses that had become acute since the Revolution. The project focused on four areas of concern that had been a continuing source of complaints – apprenticeships, violations of work agreements, theft of raw materials and false trademarks.[111] It took another year for the Council of State to complete the legislation, and a surviving draft, with marginal comments, provides some insight into the law's evolution.

The provisions regarding the structure of apprenticeships passed with little difficulty. The first article guaranteed apprenticeships freely concluded

---

[107] Napoleonica.org. *Des communautés d'arts et métiers.* Project no. 663. 27 nivôse year XI (January 17, 1803).

[108] Thibaudeau, *Mes Mémoires sur le Consulat*, pp. 345–346.

[109] Chaptal, *Mes Souvenirs sur Napoléon*, pp. 278, 288–289.

[110] AN F¹² 2178, letter to mayor of Sedan, 4 brumaire year IX (October 26, 1800); AN F¹² 2179, letter to Chavannes at Regny, 22 brumaire year X (November 13, 1801). See also Sibalis, "The Workers of Napoleonic Paris," pp. 227–228.

[111] *Journal des débats et loix du pouvoir législatif, et des actes du gouvernement*, 19 ventôse year X (March 10, 1802).

between individuals. If a master failed to observe the terms of an apprentice-ship, the arrangement could be terminated, and if an apprentice left the service of his master early, financial penalties could be levied. At the same time, in a clear effort to deny guilds an institutional foothold and to preserve the revo-lutionary ideal of freedom, the second article specified that no one could be prevented from practicing any trade because he had not served an apprentice-ship under a master.

There were also clauses pertaining to non-apprenticed workers or journey-men that were disadvantageous to these men. The articles mandated that all agreements reached between a worker and an employer on the type of work, the hours of work and the wage had to be faithfully observed by both parties. Workers could not walk off the job, and workers laid off before the expiration of their contract were to be indemnified.

The legislation required each worker to carry a passbook (*livret*), issued by the president of a panel of arbitrators, attesting to the length of time he had worked for an employer, and the passbook had to be carried from employer to employer. If an employer refused to return a passbook to a worker, the latter could appeal to the panel of arbitrators, who would judge the reasons for the employer's refusal and render a decision. Contractors who employed a worker without a passbook were subject to penalties.

These clauses were the aspects of the legislation most open to question. Although there had been a *livret* system for workers administered by guilds in the late eighteenth century, the Napoleonic worker passbook was contro-versial because insofar as it gave priority to employers, who could retain a worker's passbook, it seemed to violate the revolutionary principle of equality. Although the Consular regime was still nominally a republic, it is difficult to imagine that the *livret* would have been enacted under the Convention or Directory. It was an example of the Bonapartist regime contravening the prin-ciples of liberty and equality in favor of order, specifically labor discipline.

Employers had the right to determine the working conditions and regu-lations in their establishments, and any worker who accepted employment thereby submitted himself to those conditions and regulations. In any appeal to the panel of arbitrators, the decision rendered had to be based on the rules of each establishment.

Not surprisingly, it was the clauses dealing with coalitions or seditious gatherings of workers that provoked the most discussion. Because these arti-cles related to public authority, one member of the Council of State argued that they should be inserted at the beginning of the legislation, but the coun-cil overruled his suggestion. Key provisions made it illegal to make threats against those who were working, and worker coalitions of any kind, even by writing, formed for the purpose of work stoppages were declared as damag-ing to the free exercise of industry. Those who participated in such coali-tions could be brought to court and were subject to a fine and imprisonment, both of which would increase for repeat offenses. Furthermore, such incidents would be recorded in a worker's passbook.

In what in the draft appears to be almost an afterthought, the proposed law also forbade employers from acting in concert to lower workers' wages, subjecting them to a fine of 1,000 francs each for doing so. One member of the council believed this clause to be too vague, and noted that formerly such an action by employers would have required the intervention of a police magistrate.

The proposed legislation also dealt with trademarks on products, an aspect of production that formerly had also been associated with guilds. Among its provisions, manufacturers had to register their trademark, which had to include their name and location. Any manufacturer, producer or merchant who sold counterfeit products could be subject to legal action by the purchaser and, if found guilty, would have to refund the purchaser and pay an additional fine equal to the value of the object as well as court costs. The seller would also have to pay the costs of producing and affixing posters announcing the judgment.

The proposed legislation also provided for action against those who utilized a false trademark, and repeat offenders could be imprisoned for up to two years. In addition, there was to be a national trademark on goods made for export. Many of these provisions relating to trademarks also generated much commentary and discussion.

The last portion of the bill dealt with the panel of arbitrators mandated by the legislation. It recommended that arbitrators be drawn from among retired merchants, businessmen or producers and from among citizens in each town experienced in commerce and industry.[112]

Michel-Louis-Etienne Regnaud de Saint-Jean d'Angély presented the bill to the Legislative Body on 10 germinal year XI (March 31, 1803). Although acknowledging that guilds had originally served a useful purpose, Regnaud argued that over time they had become corrupt. In a lengthy discussion of abuses perpetrated by corporations, he noted that men who sought improvements in production were punished for departing from guild regulations. The Revolution had enacted the abolition of guilds, inaugurating a freedom of manufacture that had brought beneficial results. Since the abolition of corporations, however, that freedom had also been abused – whereas freedom had formerly been circumscribed by too many limits, unlimited license had developed. The proposed bill, Regnaud asserted, sought to address the abuses that had come into being. The Legislative Body immediately decreed that the project be sent to the Tribunate.

The Tribunate considered the bill on 19 germinal year XI (April 9, 1803), following a lengthy presentation by Claude-François Perrin. The Tribunate immediately voted unanimously to approve the legislation. Upon its return to the Legislative Body, it was adopted by a vote of 199 to 9.[113]

---

[112] AN F^{12} 501^B, dossier 28.

[113] *Archives parlementaires*, 2nd series, IV: 546–551; 599–604; 609. The police noted that the remark of Regnaud de Saint-Jean d'Angély that drew the most attention was not related to the legislation – it was one implying that the resumption of war was near. AN F^7 3831, report of 10 germinal year XI (March 31, 1803).

The bill, which became law on 22 germinal year XI (April 12, 1803), represented the most significant state intervention in the field of labor since the abolition of guilds in 1791 and the most significant piece of legislation addressing the problems created by the dissolution of guilds. To a great extent, in fact, the law resolved one of the problems created by the legislation of 1791 – how to restore regulation without reestablishing corporations. To the degree that it reintroduced punishments for workers and restored trademarks and quality standards, the legislation revived several functions of guilds without reinstating guilds themselves, which could have restricted innovation and production.[114]

The outcome was not surprising for a relatively nonideological regime that had among its goals the promotion of material prosperity as well as the maintenance of order and discipline. At the same time, however, the ambiguous character of the law – restoring major attributes of corporations without restoring corporations themselves – reflected the duality of the policy of the Napoleonic regime. On the one hand, it was not prepared to return to the structured and regulated economy of the Old Regime. On the other, it was unwilling to continue the unfettered, laissez-faire policies inaugurated by the Revolution, as evidenced, for example, by its intervention to assure the quality of products. Indeed, the legislation reflected the personal preferences of Bonaparte – according to Chaptal, he had a penchant for regulation, but was not in favor of reestablishing guilds.[115]

If the law of 22 germinal year XI sought to address a number of problems that had arisen as a result of the abolition of guilds, the Napoleonic regime had, a few months earlier, sought to deal with difficulties stemming from the legislation of September 1791, that abolished oversight of commerce and production. On 3 nivôse year XI (December 24, 1802) the government issued a decree establishing Chambers of Commerce in many cities, and the Chamber of Commerce of Paris, in particular, would become a contributor to the debate on guilds.[116]

The law of 22 germinal did not have an immediate effect, which ultimately permitted the debate on the reestablishment of guilds to continue. Indeed, despite the confidence that the Ministry of the Interior had in the legislation, which was well received by manufacturers, fraud and abuse remained.[117] In fact, during floréal year XI (April, 1803), shortly after the passage of the legislation, the Minister of the Interior ordered the head of a division of the ministry, Scipion Mourgue, to travel to Sedan and other towns to report on

[114] Reddy, *The Rise of Market Culture*, p. 71.
[115] Chaptal, *Mes Souvenirs sur Napoléon*, pp. 288–289; Sibalis, "The Workers of Napoleonic Paris," pp. 228–229.
[116] On the Chamber of Commerce of Paris, Christophe Bouneau, *La Chambre de commerce et de l'industrie de Paris (1803–2003)* (Geneva: Librairie Droz, 2003).
[117] On the confidence of the ministry in the legislation, expressed as it was being prepared, AN F¹² 1391, opinion of section of arts and manufacturing, Ministry of the Interior, 4 frimaire year X (November 25, 1801). On its reception by manufacturers, Becchia, *La Draperie d'Elbeuf*, pp. 415–416; on continuing problems with fraud, AN F⁷ 4283, extract of register of deliberations of council, 30 prairial year XIII (June 19, 1805).

the manufacture of textiles in order to make government support more effective.[118] Mourgue wrote a letter on the situation in Sedan on 1 messidor year XI (June 20, 1803) in which he noted the inadequacy of the law of 22 germinal year XI and the urgent need to put an end to the problems in manufacturing. He recommended allowing the town to form a *chambre consultative des manufactures, fabriques et métiers*, which the law of 22 germinal had authorized, to stop abuses. Mourgue sought to reassure the minister that he was not advocating the reestablishment of guilds, but he clearly believed greater action was necessary.[119]

Preserved with these documents is a long, undated description of the situation in Sedan that clearly served as the basis for Mourgue's letter to Chaptal, and it provides greater detail of the problems that existed there. Although it cannot be ascertained with certainty, it appears that Mourgue submitted it to Chaptal in order to give him a deeper understanding of the situation.

Mourgue noted that there was little discipline in the factories. In some instances, dishonest workers stole raw materials from manufacturers and then used that material when they were hired by other manufacturers, some of whom may have commissioned the thefts.

Although some aspects of production led to dispersion of the work force, the wool workers and shearers were not only concentrated, but disaffected and dangerous, particularly the shearers.[120] In fact, the shearers had sought to block the entry of apprentices into their trade to gain leverage in wage negotiations, and natural mortality had reduced their number to such a degree that current needs could not be met.[121] Mourgue informed manufacturers of provisions of the law of 22 germinal regarding apprenticeships and had been gratified to see some of them accept apprentices.

Nevertheless, Mourgue reiterated the inadequacy of the law, which was subverted by both workers and employers,[122] and recommended supplementary legislation to give local police more authority. He went on to describe other labor and production problems, including counterfeit textiles made with lower-grade materials. Indeed, Mourgue noted that in the past the syndics of a guild would have had the right to challenge producers suspected of compromising quality, and it was in this context that he sought to reassure Chaptal that he was not advocating the reestablishment of guilds.[123]

There is no record of Chaptal's response, but the report, by a trusted subordinate, was deeply pessimistic. Without question, Mourgue's mission provides insight as to why the debate on the reestablishment of guilds continued – the issue resurfaced often.[124]

---

[118] AN F¹² 654, dossier 7, letter of Chaptal to Mourgue, 5 floréal year XI (April 25, 1803).

[119] AN F¹² 654, dossier 7, letter of Mourgue to Chaptal, 1 messidor year XI (June 20, 1803).

[120] Shearers in Sedan had a long history of unrest. Farr, *Artisans in Europe*, p. 200.

[121] AN F¹² 654, dossier 7, undated list of questions and answers, no. 12.

[122] Reddy, *The Rise of Market Culture*, p. 73.

[123] AN F¹² 654, dossier 7, undated report on Sedan.

[124] AN F¹² 654, dossier 7, undated list of questions and answers, no. 13; Sibalis, "The Workers of Napoleonic Paris," pp. 229–230.

From the point of view of the Napoleonic regime, however, the legislation of 22 germinal year XI restored order and discipline in the workplace. The refusal to restore guilds, and the subjection of workers to police and public authority, would allow mechanization to proceed without challenge by guilds or worker actions.[125]

NAPOLEONIC POLICY TOWARD INDUSTRY

The Napoleonic regime remained relatively nonideological in the economic sphere. When a former master hatmaker from Paris sought to sell a method that he claimed to have perfected for the manufacture of hats – a process that he thought would be useful for outfitting troops – for a sum of 30,000 francs, the government refused his offer. The Minister of the Interior replied that the government did not have any policy of acquiring manufacturing processes, and urged the man to sell the process to a private entrepreneur.[126]

At the same time, however, the regime did not pursue a doctrinaire laissez-faire policy. From the outset, it sought ideas and showed itself willing to support and advance industry.[127] Indeed, whereas the Directory had, until late in its existence, usually refused to extend government assistance to private enterprise, the Napoleonic regime, after some hesitancy, was more accommodating in aiding and promoting manufacture and commerce, including advancing loans to entrepreneurs.[128] François Richard, known more generally as Richard-Lenoir, who became a major cotton producer in France, was refused assistance by the Directory, but initially received somewhat greater cooperation from the consular regime. When he inquired about installing a manufacturing facility in a former convent, the Minister of Finance was receptive to his request, but the government refused to loan him money to establish a cotton-spinning mill.[129] Nevertheless, Richard continued to seek favor with the government.[130] He invited the Minister of the Interior to visit one of his

[125] Costaz, *Histoire de l'administration en France*, II: 261.

[126] AN F¹² 2283, letter of Troussier to Minister of the Interior, 22 ventôse year XII (March 13, 1804); letter of Minister of the Interior to Troussier, 29 ventôse year XII (March 20, 1804).

[127] AN F¹² 2178, letter of 12 germinal year VIII (April 2, 1800); Chaptal, *Mes Souvenirs sur Napoléon*, pp. 278–283, 287.

[128] On the refusal of the Directory to assist private enterprise, AN F¹² 2178, no. 115, letter to Richard, 15 fructidor year IV (September 1, 1796); no. 145, letter to Hugues, 29 brumaire year IV (November 20, 1795). The Napoleonic regime did advance loans from an early point. AN F¹² 2178, unnumbered letters to Bernard and Boullet, 9 vendémiaire year IX (September 30, 1800); 8 brumaire year IX (October 30, 1800); 18 pluviôse year IX (February 7, 1801); Chaptal, *Mes Souvenirs sur Napoléon*, p. 287.

[129] On the response of the Minister of Finance, AN F¹² 2178, unnumbered letter to Richard and Lenoir-Dufresne, 26 floréal year IX (May 16, 1801); on the refusal to loan money, AN F¹² 2178, unnumbered letter to Richard and Company, 27 germinal year IX (April 17, 1801). See also Monnier, *Le Faubourg Saint-Antoine*, pp. 181, 183–184.

[130] It may be an indication of his early success in this endeavor that the Minister of the Interior notified Bourrienne, Bonaparte's secretary, that Richard's request for a loan had been refused. AN F¹² 2178, unnumbered letter of 27 germinal year IX (April 17, 1801).

enterprises, an invitation that the minister accepted. The minister also agreed to write to the Minister of War on Richard-Lenoir's behalf, perhaps regarding contracts for army uniforms.[131]

Two years later, the government was extending loans to entrepreneurs. One early beneficiary was James Douglas, and his example reflects the success the Napoleonic regime enjoyed in advancing mechanization and modernization of production.[132] Douglas came to the attention of the French government through the French consul in Hamburg, Meyer, a native of Bordeaux who wrote to the prefect of the Department of Gironde about him. Meyer described Douglas as an English engineer with many mechanical inventions to his credit whose goal was to improve manufacturing. The prefect, on the basis of his acquaintance with Meyer, wrote to the Minister of the Interior because of Chaptal's interest in those who could contribute to the development and improvement of French industry.[133] After receiving a favorable report on him from officials in the Ministry of the Interior, Chaptal opened negotiations with Douglas.[134]

In the fall of 1802 Douglas asked for a site for his facility,[135] which would manufacture machines for wool production, and in January 1803, after an inspection of a prototype by an official from the Ecole des Arts et Métiers to verify the usefulness of the machine, Douglas received a loan from the *Conservatoire des Arts et Métiers* to begin developing a machine to card wool.[136] The following month the Ministry of the Interior granted Douglas a patent for his machine, and he established his factory on the Ile de Cygnes in Paris.[137] Although the ministry denied his request for a loan of 288,000 francs, it did grant him loans of 20,000 francs and 5,000 francs.[138]

Douglas clearly won the confidence of the French government because even after the resumption of war with Great Britain, he not only was able to

---

[131] AN F¹² 2178, unnumbered letter to Richard and Lenoir, 12 pluviôse year IX (February 1, 1801); unnumbered letter to Richard and Cornu, 18 pluviôse year IX (February 7, 1801).

[132] On the decisive role played by the state in mechanization of production in Lodève, Johnson, *The Life and Death of Industrial Languedoc*, p. 22.

[133] AN F¹² 2207, letter of prefect of Department of Gironde to Minister of the Interior, 11 prairial year X (May 31, 1802).

[134] AN F¹² 2207, letter of head of second division and head of bureau of arts and manufacturing to Minister of the Interior, 26 prairial year X (June 15, 1802). On the critical role of Douglas in the mechanization of wool production in France, Louis Bergeron, "Douglas, Ternaux, Cockerill: aux origines de la méchanisation de l'industrie lainière en France," *Revue historique* 247 (1972): 67–80, especially pp. 67–74.

[135] AN F¹² 2207, letter of Douglas to Minister of the Interior, 23 vendémiaire year XI (October 15, 1802).

[136] AN F¹² 2207, letter of Minister of the Interior to Administrator of *Conservatoire des Arts et Métiers*, 1 germinal year XI (March 22, 1803); AN F¹² 2179, entry of letter to Molard, 1 germinal year XI; entry of letter to Douglas, 14 nivôse year XI (January 4, 1803).

[137] AN F¹² 2179, entry of letter to Douglas, 12 pluviôse year XI (February 1, 1803); Chaptal, *Mes Souvenirs sur Napoléon*, p. 99.

[138] AN F¹² 2207, letter of Minister of Interior to Douglas, 27 fructidor year X (February 16, 1802); AN F¹² 2179, entries of letters to Douglas, 27 pluviôse year X (February 16, 1802), 5 nivôse year XII (December 27, 1803), 10 pluviôse year XII (January 31, 1804).

continue his operation but also to employ British prisoners.[139] Indeed, during late 1804 Douglas became a French citizen and subsequently pledged obedience to the constitutions of the Empire and loyalty to the Emperor.[140] He went on to establish a second factory in Paris and remained in France under the Restoration.[141]

Douglas also enjoyed the support of the Society for the Encouragement of National Industry, the organization that supported mechanization.[142] Representatives of the society visited his facility and came away with a positive impression, and the society published an extremely favorable report on his machines.[143] The Minister of the Interior, Chaptal, also arranged a visit to his factory and repeatedly assured Douglas that he had "the protection of the government."[144]

The machines that Douglas produced were to belong to the government.[145] In turn, the government distributed them to enterprises throughout France to advance mechanization.[146] Furthermore, the Ministry of the Interior had a project to distribute cotton-spinning machines throughout France.[147]

The more aggressive support of mechanization of production and the development of industry was a result of the ascension of Chaptal, who made them a major priority, to the post of Minister of the Interior[148] – his revival of the industrial exhibition was also an aspect of these policies. The programs were well received also because of a perception that French manufacturing lagged that of Great Britain. After the exhibition of the year IX, many of the exhibitors

---

[139] AN F¹² 2207, letter of Minister of War to Minister of the Interior, 25 fructidor year XI (September 12, 1803); AN F¹² 2179, entry of letter to Douglas, 28 frimaire year XII (December 20, 1803).

[140] AN F¹² 2207, letter of Minister of the Interior to Prefect of Police, January 3, 1806.

[141] On the establishment of his second factory, AN F¹² 2207, Report of bureau of arts and manufacturing, 2nd division, to Minister of the Interior, August 16, 1806. AN F¹² 2206ᴮ, dossier Andelle, Ministry of the Interior, Consultative Committee of Arts and Manufacturing, note of November 17, 1831, mentions a presentation by Douglas to the Society for the Encouragement of National Industry during 1817.

[142] AN F¹²501ᴮ, dossier 31, account of efforts of council of administration of Society for Encouragement ... from 8 messidor year X to 9 messidor year XI (June 27, 1802–June 28, 1803).

[143] AN F¹² 2207, Report of Society for Encouragement of National Industry to Minister of the Interior, 5 floréal year XII (April 25, 1804); letter of Douglas to Minister of the Interior, 6 floréal year XII (April 26, 1804); *Bulletin de la Société pour l'Encouragement de l'Industrie Nationale* 2 (an XII): 153–157.

[144] On the efforts to arrange a visit, AN F¹² 501ᴮ, entries of letters to Douglas, 25 floréal year XII (May 15, 1804), 23 frimaire year XIII (December 14, 1804); on assurances of the protection of the government, AN F¹² 501ᴮ, entry of letter to Douglas, 10 ventôse year XIII (March 1, 1805).

[145] AN F¹² 501ᴮ, entry of letter to Ternaux, 14 thermidor year XI (August 2, 1803).

[146] Douglas's machines were critical in the mechanization of production in Lodève. Johnson, *The Life and Death of Industrial Languedoc*, pp. 19–20.

[147] AN F¹² 2179, entry of letter to Liancourt, 24 pluviôse year XII (February 14, 1804); Chaptal, *Mes Souvenirs sur Napoléon*, p. 99.

[148] Chaptal, *Mes Souvenirs sur Napoléon*, pp. 59, 98–101.

had had an audience with the Minister of the Interior and, in addressing the minister, the spokesman for the exhibitors had spoken of an "industrial war" with Britain,[149] reflecting a sense that France was behind in mechanization. Similarly, in a statement of purpose, the Society for the Encouragement of National Industry noted that one of its goals was to help French manufacturing retake all of the advantages that neighboring nations had gained on French industry, in an unmistakable reference to Great Britain.[150]

At the same time that the Ministry of the Interior was seeking to facilitate mechanization, however, it was also receiving reports of labor unrest in former guild trades, particularly as they became more mechanized. During the period that the ministry was dealing with Douglas, it was receiving reports of labor trouble in Paris among hatmakers.[151] Although the details of the dispute are unclear, the coincidence of labor trouble within former guild trades and efforts to advance industry and mechanization highlight the dual character of the French economy, particularly in Paris – that is, artisanal workshops existed side by side with newly emerging mechanized manufacturing enterprises.[152]

THE COEXISTENCE OF INDUSTRY AND THE POTENTIAL RESTORATION OF CORPORATIONS DURING THE EARLY NAPOLEONIC REGIME

This duality formed the basis of a dichotomy within the Napoleonic regime. On one side, Dubois, the Prefect of Police for Paris, was concerned primarily with maintaining order among workers and so continued to seek the restoration of regulations or guilds. During brumaire year XIV (November 1805), for example, Dubois wrote a four-page letter to the Minister of the Interior about complaints from wigmakers with respect to unrest in the trade. In order to correct abuses the wigmakers claimed were present, they asked that the regulations that had formerly governed the trade be reinstated and that wigmakers be required to furnish a bond.

Dubois stated that he was convinced of the validity of the wigmakers' complaints. They were, he wrote, a result of the d'Allarde law because it had opened all professions provided that one had an occupational license and because it had abolished the statutes of the former guilds.

Citing dispositions from letters-patent of December 14, 1673, Dubois noted that the provisions had offered a guarantee to the public of the practitioners' probity. A system of regulations and the requirements of a bond could achieve the same result, although he remarked that it would be necessary to allow the

---

[149] *Gazette nationale, ou le Moniteur universel*, 6 vendémiaire year X (September 28, 1801).
[150] AN F¹²502, dossier 12, Society for Encouragement of National Industry.
[151] AN F¹² 2178, entries of letter of 12 floréal year IX (May 2, 1801); 26 floréal year IX (May 16, 1801); 7 prairial year IX (May 27, 1801).
[152] A point also noted by Monnier, *Le Faubourg Saint-Antoine*, p. 292.

bond to be paid in installments. He asked the minister to consider reestablishing some regulations, but the minister refused.[153]

As this incident illustrates, on the other side, the Ministry of the Interior, seeking to advance mechanization and industry, opposed any effort to reestablish corporations, viewing them as a potential impediment to mechanization. The Ministry of the Interior sought to retain control over all questions of restoring guilds.[154] Bonaparte never decisively intervened to resolve the matter, allowing each side to continue to pursue its own policy. As a result, during the decade from approximately 1800 to 1811, the fate of guilds hung in the balance, with the prospect of their reestablishment greater than at any time since their abolition in 1791.

Within the Ministry of the Interior, the Second Division, especially its Bureau of Mechanical Arts, headed by Claude-Anthelme Costaz, and the General Council of Agriculture, Arts, and Commerce assumed leading roles in the drive toward modernization. These entities emerged during a reorganization of the Ministry of the Interior that became effective during the year X, and the mandate for the General Council reflected the dichotomous state of the French economy and the lack of a clear policy on the organization of labor.

As the reorganization moved forward, the General Council had among its projected responsibilities the state of manufacturing, and, more particularly, methods for encouraging and improving manufacturing. At the same time, however, it was to oversee regulations of corporations and the "regime of corporations" – a clear reference to a possible reestablishment of guilds.[155] Although the proposed areas of jurisdiction suggested neutrality in dealing with different realms of production, the ministry was anything but neutral – it relentlessly pursued mechanization and staunchly opposed any restoration of a "regime of corporations."

Indeed, in addition to its program of offering loans to entrepreneurs to mechanize, the Ministry of the Interior aligned itself closely with the Society for the Encouragement of National Industry – so much so that the latter came to be considered a virtual appendage of the ministry. Chaptal had been a key figure in the society's founding, although he maintained that it did not receive any government support and was funded exclusively through membership fees.[156] Nevertheless, the ministry itself had a membership in the society that

---

[153] AN F¹² 2397, dossier Prefect of Police, letter of Prefect of Police to Minister of the Interior, 20 brumaire year XIV (November 11, 1805).

[154] See, for example, AN F⁷ 2397, letter of head of Second Division and head of Bureau of Arts and Manufacturing to Minister of the Interior, 26 pluviôse year XIII (February 15, 1805), in which these officials asked the minister to notify the prefect of the Department of Loire that he should not permit the formation of a corporation of porters in his department.

[155] AN F¹² 501ᴬ, Ministry of the Interior, General Council of Agriculture, Arts and Commerce, undated. On the final outcome of the reorganization, *Almanach National de France, An X* (Paris, n.d.), pp. 96, 101.

[156] Chaptal, *Mes Souvenirs sur Napoléon*, pp. 100–101. A document that appears to be a briefing paper for the Minister of the Interior who succeeded Chaptal – prepared during July 1806 – corroborates this, stating that the Society had been formed during the year X under

included a large payment to it, a fact that has undoubtedly contributed to the debate on whether or not it was a government body.[157]

During the summer of 1804, the Ministry of the Interior sent out a circular seeking to increase membership in the society so that it could advance its programs. The circular noted that the Emperor was "at the head of its subscribers," which included other dignitaries of the Empire, ministers, members of the Council of State, senators, tribunes, deputies of the Legislative Body, prefects, sub-prefects, mayors, generals and other distinguished officers, among a host of others.[158] In fact, the relationship between the ministry and the society was perceived to be so close that several public officials – from the mayor of Tournai to the prefects of the Departments of Ardèche and Charente – sought membership in the society through the Ministry of the Interior.[159]

In addition, the society, which had submitted a favorable report on Douglas's enterprise to the Ministry of the Interior, lauded Douglas's firm in a report and claimed some credit for the favor that his establishment enjoyed within the ministry.[160] Like the ministry, the society subsidized efforts at mechanization, both in Paris and in departments outside of it.

The society believed that the prefects' efforts to publicize its existence and activities had increased its membership – it claimed to have eighty-three members in the city of Lyon alone. The Lyonnais members had formed a correspondence committee to communicate regularly with the society in Paris, and the society sought to form similar committees in Amiens, Bordeaux, Besançon and Strasbourg. Moreover, the society formed a collection of models of machines and a library of both French and foreign works relevant to the various branches of industry.[161]

The society also proclaimed its intention to disseminate knowledge useful to the improvement of methods of production.[162] In making this one of its primary goals, the society demarcated itself from the ethos of the guild system, under which, it was believed, innovation was discouraged and any improvement remained a closely guarded secret, and the distinction would have been understood by contemporaries.

the auspices of the Minister of the Interior. The report noted that membership in the society had quickly grown to 600 members and that these voluntary memberships had provided a revenue stream that had been dedicated to annual prizes that had led to many technical advances, especially in textile production. AN F¹² 506, dossier 6, Ministry of the Interior, note of July 23, 1806.

[157] AN F¹² 2179, entry of 12 thermidor year XII (July 31, 1804).

[158] AN F¹ᵃ 24, dossier year XII, circular of 14 messidor year XII (July 3, 1804).

[159] AN F¹² 2179, entry of 17 pluviôse year X (February 6, 1802), entry no. 3, 12 thermidor year XII (July 31, 1804), entry of 19 thermidor year XII (August 7, 1804); entry of 29 thermidor year XII (August 17, 1804); AN F¹² 2180, entry of 6 nivôse year XIV (December 27, 1805).

[160] For the report on Douglas, AN F¹² 2179, entry of 25 floréal year XII (May 15, 1804); on the report of the society itself, AN F¹² 501ᴮ, dossier 31, account of work of Administrative Council of Society for Encouragement, from 8 messidor year X to 9 messidor year XI (June 27, 1802–June 28, 1803).

[161] *Bulletin de la Société d'Encouragement de l'Industrie Nationale* 1 (an XI): iii, 5–6.

[162] *Ibid.*, iii.

Indeed, an early annual report of the society offers insight into the manner in which mechanization could eliminate former guild-based trades. Working apparently on a British model, a French locksmith, Koch, presented a machine that produced a new type of lock. The society commissioned models of the machine, which were to be sent to different localities, including Saint-Etienne and the Department of Somme. Historically, of course, locksmiths had been a guild-based trade, and Koch's machine obviously presented a serious threat to artisan locksmiths. The report apparently made a rare, albeit veiled, allusion to tensions between artisanal and mechanical production. It noted that if industry was threatened by a "jealous rivalry," industry could, for its part, fight and win.[163] As the passage suggests, the ideals of mechanization and modernization did not go unchallenged – the threat of a possible restoration of corporations continued.

The concerns expressed by contemporaries were not without foundation. The reorganization of bakers and butchers in Paris had already been authorized, and across France other occupations, especially bakers, were surreptitiously organizing themselves into corporations. Moreover, even after being apprised of these developments, the Minister of the Interior did not suppress the bodies – rather, he delayed taking any action pending fuller consideration.[164]

Indeed, an attempt by one group of men in Rouen, who called themselves "entrepreneur porters" (*entrepreneurs carruyers*), to organize themselves into a corporation reflects the manner in which a restoration of guilds seemed possible, particularly during the early years of Bonaparte's rule. During the year X the porters had asked the Ministry of the Interior for the exclusive right to load and unload ships – from ship to land, from land to ship and from ship to ship. After an extensive study of the request, the ministry refused to grant it because it would be inimical to commerce.

Two years later, however, during prairial year XII (June 1804), the group renewed its request, but in substantially modified form, in the hope of improving its chances of acceptance. In their revised proposal, the porters offered to become a tax-collecting entity for the city, volunteering to collect a new indirect tax. They also offered to post a bond to cover damage to or loss of merchandise and to pay 8,000 francs annually to the hospitals of Rouen, although only during peacetime.

The porters based their claim to reconstitute themselves on three issues: on the need of the city of Rouen to reestablish the services they offered; on the fact that several of their number had been porters before the Revolution had destroyed their corporation; and on the financial guarantee that their proposed corporation could offer. In addition, they asserted that their body would assure service throughout the year and that it would employ a number of workers and even assist them in their retirement.

---

[163] AN F¹² 501ᴮ, account of work of Administrative Council of Society for Encouragement, from 8 messidor year X to 9 messidor year XI (June 27, 1802–June 28, 1803).

[164] AN F¹² 2179, entries of 22 germinal year XIII (April 12, 1805); 5 fructidor year XIII (August 23, 1805); 12 fructidor year XIII (August 30, 1805).

Officials within the Ministry of the Interior again recommended the rejection of their request, but only after an extensive examination of all of the issues. The officials concluded that the benefits of a bond and the annual payment of 8,000 francs to hospitals did not outweigh the liability of the imposition of a new tax on commerce, which would ultimately diminish the volume of trade. They also noted that since the suppression of the original body during the Revolution, the commerce of Rouen had not suffered substantially. Finally, neither the Council of Commerce nor the City Council of Rouen, nor even businessmen in particular, had sought the reestablishment of a corporation of porters. To the contrary, the City Council, a majority of the members of which were businessmen, strongly opposed the reorganization.

The officials also asserted that the putative benefits for workers were overstated – the loading and unloading of ships would continue without the existence of a privileged corporation. The officials claimed that the formation of a single body "was not an indispensable necessity" and would provide little benefit other than to the members of the corporation itself. The ministry officials argued that there was "no motive of public usefulness" that militated in favor of the reestablishment of the corporation, but only a particular interest. They recommended rejection of the revised application.[165]

The request by the porters provides insight into one reason why those opposed to the restoration of guilds remained uneasy. To be sure, the ministry had refused to authorize the reorganization of the corporation, but its rejection had not been reflexive – it had come only after a careful calculation of potential benefits and liabilities. Indeed, the porters had been sufficiently confident of the prospects for reorganization that they had refined and resubmitted their original proposal. With no constitutional prohibition on guilds, and with a pragmatic regime in power, whether or not guilds would be reestablished remained an open question.

It must be remembered that mechanization was in its beginning stages and most pronounced in the textile sector, so artisanal output could potentially continue to coexist with mechanical production. The desire to maintain order was always present during the Napoleonic regime, and guilds were seen as one of the most efficacious means of assuring order among workers.

PUBLIC DEBATE ON THE RESTORATION OF GUILDS

The reestablishment of bodies of bakers and butchers in Paris had generated concern within the Ministry of the Interior,[166] particularly after the General Commissioners of Police in Lyon and Bordeaux authorized the formation of corporations of bakers in their cities and gave them greater authority over their

---

[165] AN F¹² 1560, letter of Arnould and Laine to Minister of the Interior, 14 messidor year XII (July 3, 1804).

[166] On the concern generated by their reestablishment, Costaz, *Histoire de l'administration en France*, I: 135–139.

members than was the case in Paris. Within the ministry, the head of the Second Division and the head of the Bureau of Arts and Manufacturing prepared an unusually lengthy report for the Minister of the Interior on what they termed the "illegal reestablishment" of guilds of bakers in Lyon and Bordeaux.

The report noted that the National Assembly had abolished "all corporations of the same calling and profession," which was underlined for emphasis, and stated that the Assembly had also enacted strong provisions to prevent their rebirth. They had reappeared in large cities, however, not as a result of governmental or legislative action, but by the simple act of "secondary administrations" (that is, the police) that saw the reestablishment of corporations only as a means of administrative control. The officials asked the minister to annul the actions in order to preserve freedom of work and the free exercise of industry.

They acknowledged the quasi-surreptitious decree, "neither posted nor published," that had allowed bakers in Paris to oversee the deposition of flour, but argued that it was not necessary to apply the decree in other cities – it had been put in place only with the goal of provisioning Paris. The General Commissioners of Police in Lyon and Bordeaux, however, had declared that the decree for Paris was indispensable and should be implemented in their cities, and the Minister of Justice, who, at the time the requests were made, had overseen police matters, had extended the dispositions to the two cities.

The police in the two cities had gone beyond the provisions of the Paris decree, however; the General Commissioner of Police in Lyon had issued an ordinance, approved by the prefect of the Department of Rhône, that provisionally reestablished the guild of bakers. In Bordeaux, the General Commissioner of Police had issued a decree that set up a guild of bakers, but the prefect of the Department of Gironde had refused to sanction it because of what he believed were serious problems. The police commissioner had then submitted it to the Ministry of Police, which in turn had sent it to the Minister of the Interior.

The statutes for the bakers of Lyon contained sixty-eight articles, whereas those for Bordeaux had thirty-three, and the officials argued that if the minister approved them he would be reopening the door to abuses seen under the regime of guilds. They enumerated their concerns about aspects of the regulations for each city. In both cities, the officials observed, the ordinances sought to restrict the number of bakers, or at least prevent any growth in their number, and tended toward "the exclusive." This development recalled the time when masters of each profession had united to exclude from their community those whom they regarded as enemies ready to make off with a part of their fortune, with the description of masters also underlined for emphasis.

The officials cited specific concerns about various provisions in both ordinances, from conditions for apprenticeships to requirements for admission to each guild. They repeatedly alluded to the speech that Regnaud de Saint-Jean d'Angély had made to the Tribunate [*sic*] during the year XI, in which he had criticized the liabilities of guilds.

The extraordinary length of the memorandum (24 pages), the repeated use of underlining for emphasis and the hyperbole employed (the officials twice wrote of "the pen falling from the hand" in contemplating some of the dispositions) all attest to the degree to which officials at the Ministry of the Interior regarded the reestablishment of guilds as a threat. The memorandum fulminated against "the uselessness of these rules joined to the incompetence of the authority that had prescribed them." Corporations had been abolished during June [*sic*] 1791, the officials stated, and could only be reestablished, in whole or in part, by a new law – the General Commissioners of Lyon and Bordeaux did not have the right to re-create the guilds of bakers. In doing so, they had exceeded their authority and usurped the functions of the government, which proposed laws, and the Legislative Body, which sanctioned them. Even under the Old Regime, they reminded the minister, it was not the Lieutenant-General of Police or intendants who brought guilds into existence, but *lettres-patentes* of the king.

They emphasized, again citing Regnaud de Saint-Jean d'Angély, the drawbacks of placing limits on the freedom of "industrial professions." What the government had feared to propose to the Legislative Body, the General Commissioners of Police in Lyon and Bordeaux had "boldly executed," and had compounded this "excess of power" with two others that were no less reprehensible. After pointing out those excesses, the officials asked the minister to annul the nominations of officers of these corporations and to prohibit any similar action in the future. In doing so, he would nullify the statutes and regulations of corporations that had no legal existence.[167] No action or outcome is listed on the document, but other evidence suggests that the bodies were dissolved – the Council of State discussed a corporation of bakers for Bordeaux on October 25, 1810, and established a body on September 2, 1812. Likewise, the Council of State authorized a guild of bakers for Lyon on September 15, 1813, and the prefect of the Department of Rhône established it on November 8, 1813.[168] Both acts suggest that the bodies to which the ministry had objected were, in fact, disbanded.

The officials' concerns were well founded – during the fall of 1804 the wine merchants of Paris, after receiving permission from the Prefect of Police, had met in a general assembly and had chosen a commission of twelve to draft a project for creating a corporation. Basing its proposal on Old Regime precedents, the commission drew up a set of statutes, comprising 100 articles,

---

[167] AN F¹² 502, dossier 26, undated memorandum of head of Bureau of Arts and Manufacturing and head of Second Division of Ministry of the Interior, undated (but internal evidence indicates 1805).

[168] Napoleonica.org, *Rapport et projets de décret. Mesure pour faire cesser les abus qui se sont introduits dans le commerce de boulangerie*, no. 2163, October 25, 1810; *Rapport et projets de décret relatifs au commerce de boulangerie dans la ville de Bordeaux*, no. 2717, September 2, 1812; *Rapport et projet de décret relatifs au commerce de boulangerie dans la ville de Lyon*, no. 2976, September 15, 1813; Bernadette Angleraud, *Les Boulangers lyonnais aux XIXᵉ et XXᵉ siècles* (Paris: Editions Christian, 1998), pp. 41–42.

in a bid to reorganize the trade into a body, and joined them to a petition requesting the reorganization with more than 100 signatures. The wine merchants sent a copy of their petition and proposed regulations to the Chamber of Commerce in Paris, leading the chamber to write to the Prefect of Police on 4 vendémiaire year XIII (September 26, 1804) to express its concern. The chamber stated that it presumed that the project had been submitted to the prefect because he oversaw the wine merchants and was the natural authority to decide on the means of ending abuses.

At the same time, the chamber asserted that the wine merchants' request raised major questions relating to commercial economy that merited careful consideration. Clearly uneasy, the chamber advised the prefect that it would be drafting a response to the wine merchants' request and asked him not to take any action until the chamber had presented its response.[169] Fewer than two weeks later the chamber wrote to the Minister of the Interior asking him to reject the wine merchants' "disastrous project." In a lengthy rebuttal, the chamber argued that the merchants were placing their own interests ahead of the larger interests of commerce.[170]

The Prefect of Police had responded favorably to receiving an opinion from the Chamber of Commerce of Paris, and the chamber notified him that instead of limiting itself to commenting on the details of the project it would address the principal issue – the reestablishment of corporations.[171] More than a month later, it sent the prefect three copies of the report of the commissioners who had been selected to examine the wine merchants' proposal. Apologizing for its late response, the chamber observed that the importance of the subject demanded a major effort and that it hoped the prefect would find it satisfactory.[172]

Perhaps using the opening afforded by the prefect's favorable response, the chamber also sent a report to the Minister of the Interior, but a member worried that in the communication sent to the minister it had not made its views on guilds sufficiently clear. Asserting that the question of the reestablishment of corporations could be treated at any moment in the Council of State, he proposed sending a letter on the matter to the minister. The chamber agreed, and appointed Vital Roux to draft it.[173]

A few weeks later Roux read his proposed letter to the chamber, and it was adopted a week later.[174] Three copies were sent to the minister on 4 prairial year XIII (May 24, 1805) and, reflecting the degree of concern of the chamber, it enclosed another three copies that it asked the minister to give to the emperor.[175]

---

[169] ACCIP 1 Mi 1, fols. 139–140.
[170] ACCIP 1 Mi 1, fols. 149–153.
[171] ACCIP 1 Mi 1, fol. 186.
[172] ACCIP 1 Mi 1, fol. 193.
[173] ACCIP 2 Mi 2, fol. 14.
[174] ACCIP 2 Mi 2, fols. 22–23, 24–26.
[175] AN F¹² 2471, dossier 26, undated cover note submitted with letter of Chamber of Commerce of Paris to Minister of the Interior, 4 prairial year XIII (May 24, 1805).

The letter marked the beginning of a vigorous campaign by the chamber to prevent the reestablishment of corporations in any form. Any such reestablishment, the chamber asserted, would be disastrous to industry. It claimed that current law – a reference to the law of 22 germinal year XI and the complementary law of 9 frimaire year XII – was sufficient because it covered the critical areas of apprenticeships, the rights of employers and workers and other major issues. The laws had fulfilled the views and intentions of French manufacturing and any reestablishment of corporations would be counterproductive.

The chamber strongly advocated additional industrial exhibitions, which had ceased after Chaptal left the ministry in 1804, because they highlighted the advantages of industry. It asked that the emperor put in place institutions more appropriate to the century of his reign. The chamber expressed the hope that the Minister of the Interior would order the revision of laws regulating industry instead of allowing the formation of any corporations.[176]

The closing request by the Chamber of Commerce to revise the laws regulating industry reflected a perception among some manufacturers that, despite a willingness to use them as a bulwark against the reestablishment of guilds, the laws of 22 germinal year XI and 9 frimaire year XII were inadequate – the chamber had, in fact, characterized "the collection of laws protective of industry" as "incomplete and defective."[177] Further reflecting this view, the Chamber of Commerce of Carcassonne asked for a strengthening of the legislation, particularly with respect to the theft of raw materials. For its part, however, the government sought to maintain the current legislation rather than bolster or expand it.[178]

The Chamber of Commerce of Paris refined its report in a subsequent meeting and unanimously approved it. Because the chamber agreed that preventing the reestablishment of guilds was its primary goal, it adopted the report, but as a separate motion it also decided to seek a revision of existing laws related to industry.[179]

The communication sent by the chamber to the Minister of the Interior and the Prefect of Police became the basis of a much longer pamphlet – 180 pages in length – that the chamber, in a clear bid to influence public opinion, published in 1805. Claiming that it sought to examine the "very important question" of the advantages and dangers of corporations, the chamber divided the work into five sections – a historical overview of the evolution of guilds, a treatment of their advantages and disadvantages, a consideration of their fiscal aspects,

---

[176] ACCIP 1 Mi 2, fols. 9–13.

[177] ACCIP 2 Mi 2, fol. 24.

[178] Indeed, in a report prepared for the Minister of the Interior in response to the request of the Chamber of Commerce of Carcassonne, officials in the ministry pointedly asked if one could add to the legislation without oppressing the working class. AN F¹² 509–510, dossier 1, undated report to Minister of the Interior on request of Chamber of Commerce of Carcassonne.

[179] ACCIP 2 Mi 2, fols. 24–26.

an examination of guilds as a source of oversight and discipline, and, lastly, a long commentary on the proposed statutes of the wine merchants.

The pamphlet asserted that the wine merchants' focus on particular abuses that they wanted to correct, and that the chamber conceded were present, would potentially create much larger problems of privilege and monopoly. The chamber argued that the reestablishment of a corporation of wine merchants would lead to numerous difficulties and noted that, at the beginning of the Revolution, the harm and dangers of guilds had been recognized. No one doubted the advantages of their abolition, the pamphlet asserted, but the abuses that had occurred since their suppression had led many to forget the misdeeds they had perpetrated. Although the regime of guilds had had some benefits, it also had had a number of disadvantages and, rather than choose between "two equally dangerous excesses," the chamber argued that it would be better to study what was useful and adopt such measures. It claimed that it would be dangerous to reestablish corporations and recommended against reorganizing a guild for wine merchants.[180]

The report by the Chamber of Commerce of Paris ignited a debate on whether or not guilds should be a part of the economy of the state, beginning with a long and detailed rejoinder from Soufflot de Merey, who sent a copy of his pamphlet to the Minister of the Interior. Soufflot de Merey not only offered a point-by-point refutation of the chamber's report to argue in favor of restoring the guild of wine merchants, but went on to advocate a general restoration of guilds. He proposed the establishment of eight merchant and twenty artisanal corporations.

Each corporation would pay a tax to the state, which it would apportion among its members. Soufflot de Merey argued that this would be more equitable than the system of occupational licenses and would result in fewer complaints. He asserted that only corporations could correct the problems that had arisen and scrutinize the character and behavior of their members. Inspections by the corporation would assure the quality of products and instill confidence in consumers. Furthermore, several sensitive occupations, such as booksellers, pharmacists and others, would be subject to police inspection as well.

Soufflot de Merey declared that to correct a wrong, an institution had been destroyed, and claimed it would be better to correct abuses by suppressing privileges and taking other salutary measures. He also asserted that the reestablishment of guilds would benefit both the economy and the social order of France.

In a clear effort to allay concern, Soufflot de Merey went on to state that his proposal would exempt industry from inclusion in the corporate system he envisaged. In large part, he presented this exclusion as a practical measure,

---

[180] *Rapport sur les jurandes et maîtrises; et sur un projet de statuts et réglemens pour MM. les marchands de vin de Paris, imprimé par ordre de la Chambre de Commerce du Département de la Seine* (Paris: Stoupe, 1805). For a description of wine merchants before the Revolution, *Guide des corps des marchands et des communautés des arts et métiers*, pp. 307–316.

observing that a community or corporation of manufacturers was not viable. At the same time, he did not want the perception to arise that corporations would pose a threat to the development of industry – indeed, he praised the industrial exhibitions that had been held in Paris.[181]

The pamphlet of Soufflot de Merey provoked a response from an individual named Thirion, who claimed to have had extensive experience with guilds before the Revolution. He argued strongly that one should not revert to past practices – a reference to guilds – and asserted instead that industry should be freed of all constraints and allowed to develop methods of manufacturing unimpeded. One of his implicit concerns was that corporations would limit innovation in industry.

Thirion claimed that achieving order would restore public confidence, and stated that one could not repeat too often that the manufacturer should be left to his own creative powers and allowed total independence with respect to production. In an expression of concern about the potential of guilds to restrain mechanization, he argued that loans or subsidies to entrepreneurs were less critical than accelerating the output of their production and gaining the confidence of the public. Claiming to have undertaken an apprenticeship in a guild before the Revolution, he responded to the prospective reorganization of wine merchants with a strong denunciation of corporations and a categorical rejection of Soufflot de Merey's call for their restoration.[182]

In addition, Jean-Georges-Antoine Stoupe put forward a pamphlet calling for the reestablishment of a guild of printers in Paris to curtail bankruptcies and curb abuses. When the corporation existed, Stoupe asserted, the continual surveillance it exercised over its members prevented dishonorable actions and bankruptcies. During the fifty years before the guild had been abolished, he wrote, there had been only one bankruptcy; since its abolition, there had been a multitude of them, sullying the trade in a manner heretofore unknown.[183] It was time to correct the situation, he argued, by reestablishing the guild.[184] Thereafter, the pamphlet portion of the debate died down, and the central government did not reestablish a guild of wine merchants.

The debate that occurred during 1805 was the most extensive public discussion of corporations in decades, and demonstrated that there was

---

[181] Soufflot de Merey, *Considérations sur le rétablissement des jurandes et maîtrises; précédés d'observations sur un rapport fait à la Chambre de Commerce du Département de la Seine sur cette importante question, et sur un projet de statuts et réglemens de MM. les marchands de vin* (Paris: Marchant, 1805).

[182] E. Thirion, *Mémoire à l'Empereur, sur l'amélioration des loix et règlemens commerciaux. Lettres à la Chambre de Commerce de Rouen, et au Ministre de l'Intérieur à ce sujet. Observations sur un rapport fait à la Chambre de Commerce du Département de la Seine, sur les jurandes et maîtrises et sur les considérations, publiée par M. Soufflot de Meret, sur ce rapport* (Paris: chez l'auteur, 1806).

[183] This had been noted a few years earlier in a police report. AN F7 3831, report of 15 floréal year XI (May 5, 1803).

[184] Jean-Georges-Antoine Stoupe, *Mémoire sur le rétablissement de la communauté des imprimeurs de Paris; suivi de reflexions sur les contrefaçons en librairie, et sur le stéréotypage* (Paris: chez les Marchands des Nouveautés, 1806).

a constituency that wished to restore them. During its course the debate in fact reached such proportions that the Council of State, which was drafting a Code of Commerce, briefly considered the issue of guilds. The subcommittee drawing up the code had, in the first article of the project, proclaimed that every individual had the right to undertake commerce in France, and added that "the exercise of this right is guaranteed and regulated by specific laws." The subcommittee affirmed that the provision had been drawn up in order to prevent any reestablishment of guilds or masterships, and added that it found any prospect of reestablishing corporations alarming.

Furthermore, the Interior Section of the Council of State had adopted the first part of the first article only after excluding guilds and masterships from the right to engage in commerce, and the Council of State reaffirmed its opposition to the reestablishment of corporations. Despite this stance, the idea of "corporatizing" (*corporiser*) merchants had been put forward on several occasions in the belief that it was the only means of reviving the old bonds of commerce and commercial honor. The decline in quality of goods during the Revolution, and the failure of bankruptcy legislation to ameliorate that problem, had led to a belief that the best means of restoring honor would be to submit merchants to standards and a disciplinary body. It was possible, the Council of State noted, that a return to the project could occur, and that at that time those not familiar with guilds might believe that restoring them in modified form was the best course of action.

Such an action, the council averred, would be a thousand times more disastrous for industry and commerce than any problems associated with the the abolition of guilds. There were no modifications, the council argued, that could correct the essentially vicious system of masterships and guilds. Time, however, had erased memory of the system, with its serious deficiencies, and, the council asserted, illusions could lead to reproducing that system in some form. The proposal put forward by the wine merchants was such a misconception.[185]

Ultimately, the wine merchants were not organized into a body during 1805. During June 1808, however, Dubois, the Prefect of Police, quietly organized them into a body with eight officers, which was the largest number of officials in any trade or merchant body in Paris.[186] Indeed, the formation of the wine merchants into a body marked the beginning of a wave of similar actions by Dubois – between June 1808 and June 1810 he organized twelve trades into bodies with officials.[187]

In the aftermath of the debate on wine merchants, a trusted secret counselor of Bonaparte, Joseph Fiévée, advised him during February 1806 to consider

---

[185] *La Législation civile, commerciale et criminelle de la France, ou commentaire et complément des codes français*, 31 vols. (Paris: Treuttel and Würtz, 1827–1832): 17: 369–371.
[186] Napoleonica.org. *Rapport sur l'exercice de la profession de marchand et les arts et métiers.* Project no. 2044[4er], August 11, 1810.
[187] *Ibid.*

restoring corporations, particularly for merchants, as preferable to the current situation. Fiévée argued that the system of unlimited freedom ushered in by the Revolution had harmed commerce and that in every major country in which commerce had progressed, guilds were present. Although he acknowledged the great difficulty of restoring guilds in commerce and industry in France – he termed it "impossible" – Fiévée asserted that merchants, even those in the same line of trade, were too isolated from each other. There was no vehicle for common interests to take hold – a silk merchant was as unknown to another silk merchant as a wine merchant was to a wood merchant, he claimed – and the result had been a destabilization of commerce.[188]

Confidence had been slow to reestablish itself, and the lack of structure in commerce had led to a short-term focus among merchants, rather than to a longer view, as was the case in Britain. Fiévée decried the fact that the members of the Chamber of Commerce in Paris were not businessmen, but "economic scribblers."

The government had formed notaries, bailiffs and process-servers into corporations and this had given these occupations greater stability. Returning to a system of guilds could provoke major unrest, he admitted, but it was necessary to put in place institutions that would create stability and confidence in commerce and protect it from usurers, capitalists and money merchants.[189]

Additional proposals for reestablishing guilds continued to be advanced. During February 1806, asserting that good workers had become rare and that there were many more entrepreneurs and merchants than necessary, an individual named Eméric David sent a lengthy project for reestablishing guilds to Joseph Fouché, the Minister of Police. David was particularly concerned about counterfeiting, stating that former trademarks indicating the quality of goods were now serving only to deceive the public because the names of renowned manufacturers were being affixed to merchandise of poor quality. It was necessary to reestablish both equilibrium and quality in the market, and the restoration of guilds, in modified form, David claimed, was the means of achieving those goals.[190]

"THE STATISTICAL REGIME" SURVEYS ITS WORKERS

The movement toward mechanized production was not lost on contemporaries. One guidebook to Paris during the early Empire treated the city as a virtual industrial wonderland, with an entire chapter devoted to mechanical arts

---

[188] A British visitor was made aware of the loss of confidence in commerce in 1803. *An Englishman in Paris: 1803. The Journal of Bertie Greathead*, J.P.T. Bury and J.C. Barry, eds. (London: Geoffrey Bles, 1953), p. 123.

[189] Joseph Fiévée, *Correspondance et relations de J. Fiévée avec Bonaparte, premier consul et empereur pendant onze années (1802 à 1813). Publiée par l'auteur...*, 3 vols. (Paris: A. Desrez, 1836), II: 192–203. On Fiévée, Jean Tulard, *Joseph Fiévée, conseiller secret de Napoléon* (Paris: Fayard, 1985), pp. 131–154.

[190] AN F7 4283, project and memoir of Emeric David on masterships, February 24, 1806.

and manufactures.[191] It recommended that visitors view the cotton factory of Richard and Lenoir-Dufresne on the rue de Charonne, which was impressive for its vastness and the number of workers it employed. It also made note of Douglas's factory, which manufactured machines for the production of wool, proclaiming it an establishment of the first importance. It particularly lauded Réveillon's wallpaper factory – indeed, in a footnote indicating the factory's extraordinary success since its destruction "from top to bottom" in 1789, its accomplishments were implicitly rendered as a parable of industry triumphing over the retrograde system of guilds. The guide also bestowed praise upon the Conservatoire des Arts et Métiers, the industrial exhibitions and the Society for the Encouragement of National Industry.[192]

In fact, during 1807, the government undertook two examinations of workers and the economy. In February it surveyed artisanal trades and in October it scrutinized industry. The two surveys should not be given great credence – neither was comprehensive, and in several instances respondents provided hurried replies or made subjective judgments. Despite their deficiencies, however, the surveys provide insight into the state of French labor and the structure of the economy during the middle period of Bonaparte's rule.

In response to the February survey, the Prefect of Police in Paris submitted a lengthy reply. In the first category, the prefect grouped workers associated with the city's food supply. The major groups were bakers, numbering 4,621, 2,560 of whom were in Paris itself; wine merchants, with 3,623; and butchers, with 1,269. The large numbers in these occupations, and the fact that all three were critical to the food supply, makes clear why the regime was willing to consider reorganizing them into corporations. The three groups comprised thousands of individuals, and the reestablishment of bodies would relieve the police of much of the responsibility for overseeing the safety and quality of the food supply. In all, with grocers, pastry makers and other ancillary occupations, there were 14,262 individuals in the first category.

The prefect noted that most in this category were not discontented or restive, and in general posed little threat. Bakers and butchers were two possible exceptions – the former because of their "gross ignorance and coarseness," and the latter because of the great harmony among them, implying that they would be able to act in concert. Gatherings of journeymen bakers occasionally stirred up trouble, but mostly in bars, and in any case the police kept watch on them. Journeymen butchers were fewer in number, scattered more widely throughout the city, and busier in their trade, so they posed less of a problem.

The second category cited in the prefect's report consisted of men in the building trades. The largest group in this category was masons, with 5,315

---

[191] On Paris as an industrial center under Napoleon, Louis Bergeron, *Banquiers, négociants et manufacturiers parisiens du Directoire à l'Empire* (Paris: Editions de l'Ecole en Sciences Sociales, 1978), pp. 205–210.

[192] *Panorama de Paris et de ses environs, ou Paris vu dans son ensemble, et dans ses détails...*, 2 vols. (Paris: Bailleul, 1805), especially II: 66–142.

workers. Other major components were carpenters, with 1,855 workers; stone cutters with 1,784; and excavators, with 1,200. With all allied occupations, the prefect listed a total of 24,148 workers in the building trades. He noted that it was within this group that coalitions and assemblies were the quickest to form and were the most difficult to dissipate, which he attributed to the presence of many workers at the same worksite. One agitator, he asserted, could make an inflammatory proposition, and many others would support it as a point of honor.

The third category comprised those in clothing trades. The largest group was shoemakers and boot makers, of which there were 7,474 and tailors, with 3,701, and these figures omitted 3,000 apprentices.[193] There were also 1,912 hatmakers and 1,603 hosiers. With all associated vocations, there were 17,806 workers listed in the clothing trades. The most troublesome group in this category, according to the prefect, was the hatmakers, many of whom were ready to form coalitions or were prone to violence and trouble.

The fourth category consisted of those in furniture-related trades, but this was a relatively small sector, with 5,158 workers altogether. The largest single group within it was cabinet makers, of which there were 1,865. In the view of the prefect, these workers did not pose any problem for authorities.

The fifth category was defined by men in transport, cartage and riding. This, too, was a small sector, with 3,341 workers, whom the prefect regarded as hardworking and peaceful.

The sixth category consisted of workmen in timber, and a majority of these were barrel makers. Only 1,112 men were grouped in these trades, but the prefect regarded the barrel makers as a troublesome element. Although their actions were rare, he wrote, they were problematic.

The seventh category comprised metal workers of various types, of which jewelers (1,871), goldsmiths and silversmiths (952) and founders (824) were the major groups. In all, 11,258 workers were enumerated in this classification. Not surprisingly, the prefect observed that this sector was quiescent, even during difficult economic times.

The eighth category centered on textiles, a sector in which mechanization was rapidly progressing. The prefect listed 3,215 workers in this sector, which was volatile. Indeed, in the words of the prefect, whom one would not imagine as a social reformer, the workers were "veritable machines." Not surprisingly, workers in the textile sector were discontented, particularly in the mechanized sphere. Although there were some "distinguished workers" in the cotton industry, the prefect reported that workers in cotton were notable for an "almost ridiculous inconstancy," and coalitions among them would be frequent if masters did not post rules to which workers must submit upon entry to a workshop if they wished to work. In spite of these regulations, however, there were some agitators, but in other portions of the textile industry workers did not pose a political problem.

---

[193] Almost certainly all females were excluded from the survey as well.

The ninth category consisted of workers in leather and animal skin trades, and they were a small subdivision, numbering only 1,993. Furthermore, all of these men worked out of their residence. The prefect asserted that the curriers, the majority in this sector, were politically restive.

The tenth category was made up of workers in the printing and paper trades, which the prefect enumerated at 4,467. The printers were the critical element, and the prefect asserted that new regulations were necessary to manage them. He asserted that it was among printers – the most insubordinate workers – that those most disposed toward forming coalitions and causing trouble were to be found.

The eleventh and final category, also a small one, was comprised of workers in vases and crystal. There were only 1,475 workers in this sector, the overwhelming majority in porcelain, faience and pottery. They were not a matter of concern to the prefect.

Finally, the prefect added another 2,701 workers under a heading termed "*classes isolées,*" the largest elements of which were tobacco workers (865) and dyers (535). In the prefect's opinion, these workers were also not a cause of concern.

The prefect concluded his report by calculating a total 91,946 workers in former artisanal trades in Paris. He cautioned, however, that that number excluded many who were not associated with a trade but worked at ports or food markets, or as porters and other such occupations, and their numbers were large.[194]

The prefect's response to the survey provides insight into the reason why the Napoleonic regime did not definitively foreclose the option of restoring guilds – indeed, Dubois embedded an argument for reestablishing them in his report. By emphasizing unrest among critical groups of workers – the provisioning sector, building trades, and printers – he implicitly suggested that the reinstatement of guilds would enable greater discipline to be exercised over tens of thousands of Parisian workers.

Furthermore, his warning of the potential for discontent among workers in the textile industry – those he had characterized as "virtual machines" – had been accompanied by the declaration that only the assertion of authority by masters over workers in such establishments had kept worker unrest from reaching greater levels. With mechanization not yet widespread, the prefect was clearly arguing that without action the problem of agitation among workers would only become worse, and that it was imperative to act. To a regime for which order was a primordial concern, headed by a former general whose career had received a critical boost through his suppression of a worker uprising in Paris, the prefect's arguments were highly pertinent.[195]

---

[194] AN F¹² 502, dossier 11, statistics of workers of Paris ... March 1, 1807, dated May 30, 1807.

[195] On the concern of the regime with preventing agitation or risings among workers, Alfred Fierro, *La Vie des Parisiens sous Napoléon* (Saint-Cloud: Napoléon Iᵉʳ éditions, 2003), pp. 76–78.

In addition, the minister solicited an opinion from the Chamber of Commerce of the Department of Seine, and the reply of its members echoed the prefect's concerns. The minister had sought the view of the chamber on a prospective division of work – apparently a division between artisanal work (*main d'oeuvre*) and mechanized work. The chamber was not opposed to a restoration of guilds in some modified form because the chamber viewed the imposition of regulation (*une police*) for commerce and workers, especially in Paris, as imperative. The chamber asserted that most artisanal work (*main d'oeuvre*) in Paris was limited to the luxury trades, but also noted the diffi-cult situation of workers in Paris and the confusion into which they had been thrown since the abolition of guilds. The chamber observed that there had been numerous crises during the Revolution and that workers had been sub-jected to the loss of their habitual trade or occupation. As a result, one now had a situation in which "the maker of portfolios works at making soldier's straps, the saddle maker makes boots, the painter of fans or snuff boxes tries his hand at porcelain, the steel maker becomes an armorer and so on."

In yet another reflection of the perceived inadequacy of the law of 22 germi-nal year XI, the chamber asserted that there was a need for oversight of com-merce and workers, which was lacking, particularly in Paris. The imposition of such oversight, however, had to be accomplished in a manner that would not "stifle industry under the weight of privileges of guilds." The chamber sought in particular new laws to regulate apprenticeships.[196] It did not want to reestablish the privileges of guilds, but argued that discipline could be achieved through the promulgation of clear and brief laws that would establish general principles on such matters as the nature and effects of apprenticeship con-tracts and the respective rights and duties of workers and their bosses – an additional indication of the shortcomings of the law of 22 germinal year XI, which regulated such matters.[197]

Replies from outlying departments also provide insight into the state and structure of labor during the first decade of Bonaparte's rule. The city of Grenoble offers a useful parallel case – not only did it lie well beyond the region of Paris, but it is unusually well documented because officials submit-ted thorough reports. Most importantly, however, like Paris, it had at its core formerly guild-based artisanal trades, particularly glovemaking, along with developing textile industries.

An account book for the Grenoble master glove maker Gaspard Bovier reveals the scope of the market for gloves made in the city during the early Revolution. During 1791, for example, Bovier sent gloves to custom-ers in Copenhagen, Poland, Naples, London, Augsburg, Rome, Stockholm, Rotterdam and Amsterdam, as well as Paris. By the year III, however, Bovier's

---

[196] AN F¹² 1569, dossier Seine, letter of members of Chamber of Commerce to Minister of the Interior, March 28, 1807.
[197] AN F¹² 1569, dossier Seine, letter of Chamber of Commerce to Minister of the Interior, March 28, 1807.

business had diminished considerably, and his foreign markets, except Switzerland, had virtually disappeared. The final entries were made during brumaire year IV (November 1795), with a large order destined for Paris placed that month.[198]

After the dissolution of guilds, the number of glovemakers increased, but the number of workers in the trade decreased by approximately half, mainly because many workers now produced on their own behalf rather than for a master. By the latter years of the Directory, the commerce in gloves in Grenoble had declined sharply. Indeed, French gloves were prohibited in Great Britain, Russia, Spain, Prussia and the states of the Holy Roman Empire. Because glove making was the single largest enterprise in Grenoble, the city was hard hit.[199]

During the Empire commerce in gloves had begun to recover, but the volume of trade remained about 25 percent below prerevolutionary levels, according to the prefect. He attributed the decline to the Revolution and wars, particularly the loss of colonies, to the prohibition of French gloves in Britain, to British purchases of horsehides and other skins, and the establishment of competing production centers in Britain and elsewhere. Glovemakers in Grenoble sought to prohibit the export of horsehides and the imposition of a duty on exported cowhides and other leathers. This would force French "enemies" to rely again on French suppliers and revive the commerce of Grenoble.

The glove making industry, largely artisanal, could employ a substantial number of workers. The establishment of Jean Ducruy, for example, which had been founded in 1705, employed 280 individuals in 1807.[200]

Other former guild trades were also in a parlous state, particularly tanneries, which supported the glove trade. Production in tanneries had fallen precipitously during the Revolution, due mainly to the Law of the Maximum, which had caused tanners to incur considerable losses. Production in tanneries had fallen by between two-thirds and five-sixths of prerevolutionary levels.[201]

There were other industries in Grenoble, but they, too, had suffered from developments during the Revolution. In the textile sector, the firm of Charvet Frères, which had been founded in 1724, had distinguished itself with the quality of its cloth, earning a certificate of royal manufacture in 1753. From 1766 until 1792, it had had twenty-eight looms, and as many as forty, but in 1807 it had only ten.

According to the prefect, the foundation for the firm's prosperity before the Revolution had been the intelligence of the proprietors and the constant attention they had given to the perfection of the firm's products, the special protection of the government, the regulations for production and the use of trademarks that attested to the quality of the product and the close supervision of production. All of these conditions had changed with the Revolution,

[198] BM Grenoble Ms. R 7451, especially fols. 204–253.
[199] AD Isère L 288, general account of factories and manufacturing, year VI.
[200] AN F¹² 1569, dossier Isère, general observations.
[201] AN F¹² 1569, dossier Isère, table of factories and manufactories of Department of Isère, March 25, 1807.

and the prefect asserted that the causes of the firm's decline were those that had influenced "all industry of France during the Revolution" – the abolition of regulations and total freedom in production, and the ease with which material of inferior quality could be marketed under false trademarks. All of these circumstances had enabled new manufacturers to sell their products at a lower price than had former producers, to deceive consumers and to seize markets, and had thereby forced the older enterprises to lower the quality of their cloth.

The total number of looms in Grenoble had risen from 113 in 1787 to 300 in 1807, but the quality of their output was lower for the reasons adduced by the prefect. Manufacturers sought the reestablishment of the former regulations and standards for production or, at a minimum, that standards of quality be required of producers through the use of a trademark with the name and domicile of the producer clearly indicated.

Another textile firm that had suffered during the Revolution, a print cloth firm, Perregaux Elder and Company, had opened in 1788, and until 1792 had employed 250 workers. The number of workers fell to 120 during 1793, and the facility had shut down from 1793 until 1796. It had reopened in 1796, but by the early Napoleonic era it employed only 80 workers. The most difficult factor for the firm had been the debasement of paper money, according to the prefect, but, he noted, the enterprise was beginning to rise from its ruins.

A new cotton-spinning factory had opened in nearby Saint-Marcellin during the year XIII and, producing lower-grade cotton, had become successful and deserved the government's support and protection. This facility, the prefect wrote, had introduced a new branch of industry to the region and provided employment to many who had previously been unemployed. In a harbinger of the laissez-faire industrial structure to come, the factory employed 200 to 250 men, women and children, some as young as eight. The other cotton factory, an older one that had been founded in 1778 in Grenoble, had acquired some British machines, but its production had declined sharply since the Revolution.[202]

Although he had not specifically called for the reestablishment of guilds, also implanted in the report of the prefect in Grenoble, albeit more subtly than that of the Prefect of Police in Paris, was just such an argument. Trademarks, including the name and domicile of the manufacturer, had been allowed by the legislation of 22 germinal year XI, but the prefect's comments regarding false trademarks clearly implied that the law was inadequate. Again, the prefect did not suggest restoring corporations, but it could be read into his response that a permanent, dedicated body responsible for overseeing production would be more effective and would raise the overall quality of cloth.

Whether the government survey provided the impetus is unclear, but during June 1807, rumors circulated in Paris that guilds were to be reestablished. The Chamber of Commerce of Paris, after being informed of these, discussed

---

[202] *Ibid.*

whether to send a letter to the Minister of the Interior asking him to refrain from any action until the General Council on Commerce could be consulted on the issue.

The debate produced a split in the chamber, with one side seeking to prevent any reorganization of corporations, viewing them as having the ability to place limits on industry and as a source of litigation. Another group, however, deeply concerned about the disorders in commerce, favored establishing regulations or guarantees through what they termed an "industrial code." Opponents of this argued that problems were to be found primarily in Paris and that a particular need for Paris should not lead to a code that encompassed the entire Empire. An extended discussion of the concept of an industrial code ensued, but without resolution. The chamber limited itself to writing the Minister of the Interior to inquire about the rumored reestablishment of guilds.[203]

By the time of its next meeting two weeks later, the chamber had received a reply from the Minister of the Interior in which he stated that the matter was merely a question of gaining information for the Consultative Chambers of Arts and Manufacturing; the chamber, however, remained concerned.[204] The minister's assurance did little to stem the rumors.[205]

The difficulties in commerce to which members of the chamber alluded were undeniably present,[206] and were not, in fact, limited mainly to Paris. During 1807 the Academy of Châlons-sur-Marne proposed, as the topic for its annual essay prize, "What are the best means of reestablishing order in arts, trades and manufacturing, without hindering the freedom of industry and commerce?" There was no winner that year, so the academy repeated the question for its 1808 competition. Ultimately, however, the competition received few entries in those two years, and the academy retired the question without awarding a prize.[207] The contest, as well as its outcome, reveals how intractable the issue seemed, and provides insight into how the idea of reestablishing guilds – albeit in a modified form to accommodate "the freedom of industry and commerce" – could continue to have proponents.

During the fall, the government undertook a separate survey of the state of industry and on means to accelerate and perfect it. It noted that Britain controlled three-fourths of global commerce, both in everyday and luxury items. French industry, by contrast, furnished foreign consumers with only a few luxury or fashion items from Paris, silks from Lyon, linens from northern France

203 ACCIP 2 Mi 2, fols. 149–150.
204 ACCIP 2 Mi 2, fols. 150–151.
205 ACCIP 1 Mi 2, fol. 144.
206 Munson, "Businessmen, Business Conduct and the Civic Organization of Commercial Life."
207 Ménard, *Mon Opinion sur l'organisation des manufactures, en réponse à la question suivante, proposée pour sujet de prix de l'année 1807, et réproduite pour 1808, par l'Académie de Châlons-sur-Marne* <<*Quels sont les meilleurs moyens de rétablir la police des Arts et Métiers, et des Manufactures, sans nuire à la Liberté de l'industrie et du commerce?*>> (Paris: Morisset, 1809).

and Brittany, and cloth from the Midi – otherwise, most French commerce was internal or to colonies. The Eden-Vergennes Treaty concluded before the Revolution had brought to the fore for France the clear superiority of British industry. The primary reasons for British success, the survey argued, were capital and mechanization, which enabled Britain to produce high-quality products at low cost – a lower cost than any of the countries of Europe.

According to the survey, the British government had assisted industry through various measures. The report urged the Napoleonic regime to offer its support to industry, particularly financial support. With inadequate capital to develop, French industry could not produce goods in sufficient quantities to make them competitive and to make inroads into foreign markets. The report suggested various means to offer subsidies to industry.[208]

The reports of the Prefect of Police in Paris and the prefect of the Department of Isère, along with the survey of industry and other documents, present a snapshot of the state of the economy and the structure of labor during the middle period of Bonaparte's regime. On the one hand, they suggest that the government remained concerned primarily with the issue of worker unrest and discipline and, secondarily, with the quality of production. Both of these concerns could be addressed by the restoration of corporations. On the other hand, proponents of industry argued that in order to meet the British challenge, French industry needed financial support and unfettered self-direction, which would be more difficult if guilds were restored. Although the Napoleonic regime had clearly committed itself to subsidies and support for industry, it had not settled on a position with respect to the organization of labor. An internal debate continued, and the question remained unsettled.

As the artisanal sector declined, mechanization continued apace, a process that would culminate in the factory system of the nineteenth century. In another survey of Paris by the Prefect of Police, in such traditionally artisan-based trades as hatmaking or tanning, workshops employed a maximum of a few dozen workers – in hatmaking, the smallest number was seven and the largest was sixty, with the second largest having forty. In tanning, the smallest establishment listed had two workers and the largest had thirty.

The largest category in the survey, however, was cotton spinning and production, with dozens of facilities listed. Seven of them employed hundreds of workers, and the mammoth enterprise of Richard et Lenoir had 7,900.[209]

Bonaparte himself did not make any clear pronouncements on the issues of production or the organization of labor and his view is difficult to discern. On the matter of production, although the Napoleonic government offered subsidies to industry, Bonaparte distrusted businessmen. In his view, industry and trade were to serve the state – they could not be a product of profit motive

---

[208] AN F¹² 502, dossier 27, considerations on the current state of French industry, October 7, 1807.

[209] AN F¹² 1569, dossier Seine, state of manufacturing and other establishments ... February, 1807. For an analysis of the progress of mechanization in Rouen, Daly, *Inside Napoleonic France*, pp. 169–174.

alone.[210] Indeed, in his memorandum to Bonaparte on means to alleviate the 1806 economic slowdown in Paris, the Minister of the Interior, Champagny, had explained that one reason for the slowdown was an excess of production over consumption – a suggestion that the profit motive of businessmen to produce was harmful to the state.[211] In fact, the underlying premise of the Continental System, inaugurated during 1806, was to turn the productive capacity of Great Britain into a liability.

On the question of labor, there is an insinuation in a letter that Bonaparte was more concerned with full employment than with full production. During late 1807, in a letter to the Minister of the Interior, Emmanuell Cretet, Bonaparte stated that he attached "great importance and a great sense of pride in destroying mendicity."[212] Bonaparte's public works projects are well known, and also suggest the primacy he gave to employment. At the same time, however, the vigilance that the Prefect of Police in Paris exercised over workers and worker actions on public works projects attests to the attention given to order and control.[213]

CONCERN OVER LABOR UNREST AND RENEWED EFFORTS TO RESTORE GUILDS OUTSIDE OF PARIS

In the absence of a clear proscription of guilds, and with a lack of direction from the government, public officials and workers alike undertook initiatives to reestablish them. During December 1806, the prefect of the Department of Gironde in Bordeaux submitted a plan to facilitate the policing of the workers of Bordeaux, the major component of which, he admitted, was the idea of reestablishing corporations.

The plan authorized the mayor of Bordeaux to bring together the heads of workshops, along with workers in each trade, and to create from this pool a group of inspectors and sub-inspectors. The first choice would be made by the mayor, with the others chosen by the workers. The inspectors would be renewed annually, with half to be renewed each year. The inspectors and sub-inspectors would be charged with maintaining order among workers, noting their conduct, morals and means of existence. The creation of these positions would enable authorities, on demand, to gain information that they might desire. The primary purpose of the inspectors and sub-inspectors was to exercise surveillance and police functions over their subordinates.

The prefect acknowledged that entrusting workers with electing their overseers posed some problems. More critically, however, he asserted that because corporations had been suppressed, any measure that tended to reestablish

---

[210] Chaptal, *Mes Souvenirs sur Napoléon*, pp. 274–276; Tom Kemp, *Economic Forces in French History: An Essay on the Development of the French Economy 1760–1914* (London: Dobson, 1971), p. 100.
[211] AN F^{12} 513, dossier 2, letter of Minister of the Interior to Bonaparte, February 12, 1806.
[212] BHVP Ms. 1006, fol. 217.
[213] AN F^7 3749, dossier floréal year XIII, no. 44, no. 48.

them could only occur as a result of a law or an imperial decree. Any other aspect would fall within the purview of the Minister of the Interior.[214]

In another incident, the prefect of the Department of Haute-Vienne reported during May 1806, that ten brotherhoods had been formed in Limoges and that they were, in contravention of the Concordat, observing suppressed feast days. Although the focus of the police was "religious abuse," the report noted that the brotherhoods were comprised of workers and concerned themselves with such issues as the number of days of work and other conditions of workers.[215] There was a clear insinuation on the part of the prefect that the brotherhoods were guild-like structures.

The coexistence of artisanal and mechanized production would have allowed a restoration of corporations without major disruption of the workplace.[216] Furthermore, the imposition of what the authorities called "order and discipline" on workers, which could be accomplished through the reestablishment of corporations, was an attractive prospect. Indeed, the large textile facility of Richard in Paris, which employed thousands of workers, continued to attract the attention of the police.[217] At the same time, there was a risk that the reestablishment of guilds would offer workers a platform for concerted action, including inhibiting mechanization by attacking machines.

There were some grounds for such concern. During the middle period of the Bonapartist regime, there was unrest associated with mechanization. A police report in March 1805 noted that workers in a cotton factory in Lille – a factory that employed thousands of workers and with much production still done by hand – were threatening to destroy machinery that would reduce their number. The authorities responded forcefully, arresting and prosecuting many of them.[218]

In Sedan, a center of mechanization in textiles, the mayor wrote to the Minister of the Interior after receiving a letter from a manufacturer in his town who was seeking to introduce machines into his establishment. This had provoked an action by workers, who had sung a song as a signal for a work stoppage. Although two workers had been arrested and fined, other actions – including attempting to prevent others from seeking employment at the establishment – had continued. Obviously frustrated, the manufacturer went so far as to claim that the workers represented "a privileged corporation." The mayor noted that the manufacturer had previously introduced other machines and deserved the government's protection. The government ordered the prefect of the Department of Ardennes to investigate the matter.[219]

[214] AN F⁷ 3711, report of December 18, 1806.
[215] AN F⁷ 3753, dossier May, 1806, no. 22.
[216] On the coexistence of artisanal and mechanized production, AN F¹² 1568, dossier 4, stat. 1807.
[217] AN F⁷ 3753, dossier May 1806, no. 42.
[218] AN F⁷ 3749, dossier germinal year XIII, no. 6.
[219] AN F⁷ 3758, dossier 39, report of February 13, 1808.

Artisanal and mechanized production coexisted; in Strasbourg the mayor of the city noted that it was difficult to determine lines of demarcation between *"fabriques et manufactures"* and *"arts et métiers,"* characterizing such a line as "more or less wavering and little certain."[220] At the same time, however, there can be little doubt that the artisanal sphere was in distress and decline, and that its difficulties grew worse as the relative economic prosperity during the early years of the Napoleonic regime gave way to a recession by the latter part of 1806.[221]

Even earlier, in June 1806 the prefect of the Department of Loire-Inférieure reported that many artisans from Nantes – key makers, wheelwrights and joiners – were seeking passports to emigrate to the United States, citing a lack of work. Similarly, also in June 1806, the prefect of the Department of Rhône reported that hatmakers were being recruited by unspecified agents to work in Spain.[222] Key making and hat making were, in fact, two formerly artisanal trades in which mechanization was making inroads.[223]

ECONOMIC SLOWDOWN

The regime sought to address the economic slowdown. Even as he was occupied with the war against Prussia during the fall of 1806, Bonaparte allocated a large sum for the Minister of the Interior to use for one-year, interest-free loans to industry to prevent a suspension of production. The key condition of the loans was that receiving establishments had to maintain the same number of workers. Twenty-five producers accepted loans, but when repayment came due, economic conditions had deteriorated even further and most recipients requested an additional year for repayment. The Minister agreed, but at the expiration of the grace period, a majority asked for yet another extension. By 1809, only a small percentage of the loans had been repaid.[224]

Despite such efforts, the economic situation worsened, and workers were hard hit. During January 1807, the police chief of Lyon reported that workshops were languishing and that many individuals could not find work. The number of those seeking public assistance had doubled from the previous year, and because of the lack of work, many young men were volunteering for military service.[225]

---

[220] AN F¹² 1569, dossier Bas-Rhin, preliminary observations of mayor of Strasbourg, May 10, 1811.
[221] On the situation in Elbeuf, Kaplow, *Elbeuf During the Revolutionary Period*, p. 122.
[222] AN F⁷ 3753, dossier June 1806, no. 59, no. 60.
[223] AN F¹² 2283, letter of hat manufacturers of Lyon to Minister of the Interior, February 9, 1808; *Rapport du jury sur les produits de l'industrie française, présenté à S.E. M. de Champagny, Ministre de l'Intérieur; précédé du procès-verbal des opérations du jury* (Paris: Imprimerie Impériale, 1806). See also AN F¹² 1569, dossier Bas-Rhin, State of manufacturing ... May 10, 1811.
[224] AN F¹² 1559, dossier 1, *liasse* 4, notice on loans..., October 8, 1809.
[225] AN F⁷ 3755, no. 58.

During the following month, the police chief offered a less pessimistic assessment of the situation in Lyon, asserting that the hardship was concentrated among silk workers. The overriding concern of the regime was evident, however, in his observation that although many were suffering from the stagnation in commerce, discontent with the government had not yet been heard.[226] More than a year later, as unemployment continued to rise, the situation in Lyon remained a matter of concern.[227]

In some regions, the slowdown was so severe that even mechanized producers sought to emigrate.[228] A report from Toulouse during March 1807 noted that many French mechanics were leaving for Spain to establish cotton-spinning mills, leading to a suggestion that the government consider prohibiting the export of machines to Spain.[229] Indeed, during the year XIV (1805), a request by a French entrepreneur to send cotton-spinning machines to Spain had been decided by the Minister of the Interior personally, and he had refused to permit it.[230]

At the same time, other areas prospered, particularly Rouen and Alsace, with production surging between 1806 and 1808. Both of these regions, however, had a reliable supply of raw cotton, which was not the case elsewhere.[231]

During June 1808, the prefect of the Department of Aube reported that a placard had been posted in Troyes complaining of the high price of cotton and the layoffs that had resulted from those prices. Furthermore, the placard accused the prefect and the mayor of Troyes of contributing to the hardship among workers by allowing the employment of prisoners of war – a common practice during the Empire.[232]

For its part, the government sought to present prisoner labor as an economic benefit – in a state of the Empire draft during 1808, the use of prisoners was noted in a section entitled "support of industry."[233] Indeed, in some instances the use of British prisoners brought technological advances.[234]

To be sure, the use of prisoners was a benefit to producers because, although many worked on public works projects,[235] some worked in factories or on farms for public employers. During July 1806, the proprietor of a cotton-spinning facility in Creteil-sur-Marne sought permission from the Ministry

---

[226] AN F⁷ 3755, no. 76.

[227] AN F⁷ 3759, no. 39.

[228] On declines in textile production, Reddy, *The Rise of Market Culture*, pp. 68–69.

[229] AN F⁷ 3755, no. 90.

[230] AN F² 2180, dossier vendémiaire year XIV, 19 vendémiaire year XIV (October 11, 1805), no. 6; 26 vendémiaire year XIV (October 18, 1805), no. 3.

[231] Daly, *Inside Napoleonic France*, pp. 174–177; Ellis, *Napoleon's Continental Blockade*, pp. 157, 166, 178–179, 185–189.

[232] Indeed, there were 1,200 prisoners at Troyes working on a canal and the unemployment of workers was a matter of concern to Bonaparte. BHVP Ms. 1006, fol. 230. For more on the use of prisoners, AN F⁷ 3751, no. 56; AN F⁷ 3758, no. 7, no. 61.

[233] AN F¹c I 13, dossier Public Spirit (1808).

[234] Chassagne, *Le Coton et ses patrons*, pp. 254–255.

[235] See, for example, BHVP Ms. 1006, fol. 230.

of War to employ an English prisoner in his enterprise, and it was granted.[236] In Nevers, during the year XIV (1804), 191 of 1,517 prisoners held there were employed as workers.[237]

The use of prisoners on public works projects, such as canals, is not surprising, but their use in factories and on farms would have contributed to a lowering of wages or even unemployment. The anger among workers, then, is understandable – according to the prefect there were 10,000 unemployed individuals in Troyes.[238]

During April 1808, the prefect of the Department of Seine-Inférieure reported that producers had laid off a portion of their workforce and reduced the hours of remaining workers. There would soon be 12,000 unemployed in Rouen, and Elbeuf, Bolbec, Yvetot and other towns of the department were in the same situation. The prefect suggested that the government subsidize the cost of raw materials for producers in order to maintain production and prevent more layoffs.[239]

The prospect of massive unemployment, which the Napoleonic regime had not yet had to confront, was undoubtedly unsettling. The law of 22 germinal year XI provided for discipline of workers in the workplace, but outside of the workshop there was no institution, except the police, to oversee workers, as guilds had done under the Old Regime. Whether or not the reports of rising unemployment instigated them is not clear, but it is indisputable that during the period after these reports were furnished, the Prefect of Police in Paris, as well as other officials, renewed their efforts to restore corporations. Furthermore, there is a correlation between the trades earlier listed by the prefect as potentially volatile and those in which attempts at reestablishment occurred.

One critical group cited by the prefect in his report of March 1807, a group with a significance out of proportion to its numbers, was that listed as "printing and paper." The prefect had asserted that there did not exist workers "more insubordinate, more inclined toward coalition and tumult."[240] The years of the Consulate had seen a crisis in the publishing world, with several bankruptcies, and some printers sought a reduction in the number of printers from the government to restore stability to the trade.[241] Booksellers, who were of course closely associated with printers, also sought reregulation from the government, with one of them pointing out that in 1776 Turgot had exempted the printing and publishing trades from his edicts for reasons of public order and safety. Although there was some disagreement among booksellers on the degree of reregulation to seek, the desire for it was strong. As a result, during

---

[236] AN F^{12} 2180, dossier July 1806, entry of July 25, 1806.
[237] AN F^7 3751, no. 76.
[238] AN F^7 3759, no. 42.
[239] AN F^7 3759, no. 97.
[240] AN F^{12} 502, dossier 11, statistics of workers of Paris, May 30, 1807.
[241] What follows is based on Hesse, *Publishing and Cultural Politics in Revolutionary Paris*, pp. 205–228.

1808, despite the opposition of the Ministry of Police to the reorganization of the book trade in particular and to the reestablishment of guilds in general,[242] the Council of State began to hold discussions on regulations for the book trade, and in February 1810, primarily for the purpose of surveillance of it, the government established the Administration of the Book Trade.

The new body cannot be considered analogous to a guild, not least because its jurisdiction was national, whereas the guilds of printers and booksellers had been municipal in scope. At the same time, however, the Administration of the Book Trade limited the number of printers in Paris and required each to have at least four presses, and all new publishers and booksellers had to offer evidence of "clean living and good morals, as well as their attachment to the fatherland and the sovereign." The legislation also provided for a group of inspectors to oversee the book trade, along with police and customs officials.

Again, although it should not be regarded as a guild, the Administration of the Book Trade reinstated many of the qualities of guilds. By setting a limit on the number of printers, it overturned the free market in labor and access to all trades that had been in place since the abolition of corporations. Furthermore, by exercising oversight of members and acting as an auxiliary to public authority, the establishment of the administration indicated that the Napoleonic regime was assuming a stance at least compatible with the reestablishment of guilds.

Another group the prefect had cited as particularly volatile were men associated with building trades, and during 1810 he took action in this sector, as well. Dubois sought the advice of the Minister of the Interior, who asked that the heads of the Second and Third Divisions of his ministry work on a response to a project to police masons, carpenters, joiners and key makers in Paris.

Fauchot, the head of the Second Division, which was responsible for subsidies to aid the development of industry and had consistently opposed any restoration of corporations, protested that the project's first article presupposed as settled a question that was not yet decided – the reestablishment of guilds. He sought a rewording of the article in a manner that was more ambiguous, arguing that the suppression of guilds did not appear to prohibit the right of assembling masters and giving them representatives who would become their conduit to public authority, as had already been done with bakers and butchers. Fauchot proposed that the masters of each *arrondissement* form a syndicate to name "a central representative" who would be in contact with the Prefect of Police.[243]

Despite Fauchot's request, the project, which was presented to the Council of State on July 14, 1810, maintained the word *"corporation"* – each of the four occupations would be organized into one. The proposal also referred to the "privileges of masters," which included the exclusive right to practice

[242] AN F^{12} 268^1, no. 56 (April 10, 1808).
[243] AN F^{13} 521, letter of Fauchot, April 2, 1810. I would like to thank Allan Potofsky for calling my attention to this document.

their trade – "a natural consequence of the establishment into a corporation," according to the report.

Although the bill required a proof of skill before one could become a member of a corporation, it is clear that the primary purposes of the proposal were surveillance and control. The Council of State made clear that it wanted to avoid general assemblies of workers. In addition, each guild had to deposit a bond that would serve as a guarantee that the masters would carry out the obligations imposed on them – the council, in fact, characterized the bond as a "restraint." Furthermore, the project called for stricter enforcement of regulations related to workers' passbooks, as these were widely ignored in building trades.[244]

The judgment of Allan Potofsky on the reestablishment of a corporate structure in the building trades is applicable to most of the guild-like bodies organized by the Napoleonic regime:

In the *ancien régime* idea of corporations, the police and the masters, on paper at least, celebrated their organic cohesion. During the Napoleonic revival, they openly regarded each other with distrust about each others' natural penchant for, respectively, control and profit.[245]

His conclusion that "in reviving guilds, Napoleonic administrators thus transformed them into rational instruments of social administration" is even more apposite.[246]

Indeed, during 1810 the regime contemplated a more comprehensive plan for restoring guilds. During 1810 the Minister of the Interior, Jean-Pierre Bachasson, Comte de Montalivet, asked Regnaud de Saint-Jean d'Angély for a plan that the latter had drafted during the year XI on *"la police des arts et métiers."* Regnaud sent the plan in March, with an observation that Montalivet would find in the project "the organization of guilds as I knew it and as I conceive it still."[247] Because Regnaud asked that the plan be returned to him, which it was on April 27, it is unfortunately not joined to the cover letter in the archives. Although the minister's focus seems to have been issues in the building trades, there was clearly a larger effort under consideration.[248]

The existence of a potentially more comprehensive project is corroborated by an allusion made by Fiévée in July 1810 to a discussion soon to open in the Council of State "on the utility or danger of the reestablishment of guilds." He wrote Bonaparte that he would not address the issue of their utility or danger,

---

[244] Napoleonica.org, *Projet de décret présenté par le Conseiller d'état Préfet de Police, sur le réunion en corporations des maçons, charpentiers, serruriers et menuisiers*, no. 2044bis, July 14, 1810.

[245] Potofsky, "The Builders of Modern Paris," pp. 356–357.

[246] *Ibid.*, p. 357.

[247] AN F[13] 521, letter of Regnaud to Montalivet, March 28, 1810.

[248] AN F[13] 521, letter of Minister of the Interior to Regnaud de Saint-Jean d'Angély, April 27, 1810. Once again, I would like to thank Allan Potofsky for bringing this carton to my attention.

but there was a possibility of their reestablishment, and his conclusion was that their "resurrection" was impossible.

Although some bodies had been reestablished, this had been done under the authority of the police because they were related to the provisioning of the city or as a result of security needs. With respect to commerce and industry, however, it would be impossible to make classifications, and especially to "imprison them in regulations," and he reiterated that he believed that it was impossible "to put the majority of material interests in guilds."[249]

On July 14, 1810, the same day the project for corporations in the building trades was considered, Regnaud de Saint-Jean d'Angély put forward a preliminary report on the profession of merchants and on arts and trades. The project was structured as a series of seven questions that summarized the view of the Interior Section of the Council of State. The first question posed was whether there would be corporations of merchants and of trades, and the answer was affirmative. To the question of where they would be established, the section responded that they would be set up in towns in which it would be appropriate either because of the size of their population or the extent of their industry. According to the third query, they would be established by public administration regulations, through the Ministry of the Interior acting on the advice of the mayor, sub-prefect and prefect. The remaining questions stipulated that various analogous or non-analogous professions could be in the same body, that apprenticeship and a journeyman period, along with a test of skill, would be required and other matters.[250]

Regnaud de Saint-Jean d'Angély presented a fuller report to the Council of State on August 11, 1810. The project opened with a statement that the administration demanded new regulations for oversight of merchants and artisans and further asserted that those engaged in these activities sought new regulations. The questions of the utility and necessity of corporations had long been discussed and different ideas had been put forward and debated.

According to Regnaud, Bonaparte, momentarily discarding all systems and not sanctioning any theory, wished to determine the facts by referring to experience. Regnaud informed the Council of State that he wished to present a small number of facts and to establish the questions to which these facts had given rise.

In a reflection of the regime's priorities, the first section of the project addressed discipline and control. In major and even smaller towns, the report claimed, administrators complained of the difficulty and even impossibility of surveillance over artisans and workers – it asserted that even the number of those who practiced various occupations was unknown. To indicate the abuses that were present, the report cited a particularly egregious case in which a key

---

[249] Fiévée, *Correspondance et relations … avec Bonaparte*, III: 71–76.
[250] Napoleonica.org, *Projet sur la profession de marchand et sur les arts et métiers*, no. 2044ter, July 14, 1810.

maker had been affiliated with a ring of burglars.[251] It adduced several other problems and stated that difficulties were to be found all over France.

Many areas were clamoring for councils of arbitrators (*conseils de prud'hommes*) as a solution to abuses, but the report argued that such councils were not suitable for all towns. The councils had been established initially in Lyon in 1806. They sought to use arbitration rather than the force of public officials to resolve labor disputes – the law of 22 germinal year XI had given police and municipal authorities jurisdiction in these matters. Similar bodies were subsequently established in other localities, and contemporaries regarded them as successful, rendering prompt and impartial decisions.[252] The report contended, however, that even in those towns in which they operated, the councils of arbitrators did not eradicate malfeasance because they did not have jurisdiction over all categories of work.

The report noted that the Council of State had, on many occasions, refused requests to reestablish guilds or to allow trades or occupations to elect officials – refusals that had been driven by "the nature of things" and "the force of circumstances." The report noted that a number of trades in Paris had been organized under the authority of the police, although it appeared to express skepticism about the legality of these bodies, stating that in forming them the police had been driven by a sense of the advantages of doing so and that they would be all the more welcome if their organization had the legality that was otherwise lacking. It praised the results of the reorganization of bakers and butchers in Paris, both of which had been approved by the central government.

After examining other aspects of the issue, the project asserted that in the current state of affairs commerce had no organ for addressing itself to administration and administration had no organ for making itself heard. The report advocated a reestablishment of guilds of merchants and artisans, as well as regulations on certain types of manufacturing.[253]

Regnaud's recommendations were not adopted, and never again did the Council of State consider a broad reestablishment of corporations. It did, however, authorize the establishment of a guild of bakers in Bordeaux on October 25, 1810, and organized many corporations of bakers in subsequent years.[254]

This is not surprising, since assuring the bread supply was a means of stemming worker unrest. Indeed, the regime's deep concern over labor unrest is

---

[251] Whether it was in response to Regnaud's assertion that the number of workers in various occupations was unknown cannot be determined, but during 1811 a survey of Paris was conducted that included the number of workers in various trades, including key makers. The survey should not be considered a reliable guide, but it does demonstrate the survival of artisanal sectors even without corporations. BHVP Ms. 35.

[252] Costaz, *Histoire de l'administration en France*, 2: 255–259.

[253] Napoleonica.org, *Rapport sur l'exercice de la profession de marchands et les arts et métiers*, no. 2089, August 11, 1810.

[254] Napoleonica.org, *Rapport et projets de décret. Mesure pour faire cesser des abus qui se sont introduits dans le commerce de boulangerie*, no. 2163, October 25, 1810.

evident in its handling of a situation involving building workers at Versailles during the spring of 1810. In May that year workers employed at the palace and the two Trianons had come together to seek an increase in their daily wage, and by threats of incitement were preventing others from working at the site. The prefect of the Department of Seine-et-Oise, citing the law of 22 germinal year XI, ordered the mayor of Versailles "to maintain subordination among workers" and placed substantial armed force at his disposition in order to break up gatherings of workers and arrest instigators.[255] As a work site, the palace at Versailles was relatively isolated, but the Napoleonic authorities did not want labor unrest spreading to Paris, which was itself experiencing worker actions.

The magnitude of force to be deployed against workers reveals the regime's apprehension and a reason why the idea of reviving guilds made a resurgence. Nevertheless, although corporations of bakers would be reestablished in several provincial cities during 1813, the movement to restore guilds had crested.

During July 1810, a fire occurred at the Hôtel Schwarzenberg, the Austrian embassy, during a ball given in honor of the marriage of Napoleon and Marie-Louise, leading to an evacuation that produced many injuries. Dubois, the Prefect of Police, was not in attendance, although he had been invited, and his absence angered Bonaparte. The incident led to Dubois's disgrace and on October 14, 1810, he was called to the Council of State, bringing his career as prefect to an end.[256] Dubois had been a major figure in the effort to restore guilds – of the thirteen bodies cited by the Council of State as organized by the prefect, twelve had been created since 1808 – and his departure slowed the drive for their reestablishment.

If the dismissal of Dubois was the most immediate cause of the loss of momentum, two other factors would have a significant role in stemming any further attempts to restore guilds. On June 26, 1810, the government founded the General Council on Factories and Manufacturing (Conseil général des fabriques et manufactures), a body of sixty men chosen by Bonaparte from a list of active manufacturers submitted by the Minister of the Interior. The decree specified that the textile industry in particular had to be represented in the council's membership and, because the textile sector was the most advanced in mechanization, the Council on Manufacturing would become a staunch opponent of any effort to reestablish guilds.[257]

The Minister of the Interior was the *ex-officio* president of the council, but the vice-president – chosen by the minister from the council – conducted the

---

[255] AN F¹³ 521, decree of prefect of Seine-et-Oise, May 28, 1810.

[256] *Dictionnaire de biographie française*, 11: 956; Jean Tulard, *Paris et son administration (1800–1830)* (Paris: Commission des Travaux Historiques, 1976), p. 119.

[257] On the founding of the council, *Almanach Impérial 1811*, p. 205; the best treatments of the early history of the council are Bertrand Gille, *Le Conseil général des manufactures: Inventaire analytique des procès-verbaux 1810–1829* (Paris: S.E.V.P.E.N., 1961) and Richard J. Barker, "The Conseil général des Manufactures under Napoleon (1810–1814)," *French Historical Studies* 6 (1969): 185–213.

meetings. The vice-president was Guillaume Ternaux, an important textile manufacturer who employed thousands of workers in several factories across France. Ternaux had gained recognition for his innovative manufacturing efforts, winning gold medals at the industrial exhibitions of the years IX and 1806, and he provided dynamic and effective leadership to the council.[258]

From the beginning, in fact, the council found itself dealing with the question of guilds. At its ninth meeting, on October 25, 1810, the council, without any old or new business on its agenda, undertook an examination of the issues of greatest importance to manufacturing and the arts. The first issue to emerge was that of the advantages and disadvantages of corporations, along with regulations that would facilitate manufacturing – the two recommendations made by Regnaud in the Council of State on August 11. The two issues were linked, because consideration of regulations on fabrication, particularly with respect to quality, brought discussion back to the old mode of inspections by guild officers to enforce quality.

The council unanimously opposed any reestablishment of guilds and sought a system more favorable to enterprise and industry. Reflecting continuing discontent with the law of 22 germinal year XI, the issues on which the council sought improvement were the relationship between employers and workers and workers and apprentices – indeed, the council wanted to achieve more precision on the means "to maintain order and subordination." The members of the council also recognized that it would be inadvisable to impose production regulations in different areas of manufacture, but wanted to make it possible to offer guarantees to consumers about the quality of products.

The council realized that these matters were too extensive to be resolved at a single meeting, but aspired to draft a "manufacturing code" that would encompass many of the issues of concern. The council members decided that they would make the reputation of French industry their primary responsibility. They also agreed to discuss these issues at greater length when there were no old or new items on the agenda.[259] Throughout this early period, however, the council maintained a consistently strong stand against reestablishing guilds or specifying modes of production.[260]

The second factor in slowing any effort to reestablish guilds was a reorganization of the Ministry of the Interior in early 1812. The Second Division, which had labor and manufacturing as part of its responsibilities, was removed from the Ministry of the Interior and elevated to a separate ministry, the Ministry of Manufacturing and Commerce. The new, enhanced status for a branch that had consistently opposed the reestablishment of guilds and

---

[258] On Ternaux, the definitive work is that of L.M. Lomüller, *Guillaume Ternaux, 1763–1833: Créateur de la première intégration industrielle française* (Paris: Cabro d'Or, 1978). See also *Biographie universelle, ancienne et moderne*, 41: 164–166; *Nouvelle biographie générale*, 44: 1002–1004.

[259] AN F¹²* 194, fols. 17–18.

[260] AN F¹²* 194, fols. 27–29.

favored industry gave it greater influence over the direction of both labor policy and economic development.

The renewed debate on guilds and the formation of the Council on Manufacturing occurred at the beginning of a major economic crisis that lasted for the remainder of the Napoleonic regime.[261] Indeed, Odette Viennet argued that the crisis was the catalyst for the creation of the new Ministry of Manufacturing and Commerce.[262] Although she treated the crisis mainly as a turning point in the attitude of much of occupied Europe toward France, within France it revealed the disadvantages of industrialization. The four industrial exhibitions had created a positive image of industry as modern and efficient, but the crisis now served to reveal the potential problems of industrial production.

The regime of guilds had never been associated with a crisis of this magnitude, which may have prolonged the idea of their reestablishment as worthy of consideration. In fact, after the restoration of the Bourbon monarchy there was an expectation that guilds would be restored, but the Crown ultimately chose to forego their reestablishment and to continue its commitment to mechanization of production and development of industry.

* * * * * * *

The overthrow of the Directory by Napoleon Bonaparte in 1799 did away with the Constitution of the Year III, destroying the constitutional proscription of corporations and effectively reopening the question of their reestablishment. Indeed, from its beginning the Bonapartist government considered reestablishing guilds, and the issue resurfaced on multiple occasions during the first decade of the regime, in both governmental deliberations and public debate. These were, in fact, the most extensive discussions on corporations since their abolition by Turgot nearly a quarter of a century earlier. Such examinations usually occurred during times of economic difficulty and were intended to maintain stability and order, again illustrating the contingent and often reactive nature of Napoleonic policy on corporations.

The Napoleonic administrators and counselors who advocated the reestablishment of guilds were not nostalgic sentimentalists seeking to hold back modernity. Rather, they were practical men who understood the inadequacy of previous legislation, especially the law of 22 germinal year XI. However comprehensive it may have appeared on paper, the law had failed to correct the problems it was supposed to address. The police in Paris and prefects in the departments were aware of the law's deficiencies, but in the more rarefied environment of the Ministry of the Interior they were virtually unknown. This is why Morgue had been shocked by the conditions he encountered in Sedan

---

[261] Odette Viennet, *Napoléon et l'industrie française: la crise de 1810–1811* (Paris: Plon, 1947). For examinations of the crisis in one locale, Kaplow, *Elbeuf During the Revolutionary Period*, pp. 123–126; Becchia, *La Draperie d'Elbeuf*, pp. 434–435.

[262] Viennet, *Napoléon et l'industrie française*, pp. 275–276.

and why he was so apologetic that his correspondence could be interpreted as supporting a restoration of corporations. In retrospect, however, it appeared that guilds had been more effective in areas such as maintaining worker discipline and quality in production. In addition, they were known and familiar, which is why the idea of reviving them recurred – it was a matter of officials continuing to seek a solution to lingering problems.

As much as stability and order were of paramount importance, the Napoleonic government remained concerned that a reestablishment of corporations could provide a platform to oppose or hinder mechanization of production. The potential disruption that a restoration of guilds could pose to mechanization became a primary argument against their re-creation.

Just as the public debate was divided on the issue of guilds, so, too, was the Napoleonic government. Seeking to assure the safety and integrity of the food supply of Paris, the central government reestablished bodies of bakers and butchers in the city under the Consulate. With that precedent established, during the Empire – primarily between 1808 and 1810 – the Prefect of Police in Paris organized bodies of many other trades. Emulating the prefect, the General Commissioners of Police in Lyon and Bordeaux reestablished bodies of bakers in their cities, although these appear to have been quashed by the central government. In addition, prefects of departments considered reestablishing corporations within their jurisdiction.

Within the government, the Ministry of the Interior led the opposition to the reestablishment of guilds and, after the reorganization of bakers and butchers in Paris, the Council of State reinforced this resistance. After the General Council on Factories and Manufacturing came into existence during June 1810, it formed an additional rampart against any reestablishment of guilds.

In the final analysis, it is apparent that the Napoleonic government had recognizable criteria from which to define limits on the reestablishment of bodies reminiscent of the former guilds. Initially, in fact, the boundaries of the economy and government were being worked out – the reestablishment of the corporation of butchers, in particular, was justified in terms of public health more than police of the trade. With the benefit of hindsight, it is evident that in matters of public order or safety of the food supply, as with bakers and butchers, or if it was a question of control of public opinion or politics, as with printers and booksellers or barristers, organized in 1810 and 1811, respectively, the Bonapartist government was willing to establish bodies evocative of Old Regime corporations.[263]

If the guidelines for bodies restored by the central government are readily identifiable, the *corps* formed by the Prefect of Police in Paris presented a more confusing picture – it is difficult, for example, to discern a public

[263] See Hesse, *Publishing and Cultural Politics*, pp. 205–248; Michael P. Fitzsimmons, *The Parisian Order of Barristers and the French Revolution* (Cambridge, MA: Harvard University Press, 1987), pp. 154–192. Another corporate-like institution created by the Bonapartist government for political control could also be cited – that of the electoral colleges established by Bonaparte. Sydenham, *The First French Republic*, p. 300.

policy consideration behind a body of wallpaper manufacturers and sellers. Indeed, between 1791 and 1801, the Parisian public had seen an official policy of absolute prohibition of corporations; between 1801 and 1810, however, it had seen fifteen trade or service occupations organized into bodies analogous to guilds. The creation by the central government of a body of printers and booksellers in 1810 and the resurrection of the Order of Barristers in Paris in 1811 seemed to represent a continuation of this trend.

It is not surprising, then, that contemporaries, especially in Paris, continued to view the prospect of a return of guilds as not only possible, but probable. The extension of bodies of bakers to numerous cities and towns across France after 1810 undoubtedly strengthened this belief, as did the absence of a clear decision against them by the government.

If there was a time during the revolutionary and Napoleonic epoch when guilds might have been restored, it was the first decade of Bonaparte's rule – the Bonapartist government was more pragmatic than ideological, and during most of its existence the regime continuously thought of itself as evolving.[264] The Bonapartist government did seek to address many of the problems created by the abolition of corporations more comprehensively than any of its revolutionary predecessors. The laws of 22 germinal and 12 frimaire year XI dealt with apprenticeships, quality control and oversight of workers, but were often viewed as inadequate.

Ultimately, however, the regime did not reorganize corporations – it elected to commit itself to modernization and mechanization of production, a decision signified in particular by the establishment of the General Council on Factories and Manufacturing and of the Ministry of Manufacturing and Commerce. This commitment, however, occurred in the midst of a major economic crisis that continued until the end of the Napoleonic era. The crisis revealed the disadvantages of modernization and mechanization of production, and the return of the Bourbon dynasty after the fall of Bonaparte led to an expectation that Revolutionary reforms would be overturned, and one aspect of that policy would be a reestablishment of guilds.

[264] Sydenham, *The First French Republic*, p. 297.

4

The Triumph of Mechanization, 1812–1821

> The king did not wish that honorable perseverance and new claims to national gratitude remain unrewarded. His Majesty has conferred the title of baron upon MM. Ternaux and Oberkampf, who have rendered, and continue to render, distinguished services to our industry.
>
> *Gazette Nationale, ou le Moniteur universel*, December 6, 1819

In January 1812, the government reorganized the Ministry of the Interior, removing the Second Division, which favored mechanized industry and opposed the reestablishment of guilds, and elevating it by creating a new ministry, the Ministry of Manufacturing and Commerce. From this larger platform, the new ministry continued to support mechanization of production and to stem any movement toward restoring corporations. In 1814, in an action that seemed to presage a rolling-back of revolutionary and Napoleonic reforms or policies, the restored Bourbon monarchy abolished the Ministry of Manufacturing and Commerce and reintegrated it into the Ministry of the Interior. Amid expectations that the Bourbon regime would reestablish guilds, which were perceived as a quintessential monarchical institution, a pamphlet debate began on that issue. The monarchy temporized, but in 1819 the Ministry of the Interior revived the industrial exhibition, thereby signaling its endorsement of mechanization over the reestablishment of guilds.

THE CREATION OF THE MINISTRY OF MANUFACTURING AND COMMERCE

A decree of January 19, 1812, had created the Ministry of Manufacturing and Commerce, with a mandate to manage all internal and external trade, as well as the formation and administration of the manufacture of "indigenous products." It may have been this mandate, particularly the use of the word "administration," that gave hope to a former inspector of manufactures that this position, or one analogous to it, would be reestablished.[1]

There were four divisions within the new ministry, all of them drawn from the Ministry of the Interior. Indeed, the duties assumed by the Ministry of Manufacturing and Commerce had been regarded as among the most important functions of the Ministry of the Interior.[2] Although much of his concern was the prospect of large-scale unemployment, as early as March 1807 Bonaparte had made it abundantly clear that he wanted the government to assist large enterprises rather than artisanal trades,[3] and the creation of the Ministry of Manufacturing and Commerce reflected this priority.

The change of focus is evident in the office led by Claude-Anthelme Costaz. Within the Ministry of the Interior, he had headed the Office of Arts and Manufacturing, with the first part of the term – arts – encompassing artisanal trades (*arts et métiers*). In fact, the responsibilities of the Office of Arts and Manufacturing had included artisanal trades, the policing of workshops and workers, and laws related to manufacturing and artisanal trades (*manufactures et aux arts*).[4] Within the new Ministry of Manufacturing and Commerce, however, Costaz led the division of Factories and Manufacturing (*Fabriques et Manufactures*). The first office of this division had among its responsibilities the perfection and statistical tracking of manufacturing and oversight of the Council on Manufacturing and other bodies associated with manufacturing. In the enumeration of duties, there was no reference to *arts* or to *arts et métiers*.[5]

The Minister of Manufacturing and Commerce was Jean-Baptiste Collin, Comte de Sussy, a lesser figure of the Empire of whom relatively little is known. He was a customs official when the coup of Brumaire occurred, and shortly thereafter he attracted the attention of Bonaparte, who was seeking capable men to serve him. Collin became a member of the Council of State in the section on finances and, after demonstrating his abilities by carrying out several important missions, Bonaparte appointed him in 1801 as Director-General of the Customs Bureau – indeed, he received the post after he presented the proposal for establishing the bureau to the Legislative Body. He was made a count of the Empire – the Comte de Sussy – and received the Cross of the Grand Officer of the Legion of Honor. Ultimately, it was recognition of the influence that customs policy had on commerce that led to the idea of removing commerce from the purview of the Ministry of the Interior and establishing a separate ministry, that being the Ministry of Manufacturing and Commerce.[6]

[1] IISH Bruyard Papers, *liasse 196, liasse 197.*
[2] AN AF IV 1291[A], dossier 226, fol. 36, report of June 28, 1812.
[3] AN F[12] 4639, dossier 4, copy of letter of Bonaparte, March 27, 1807.
[4] *Alamanach Impérial 1811*, pp. 202–203.
[5] *Almanach Impérial 1812*, pp. 254–255.
[6] *Biographie universelle et portative des contemporains, ou Dictionnaire historique des hommes savantes, et des hommes morts depuis 1788 jusqu'à nos jours, qui se sont fait remarquer chez la plupart des peuples, et particulièrement en France, par leurs écrits, leurs actions,*

Another figure of critical importance was Costaz, who became head of the Third Division – Factories and Manufacturing – in the new ministry. Also known as a capable administrator, he had been in the Ministry of the Interior – in the section on commerce and agriculture, where he had had responsibilities for both artisanal and mechanized production – for more than fifteen years. In his new post, however, shorn of any responsibilities for trade crafts, Costaz could pursue in an untrammeled manner the industrial policy that he had long favored, and contemporaries credited him with aiding the advance of industry in France.[7]

The Ministry of Manufacturing and Commerce had a short life, and unfortunately there are few records that offer insight into its deliberations or operations. Given the outlook of Collin de Sussy and Costaz, however, there can be little doubt that the ministry pursued a policy that favored mechanization and the maintenance of order among workers. In response to a question from the prefect of the Department of Rhône, for example, one of the first decisions rendered by the ministry declared that female workers in the factories of Lyon – a large percentage of workers – were subject to the law requiring passbooks. This was the only trade in which women were subject to the *livret*, but because there was some concern that employers might seek to extort sexual favors from women in return for satisfactory notations, the authorities were willing to allow greater latitude for them in meeting the requirement.[8] Nevertheless, the goal of providing advantageous conditions for factory owners, especially through subjection of workers to discipline, is clear.

In another instance, in response to a question from Troyes, the ministry reaffirmed an earlier decision of the Ministry of the Interior under which the only unfavorable information that could be entered into a worker's passbook was that related to performance in the factory or workshop. Any activities outside of the workplace that might fall under "morals and probity," such as drinking and fighting, could not be included. Employers had to limit themselves to the matter of whether a worker had fulfilled the obligations of the contract into which he had entered. Unfavorable comments that were not related to work performance – from "another order of things," as the minister characterized it – could lead to difficulties for workers in procuring future work, and to possible hardship or death.

On this occasion, the ministry's concern was not solicitude for the situation of workers, but to assure a reliable workforce, and it did not want to see

leurs talents, leurs vertus ou leurs crimes, 5 vols. Alphonse Rabbe, Claude Augustin Vieilh de Boisjolin and Charles Claude Birret de Sainte-Preuve, eds. (Paris: F.G. Levrault, 1834), I: 1040.

[7] *Ibid.*, I: 1112. On his devotion to mechanization and industry, Claude-Anthelme Costaz, *Essai sur l'administration de l'agriculture, du commerce, des manufactures et des subsistances* (Paris: Huzard, 1818), pp. 163, 297–298, 305–306, 402–405.

[8] AN F^{12} 4648, dossier 1, letter on behalf of prefect of Department of Rhône to Minister of Interior, January 3, 1812; letter of Minister of Manufacturing and Commerce to prefect of Department of Rhône, January 18, 1812.

the labor pool reduced for extraneous reasons. The intent of the decision on *livrets* was simply to distinguish "the faithful and hardworking man from the one who is not."[9]

Another responsibility assigned to the Ministry of Manufacturing and Commerce was that of the food supply, and this task produced an ironic turn of events – the Ministry of Manufacturing and Commerce, which strongly opposed the reestablishment of guilds, restored bodies of bakers throughout France. During late 1811 a provisioning crisis began to develop in Paris, compounded somewhat by individuals manipulating the use of government-subsidized flour to their benefit. One response was the transfer of responsibility for the food supply from the Ministry of the Interior to the Ministry of Manufacturing and Commerce, due mainly to a belief that Collin de Sussy understood the nature of the grain trade better than Montalivet, the Minister of the Interior.[10] Shortly afterward, however, during the spring of 1812, the price of flour rose precipitously, leading Bonaparte to convene an extraordinary meeting of the Subsistence Council. Unrest mounted in Paris and beyond, especially in Normandy – indeed, a violent uprising occurred in Caen, which the government severely repressed.[11]

During May Bonaparte convened a meeting at Saint-Cloud at which he ordered the Prefect of Police to search the forty or fifty individuals in Paris and its suburbs who conducted commerce in grains and flour, all of whom would have to reveal their purchases and prepare an inventory of the grains and flour in their possession. The prefect would verify each declaration and then the stocks were to be sent to the food markets in Paris. The prefect was to report to Bonaparte the following day on the results of this operation. Bonaparte also prohibited bread from leaving Paris and ordered flour to be distributed throughout the city, among other measures.[12]

Bonaparte's intervention has been characterized as a nearly Jacobin solution, and culminated in two decrees. The first limited all grain sales to public market sites and was designed to bolster public confidence in the grain supply. The second mandated price controls over grains – the 1812 Maximums.[13]

Clearly, however, more than dramatic interventions were required to stabilize the grain supply. Ultimately, as Judith Miller noted, Napoleonic administrators of the food supply resorted to several Old Regime methods,[14] and the reestablishment of guilds of bakers was one of them.

---

[9] AN F[12] 4648, dossier 1, letter of president of *Conseil des prud'hommes* of Troyes to Minister of Manufacturing and Commerce, November 28, 1812; undated draft of reply of minister to president of *Conseil des prud'hommes* of Troyes, with the quotation from the latter.

[10] Etienne-Denis Pasquier, *Histoire de mon temps: Mémoires du Chancelier Pasquier*, 3 vols. (Paris: Plon-Nourrit, 1894), I: 502.

[11] *Ibid.*, I: 503–509.

[12] *Ibid.*, I: 504–507.

[13] Judith A. Miller, *Mastering the Market: The State and the Grain Trade in Northern France, 1700–1860* (New York: Cambridge University Press, 1999), p. 199.

[14] *Ibid.*, p. 203.

Throughout 1813, in an attempt to assure the bread supply, the Ministry of Manufacturing and Commerce sought to establish bodies to conduct commerce for bakers in cities and towns in departments outside of Paris. It established guilds of bakers in such cities and towns as Lille, Besançon, Strasbourg, Nantes, Troyes, Dijon, Versailles, Rouen, La Rochelle, Amiens, Nîmes and Rochefort.[15] It also addressed aspects of the food supply in Paris – the wine trade, the sale of freshwater fish and abuses in the bread trade.[16]

One of the members of the Subsistence Council established by Bonaparte was Dubois, the former Prefect of Police in Paris. He had organized the bakers of Paris during 1801, and the Paris structure was the model used in reorganizing guilds of bakers in outlying cities and towns during 1813.

The guild of bakers in Lyon, for example, based on a project presented by Dubois in the Council of State in late September 1813, was reorganized on November 6, 1813, and placed under the authority of the prefect of the Department of Rhône. In accordance with the Paris prototype for bakers, exercise of the trade required the authorization of the prefect, a mandatory deposit of flour in a public warehouse and a stock of flour equivalent to three months of bread production at one's domicile. The requirement varied according to one of three classifications, based on one's daily output of baking. The bakers were also to choose from among their ranks twenty-four electors, who in turn would elect four syndics to oversee the flour deposits. Finally, the regulations stipulated the qualities, weights and prices of breads.[17]

A scholar of the bakers of Lyon noted that the syndic and his assistants comprised a police of the trade, in the service of the municipality but at the expense of bakers. She argued that the originality of the Napoleonic regulations did not lie in the requirement of a flour reserve, but in removing the police from the supervision of bakers' grain stocks.[18]

Although there were regional variations, in Lyon the reestablishment of the bakers' guild was followed by a long period of stable, relatively low grain prices, except for a crisis during 1817.[19] In a similar vein, Judith Miller asserted that "the Restoration represented a significant moment in the maturation of provisioning policies."[20] It is unclear whether contemporaries perceived a correlation between the reestablishment of bodies of bakers and the stabilization of grain prices, but if so, it would undoubtedly have strengthened the case of those who argued for the reestablishment of guilds under the Restoration.

The provisioning crisis that led to the restoration of guilds of bakers throughout France during 1813 was a component of the larger economic crisis that had

---

[15] AN F[12] 511[B], Ministry of Manufacturing and Commerce, reports of projects and decrees to send back to Council of State, *passim*.

[16] *Ibid.*, entries of January 20, 1813; July 21, 1813; November 24, 1813.

[17] Napoleonica.org., *Rapport et projets de décret relatifs au commerce de la boulangerie dans la ville de Lyon*, no. 2976, September 23, 1813; September 27, 1813; Angleraud, *Les Boulangers lyonnais*, pp. 41–42.

[18] Angleraud, *Les Boulangers lyonnais*, p. 43.

[19] *Ibid.*, pp. 33, 36.

[20] Miller, *Mastering the Market*, p. 237.

engulfed the Empire beginning in 1810. The magnitude of the crisis and the degree of concern it generated at the highest levels of government are apparent in correspondence between the Minister of Police and the Minister of the Interior. During March 1811, the Minister of Police wrote to the Minister of the Interior and, specifying that the letter be read by him only, notified him that the prefect of the Department of Seine-Inférieure had apprised him of the difficult conditions of workers in his department. Many production facilities, particularly in Rouen and Yvetot, had closed and the prefect was deeply concerned about public order. The prefect asked that government funds be advanced to manufacturers in his region, and the Minister of Police observed to the Minister of the Interior that the situation in the department deserved special attention.[21]

Within a week the Minister of the Interior submitted a report to Bonaparte on the layoffs at the "better factories" in the department. Citing the letter of the Minister of Police, he told Bonaparte that the cluster of industrial establishments located in the Department of Seine-Inférieure made it worthy of great interest and recommended that assistance be provided.[22]

The next day the Minister of Police notified the Minister of the Interior that the situation of workers in the Department of Nord was as difficult as it was for those in the Department of Seine-Inférieure. He indicated that 20,000 workers were affected and that he was deeply concerned about the ramifications of the impoverishment of so many unemployed individuals.[23]

As difficult as conditions were in 1811, they were perceived as even worse in 1812. A report on production facilities in Bordeaux noted that, in 1790, some 12,000 workers had been employed in the city, but in a letter of December 6, 1811, the prefect claimed that the number of employed had been reduced to 900. The report observed that all of the correspondence for 1812 indicated that there was greater economic stagnation than in 1811.[24]

The Continental System made importation difficult, and supplies of raw cotton, in particular, fell sharply.[25] Indeed, the cotton industry suffered a sharp decline between 1810 and 1812, and it was cotton that had been one of the cornerstones of mechanization.[26]

In Paris, among the enterprises that were particularly hard hit were those the government had substantially aided – those of Richard-Lenoir in cotton and Douglas in machine construction.[27] David Landes characterized the French economy during the last five years of the Empire as "years of spasmodic crisis

[21] AN F¹² 2467, letter of Minister of Police to Minister of the Interior, March 19, 1811.
[22] AN F¹² 2467, report of Minister of the Interior to Emperor and King, March 25, 1811.
[23] AN F¹² 2467, letter of Minister of Police to Minister of the Interior, March 26, 1811.
[24] AN F¹² 2467, undated note on factories and Bordeaux.
[25] David S. Landes, *The Unbound Prometheus: Technological Change and Industrial Development in Western Europe from 1750 to the Present* (Cambridge: Cambridge University Press, 1969), p. 159.
[26] *Ibid.*, p. 143.
[27] *Ibid.*, pp. 143–144. Douglas appears to have been the largest recipient of government aid under the Empire. AN F¹² 513, report to His Majesty, February 4, 1808.

that left the economy much enfeebled and momentarily helpless to meet the rash of cheap British products that came with peace."[28]

It is not surprising, then, that contemporaries particularly recalled the difficulties of the last years of the Empire – Pasquier recounted its hardships, principally among the working classes. Pasquier, who was Prefect of Police, sought to ameliorate the distress among workers in the *faubourg* Saint-Antoine by ordering furniture for imperial palaces, and undertook public works improvements in the Luxembourg Gardens to provide relief for workers in the *faubourg* Saint-Marceau.[29]

The demands of conscription, which fell heavily on workers as well as peasants, also compounded the situation of workers.[30] An undated internal document from the Ministry of the Interior noted the pernicious effect of conscription on the French economy because it removed many workers needed by French manufacturers from the labor pool.[31] Once again, Pasquier presented this period in stark terms, as one in which "the hardships of war were so heavy, when the enormous consumption of men could generate despair in the population, the consequences of which could be incalculable."[32]

During 1813, after the debacle in Russia and the loss of much of the Empire, the government sought to conscript 840,000 men,[33] and, in a cynical move, during January 1814, Bonaparte sought to take advantage of the high level of unemployment by seeking to form regiments of unemployed workers in Rouen, Amiens, Alençon, Caen, Lille, Reims, St. Quentin, Louviers, Elbeuf and other towns. The workers would serve until the enemy had been driven from French soil, after which they would return to the factory from which they had come. The government would support the wives and children of volunteers with a stipend to be paid through the head of their factory or workshop. On January 15, 1814, the Ministry of Manufacturing and Commerce summoned many leading manufacturers, including Richard-Lenoir, to convey the offer, but there was little response among workers.[34]

By force of circumstance, the British naval blockade shifted the axis of French commerce toward continental markets, and the Continental System established by Napoleon had been designed in part to institutionalize external markets for French manufacturers and undermine potential economic competitors in continental Europe. Alsace was a beneficiary of the Continental System, and with advances in mechanization its cotton industry developed. The economic crisis of 1810–1812, however, led to a substantial decline in production throughout

[28] Landes, *The Unbound Prometheus*, p. 144.

[29] Pasquier, *Histoire de mon temps*, II: 61–62.

[30] On the effects of conscription on artisans and manual laborers, Fierro, *La Vie des Parisiens sous Napoléon*, pp. 73–74.

[31] AN F¹² 2473, undated (but after June 1810) proposition on customs duties.

[32] Pasquier, *Histoire de mon temps*, II: 61.

[33] *Ibid.*, II: 88.

[34] AN F¹² 2203, list of persons summoned by Minister of Manufacturing and Commerce, January 15, 1814; letter of Minister of Manufacturing and Commerce to president and members of *Chambre consultative des manufactures et fabriques* of Nogent-le-Rotrou, January 17, 1814.

the region – a 20 to 30 percent decline from 1810 to 1811 alone, according to Geoffrey Ellis – and this was followed by the loss of continental markets, invasion and military defeat.[35] Similarly, in Marseille, the value of industrial output for the year 1813 was 12 million francs, compared to 50 million in 1789.[36] As the Empire crumbled, the French labor market and economy fell into severe disarray, with high unemployment and lower production.

The predicament of the French economy can be gleaned from a *mémoire* on the state of commerce prepared by the Paris Chamber of Commerce in late 1810. It noted that many manufacturers were in a state of "absolute dependence" on external trade, with a great number of them unable to sustain themselves without it.[37] The strain extended throughout France; the prefect of the Department of Vendée – never a very economically developed region – advised the Minister of the Interior in February 1814 that the department was experiencing a "complete stagnation of every type of commerce."[38]

With widespread unemployment, and no institution to regulate or control jobless workers, the reestablishment of corporations had a particular pertinence and attraction. Furthermore, with the anticipated return of the Bourbon dynasty, and the prevalent belief that it would reverse the reforms of the Revolution, the stage seemed set for a restoration of guilds.

THE BOURBON RESTORATION AND THE EXPECTATION OF A RETURN TO THE SYSTEM OF PRIVILEGE

On April 2, 1814, the Senate deposed Bonaparte, who unsuccessfully sought to abdicate the throne in favor of his young son. The sequence of events that ended Bonaparte's regime cleared the way for the restoration of the Bourbon dynasty by the allies, and the Comte de Provence came to the throne as Louis XVIII. The Bourbon dynasty returned to a country in which there had been "a powerful outburst of industrialization" between 1802 and 1810, yet also one in which, because of the dislocations of war, the volume of industrial production was not significantly above the levels of the 1780s.[39] Not returning to a smoothly functioning economy left the Bourbon regime with more latitude in charting a future course for the country, particularly in the aftermath of the economic crisis of the last years of the Empire.[40]

[35] Ellis, *Napoleon's Continental Blockade*. It is important to note, however, that Ellis's overall argument is that the economic development made possible by the Continental System until 1810 outweighed the deleterious effects of the following years.

[36] François Crouzet, "War, Blockade and Economic Change," p. 571. Because port cities suffered disproportionately, this figure should not be regarded as typical, but it is a reflection of the economically exhausted state of France by 1814.

[37] AN F¹² 2712, dossier 5, *mémoire* on current state of commerce, December 5, 1810.

[38] AN F¹² 506, letter of prefect of Department of Vendée to Minister of the Interior, February 23, 1814.

[39] Crouzet, "War, Blockade and Economic Change," p. 585.

[40] On the faltering of mechanized production as a result of the crisis of 1811 and a look to the past in search of prosperity, David Higgs, *Ultraroyalism in Toulouse: From its Origins to the Revolution of 1830* (Baltimore, MD: The Johns Hopkins University Press, 1973), pp. 52, 72.

The general sense with which a return to a system of privilege was anticipated is evident in the effort of former free-port cities to reclaim their privileged status under the restored Bourbon regime. These cities, which had been designated by Colbert during the 1660s and 1670s, were Marseille, Bayonne and Dunkirk, with Lorient added later. At all the free ports cargo was exempted from duties, but the most favored was Dunkirk, where all merchandise went through without duties or declarations.[41] The free-port system had escaped proscription during the reforms undertaken by the National Assembly between 1789 and 1791, but the National Convention had abolished it in February 1795.[42]

In June 1814, only weeks after the return of the Bourbons, representatives of the Chamber of Commerce of Marseille requested the reestablishment of the city's free-port status, arguing that this would increase the prosperity of both Marseille and France. The representatives, however, were sensitive to the perception that Marseille was seeking to reclaim a privilege, which in the case of commerce, they stated, was always odious. They argued that the city was not seeking a privilege, but merely recognition from the government of the advantages that the port had to offer. They cited the fact that the government established a fair at Beaucaire rather than Tarascon because of geographical features, even though both towns were located on the Rhône River. Marseille, they asserted, was like Beaucaire. The *mémoire* argued that seeking to destroy all privileges in favor of a spirit of uniformity was appealing only to mediocre minds. A few months later, the General Council of the Department of Landes sought to regain the privileges of the port of Bayonne.[43]

The most aggressive campaign to revert to the system of privilege, however, was that waged by the town of Dunkirk, which, beginning in 1814, vigorously sought to regain its free-port status. Dunkirk, along with Bayonne, had been among the most active in resisting the abolition of free ports,[44] and during October, 1814, renewing what had apparently been an earlier request by the town, the Chevalier de Coppens began an effort to place before the monarch a request to restore its free-port status. Coppens had fifteen copies of the original request printed for distribution to ministers and the private council of the king, if the king believed it appropriate.

The fifteen copies had been given to the Minister of the Interior, and the rationales put forward in the request are illuminating. The first was the attachment of the inhabitants of Dunkirk to the person of the monarch and the second was the wisdom of former institutions created by men of superior genius that had contributed to making the reign of Louis XIV so illustrious. In short, Dunkirk offered no grounds of utility for the restoration of privilege – only

[41] Marcel Marion, *Dictionnaire des institutions de la France aux XVIIe et XVIIIe siècles* (Paris: A. Picard, 1923), p. 446.

[42] Nussbaum, *Commercial Policy in the French Revolution*, pp. 184–192.

[43] AN F¹² 633–637, dossier 101 (Marseille); Pierre Perron, Pierre Plasse, Pierre-Honoré Roux, *Au Roi* (Marseille: Eberhart, 1814); AN F¹² 638, dossier 236 (Bayonne).

[44] Nussbaum, *Commercial Policy in the French Revolution*, p. 191.

loyalty to the monarch and the weight of past tradition. In abolishing the privileges of Marseille, Bayonne and Dunkirk, the *mémoire* claimed, the National Convention had reduced the ports to an equality of calamity and misery.[45]

The General Council of the Department of Nord endorsed the request to restore the privileges of the port of Dunkirk.[46] Even during the Hundred Days in May 1815, Coppens continued to pursue the restoration of Dunkirk's privileges.[47]

The wish to revert to the *status quo ante* of privileged corporatism was also seen in the mayor of Dunkirk's attempt to reestablish guilds in the town during September 1814. The prefect of the Department of Nord wrote to the Director-General of Agriculture, Commerce and Arts and Manufacturing – the new title of what had formerly been the Minister of the Interior – to inquire as to what course he should follow. In an indication that the restored Bourbon regime, contrary to the expectations of its more conservative adherents, would not act reflexively or precipitately, the Director-General responded guardedly, cautioning the prefect that any reestablishment of corporations required careful consideration. The Director-General stated that such an examination would be undertaken at an appropriate time, but until a decision was made, the prefect was free to collect any views or information that could serve to guide the discussion.[48] Indeed, in the absence of any clear resolution or even guidance, efforts to reinstate free-port status to and reestablish guilds in Dunkirk continued over the next few years and became issues of national import.

There was, in fact, a widespread belief that the restored Bourbon regime would overturn the work of the Revolution.[49] Not only was the dissolution of guilds one of the major achievements of the Revolution, but they were seen to be closely associated with the monarchical system. During June 1814, only weeks after the return of the Bourbons, merchants in Arras requested that the Crown reestablish corporations.[50] Similarly, in December 1814, the grocers/druggists of Paris requested the reestablishment of guilds in that city, claiming their abolition had "opened the door to abuse, fraud and demoralization" in commerce and production.[51]

Also during 1814, a *mémoire* advocated the reestablishment of guilds on fiscal grounds. A rebuttal sought not only to refute the fiscal argument but attacked any restoration of corporations as inimical to industry, which it contended was the major issue. The abolition of the "empire of guilds and

45 AN F¹² 633–637, dossier 169, extract from *mémoire* addressed to Director-General by Chevalier de Coppens, October 4, 1814.
46 AN F¹² 638, dossier 237.
47 AN F¹² 2187, dossier 1815, entry of May 3, 1815.
48 AN F¹² 2188, letter of Director-General of Agriculture, Commerce and Arts and Manufacturing to prefect of Department of Nord, September 30, 1814.
49 IISH Bruyard Papers, *liasse* 198; Higgs, *Ultraroyalism in Toulouse*, pp. 58, 73; Sibalis, "The Workers of Napoleonic Paris," p. 424.
50 AN F¹² 633–637, dossier Rége. A, no. 65.
51 AN F¹² 638, dossier 245, request dated December 31, 1814.

regulations" meant that "the domain of the arts became the patrimony of all," leading to improvement in all types of manufacturing and the development of new products through industry. The system of guilds, masterships and regulations, by contrast, constituted a "code of uniformity and routine" and would lead to restrictions, inconveniences and abuses. A return of corporations would not bring any advantage to the state.[52]

In January 1815, Louis-Pierre Deseine sent a lengthy *mémoire* to the Minister of the Interior vigorously arguing for the reestablishment of guilds, and later published it as a pamphlet. Deseine claimed that the public desired the restoration of corporations in order to put an end to the disorder that had been introduced in all branches of national industry through the *patente*, which had given each individual the right to practice whatever occupation he wished. The abolition of guilds, he asserted, was an attempt by revolutionaries to attract the support of the masses, and reestablishing them would serve to redirect minds toward the monarchical ideal.

Deseine argued that there should be a proof of skill required to practice a trade, and guilds had formerly had the right to judge their peers. He went on to offer a defense of the role that corporations had played in ensuring quality, and contrasted it with the decline in workmanship and quality that had occurred since the guilds' abolition and the introduction of the occupational license.

Deseine argued that reestablishing guilds would be in the general interest because it would lead to higher quality in all branches of industry. He also claimed that their restoration would not be contrary to the principles of equality, and extolled the charitable functions that corporations had performed under the Old Regime. In the final analysis, the reestablishment of corporations would restore confidence and respect to commerce.[53] Although one must recognize the norms of politeness and social convention in his reply, François Xavier de Montesquiou, the Minister of the Interior – his title had reverted to that of his predecessors – claimed to have read "with much interest" Deseine's observations "on this important question," suggesting at least an openness to considering the restoration of guilds.[54] Indeed, during the following month a division of the Ministry of the Interior approved a proposal to send to the Council of State a project to organize a body of peat ash carriers at Amiens.[55]

Some actions by the early Bourbon government seemed to portend the restoration of corporations. On May 18, 1814, just six weeks after returning to power, the Bourbon government abolished the Ministry of Manufacturing and Commerce. In its place, the regime created a Director-General of Agriculture, Commerce and Manufacturing, which was placed within the Ministry of the

---

[52] BNU Strasbourg Ms. 559.

[53] Louis-Pierre Deseine, *Mémoire sur la nécessité du rétablissement des maîtrises et corporations, comme moyens d'encourager l'industrie et le commerce...*(Paris: Fain, 1815).

[54] AN F^{12} 638, dossier 299, undated letter and *mémoire* of Deseine to Minister of the Interior; letter of Minister of the Interior to Deseine, February 6, 1815.

[55] AN F^{12} 2182, entry of February 20, 1815.

Interior.[56] After slightly more than two years of operation, then, a leading vehicle for promoting mechanization of production, and a leading center of opposition to the reestablishment of corporations, had been disbanded.

At the same time, although there was a perception that guilds would be reestablished, and although it abolished the Ministry of Manufacturing and Commerce, the restored Bourbon regime did not act precipitately on the issue of guilds. During October 1814, the Ministry of the Interior refused to allow the city of Lyon to revert to regulations of 1744 governing production facilities, which had been abolished during the Revolution.[57]

More significant, however, was the attitude of the Bourbon monarchy toward the Council on Manufacturing. The council was apprehensive about the transition to the monarchy – like the Ministry of Manufacturing and Commerce, it was a recent creation of the deposed imperial regime and therefore faced an uncertain future. The council met on May 18, 1814, the same day that the Ministry of Manufacturing and Commerce was abolished, and prudently redated the sequence of its meetings to reflect the change of government – meaning that May 18, 1814, was listed as the first meeting instead of continuing the numerical sequence from the Napoleonic period. Indeed, undoubtedly in reference to the suppression of the ministry that day, the council noted that until the "new order" established itself, it did not even have a meeting place.[58]

The next day, on May 19, the council went to the meeting room of the Ministry of the Interior to meet with the minister. Ternaux, the vice-president, conveyed the greetings and hopes of the council and expressed the uneasiness of its members at the competition of foreign industry – a discreet reference to Great Britain. The minister responded in a favorable manner, although he declined an invitation to preside personally over the council's meetings.

A general conversation ensued and Ternaux was sufficiently encouraged by its tone to ask the minister to arrange a meeting of the council with the king. The minister said that he would attempt to arrange it promptly.[59]

In fact, the minister acted so quickly that the council was caught unprepared. The Grand Master of Ceremonies notified it at 7:00 p.m. on May 23 that the council would be presented to the king the next day at 11:30 a.m., but the council had to ask for a later meeting because not enough of its members were in Paris. As a result, the meeting took place on May 27, and after Ternaux offered a prepared statement on behalf of the council, Louis, in a reply that should have encouraged the delegation, stated that he understood the role of manufacturing in the well-being of the state and that the council could rely on his protection.[60]

56 AN F¹² 509/510, dossier 16.
57 AN F¹² 2182, entry of October 25, 1814.
58 AN F¹²* 194, fol. 486.
59 AN F¹²* 194, fols. 488v°–489.
60 AN F¹²* 194, fols. 489–490.

Within days, however, it also became clear that some members of the royal family were rooted in the Old Regime and were unfamiliar with the economic changes that had occurred during the Revolution. On May 30, members of the council met with the Duchesse d'Angoulême, who was seeking details on which areas of French manufacturing had suffered most, and she wanted to know about Lyon, in particular. After receiving answers from Ternaux, the duchesse learned, "with astonishment," how great a number of workers were employed in the manufacture of cotton and how great their suffering was. She concluded the meeting, however, by observing that the king wanted prosperity for all manufacturing and that the council could rely on her cooperation also.[61]

These events encouraged the council to seek to increase its membership closer to its authorized number. On June 21, 1814, the secretary of the council wrote to the Director-General to inform him of the shortfall in its membership – the council, which was supposed to be comprised of sixty members, had only thirty. The secretary explained that this number would be more than sufficient if all the members resided in Paris, but this was not the case. Only ten lived in Paris, and it was rare to have all of them at the same meeting. The number of members living outside of Paris had fallen to eighteen, and it was even more unusual to have them attend meetings. As a result, at most meetings only five members were in attendance, and often fewer than that.

The secretary stated that it would be useful to augment the number, especially with men who resided in Paris or frequently visited the city. Knowing that the ministry wanted to choose the members of the council, the secretary submitted a list of names of prospective members. Ten days later, the council submitted a list of twenty-five names to the ministry as candidates for membership.[62] The Director-General began to appoint members in September 1814 and the first two named were drawn from the list of desired candidates submitted by the council. The next month the Director-General received a proposal from his subordinates to name an additional twenty-three members, bringing the council closer to its authorized strength.[63]

Like the Council on Manufacturing, the Society for the Encouragement of National Industry was apprehensive about the future. It, too, had come into existence during the Napoleonic regime and, although it was not an official government body, it had had close ties to the Napoleonic Ministry of the Interior. Only weeks after the return of Louis XVIII, the society decided to name a deputation to assure the monarch of its respect and devotion and to offer him a set of its publication. Chaptal wrote the address, and the delegation met with Louis on May 19; he assured it, as he had the Council on Manufacturing, that it could count on his protection.[64] In addition, during the

[61] AN F¹²* 194, fol. 491.
[62] AN F¹² 618, letters of secretary of General Council on Manufacturing to Director-General of Agriculture, Commerce and Arts, June 21, 1814, July 1, 1814.
[63] AN F¹² 2182, entries of September 13, 1814; October 18, 1814.
[64] *Bulletin de la Société d'Encouragement pour l'Industrie Nationale* 13 (1814): 128–130.

late summer of 1814, apparently in response to an inquiry from the society, the Director-General wrote to the leadership of the society to assure them that it could rely on the protection and good will of the government.[65] At the same time, it is a reflection of the uncertainty surrounding the issue of mechanization generally and the society in particular that the society experienced a sharp drop in new members during 1814.[66]

During the meeting of the General Council on Manufacturing with the minister, Ternaux had mentioned the council's concern about competition from foreign industry. In fact, amidst the acute economic dislocation of the Empire's final years, the end of the Continental System was an eventuality many French businessmen viewed with trepidation. The belief that Louis XVIII was deeply indebted to Great Britain for his restoration to the throne and would therefore revive free trade between the two countries was particularly disconcerting. Just weeks after the Restoration, the Chamber of Commerce of Rouen wrote that rumors of a trade treaty with Britain that was to follow a general peace treaty had become so widespread that the chamber believed it necessary to write in advance to the Minister of the Interior to argue against it.

The Minister of the Interior forwarded the *mémoire* to the Council on Commerce for consideration in anticipation of trade treaties that would have to be renewed with different countries. The council decided to take as its starting point for deliberation the trade treaties that had been broken by the wars of the Revolution. The following month, during a discussion on wool, the council declared itself in favor of free trade.[67]

The degree to which the prospect of free trade unsettled French businessmen is evident in another letter from the region of Rouen. During the fall of 1814, an inhabitant of a town near Rouen wrote to the Minister of the Interior to support the request by the Chamber of Commerce of Rouen that no trade treaty with Britain be concluded and that the protective system be maintained.[68]

A restoration of guilds would also have been antithetical to most notions of free trade, but, as had been the case during the Napoleonic regime, some did advocate for their restoration. Indeed, during late 1814 and early 1815 the Bourbon government continued the policy of the Napoleonic regime of reconstituting corporations of bakers, but, without calling them guilds, made some changes that aligned the bodies more closely with the former guild model. In reorganizing a corporation of bakers in Aix-en-Provence, for example, the election of a syndic and two assistants for the body was limited to ten of the most experienced bakers in the town, all of whom would be chosen by the mayor. Masters had largely controlled guilds before 1789, of course, and the vesting of the election of officers with a small group of senior members was closer to the Old Regime ideal than the Napoleonic one, in which all bakers

[65] AN F¹² 2182, entry of August 30, 1814, no. 419.
[66] *Bulletin de la Société d'Encouragement pour l'Industrie Nationale* 13 (1814): 302.
[67] AN F¹² 2473, minutes of General Council of Commerce, June 11, 1814, July 23, 1814.
[68] AN F¹² 506, letter of Minister of the Interior to Gaillard, October 19, 1814.

participated in elections for officers. The model established for Aix was subsequently extended to Orléans, Rennes and Nancy. Furthermore, the government added a requirement of *"bonne vie et moeurs"* to join the body and
mandated the completion of an apprenticeship to become a baker.[69] Again, all
of these measures represented a greater regression toward Old Regime-style
guilds than had occurred during the Bonapartist regime.

THE HUNDRED DAYS AND THEIR AFTERMATH

In whatever direction the Bourbon monarchy may have been moving with
respect to the issue of guilds, the restored government was displaced by the
return of Bonaparte to France during March 1815. As was the case with many
aspects of French life, Bonaparte's return produced turmoil in the world of
work as the Allies' refusal to negotiate led to a renewal of hostilities. The
shift to a war footing, and especially the prospect of greater regimentation of
labor, led to agitation among workers – indeed, during June 1815, on the eve
of the Battle of Waterloo, the police had to deal with worker unrest in an arms
workshop over reductions in wages and other issues.[70]

Bonaparte's return also sparked a revival of Jacobinism among workers –
on May 11 workers in the *faubourgs* Saint-Antoine and Saint-Marceau urged
their fellow citizens to join together to defend Paris. A moderate newspaper,
reporting on this the next day, praised the workers' patriotism but pointedly
added that it hoped that their zeal would not be carried too far.[71]

The newspaper stated that it wanted freedom, but not that of 1793, and
quoted a phrase from the appeal that it found "reprehensible" – "we also
want, by our attitude, to strike terror [in] the traitors who would once again
wish to see the degradation of their fatherland." In a free state ruled by just
laws, the newspaper asserted, only the law should strike terror among traitors. Armed citizens should only be instruments of the law and the protectors
of order and prosperity. The word "terror," the newspaper claimed, recalled
painful events – it would perhaps be more appropriate to form into companies
workers whose patriotism was not suspicious.[72]

All of these undertakings ended with the decisive defeat of Bonaparte at
Waterloo, but the Hundred Days led to a revision of the peace treaty with
France, including an extensive occupation of the country. One consequence
in Paris was a requisition of material and labor by Prussian forces, including

---

[69] AN F¹² 2712, dossier 8.
[70] BHVP Ms. 1013, fol. 126. The quasi-Jacobin spirit of the Hundred Days raised the prospect
of a return to a war economy – during May, 1815, for example, a Parisian tanner sought to
negotiate a contract with the Ministry of War for a total of 90,000 boots and shoes. BHVP
Ms. 1013, fol. 119.
[71] On the fear inspired by the movement, R.S. Alexander, *Bonapartism and Revolutionary
Tradition in France: The Fédérés of 1815* (Cambridge: Cambridge University Press, 1991), pp.
193–203.
[72] *L'Indépendant, chronique nationale, politique et littéraire*, May 12, 1815.

the requisitioning of shoemakers to produce boots and shoes for the Prussian army.[73] Aside from causing resentment, such requisitions delayed a return to a peacetime economy.

Bonaparte's defeat at Waterloo led to what has become known as the Second Restoration, which was more bitter than the initial return of Louis XVIII to power in April 1814. Not only did the Allies revise the peace treaty with France to make it harsher, but the internal political climate sharply deteriorated. As one scholar noted, all those who had abandoned the Bourbons in favor of Bonaparte "were marked with an indelible stigma which was to make them irreconcilable enemies of the monarchy."[74]

The atmosphere of bitter mistrust became pervasive, and this was true even with respect to the Council on Manufacturing, whose developing relationship with the Bourbon government was severely undermined. Although the council had not convened during the Hundred Days, during that time Richard-Lenoir had met with Bonaparte, speaking with him about a wool-spinning process.[75] Richard was removed from the Council on Manufacturing, and during September 1815 the Minister of the Interior ordered the prefect of the Department of Seine to investigate the political conduct of members of the council.[76]

At least one member resigned, and the Minister of the Interior followed the investigation closely, asking the prefect to expedite his report on the conduct and political opinions of the council members who resided in Paris. Indeed, the minister expanded the scope of the investigation.[77] Two weeks later, he was again insisting on receiving the report from the prefect on council members in Paris.[78] During late December 1815, several members of the council were removed and the secretary was relieved of his duties, although he was permitted to continue to attend the council's meetings.[79]

Another dismissal occurred in January 1816, and the government began to name replacements, apparently without consulting the council. Only in April 1816 did the government notify Ternaux that he would be retained as vice-president, albeit on a provisional basis.[80] A few days later the Minister of the Interior proposed a reorganization of the General Council on Manufacturing.[81]

Unlike the General Council on Manufacturing, the Society for the Encouragement of National Industry did hold a general meeting during the

---

[73] BHVP Ms. 1014, fols. 79–81, 98, 101, 105–140.

[74] Guillaume Bertier de Sauvigny, *The Bourbon Restoration* (Philadelphia, PA: The University of Pennsylvania Press, 1966), p. 115.

[75] AN F^{12} 2182, entry of May 17, 1815, no. 1064. On the suspicion that fell on Richard, Alexander, *Bonapartism and the Revolutionary Tradition*, pp. 213–214, 216.

[76] AN F^{12} 2182, entry of September 29, 1815, nos. 190–191.

[77] AN F^{12} 2182, entry of October 30, 1815, nos. 348–351.

[78] AN F^{12} 2182, entry of November 14, 1815, no. 445.

[79] AN F^{12} 2182, entry of December 26, 1815, nos. 113–114, no. 118.

[80] On the dismissal, AN F^{12} 2183, entry of January 12, 1816, no. 115; on Ternaux, AN F^{12} 2183, entry of April 23, 1816, no. 1493.

[81] AN F^{12} 2183, entry of April 27, 1816, no. 1542.

Hundred Days. On May 10, 1815 the administrative council of the society sent a *mémoire* to the Minister of the Interior asking that the exhibition of products of French industry be revived.[82] This was an implicit recognition of the legitimacy of the Bonapartist regime and led to a sharp breach with the Bourbon monarchy after its return. Indeed, there was no general meeting of the society for the remainder of the year. Moreover, during early 1816 the Ministry of the Interior substantially cut back the amount that it paid to the society for its bulletin – from 6600 francs to 4000 francs, a reduction of nearly 40 percent.[83]

Not only had leading advocates for mechanization and industry been compromised, but, more broadly, in the more conservative climate of the Second Restoration, the idea of reestablishing corporations gained new momentum. Indeed, the question became a matter of considerable debate both inside and outside of government, and the attitude of the government itself seemed unresolved. During November 1815, for example, the Minister of the Interior had written to a correspondent that it was impossible to restore guilds, but by March 1816, his stance on the question of corporations had become more equivocal – "for the present," he wrote, it was not possible to reestablish them.[84] Moreover, the ministry continued to receive *mémoires* on the reestablishment of guilds.[85]

In addition, in March 1816, rather than refusing permission for master joiners to group themselves into a corporation, the minister asked for additional information.[86] During the spring and summer of 1816, however, the minister did refuse permission to enact regulations grouping locksmiths in Marseille and ash carriers in Amiens into corporations – the latter a second request.[87] During August 1816, the ministry refused to allow the mayor of Nantes to allow nailsmiths to form themselves into a corporation.[88] Six weeks later, however, in what seemed to be a reversal, the minister was suggesting that it might be possible to reinstitute worker corporations in Dunkirk.[89]

The uncertainty surrounding the situation of guilds was particularly apparent in Dunkirk. On October 8, 1814, the sub-prefect had advised the mayor of Dunkirk of the recommendation of the Director-General to the prefect to gather information and views on the reestablishment of guilds.[90] Clearly interpreting the equivocal response as an opening to proceed, in February 1815 the

---

[82] *Bulletin de la Société d'Encouragement pour l'Industrie Nationale* 14 (1815): 113.

[83] AN F¹² 2183, February 26, 1816, entry no. 754.

[84] AN F¹² 2182, entry of November 7, 1815, no. 375; AN F¹² 2183, entry of March 4, 1816, no. 829.

[85] AN F¹² 2183, entry of April 23, 1816, no. 1492.

[86] AN F¹² 2183, entry of March 16, 1816, no. 1058.

[87] AN F¹² 2183, entry of May 15, 1816, no. 1746 (Marseille); AN F¹² 2183, entry of May 27, 1816, no. 1857 (Amiens). The ash carriers in Amiens had submitted the same request during 1815.

[88] AN F¹² 2183, entry of August 21, 1816, no. 2921.

[89] AN F¹² 2183, entry of October 3, 1816, no. 3586.

[90] AN F¹² 2188, note relative to correspondence begun in 1814…, March 5, 1817.

mayor wrote a long letter to the sub-prefect restating the putative benefits for the town of restoring guild-like bodies.[91]

During July 1815 responding, he claimed, to the advice of the Director-General to the prefect to collect views and information on the reestablishment of guilds, the acting prefect of the Department of Nord wrote to the Director-General to offer the statutes drawn up by the mayor. The acting prefect stated that the mayor had convinced him of the need for the bodies, and he appropriated the mayor's arguments to advance his case.

The bodies at issue, he declared, were not "properly speaking" the same guilds that had been abolished in 1791. Instead, he argued that they could be regarded as regulatory vehicles that would determine the obligations of these "societies of workers" in services to be provided to the public as well as setting the wages that workers could demand. The prefect observed that, with a few modifications, the proposed regulations could quickly be put into effect.[92]

During the fall of 1815, the Chamber of Commerce of Dunkirk also took up the cause, writing to the Minister of the Interior in support of reestablishing corporations. The minister's reply is one of the few that did not pass through the channels of prefect, sub-prefect and mayor in which knowledge of the ramifications of the issue was assumed – it is a letter from the minister to a nongovernmental entity.

In it, the minister acknowledged that the reestablishment of guilds of workers associated with the port was supported by the municipal authorities of the town, but that that desire had to be subordinated to the fact that the suppression of corporations had been ordered by law. This fact, the minister declared, trumped "the well-recognized advantage that commerce would find in this reestablishment." At the same time, however, the minister stated that in a matter of such importance he could not excuse himself from gathering their views. He therefore invited the chamber to inform him of the advantages and disadvantages of putting into effect, "except for modifications necessitated by the changing of circumstances" – an extraordinarily elliptical allusion to the Revolution – the former regulations.[93]

The letter seems to indicate a willingness, and perhaps even a readiness, on the part of the minister to reestablish guilds, but this would have to be done in a manner that would not violate the d'Allarde law, which was virtually impossible, or the d'Allarde law would have to be repealed. The latter action would have been contentious, not only within the Ministry of the Interior, but within society at large.

After a change of minister at the Ministry of the Interior, the Chamber of Commerce of Dunkirk wrote to the minister in May 1816 to inquire about the

[91] AN F¹² 2188, copy of letter of mayor of Dunkirk to sub-prefect of Dunkirk, February 13, 1815.
[92] AN F¹² 2188, letter of acting prefect of Department of Nord to Director-General of Commerce, Arts, etc., July 14, 1815.
[93] AN F¹² 2188, letter of Minister of the Interior to Chamber of Commerce of Dunkirk, October 26, 1815.

possibility of organizing a number of trades into corporations. The idea, the chamber claimed, had wide support in Dunkirk, from the city council to the workers themselves. Under a plan drafted by the mayor and the Chamber of Commerce, each restored corporation would be directed by a head (*doyen*), with two assistants drawn from skilled workers of known probity. All of the restored corporations would be overseen by either a magistrate, a member of the Chamber of Commerce or a respected inhabitant of the town, and the individual selected for the task would have the title of "notable." Although there had been abuses during the Revolution, the chamber assured the minister that men who had practiced in the proposed trades since the Revolution would be included in the restored guilds, and concluded by asking the minister to approve the request to reestablish corporations.[94]

During July 1816 a new mayor of Dunkirk sent the sub-prefect a petition drawn up by workers who had formed themselves into an association to oversee the tasks of commerce. The petition asked that the workers be reintegrated into corporations with all of the attributes that they had formerly enjoyed. The new mayor also pointedly reminded the sub-prefect of his predecessor's requests.

A week later the sub-prefect replied that the prefect had authorized him to convene an extraordinary meeting of the municipal council to deliberate the issue of reestablishing guilds of workers. The council met on August 6 and passed a resolution asking for reestablishment and enumerating the advantages to be realized from this. The resolution asked the higher authorities to take all necessary measures to reestablish corporations as quickly as possible. It received an endorsement from the Chamber of Commerce of Dunkirk, and was sent to the sub-prefect on August 8.[95]

Indeed, by the fall of 1816 the minister was instructing the prefect of the Department of Nord on the means through which the restoration of corporations in Dunkirk could be achieved.[96] The minister observed that former usages could be put into effect only by a general measure passed legislatively, but, while awaiting such an act, public authorities had the right to oversee professions vital to public order and submit them to regulations that this demanded. The joining of these professions under syndics and a "wise organization" of the syndicates were means that could be efficaciously utilized.[97]

WORKERS, THE DEBATE ON GUILDS AND MECHANIZATION

One indication of a sense of hope among artisans during the Restoration not only that guilds might be restored but also that mechanization might be checked is found in a petition from shoemakers and bootmakers in Paris.

[94] AN F¹² 2188, letter of Chamber of Commerce of Dunkirk to Ministry of the Interior, May 11, 1816.
[95] AN F¹² 2188, note relative to correspondence begun in 1814…, March 5, 1817.
[96] AN F¹² 2183, entry of October 3, 1816, no. 3586.
[97] AN F¹² 2188, note relative to correspondence begun in 1814…, March 5, 1817.

During December 1815, they proposed to the Minister of the Interior, the ultra Vincent-Marie Viénot, Comte deVaublanc, that a tax be levied on shoes and boots that were produced mechanically. Along with the proposed tax, the petition requested that a limit of 600 pairs of shoes and 200 pairs of boots per day be placed on mechanical manufacture. Without these measures, they claimed, artisan shoemakers would be reduced to misery. The ministry undertook an investigation that discovered that the mechanical process for producing shoes and boots had been imported from Britain. It did not, however, take any action on the petition.[98]

A public debate began during 1816, with the publication of a pamphlet by Costaz that extolled the previous twenty years of industrial policy. Costaz admitted that the abolition of guilds had led to "a kind of anarchy" in production sites that had lasted for years and had resulted in a desire to return to the guild system as a means of restoring order and discipline. This longing, Costaz argued, was misplaced and short sighted because in order for new legislation to be advantageous it was necessary to destroy all aspects of the former system, and from such a vantage point, he asserted, the Bourbon monarchy was in a far more promising position than that seen in 1789.

As a result of laws passed during the Revolution, the Bourbon regime had been freed from institutions that could oppose the development of industrialization and was better placed to undertake policies that could produce prosperity for manufacturing. The pamphlet traced many of the steps that had been taken during the Bonapartist regime and asserted that it had put in place an excellent system for the policing of factories and workshops – an implicit plea against a restoration of guilds that would have been understood as such by contemporaries. It concluded with an exhortation that the current regime follow the course that had brought the development of industry and prosperity.[99]

Costaz was not, of course, a disinterested observer. From his position in the Ministry of the Interior, he had played a central role in developing and carrying out the policies that he praised in the pamphlet. Nevertheless, his concerns were well founded. During the summer of 1815 elections produced the body known as the "Incomparable Chamber," a body in which extreme royalists, known as ultras, comprised a large majority, and during March 1816, in the course of budget hearings, one of them launched an effort to restore guilds. During a meeting of the Chamber of Deputies on March 9, Etienne-Antoine Feuillant, second reporter on the budget commission, offered a report on indirect taxes.

Feuillant was a royalist who had established a newspaper during 1814 – the *Journal Général de France* – that became successful. He had stood as a

---

98 AN F¹² 2283, letter to Minister of the Interior from widow of M. Demorelle, December 29, 1815; report of January 10, 1816.

99 Claude-Anthelme Costaz, *Mémoire sur les moyens qui ont amené le grand développement que l'industrie française a pris depuis vingt ans* (Paris: Firmin-Didot, 1816), especially pp. 14–15, 26, 57–58.

candidate in elections in the Department of Maine-et-Loire in 1815 and won. As a deputy, using his position on the budget commission, he vigorously promoted the ultra program, albeit with little success.[100]

The month of March 1816 was the zenith of ultra influence,[101] and the meeting of March 9 offers an example of their ascendancy. After presenting a series of recommendations on indirect taxes to the chamber, Feuillant stated that the budget commission believed that it was necessary to reestablish guilds.[102]

The full report provides insight into the motives that underlay the effort to restore guilds during the Second Restoration. Although the proposal was couched primarily in fiscal terms – as a means to reform taxation – there were other reasons.

The "benefit" of these "eminently monarchical" institutions would be not only to introduce advantageous changes in state finances, which would strengthen the state, it would also ease policing, thereby rendering it less severe. Through the reestablishment of guilds, each Frenchman, Feuillant asserted, would "necessarily belong" to a category of citizens. Exceptions would be rare, which would eliminate the many difficulties currently in existence, especially in large cities, as a result of "the confusion of all estates, of all professions." "This return to our former organization," he argued, would clarify morals, and the spirit of corporations would imbue public life.

This argument, Feuillant conceded, was not a report on finances, but he hoped that the commission's view would reverberate across France and soon be placed at the foot of the throne. If the proposal was realized, he stated, it would once again root monarchy very deeply among the classes of society.[103] Against the backdrop of Jacobin sentiments among workers in Paris less than a year earlier that had alarmed even moderates, such arguments were attractive to a strongly conservative body.

Indeed, although the author of the bill is not identified – it may or may not have been Feuillant – a bill to reestablish guilds was drawn up during 1816, a period of ultra ascendancy in the chamber. Reflecting the conservative climate of the Second Restoration, the bill stated that the government wanted to encourage "by all the means that Providence has given us moral recovery and the development of industry." The law proposed revoking the occupational tax, with the 488 occupations subject to the tax being divided into ten groups, and each group subdivided into ten corporations.

Each corporation would be governed by three syndics and twelve board members, all of whom were to be elected by the membership of the entire corporation from a triple list provided by the body's five oldest members. The

[100] *Dictionnaire des parlementaires française*, 13: 1222.
[101] Robert Alexander, *Re-Writing the French Revolutionary Tradition: Liberal Opposition and the Fall of the Bourbon Monarchy* (Cambridge: Cambridge University Press, 2003), p. 52.
[102] *Gazette nationale, ou le Moniteur universel*, March 10, 1816.
[103] *Gazette nationale, ou le Moniteur universel*, March 13, 1816 (supplement).

syndics and the board would serve a one-year term, but could be reelected, and had to meet at least once a month. Only the officers and board could call a general meeting of the corporation, but the convocation required prior approval by the prefect.

Each corporation would also have honorary officers, including the local prefect, military commander, bishop, president of the royal court, president of the court of first instance and justice of the peace. They could attend when they believed it appropriate, but had only an advisory role.

The general assembly of each corporation had to be presided over by one of the syndics and the assembly could propose rules for the body's internal governance, but any regulations enacted could be carried out only after being approved by the Ministry of the Interior. The remaining articles specified the conditions under which one could practice an occupation in France and stipulated transgressions that could lead to exclusion from the corporation.[104]

Although there is no evidence that this bill was ever submitted for consideration, the project is nonetheless of interest. The plan indicated that any restoration of corporations would not be a simple reversion to the *status quo ante*. Indeed, the division of occupations into ten groups recalled the systematization utilized by Dubois in his 1807 survey of artisanal trades in Paris. Furthermore, the subordination of the proposed corporations to the prefect, and the titular membership accorded to bishops, administrative, judicial and military officials made clear that the "new corporations" would not have the quasi-autonomous status of prerevolutionary guilds.

The threat that a reestablishment of corporations could pose to mechanization and industrial development is again apparent in a contemporaneous event involving shoemakers in Paris. During late 1816 a large number of shoemakers in the city renewed their complaints about mechanical production of shoes and boots. On this occasion, however, they asked not for a limit on production, but for the outright suppression of machinery, without which, they asserted, they would be ruined.

An official in the Ministry of the Interior advised the Prefect of Police that the fears of the shoemakers seemed unfounded. Furthermore, the inventor, Olivier, had a patent on the process, and patent legislation guaranteed him the free use of his discovery. As a result, the government had no right to oppose either his enterprise or the sale of his products. He asked the prefect to convey these facts to the shoemakers and also to take all measures to quell their unrest.[105]

A TRADE FORMED INTO A BODY: THE EXAMPLE OF SHOEMAKERS

Any effort to set policy or enact new legislation was complicated by the fluidity of the structure of the world of work. Legally, corporations had been

[104] *Projet de loi pour l'établissement de nouvelles corporations* (N.p., 1816) [BHVP 6364].
[105] AN F¹² 2283, letter from Fourth Bureau of Third Division of Ministry of the Interior to Prefect of Police of Paris, October 9, 1816.

abolished and the occupational license continued to be in force, but at the same time public authorities had formed many trades or occupations into bodies (*corporiser*) that were largely self-governing. They were guilds in all but name, although the vocabulary was carefully controlled – they were referred to as *corps* and never as *corporations*.

These bodies had been formed administratively rather than legislatively, and their formation was based on the premise that unlimited freedom could not be extended to all trades – regulations and ordinances had to be imposed on some in the general interest of all. The process had begun with the reestablishment of the guild of bakers in Paris in 1801, which was was followed by the creation of the body for butchers in the city a year later.

Because problems with adulterated bread and rotten or diseased meat were seen during the years after the abolition of guilds, as a matter of public good an argument for the creation of bodies to govern and police these trades could be made. Indeed, similar organizations for bakers and butchers had been formed in other cities.[106]

In Paris, however, the Prefect of Police had established bodies (*corporisé*) of other trades or occupations. Some of these, such as pork-butchers (*charcutiers*), grocers and wine merchants, were associated with the food supply, so their formation into a body could be seen as a logical extension of the structure accorded to bakers and butchers. For others that the prefect organized – masons, roofers, carpenters and others – a public-policy argument that the safety of buildings needed to be assured could be put forward. Perhaps even the organization of wood merchants and coal merchants that had been carried out could be defended on the basis of public policy.

By contrast, however, the organization of other trades into bodies appears not to have been rooted in a concern for the greater good and suggests that the Prefect of Police was seeking a *de facto* reestablishment of guilds through surrogate bodies. It is difficult, for example, to discern a broad public benefit from forming wallpaper manufacturers and sellers into a *corps*. Moreover, the Ministry of the Interior did not possess any copies of the regulations that the Prefect of Police had established for these bodies.[107]

The Prefect of Police in Paris during most of this era was Jules Anglès, who held the position from September 1815 until December 1821. The son of a magistrate at the *parlement* of Grenoble who emigrated, Anglès was named Minister of Police during the Provisional Government of April–May 1814, before becoming Prefect of Police.[108] As prefect, Anglès continued the practice of organizing trades into bodies, which had ceased after Dubois had moved to the Council of State. Once again, some of the trades that received such status seem to have had little to do with considerations of public safety or the greater good. One example is the formation of shoemakers – both makers

[106] AN F¹² 2188, memorandum of 3rd Division of Bureau of Arts and Manufacturing, May 22, 1816.

[107] *Ibid.*

[108] *Nouvelle biographie générale*, 2: 659.

and merchants – into a body by the Prefect of Police in September 1817. Furthermore, the body of shoemakers seems to be one of the few for which regulations have survived.

The Ministry of the Interior had asked the prefect to take all measures to quell the shoemakers' unrest, and this may have been the mechanism that the prefect devised to that end. Indeed, the rationale for the body's creation was to provide the trade with representatives to deal with public authorities, and their deliberations had no force until they were approved by the Prefect of Police. Forty-eight electors chose three delegates and three deputies – at the expiration of their two-year term, the three delegates were to be replaced by their deputies.

The delegates would manage both the affairs and funds of the body, and were also charged with maintaining discipline and regulations among its members. The body was to ensure that all those practicing the trade of shoemaker or boot maker possess the proper occupational license and would identify to the authorities those who did not. The delegates were also to investigate disputes between merchants, shoemakers and workers, but only to act as conciliators when a matter was submitted to them. The delegates and deputies were to prepare a list of all practicing shoemakers and boot makers in Paris and submit it to the prefect each year. The members paid dues to the body to support it – the body had a chaplain and a barrister, and an office that would be open daily from 9:00 a.m. until 4:00 p.m. – and to provide for indigent workers. The dues were to be set by the electors and were divided into three levels, according to one's standing in the trade. The dues were paid in two installments, on January 1 and July 1.[109]

With their earlier overt opposition to mechanization, the shoemakers were an unusual choice of trade to be *corporisé*, despite the minister's order to the prefect to quell their unrest. Even with the oversight of the Prefect of Police, the body offered a potential platform for shoemakers to oppose modernization of production.

The increasing number of trades formed into bodies in Paris leaves little doubt that Anglès deliberately sought to form as many occupations as he could into guild-like structures. At the same time, however, the regulations for shoemakers provide insight into his reasons for pursuing this policy, and they were unrelated to the question of artisans versus modernization or mechanization of production. Rather, the prefect viewed the bodies much as his analogues under the Old Regime had looked upon them – as an extension of the police.

The experience of the 1790s had shown the futility of the police attempting to oversee the safety of the food supply of Paris; it was simply too great a responsibility along with the other duties they were required to perform.

---

[109] *Arrêté de S.E. le Ministre d'Etat, préfet de police, qui autorise les Marchands-Fabricans-Cordonniers de la ville de Paris, à avoir, pour les représenter, dans leurs relations avec l'autorité, des délégués et des adjoints, et à nommer des électeurs pour les choisir, etc.* (Paris: Doublet, 1817) [BHVP 8° 132060].

Indeed, many of the early actions of Dubois as Prefect of Police concerned the city's food supply.[110] The problems of adulterated bread or diseased meat had diminished substantially with the formation of bodies of bakers and butchers, and successive prefects clearly found the structures useful. If the statutes for the shoemakers are typical, and there is no reason to believe they are not, the police would be relieved of overseeing enforcement of the *patente* and of resolving disputes in the trade. Indeed, each trade would finance and administer itself and the police would thereby be freed for other duties.

From the vantage point of the Council on Manufacturing, however, the formation of trades into bodies was a threatening development. The proliferation of occupations that were *corporisé* appeared to represent a possible precursor to a more comprehensive restoration of guilds, which might oppose mechanization of production. Such fears could only have intensified when, shortly after the organization of the shoemakers into a body, a group of merchants and artisans in Paris launched a major attempt to restore corporations.

As efforts by various trades across France to group themselves into self-governing bodies continued, the Council on Manufacturing remained inactive. Unsettled by the reshuffling – one might even say purge – of its membership, the council did not officially react to the attempts to reestablish guild-like structures during 1816. The position of Ternaux was tenuous and the council had to find a new internal chemistry after the replacement of several of its members, leaving it in a disadvantageous position to counteract the movement to reestablish corporate structures in trades.

With the council weakened, the only major impediment to the restoration of worker corporations was the Ministry of the Interior, and its stance was ambiguous. On the one hand, it refused to permit the reestablishment of trade corporations on an individual basis in various cities, but on the other it was willing to explore broader proposals in selected cities.

In Dunkirk, for example, after the prefect of the Department of Nord had been authorized by the Ministry of the Interior to explore the possibility of restoring worker corporations in that town, its mayor submitted a plan to the minister Joseph-Henri-Joachim Lainé, a moderate centrist, during early 1817. The mayor conceded that because such corporations had been suppressed at the beginning of the Revolution, former usages and the bodies themselves could be reestablished only by means of a general measure passed legislatively. The mayor observed, however, that the minister had stated that until such an action occurred it was possible for local officials to enact measures that would not contravene existing law nor exceed local authority, including the right to oversee trades that affected public order and to submit them to regulations that this responsibility required.

One means was to have meetings of tradesmen under the supervision of syndics because intelligent organization of "syndicates," as the mayor called them, was a device to which police had had recourse, not only in Paris but in

[110] *Collection officielle des ordonnances de police*, I: 5–7, 12–15, 18–19, 25–26.

other cities as well. The minister had also indicated that it should be clearly understood that individuals exercising the same trade could, under the supervision or even on the invitation of public authorities, join together "freely and spontaneously" in a mutual provident society modeled after similar institutions found in other cities for the purpose of social assistance – care for the elderly and the sick or assistance to the widows and children of men who practiced the trade.

If, after all of these dispositions, what the mayor referred to as "the current legislation" on the reestablishment of corporations was still not passed, local officials, he asserted, could use their existing powers to oversee trades that affected public order and impose regulations. Because the suppression of guilds had had an adverse impact on both workers and commerce, the mayor argued, and because experience had demonstrated the need to organize workers provisionally until a "regular and definitive" arrangement could be forged, he claimed that it was imperative to organize several trades into a provident society under the supervision of the office of the mayor.

Indeed, only workers grouped into such bodies would have the right to practice these trades, whether in the port or in the city, and each member would confine himself to practicing the trade into which he was grouped. One could be admitted into the proposed body only if he had resided in Dunkirk for one year and was of good character and morals, and he would have to present himself to the mayor, who would determine his admission to or exclusion from the "syndicate."

The syndic of each body would be selected by the mayor and the Chamber of Commerce, and the office would be renewed every three years. The mayor also outlined proposed disciplinary measures for infractions by members, the responsibilities of workers and other such issues in his letter.

The sub-prefect based in Dunkirk endorsed the project put forward by the mayor because it sought to provide to commerce the guarantees that the interest of workers and the maintenance of public order required. He recommended that the minister approve the plan.[111] The prefect forwarded the project with his approbation to the Minister of the Interior, noting that it conformed to all of the guidelines specified by the minister in his October 1816 letter as necessary in order for bodies to be reestablished.[112]

Although the multiyear correspondence, which spanned two mayors of Dunkirk and five ministers of the Interior, would appear to indicate an attempt by public authorities to circumvent the abolition of guilds by establishing analogous bodies under the guise of charity and maintenance of order, the effort abruptly collapsed when it was explicitly characterized in this manner by an official. The proposed regulations drafted by the mayor were not approved – the undersecretary of the Ministry of the Interior, claiming that

---

[111] AN F¹² 2188, letter of mayor of Dunkirk to Minister of the Interior, January 17, 1817.
[112] AN F¹² 2188, letter of prefect of Department of Nord to Minister of the Interior, February 4, 1817.

the project, which he termed a "reprehensible initiative," was a veiled criticism of existing law that sought to reestablish corporations by disguising them under another name, refused to sanction them.[113]

The undersecretary, François-Louis Becquey, had been a deputy to the Legislative Assembly, achieving some distinction as one of the seven deputies to vote against the declaration of war in 1792. He had gone into hiding in his native region of Vitry-le-François (Marne) during the Terror, but returned to Paris under the Directory. He became associated with royalists seeking the return of Louis XVIII, but the group dissolved when Bonaparte became First Consul. Becquey served the Napoleonic regime as a deputy to the Legislative Body and as an officer of the Imperial University, but rallied to the Bourbons in 1814. He won election to the Chamber of Deputies in the elections of 1815 and became a member of the moderate minority, opposing various ultra initiatives. He became undersecretary when Lainé became Minister of the Interior and his appointment can be viewed as part of the movement against the ultras that began in May 1816.[114] His sudden termination of the effort to restore guilds in Dunkirk may similarly be understood as part of his opposition to ultra undertakings.

Clearly stunned by the tone of the undersecretary, the mayor of Dunkirk sent an angry letter to the sub-prefect in which he vigorously defended his attempt to reorganize workers, even though the effort had begun under his predecessor and he had simply continued it. The mayor noted the support that the measure had consistently enjoyed in Dunkirk, but, citing the gravity of the undersecretary's insinuations against him, he offered to resign, although he would remain proud of the regard in which his fellow citizens held him.[115]

Seeking to mediate, the sub-prefect wrote to the prefect that the mayor's intentions had been pure and that the undersecretary may have misunderstood the effort to conform to the October 1816 guidelines put forward by the minister. The sub-prefect asserted that the mayor sought only to propose means of security for commerce and order among workers in Dunkirk. He asked the prefect to make known to the minister that the mayor respected the principles of government and sought to make them the basis of his administration.[116]

For his part, the prefect also took a conciliatory stance. Although it was the undersecretary who had responded, he wrote to the minister that he had conveyed to the sub-prefect that the minister had not intended to offend the mayor and that the minister hoped that the mayor would respond to the confidence of his fellow citizens and remain in office. The prefect added that he had asked that another proposed set of regulations be drawn up, arguing that

[113] AN F¹² 2188, letter of mayor of Dunkirk to sub-prefect of Dunkirk, March 7, 1817, letter of sub-prefect of Dunkirk to prefect of Department of Nord, March 10, 1817.

[114] *Dictionnaire des parlementaires français*, 1: 233–234; on the beginning of the movement against the ultras, Alexander, *Re-Writing the French Revolutionary Tradition*, p. 55.

[115] AN F¹² 2188, letter of mayor of Dunkirk to sub-prefect of Dunkirk, March 7, 1817.

[116] AN F¹² 2188, letter of sub-prefect of Dunkirk to prefect of Department of Nord, March 10, 1817.

"disciplinary regulations on certain classes of workers in cities were indispensable and generally demanded." He also declared that local authorities should be able to make known to higher authorities any problems and to submit suggestions for ameliorating them. It was up to the minister, the prefect concluded, to judge if the mayor of Dunkirk had exceeded his authority, but the prefect averred that the mayor's intentions had been honest and respectable.[117]

The undersecretary of the ministry wrote directly to the mayor of Dunkirk to declare that he knew all that one could argue with respect to the advantages of guilds. The opposing argument, he observed, was the progress that unfettered industry had made in many sectors, and that, whatever position one took, current law alone should rule. If the government had no part in proposing another law, it was appropriate that authorities not announce a change that did not exist, which was the instruction that he had given to the prefect of the Department of Nord.[118]

The undersecretary's letter clearly demonstrated the futility of authorities in Dunkirk continuing to seek the reestablishment of guilds administratively, through the Ministry of the Interior. If elements in the town wished to restore corporations, they would have to work through the legislature. In fact, the following year a group of workers from Dunkirk petitioned the Chamber of Deputies, seeking official recognition for a status closely resembling that of a former guild.[119] On April 2, 1818, however, the chamber refused to consider the petition and instead sent it to the Minister of the Interior for resolution.[120]

The undersecretary of the ministry sent a stern letter to the prefect of the Department of Nord stating that it was irregular for workers who were not allowed legally to comprise a corporation to send a petition to the chambers. Alluding to the correspondence of the preceding year, he reminded the prefect that the mayor's request to form seven occupations, including the one that had petitioned the chamber, had been refused.[121] After a final attempt some months later by four workers to circumvent the Ministry of the Interior by writing to the Duc d'Angoulême, which seems to have been ignored, the effort to reestablish guilds in Dunkirk ended.[122]

RENEWED EFFORTS TO RESTORE GUILDS

Although Feuillant's suggestion during the 1816 budget hearings to restore corporations was not acted on, it may have reflected a growing concern with

[117] AN F¹² 2188, letter of prefect of Department of Nord to Minister of the Interior, March 12, 1817.
[118] AN F¹² 2188, letter of undersecretary of Ministry of the Interior to mayor of Dunkirk, March 15, 1817.
[119] AN F¹² 2188, undated petition to president and members of Chamber of Deputies.
[120] AN F¹² 2188, Chamber of Deputies, meeting of April 2, 1818.
[121] AN F¹² 2188, letter of undersecretary of Ministry of the Interior to prefect of Department of Nord, May 7, 1818.
[122] AN F¹² 2188, letter of tradesmen to Duc d' Angoulême, December 3, 1818.

what was perceived as the ever increasing number of workers in Paris – during April 1817 the Prefect of Police wrote to the Minister of Police about this issue. It was the time of year, the prefect wrote, when seasonal workers, especially those in the building trades, streamed into the city seeking work. A subsistence crisis in several areas of France, along with special efforts made to provision Paris, had led to a larger influx than usual.[123] The city already had a large number of workers, and more were arriving daily. They were congregating at the traditional sites from which workers were hired, but the current amount of work was not sufficient to employ them all. Furthermore, the economic slowdown indicated that little improvement would be forthcoming. The prefect suggested an expansion of the public works program to occupy workers. Even if order had been maintained thus far, he stated, there was much to fear from prolonged idleness and the resulting misery. The workers would begin returning to their native regions in August, but the prefect was particularly concerned about the months of May and June.[124] In another reflection of the prefect's degree of concern, the following week he prohibited any bread from leaving the city.[125]

Against this background, it is not surprising that a new effort to restore guilds in Paris occurred during 1817. In September 1817, after an audience with Louis XVIII, a group of merchants and artisans from Paris, with the assistance of their counsel Levacher-Duplessis, drew up a *mémoire* on the need to reestablish the merchants body and guilds (*corps de marchands et les communautés des arts et métiers*) in Paris and submitted it along with a formal request that these actions be taken.

The cover letter of Levacher-Duplessis's request denounced the "innovating spirit of the last century," which had been turned loose especially on corporations, and asserted that corporations were a powerful means to assure order and public morality. The letter observed that since guilds had been abolished, industrial and commercial professions had been subjected to shameful license – there were no longer any regulations, limits or policing. Insubordination, the letter claimed, reigned in the workplace and bad faith, rather than order and probity, was the rule in retail commerce. In Paris, the most scandalous efforts were used daily to deceive the public, and honest merchants were powerless to stop them.

In craft trades, other problems were apparent. Masters had no authority, and the indiscipline of workers knew no limits. Apprenticeships had virtually disappeared because the terms of their conditions were no longer enforced.

Such was, the *mémoire* asserted, the "sad but faithful portrait of commerce and industry" in Paris, and it was for this reason that the group was asking the monarch to reestablish the merchants' body and guilds in the city. The cover letter asserted that they were not asking to restore privileges that restrained

---

[123] On the crisis, Miller, *Mastering the Market*, pp. 246–253.
[124] AN F7 9787, copy of letter of Prefect of Police to Minister of Police, April 24, 1817.
[125] APP DB 305, ordinance prohibiting bread from leaving Paris, May 1, 1817.

commerce and industry; they were asking only for the repression of license. The cover letter bore no names or addresses, but Levacher-Duplessis claimed that it had been signed by members of thirty-four commercial and industrial professions.

The attached *mémoire* underscored the degeneration that had resulted from a system of "unlimited freedom" and stated that in Paris and elsewhere there had been appeals to reestablish guilds. After thirty years, the *mémoire* argued, the system brought in by the Revolution could no longer be defended – there was a sense of exhaustion after so many unfortunate innovative efforts.

Whereas Costaz had earlier praised the legislation and industrial policy of the Directory and especially that of the Napoleonic regime, Levacher-Duplessis's *mémoire*, although conceding that some laws had slightly improved the conditions of commerce and labor, argued that most of them had been ineffectual, primarily because of a lack of enforcement. The marketplace, the *mémoire* asserted, remained in a degraded state due to poor quality, deceit and dishonesty by unscrupulous producers. It argued that the government should disregard the notion that the marketplace would reestablish itself and recognize that there was an urgent need to correct the many deficiencies still present.

The *mémoire* disputed the idea that the reestablishment of corporations would impede industrial progress. It argued instead that the restoration of quality that would result from their reestablishment would facilitate industrial development.

The *mémoire* alluded to the reorganization of various bodies – from those of bakers to barristers – and noted that conditions had improved in all of these occupations since their reestablishment. The *mémoire* also asserted, without documenting the claim, that the Napoleonic Council of State had voted by a majority to reestablish guilds, but that this had been averted by "political circumstances" that were not specified. Levacher-Duplessis concluded by declaring that the *mémoire* refuted all possible arguments against restoring corporations and asked Louis XVIII to reestablish them.[126]

Others had drafted *mémoires* asking Louis XVIII to reestablish guilds,[127] but Levacher-Duplessis and his clients followed their *mémoire* with a more systematic, sustained effort to restore the merchants' body and guilds. In fact, on October 7, shortly after the meeting with the monarch, commissioners of the group had had a brief meeting with the Minister of the Interior, during which the minister had offered some noncommittal remarks.

Dissatisfied, representatives of the group, who claimed that their *mémoire* had been signed by 2,000 individuals, wrote a letter seeking a longer audience

---

[126] *Requête au roi, et mémoire sur la nécessité de rétablir les corps de marchands et les communautés des arts et métiers; présentés à Sa Majesté le 16 septembre 1817, par les marchands et artisans de la ville de Paris, assistés de M. Levacher-Duplessis, leur conseil* (Paris: J. Smith, 1817).

[127] In addition to those already mentioned, see AN F¹² 1560, undated *mémoire* of Pierre to Louis XVIII.

with the minister in order to explain their request. They argued that they were not simply seeking to assist some merchants or artisans, but were taking on such larger issues as order, license and public morality.

From the brief conversation the minister had had with the commissioners, the commissioners noted that they had been unable to ascertain when the minister might act on their request – perhaps a year or even longer. The letter insisted again that the matter be submitted for consideration and discussion to the Council of State immediately. During their meeting, the minister had mentioned to its commissioners that the group had "numerous adversaries," and the commissioners acknowledged that this was indeed the case. They argued, however, that they had made their principles, reasons and proofs public in their published *mémoire*, and asked that an honest dialogue begin and that the minister back their cause.[128]

Four members of the group also delivered a copy of the *mémoire* to the Chamber of Commerce of Paris, which discussed it in a meeting during October. The chamber noted that the request was signed only by Levacher-Duplessis, and said that nothing justified the alleged mission of the signatories of the letter. It was misleading, the chamber stated, to present the request as being the work of the merchants and artisans of the city of Paris.[129]

As to the request itself, the chamber observed that its opinion on the matter had long been known. Attempts to restore guilds had been made during 1805 by the same means currently being employed, and in 1805 the Chamber of Commerce of Paris had published a report on the issue. There could be no doubt, the chamber asserted, about the deleterious effects that could be expected from the reestablishment of corporations and privileges.

Time and reflection, the chamber argued, had served only to strengthen its opinion, which the chamber believed it had a duty to make known. The chamber also decided that it would appoint a deputation that would seek a meeting with the undersecretary of the Ministry of the Interior to express its concern about the effort to reestablish guilds.[130] As a result, by unanimous consent, the chamber sought to make an extract of its minutes public, and it appeared in several newspapers.[131]

After the chamber had made its view public, Levacher-Duplessis responded with a lengthy set of observations to the ministry on the opinion of the Chamber of Commerce. He asserted that the chamber had claimed, "perhaps with a little too much assurance," that it had definitively settled this important

---

[128] AN F¹² 2188, undated (but between October 7 and 17, 1817) letter of delegates of merchants and artisans of Paris to Minister of the Interior.

[129] The issue of the legitimacy of the claim to represent the merchants and artisans of Paris would become a common critique. Michel Frédéric Pillet-Will, *Réponse au mémoire de M. Levacher-Duplessis, ayant pour titre "Requête et mémoire sur la nécessité de rétablir les corps de marchands et les communautés des arts et métiers," par Pillet-Will* (Paris: Didot l'aîné, 1817).

[130] ACCIP 2 Mi 3, fols. 230–231.

[131] *Gazette nationale, ou le Moniteur universel,* October 16, 1817.

question. He stated that in preparing his *mémoire* he had, in fact, consulted the 1805 opinion of the chamber, but added sarcastically that he was far from regarding his opinion as being as lofty and that he did not regard his opinion as a final verdict without appeal. Levacher-Duplessis noted that he had addressed the critical points of the 1805 opinion in the third chapter of his *mémoire* but had not cited it because he sought to be objective rather than personal in his arguments.

Because the chamber had thrown the first punch, however, he would answer, and he put forward a lengthy rebuttal. He asserted, with underlining for emphasis, that instead of making a conclusive case for the deleterious effects of guilds, the chamber's report implicitly demonstrated the necessity of reestablishing them.[132]

The chamber's publication of its opinion led to a widening of the debate. One newspaper, for example, which had published neither the original request to the king nor the opinion of the Chamber of Commerce, felt compelled to publish both by the end of the month. The newspaper explained that it wished to keep readers informed as discussion of this important issue established itself.[133]

Although couched in polite terms, the letter of the group led by Levacher-Duplessis to the Minister of the Interior was strong, even aggressive, in tone, and the minister replied in a firm tone as well. On October 25 he wrote to the group that a question as important as that raised in the *mémoire* presented to the king unquestionably deserved the most serious attention. Although the issue had long been discussed and debated, and although powerful arguments in favor of the reestablishment of corporations had been brought forward many times, the minister believed it his duty to observe that even if the issue remained unresolved, it was because serious objections had been raised against the project and that advocates of the opposite policy had also been able to raise issues of great weight. In this situation, the minister noted, it was not possible to enact such a request until the subject had been more deeply explored and an unflinching discussion within the government had taken place on the possible advantages or disadvantages of adopting a system almost entirely antithetical to the legislation currently in force. He concluded by assuring the group that they should not doubt the care and attention that would be given to the matter.[134]

However direct, the theme of the letter – indeed, the summary given to it by the ministry itself – was that the request of Levacher-Duplessis and his group would be considered. As a result, they continued their efforts and the issue of the restoration of guilds lingered.

[132] AN F¹² 2188, observations on the report of the Chamber of Commerce of Paris, relative to guilds and masterships, undated.
[133] *Journal des débats politiques et littéraires*, October 30, 1817.
[134] AN F¹² 2188, letter of Minister of the Interior to merchants and artisans of Paris, signatories to the *mémoire* presented to the king in favor of the reestablishment of corporations, October 25, 1817.

In fact, a few days later, on October 29, the minister asked the Council on Manufacturing to examine it. The importance of the request, the publicity that it had received and the dissension that it had generated led the minister, he declared, to consult the council on the matter. The minister notified the council that he had just informed the petitioners' leaders that their request would be examined with great care and serious attention.

The minister recommended the 1805 report of the Chamber of Commerce of Paris to the council, asserting that it provided useful insights as the question arose once again. He sent the council a copy of the report as well as copies of the minutes of the chamber, including those of the October 8 meeting at which it had discussed the *mémoire*. The minister wanted these items, along with the *mémoire*, to serve as the basis for the council's deliberations.

He asked the council to take up the matter as quickly as possible. In addition, he requested that the council consider whether matters should be left as they were or whether the minister should create syndicates similar to those that were in existence in various professions.[135]

THE COUNCIL ON MANUFACTURING DELIBERATES

Weeks before the minister had asked the council to examine the issue, however, the council had become aware of the request and had begun to discuss it. On October 2, a member of the council had submitted copies of the *mémoire* to the body, and a week later, at the next meeting, a member inquired as to how the *mémoire* had come before the council. The reply came that it had been brought by a member who had received it directly from Levacher-Duplessis and that no discussion of it had occurred. An exploration of the *mémoire* followed, focusing on the manner in which it had originated and the propriety of the signatories' claim to represent all of the merchants and artisans of Paris. Anticipating that the petition given to the monarch would be forwarded to the Minister of the Interior and that the council would be consulted on it, it terminated the discussion.[136]

It was during the next week that the excerpt from the minutes of the Chamber of Commerce of Paris appeared in several newspapers. The Council on Manufacturing met on the same day that the extract appeared, which led to further discussion of the *mémoire*. One member, in reviewing the minutes of the previous council meeting, wanted the title of the *mémoire* recorded more accurately and to emphasize the council's displeasure that it seemed to claim to speak for all merchants and artisans of Paris. The council corrected the title in its minutes, but did not address the presumption of the *mémoire* that it represented all Parisian merchants and artisans. Another member took the opportunity to advise the council of the insertion in many newspapers of

---

[135] AN F¹² 2188, letter of Minister of the Interior to members of Council on Manufacturing, October 29, 1817.
[136] AN F¹²* 195, fol. 90, fols. 104–105.

the extract of the Chamber of Commerce opposing the reestablishment of guilds. He noted that publication of its minutes by the chamber was irregular because an administrative decision had prohibited it from doing so.[137]

This observation provoked an animated discussion, both on the issue of the reestablishment of guilds and the means used to support or oppose this. The meeting ended, however, with the council deciding that it had not been called upon to approve or censure the conduct of the authors of the *mémoire* or that of the Chamber of Commerce.[138]

Comte Christophe Chabrol de Crouzol, a former member of the Council of State who had recently been named undersecretary of the Ministry of the Interior,[139] solicited the opinion of the Council on Manufacturing on October 30, 1817. The council quickly decided to name a subcommittee of seven members to examine the issue and to report back to it. Another member, who supported the proposal to form the subcommittee, suggested that the group headed by Levacher-Duplessis be asked for a concrete plan on the means to be employed in reestablishing corporations because neither the request nor the *mémoire* contained a specific proposal. It would be useful for the authors of the project, he said, to make explicit the structure of their proposed system.

Several members of the council opposed this suggestion, with some stating that such a request would prejudge the question. Others, however, asserted that the letter of the Comte de Chabrol appeared to give the council sufficient latitude to make the request. In addition, the council informally agreed that it would suggest dispositions that would be appropriate to add to existing legislation on commercial and industrial professions.

The council then proceeded to elect the subcommittee, which included Ternaux. All but one of the members selected were present at the meeting, and they set a date and time for the subcommittee to meet at Ternaux's residence.[140]

The subcommittee presented its report to the council on November 20, but it quickly became enmeshed in various procedural issues, such as whether the subcommittee or the council itself would make changes to the report. Ternaux acknowledged the validity of the observations, and because the subcommittee, which had met shortly before the council meeting, had not had time to complete its discussion of the report, he cut the reading of the report short and opened the floor to members so they could continue the discussion. After comments by members of the subcommittee, changes were made to the report.

The council discussed whether, with respect to the exercise of commercial and industrial professions, the current state of affairs should continue to exist or whether it would be useful to adopt some new measures. Opinion on the issue was divided, with some members noting that the council was unaware

[137] Indeed, those who favored the reestablishment of guilds believed that the extracts of the minutes of the chamber had been planted by the police. BHVP Ms. N.A. 477. fols. 268–269.

[138] AN F^{12}* 195, fol. 105.

[139] AN F^{12}* 195, fol. 105.

[140] AN F^{12}* 195, fol. 112.

of many current regulations among professions that had already been formed into syndicates. Ternaux sought to summarize the various matters raised during the discussion and argued that the subcommittee could not resolve whether the current situation should continue or whether it should determine changes to be made without having fully discussed the proposed means, particularly because the discussion could, he declared, result in a political outcome contrary to many innovations.

The unnamed member who had had the floor before Ternaux asked if he could continue to speak and inquired as to whether he could present in a more systematic fashion some of his ideas. The council accepted this request and he began to read his text, but Ternaux interrupted, stating that if every or even just several of the council members wrote on the issue, the council could not truly discuss it until after all such readings, which could take an enormous amount of time. He therefore asked that all discussion be verbal in order to examine all of the various opinions, and the council agreed.

The minutes do not indicate whether the text that the member had sought to read had favored the reestablishment of guilds, but that is evident from what immediately followed. Another member of the council was given the floor, and he observed that for more than ten years the council had been consulted many times on the reestablishment of corporations and that it had consistently and almost unanimously voted against this. This was well known to the only member of the council who held the opposite view, who dared now hope that his view would triumph or flattered himself that he could convince the council of its correctness at this meeting after it had already indicated its opposition to many different versions. The view of the council seemed fixed and unyielding, he asserted, and attempts to change that would do little more than waste time.

The council heartily welcomed this observation, and Ternaux claimed that it would be useless to continue discussion because nearly all members considered it superfluous since it would do nothing to change the council's opinion. Consequently, Ternaux proposed that the council proceed with a vote on two questions presented by the subcommittee. The first was whether the reestablishment of the merchants' body and guilds in the manner in which they had existed before the Revolution was beneficial to the interests of commerce and industry. The council voted unanimously that it was not.

The second question was whether their reestablishment with modifications would be advantageous. Again, the council voted that this would not serve commerce and industry, but this time there was one dissenting vote.

The subcommittee also put forward a third proposition – whether consideration should be given to different measures that could be adopted to "regularize" the practice of industrial and commercial professions. Ternaux stated that he thought that the necessity of some dispositions was generally recognized and desired. He offered as an example commerce with the Ottoman Empire, which had formerly been successful because regulations on the production of textiles had provided a material guarantee for Ottoman consumers. The abandonment of these regulations, he claimed, had enabled foreign producers to enter markets in the Ottoman Empire at the expense of France.

Ternaux's belief, however, was not shared by many members of the council, who argued that currently successful foreign products were not made by manufacturers who were subject to strict regulations. They stated that freedom of industry should not be overturned, and one member opined that the loss of markets was due to other causes rooted in the Revolution, such as the Maximum. Another member spoke against strict production regulations as harmful to industry. Ternaux ended the discussion, stating that this was not the moment to discuss all of its ramifications – it could be done when the matter of measures to be enacted arose.

The meeting was about to be adjourned when a member asked if he could propose that the council explicitly state the reasons for its opposition to the reestablishment of corporations. If this was done, the view of the council could serve as a direct refutation of both the request and the *mémoire* that sought their reestablishment. Ternaux stated, however, that the subcommittee or the entire council could take up the request when the final report was adopted, after full deliberation on the matter.[141]

The minutes of the council do not provide the names of speakers, making it difficult to identify the member who sought the reestablishment of guilds with modifications. The evidence suggests, however, that it was Eugène de Bray – de Bray had been mentioned by Levacher-Duplessis as having assisted in the preparation of the *mémoire* that he submitted.[142]

De Bray, of whom little is known, was a cotton-spinning mill owner from Amiens, but he had a residence in Paris, which enabled him to attend the council's meetings on a regular basis.[143] Unlike many of his colleagues on the council, he does not seem to have served on the Tribunal of Commerce for the Department of Seine.[144] Following the Hundred Days, he wrote a paean to Louis XVIII in which he asserted that the Bourbons had brought freedom, peace and happiness, whereas Bonaparte had replaced these with despotism, civil war and foreign war.[145] On the issue of privileges for the port of Dunkirk, particularly its free-port status, on which members of the council had published a pamphlet, de Bray had stood with the council in opposing the town's claims.[146]

On the matter of corporations, however, de Bray seems to have acted as an informer for Levacher-Duplessis and his group because only days after the council meeting on the reestablishment of guilds, a delegation from Levacher-

[141] AN F¹²* 195, fols. 118–120.
[142] *Requête au Roi et mémoire*, pp. 58–59.
[143] On his origins in Amiens and his occupation, AN F¹² 618, letter of secretary of Council on Manufacturing to Director-General of Agriculture and Manufacturing, July 1, 1814; on his Paris residence, *Almanach Royal 1816*, p. 135.
[144] AN F¹² 941, dossier Seine (1815), dossier Seine (1817).
[145] Eugène de Bray, *Le Règne de Louis XVIII, comparé à la dictature de Napoléon, depuis le 20 mars 1815 jusqu'au 31 mai suivant*, 2nd ed. (Paris: Ofigez, 1815), especially p. 48.
[146] *Observations sur le rétablissement de la franchise du port et de la ville de Dunkerque, présentés aux deux chambres* (Paris: Bailleul, n.d.).

Duplessis's group wrote to the Comte de Chabrol about the meeting. Its members began by notifying Chabrol that they had learned that the request and the *mémoire* had been submitted to the Council on Manufacturing for its opinion. Because the council was an advisory group to the Minister of the Interior rather than a public body, the fact of the meeting would not necessarily have been public knowledge, particularly so quickly after it had occurred.

The letter to Chabrol stated that although the council undoubtedly had many men knowledgeable in industry and manufacturing, it did not have a single member corresponding to the professions represented by Levacher-Duplessis's group who could enlighten the government about the problems they confronted. Who, they asked, knew better than they the problems afflicting them and the solutions to them?

They requested a meeting with Chabrol at which they could explain further their request to the king. They had not, they claimed, said everything they wanted to say in their *mémoire* and wished to add more to the discussion. They asked Chabrol to receive six of them in an audience – three members from retail trades and three from trade crafts, along with Levacher-Duplessis. In late November, Chabrol agreed to meet with them.[147]

Even as the Minister of the Interior was taking a careful and measured approach to the issue, Chabrol actively assisted the petitioners. Chabrol was newly installed as undersecretary of the Ministry of the Interior, having assumed his duties only on September 24. The son of a conservative noble deputy to the Estates-General, Chabrol, along with his family, had been imprisoned during the Terror, and were released in 1795.

He had entered public life during the Consulate and had held a series of posts under the Napoleonic regime. He went over to the Bourbon regime in 1814 and was made a member of the Council of State before being named prefect of the Department of Rhône in November 1814. During the Hundred Days he attempted to mount a defense of Lyon, but when the futility of that effort became clear, he fled as Bonaparte entered and rejoined the Comte d'Artois, who had initially assisted him in making preparations for defense of the city. Chabrol returned to Lyon only in July 1815, and reassumed his duties as prefect, although the city was under Austrian occupation.

His second tenure as prefect was sullied by the eruption of the White Terror in Lyon, which raged for more than a year – from June 1816 until September 1817, when Louis XVIII sent General Marmont to restore order in the city. A reactionary general who had spearheaded the White Terror in Lyon, General Canuel, was relieved of his command in Lyon and Chabrol was removed as prefect. As compensation for the loss of the prefecture, he was named undersecretary at the Ministry of the Interior.[148]

---

[147] AN F¹² 512, letter of delegates of merchants and master artisans of Paris to Undersecretary of State at Ministry of the Interior, November 25, 1817; letter to delegates on behalf of undersecretary, November 28, 1817.

[148] *Dictionnaire des parlementaires français*, 2: 17–18; *Nouvelle biographie générale*, 9: 541–542.

Chabrol had not been a participant in the White Terror, but he had done nothing to oppose it. After witnessing turmoil for more than a year in the second-largest city in France, including the permanent placement of a guillotine in the city, Chabrol would almost certainly have been susceptible to arguments in favor of order in society. Whatever his motivation, it is clear that he sought to promote the restoration of guilds.

A few days after his meeting with the delegation, Chabrol, during a session over which he personally presided, consulted the Council on Commerce on the question of the reestablishment of the merchants' body and guilds, although only four members of the council were present. After distributing some documents, Chabrol informed these members that the matter had been discussed during several meetings of the Council on Manufacturing, which had recommended against it, even with modifications.

Despite the fact that the majority of members of the Council on Commerce agreed with the view of the Council on Manufacturing, Chabrol, without dismissing their position but clearly determined to pursue the issue, argued that the question could be approached from a different point of view. According to him, fine minds who could not be accused of favoring a return to the regulated system for factories nevertheless believed it necessary to enact some regulations, particularly with respect to relations between masters and workers.

He cited different types of complaints that had arisen in many locales regarding production, unrest and abuses that, he claimed, broke the bonds of subordination on the part of workers, destroyed confidence between them and masters, and even struck at the honesty of arrangements. On one side, Chabrol asserted, political considerations related to commercial relations with foreign countries where it was important to maintain markets acquired through a deserved reputation for quality of production, and, on the other side, considerations of order and public confidence converged to make actions appropriate to current circumstances desirable.

One member then asked if he could read a work that he had prepared on this matter that included general views that harmonized with those expressed by Chabrol. He began reading until he reached a point at which he believed it necessary to ask that the measures he was preparing be enacted in the grain trade to correct abuses that he claimed existed. He acknowledged, however, that this touched on an infinitely sensitive sector and could be put in place only after a discussion by the council.

Because it was late in the meeting, however, the reading was suspended. Chabrol asked the council if it was amenable to continuing to examine the issue, which, he admitted, ought to be treated by the Council on Manufacturing. A member observed that an insufficient number of members were present to appoint a subcommittee, so he suggested holding an extraordinary meeting of the council to name a subcommittee. Chabrol argued that it would be useless to convene a special meeting to which many members who rarely attended could still excuse themselves when it was only a matter of a single item. Rather, he believed that the members in attendance could well appreciate all of the considerations of public good that were involved in this important question. "Despite this observation," according to the minutes, the council elected not to pursue discussion of the matter and adjourned without taking any action.[149]

In the meantime, the Council on Manufacturing continued its investigation of the "existing system," particularly the degree to which trades had already been organized into bodies or syndicates. On December 11, it received a letter and documents sent by Chabrol the previous day relating to some of the professions "syndicated" in Paris. The council had sought this information to inform itself during its consideration of the reestablishment of corporations, and decided to forward the documents to its subcommittee.[150]

It appears that the subcommittee asked Chabrol for additional information, because on December 26 an official in the Ministry of the Interior, citing that the issue of the reestablishment of guilds had been raised, wrote to the Prefect of Police in Paris to seek clarification about which industrial trades or professions were already organized into corporations with delegates or syndics, conferring upon them "a kind of special accommodation or policy."

According to a list drawn up in 1816, the official wrote, it seemed that syndics or delegates for whom the prefect had authorized elections numbered thirteen, which he listed. According to the author of the letter, however, the *Almanach Royal* had not included three of the trades included in that list. Similarly, the *Almanach Royal* listed eight other trades as having been formed into bodies for which Chabrol had no record. He asked the prefect to provide him as quickly as possible with a precise list of all the groups of merchants or workers who were currently led by syndics or delegates under his authorization. The official also requested the regulations that governed these trades.

A list of trades that had been formed into bodies that was enclosed indicated that those of bakers and butchers had been organized by the central government during the years X and XI. The remaining thirteen had been established by the prefect, with the vast majority of them organized during 1809 and 1810.[151]

The letter suggests that the grouping of trades into corporations had virtually escaped the control of the central government. The Ministry of the Interior did not have a full grasp of the situation, and the incertitude of the Council on Manufacturing with respect to the "existing situation" is understandable. The results of the investigation by the Prefect of Police were sent to the Council on Manufacturing on January 17, 1818.[152]

---

[149] AN F^{12}* 192bis, fols. 54v°–55.

[150] AN F^{12}* 195, fol. 126.

[151] AN F^{12} 2188, letter of Undersecretary of Ministry of the Interior to Prefect of Police, December 26, 1817. See also AN F^{12} 2183, December 26, 1817 (no entry number).

[152] AN F^{12} 2183, January 17, 1818, nos. 143–144.

THE PERSISTENCE OF EFFORTS TO RESTORE CORPORATIONS

On December 26, the same day that the official wrote to the prefect, delegates of "entrepreneur roofers" wrote to Louis XVIII through their president. In a reflection of the fluidity of the organization of trades or occupations into guild-like bodies, the roofers stated that they were "organized into a provisional corporation" and asked that their guild be reestablished. They argued that its restoration would be a sure method of correcting the large number of abuses that were occurring under the system of isolated individuals practicing the same trade. It was well known, they asserted, that the sense of honor connected with a constituted corporation was one that individuals feared compromising much more than if they lived and operated in isolation.

The building trades in Paris employed a great number of workers, and therefore required greater supervision, they argued. Both as a matter of private interest and public good, the trade had attracted the government's attention. In the past, only masters had had the right to practice the trade of roofer, and prospective members had been admitted to the guild only after demonstrating proof of good character and having satisfactorily answered different questions posed by officers of the guild. Currently, however, the lowest grade of occupational license sufficed to enter and practice the trade.[153]

More systematically, Levacher-Duplessis and his clients continued their effort to reestablish the merchants' body and guilds of Paris. Buttressing the belief that de Bray – or someone else – within the council was informing Levacher-Duplessis of the critique of the *mémoire* within the Council on Manufacturing, Levacher-Duplessis published a supplement to his original *mémoire*. The supplement sought to "end all incertitude" by explaining the means to reestablish guilds and went on to enumerate the requirements to be admitted into a guild.

The former statutes had established a minimum age of twenty in order to become a master, but except that the age of eighteen had been set in order to receive an occupational license, no regulations had replaced the old ones. Levacher-Duplessis advocated a minimum age of twenty-one.

He also argued for a mandatory apprenticeship, which should be regulated "with moderation and wisdom" and the duration of which should be "neither too short nor too long." Although Levacher-Duplessis did not want to establish a uniform length of apprenticeship for all occupations, he proposed four years and put forward guidelines for this.

Levacher-Duplessis also asserted that all of the laws enacted in the economic sphere during the Napoleonic regime had been so detailed and had multiplied to such a degree that they were difficult to enforce. The restoration of corporations, he argued, would be an effective means of oversight.

Levacher-Duplessis claimed that the government and the two chambers were sympathetic to his ideas. He concluded the supplement with the claim that "public freedom" did not consist of "vain theories" or in "abstract principles

---

[153] AN F¹² 2188, letter of delegates of entrepreneur-roofers of Paris to Louis XVIII, December 26, 1817.

consigned to a Charter," but were to be found in "a joining of similar interests in a common association."[154]

In Paris, the initiative led by Levacher-Duplessis elicited a public expression of support. Although he believed the request put forward by Levacher-Duplessis and his group was too cutting in tone, one contemporary strongly supported the push to reestablish corporations.[155]

Beyond Paris, the effort by Levacher-Duplessis to restore guilds drew different responses from two disparate areas of France. The Consultative Chamber of Manufacturing and Arts and Trades of St. Quentin – a town of concentrated mechanized textile production – wrote a response to Levacher-Duplessis and sent it to the Minister of the Interior.[156] The chamber stated that Levacher-Duplessis was an eloquent defender of the reestablishment of guilds, but questioned whether the issue had been correctly presented to him. The chamber sought, it claimed, to put forward a "circumspect refutation" but one "sufficiently extensive" to support their opinion.

The arguments advanced by the chamber are familiar and do not need to be treated at length – the reorganization of corporations would stifle innovation and individual initiative. The current problems under consideration, the chamber asserted, had not resulted from the absence of guilds.[157]

By contrast, artisans from Bordeaux wrote to the king to support the petition of Levacher-Duplessis. Stating that the experience of twenty-five years had destroyed all illusions, the artisans endorsed the petition and, once again, the arguments were familiar.

In 1791, they claimed, "in the name of freedom" guilds and masterships had been suppressed. With each individual having received the right to practice any trade or profession, all subordination and discipline had been destroyed. Although it did not refer to the Napoleonic regime by name, the petition asserted that it had limited itself to half-measures – establishing "a kind of discipline for workers and apprentices," an allusion to the law of 22 germinal year XI. These "incomplete measures" had not produced any results, and the disorder they sought to prevent or at least diminish continued.

The problems that were merely a nuisance to consumers were a source of discouragement and ruin to honest merchants and artisans, a point that was emphasized through underlining. Just as the petition of Levacher-Duplessis did, the artisans of Bordeaux asked, among other things, that each trade or profession have a mandatory apprenticeship, that proofs of competence and probity be required and that each corporation have its own internal discipline.[158]

[154] Levacher-Duplessis, *Appendice du Mémoire sur les corporations* (N.p., 1818).
[155] G.P. Legret, *Sur les corporations* (Paris: Scherff, 1818).
[156] It also sent a copy to the Chamber of Commerce of Paris, which sent a letter of thanks. ACCIP 2 Mi 3, fol. 234; ACCIP 1 Mi 4, fols. 81–82.
[157] AN F^{12} 2188, letter of Consultative Chamber of Commerce on Manufacturing, Arts and Trades of St. Quentin to Levacher-Duplessis, October 23, 1817.
[158] AN F^{12} 2188, letter of artisans of Bordeaux to king, undated; letter of transmission to General Council on Manufacturing, January 1, 1818.

Both documents were sent to the Council on Manufacturing, which, in turn, forwarded them to its subcommittee examining the issue of the reestablishment of guilds.[159] A few weeks later the council also received a notice that the Ministry of the Interior had asked the Prefect of Police to provide him with information on the different regulations and ordinances relative to the syndicates or corporations of certain "industrial professions" that had their own special discipline. The minister also sent to the council the request of the entrepreneur roofers of Paris to form themselves into a guild.[160]

Although the focal point of the Council on Manufacturing was Paris, an inventory of documentation given to the council to consider in its examination of whether to reestablish guilds involved statutes or regulations of different occupations across France – from Bordeaux, Versailles, Cambrai, Lille, Nantes and Marseille.[161] Its decision would have a national impact.

AWAITING THE DELIBERATION

Whether or not it was in response to the observation in the appendix to the *mémoire* of Levacher-Duplessis that the various laws on worker discipline were not being enforced cannot be determined, but in early 1818 the Prefect of Police of Paris wrote to the Minister of Police about the necessity of strongly and uniformly enforcing regulations on workers.[162] On January 10, the Minister of Police sent a circular to prefects of the departments instructing them to enforce the laws and to reduce the number of workers coming to Paris by limiting the number of passports they granted.[163]

In the absence of a decision by the Council on Manufacturing during 1818, workers continued to seek to arrange themselves into guild-like structures. During mid-1818, for example, artisans in Marseille asked to be grouped into corporations, and their request was passed along to the Council on Manufacturing.[164]

In fact, in an indication of awareness that matters had escaped the control of the central government, in mid-1818 the Minister of the Interior sent a circular to prefects in which he expressed concern about the efforts of some municipal authorities to reestablish guilds. In many instances, the minister advised the prefects, municipal officials had gone beyond the limits of the law and had sought to bring back guilds that had been abolished.

---

[159] AN F¹² 2188, letter of Minister of the Interior to Council on Manufacturing, December 26, 1817; AN F¹²* 195, fol. 142 (St. Quentin); AN F¹²* 195, fol. 224 (Bordeaux).

[160] AN F¹² 2188, communication of Ministry of the Interior to General Council on Manufacturing, January 17, 1818.

[161] AN F¹² 2188, letter of Minister of the Interior to Council on Manufacturing, December 10, 1817, documents communicated to date to Council on Manufacturing on question of reestablishment of corporations, December 22, 1817.

[162] AN F⁷ 9786, letter of Minister of Police to Prefect of Police, January 7, 1818.

[163] AN F⁷ 9786, letter of prefect of Department of Jura to Minister of Police, January 14, 1818; letter of prefect of Department of Manche to Minister of Police, January 26, 1818.

[164] AN F¹² 2183, July 1, 1818, entry 646.8.

Although the motives of municipal officials may have been laudable, they had often not sought approval from higher authorities. In other instances, prefects had assumed that these were local matters and they had approved or tolerated the actions without reviewing them. Each such example, the minister declared, served to authorize a great number of more or less analogous efforts.

The cumulative effect had been to generate much confusion and many complaints. In turn, the complaints had made the Ministry of the Interior aware of the bewildering array of ordinances and regulations that existed but had never been forwarded to the ministry. It was the responsibility of the Ministry of the Interior to ensure that measures taken in each locale not contravene general laws, which meant that examination and authorization of these acts were indispensable. In addition, some of the attributes that mayors had arrogated to themselves were illegal, especially those allowing them to judge infractions, which was the duty of the justice of the peace.

The minister instructed the prefects to examine the disciplinary ordinances or regulations established by mayors with respect to workers that had been established in their department without the minister's approval. For those arrangements that had been approved, the prefect should indicate the date of approval. Lastly, the minister ordered the prefects not to approve any measure without having first received permission from the ministry.[165]

RAPPROCHEMENT BETWEEN THE BOURBON GOVERNMENT AND THE SOCIETY FOR THE ENCOURAGEMENT OF NATIONAL INDUSTRY

Also during 1817, as the council continued to work on its report, a *rapprochement* between the Ministry of the Interior and the Society for the Encouragement of National Industry began. After the ministry had substantially reduced its financial support for the society, there had been a lessening of cooperation between them. It is, in fact, a measure of how strained relations between the society and the Crown were, particularly after the Hundred Days, that the society felt compelled to separate itself from its Napoleonic roots by fictionalizing its origins in the *Almanach Royal*. As a history written by an official of the society stated, and as had been described in editions of the *Almanach Royal* and *Almanach Impérial* going back to 1806, the society had been founded under the Napoleonic regime during the year X (1802). By 1817, however, the description of the society in the *Almanach Royal* claimed that it had been founded "many years before the Revolution" and had been "reestablished" in 1802.[166]

Under the ministry of Lainé, a moderate who took office in 1816, reconciliation began. On January 31, 1817, the ministry sent a circular to prefects

[165] AN F^{Ia} 33, dossier 1818, circular of July 3, 1818.
[166] *Almanach Impérial 1806*, p. 778; *Almanach Royal 1817*, p. 887.

praising the work of the society and instructing each prefect to make its work known in every corner of his department.[167] The circular was accompanied by the program for the prize competition of the society for 1817 and 1818, and late in the year the ministry forwarded the prize competition announcement for 1818, 1819, and 1820.[168] Moreover, the circular announcing the prize competition for 1818, 1819, and 1820 praised the "useful works" of the society and noted the importance of the results of its efforts. The ministry declared its pleasure that prefects had been attempting to promote participation in the society within their jurisdictions.[169]

In early 1818 the Ministry of the Interior received a brief history of the society that had been written by E.J. Guillard-Senainville, an official of the society, in 1814, which he had updated with a supplement in 1817.[170] Chabrol, the undersecretary of the Ministry of the Interior who had promoted the reestablishment of guilds, read it and wrote a warm letter to Guillard-Senainville to inform him of how impressed he was with the society's work.[171] Indeed, the following month, February 1818, Chabrol became a member of the society.[172] During September, the secretary of the society invited the Minister of the Interior to its ceremony for the distribution of prizes.[173] By the end of the year, the ministry was purchasing additional copies of the work by Guillard-Senainville, which it distributed to prefects.[174]

Indeed, by 1818 the society felt sufficiently confident to advocate the revival of the industrial exhibition – the very act that had brought it into disfavor with the Bourbon government when it had made the same request during the Hundred Days. In June 1818 the society's publication reported that an exhibition of products of industry had been held in Cassel during the spring. Before providing details on the exhibitors and their products, however, the article noted that it was France that had given rise to such exhibitions and it lamented their suspension for so many years. One could hope, the article stated, for their reestablishment.[175]

Two months later the society wrote about textile samples, along with some other products, that it had received from the Society of Agriculture of

---

[167] AN F¹ᵃ 33, dossier 1817, circular of January 31, 1817.

[168] AN F¹² 2183, January 31, 1817, entry no. 260, December 3, 1817, entry no. 4741.

[169] AN F¹ᵃ 33, dossier 1817, circular of December 8, 1817.

[170] For the history, AN F¹² 2333, notice on the Society for the Encouragement of National Industry (undated), supplement to notice on Society for the Encouragement of National Industry, December 12, 1817; on its arrival at the ministry, AN F¹² 2183, January 7, 1818, no. 145. In contrast to the description in the contemporaneous *Almanach Royal*, the notice declared that "the enthusiasm inspired by the exposition of the year IX gave birth to the Society for the Encouragement of National Industry."

[171] AN F¹² 2333, letter of undersecretary (of Ministry of the Interior) to Guillard-Senainville, January 7, 1818.

[172] AN F¹² 2183, February 17, 1818 (no entry number).

[173] AN F¹² 512, letter of secretary of Society for Encouragement of National Industry to Minister of the Interior, September 22, 1818.

[174] On the purchase, AN F¹² 2183, December 14, 1818, no. 4721; December 19, 1818, no. 4786. On the distribution to prefects, AN F¹² 981–984.

[175] *Bulletin de la Société d'Encouragement pour l'Industrie Nationale* 17 (1818): 193.

Châteauroux – the Society of Agriculture wished to increase awareness of progress made in the manufacture of wool in the town with the assistance of machines from Douglas. The Mechanical Arts Committee of the Society for the Encouragement of National Industry reported favorably on them, and praised in particular the high quality and modest cost of the wool. The society published the evaluation in its *Bulletin*, along with a report on manufacturing in the Department of Indre. In a more indirect endorsement of reviving the exhibition, the *Bulletin*, in its report on the Department of Indre, devoted extensive coverage to an exhibition of products of industry organized by the prefect of the department in September 1817.[176]

At a meeting of the leadership of the Society for the Encouragement of National Industry on September 23, 1818, officers observed that many individuals from outlying departments had offered to send the society samples of their products. The society's officials expressed satisfaction with the spread of industry and stated that it augured well for the next exhibition of products of French industry.[177]

THE COUNCIL ON MANUFACTURING CONVENES

As the council awaited the report on guilds from its subcommittee, several worker actions occurred throughout France, some of which revealed the types of problems that could result from the reestablishment of corporations. In the Department of Isère, which had been in a state of tension for years,[178] worker unrest had broken out during late 1818 when journeymen in Vienne had scuffled with the National Guard, leading to the arrest of seven.[179] The discontent escalated in early 1819 with news of the imminent arrival in Vienne of a new machine to cut fabric. Fabric cutters of the region had submitted a petition to local authorities seeking to prohibit the machine's introduction into their workshops.

The Ministry of the Interior looked into the incident because it was seeking to assist enterprises that had as their goals the acceleration of industry and the greater prosperity of production facilities. Indeed, the head of a division of the ministry had written to the sub-prefect at Vienne instructing him to take all necessary measures to reassure manufacturers that the government would not only protect their property, but also their right to innovate and promote industry.[180]

As a result, authorities visited the workshops of fabric cutters and collected information on workers in them in advance of the machine's arrival, and the

---

[176] *Bulletin de la Société d'Encouragement pour l'Industrie Nationale* 17 (1818): 229–233.

[177] *Bulletin de la Société d'Encouragement pour l'Industrie Nationale* 17 (1818): 262.

[178] Alexander, *Re-Writing the French Revolutionary Tradition*, pp. 56–58, 71–73, 75.

[179] AN F7 9786, dossier Isère, letter of prefect of Department of Isère to Minister of Police, November 12, 1818.

[180] AN F7 9786, dossier Isère, letter of head of Third Division of Ministry of the Interior to Minister of the Interior, February 19, 1819.

prefect observed that this measure had made an impression on some of them. The workers were informed of the punishments that could be levied if they persisted in any plan to destroy the machine. Although some workers had spoken of the misery that installation of the machine would bring them, three said that they still intended to destroy it. These three, along with eight others, were subsequently pointed out at a meeting and the prefect planned to take action against them, which he hoped would have the desired effect.[181]

There is no indication that the Council on Manufacturing was aware of what had occurred in Vienne, but the episode illustrates why the council opposed any reestablishment of guilds. Whatever arguments might be marshaled in favor of their restoration – quality control, order among workers – the council gave absolute primacy to innovation, mechanization and the development of industry. Indeed, during 1815 one member of the council had asserted that France was engaged in an "industrial struggle" with "our eternal enemies,"[182] and this outlook dominated its deliberations. The critical element in this "industrial struggle" was mechanization of production, and to allow corporations to be reestablished would provide a platform for any opposition to this.

The project languished within the council for more than a year, coming up again only in March 1819 and then only because of a petition forwarded to the council by the Minister of the Interior. On March 25, the minister sent the council a request by a group of fabric producers in Paris to establish a council of arbitrators (*conseil de prud'hommes*), modeled after those in other manufacturing centers of the kingdom – by the end of 1819, there were *conseils de prud'hommes* in forty-one cities and towns.[183] The producers asked for the establishment of such a body to resolve disputes "between masters and workers" in this sector because the justices of the peace, before whom such disputes were currently adjudicated, did not have a sufficient understanding of the issues to resolve them impartially.

After the petition was read to the council, a member mentioned that it lent itself to the project of the subcommittee appointed to consider disciplinary regulations for factories and workshops, which was one aspect to be examined by the subcommittee looking into the reestablishment of guilds. He proposed a reading of the report, which was now complete and took a position particularly applicable to the petition. As a result, the subcommittee's report was brought before the council, but because it was late and many members of the council were not present, discussion of it was postponed until the next meeting.[184]

On April 1, the meeting opened with consideration of the subcommittee's report, which, it was noted, had been appointed at the same time as

[181] AN F⁷ 9786, dossier Isère, letter of prefect of Department of Isère to Minister of the Interior, March 9, 1819.
[182] AN F¹²* 194, fol. 543.
[183] Costaz, *Histoire de l'administration en France*, 2: 256–257.
[184] AN F¹²* 196, fols. 66–67.

the reestablishment of corporations had been requested. The subcommittee, which had included de Bray in its membership, acknowledged that complete freedom of commerce and industry produced continuing complaints everywhere, and further acknowledged that the abuses that led to such outcries were substantial and real. The subcommittee argued, however, that the most widely proposed solution, the reestablishment of guilds, was not a beneficial course of action. Guilds, it asserted, had hindered industry and held back useful discoveries, and the progress of industry since the Revolution demonstrated that a return to that system would be self-defeating.

The subcommittee recognized a need for regulations in commerce and manufacturing and asserted that the law of 22 germinal year XI had been the first step toward such specialized oversight, and went on to cite subsequent legislation. Although some minor changes might be in order – the subcommittee suggested creating officials to assure enforcement of laws and regulations – the position of the subcommittee was that making current laws known and enforcing them more strictly would be adequate.[185]

After the reading, which consumed a large amount of time – the report was thirteen pages in printed form – the council held a discussion. In view of the extreme importance of the issue, a member argued, and to ensure that the discussion was as comprehensive as possible, the summary should be printed and circulated not only to members of the council in Paris, but also to members residing in departments, as well as members of the Consultative Chamber of Commerce. In this manner, he asserted, all possible objections and observations regarding the plan would be made known.

Another member, although not opposed to printing the summary, and also seeking as exhaustive a discussion as possible, argued against distributing the report beyond the members of the council residing in Paris. He asserted that sending it could appear to represent a tacit endorsement by the council of a project that it would not yet have discussed. Furthermore, he claimed that the discussion could result in substantial changes to the plan or even rejection of it. In either case, he argued, sending the project would be incomplete or superfluous. His comments drew support from many members of the council.

The speaker went on to offer additional ideas. If, he asked, as the subcommittee had indicated in its report, current laws and regulations were for the most part sufficient to deal with abuses, why should the subcommittee not simply limit itself to compiling a specific collection of all of the pertinent legislation? Such a compilation would have the advantage of making available a single source for this specialized field of knowledge to businessmen, manufacturers and workers alike – information that heretofore had been ignored

---

[185] Although it remained an internal document, it was printed as *Rapport rélatif au rétablissement demandé des corps de marchands et des communautés d'arts et métiers, et contenant la discussion des mesures proposées pour la police du commerce, des manufactures et des ateliers* (Paris: Imprimerie Royale, 1819) and was available at AD Seine-Maritime 10 M 1

or unknown. This course of action, he argued, would be preferable to adding new laws or creating an institution that could alarm commerce and industry through the fear of stalling their development. An opposing speaker, however, contended that the main aim of the report was to make up for the current lack of enforcement of laws and regulations that the commission regarded as the cause of the abuses that had led to complaints.

Other members advanced arguments both for and against the subcommittee's plan. The strong divergence of opinion that emerged, coming after only a cursory reading that had not allowed for extensive discussion, led the council to conclude that a more in-depth examination was necessary. Consequently, the council decided that the report would merely be printed and regarded as a matter under consideration and would be distributed only to members residing in Paris. After a careful reading, each member could bring his views of the project to a meeting. Only after a serious discussion by the council had occurred would the project be printed and distributed to departments.[186]

A member then raised the issue of the council of arbitrators for Paris – the request that had brought forward the project of the subcommittee and on which the Minister of the Interior had asked for an opinion – and asserted that although it was secondary in the work of the subcommittee, it had major implications for the interests of industry in Paris. He suggested that the matter be discussed during the next meeting at which the minister presided.

It would be easy, he claimed, to detach the question of a *conseil de prud'hommes* from the larger issue because current legislation gave the government the power to create one in any locale that believed would benefit from it. The request to establish one in Paris, he asserted, required a much more extensive examination because of the great number and variety of industries in Paris. The distribution of workers throughout the capital complicated the question, presenting different and perhaps opposing interests, so that any discussion of jurisdiction would have to reconcile many considerations.[187]

The request for a council of arbitrators in Paris illustrates the manner in which the potential reestablishment of guilds intersected with other issues, and how vigilant the council was in regard to any undertaking, surreptitious or overt, that could lead to that outcome. One study has characterized the *conseil de prud'hommes* as filling "the gap between the guild system of the *ancien régime* and the modern trade union,"[188] and, with modern trade unions in the future, it was its close approximation to the guild system that concerned the council.[189]

---

when Jeff Horn consulted it for *The Path Not Taken*. When I consulted the carton on March 16, 2007, however, the document was missing. I would like to express my deep gratitude to Jeff Horn for generously allowing me to utilize the photocopy that he had made.

[186] AN F^{12}* 196, fols. 67–69.

[187] AN F^{12}* 196, fol. 69.

[188] Chester P. Higby and Caroline B. Willis, "Industry and Labor under Napoleon," *The American Historical Review* 53 (1948): 465–480, with the quotation from p. 465.

[189] On the proximity between the *conseil de prud'hommes* and guilds, Reddy, *The Rise of Market Culture*, pp. 72, 83.

The Council on Manufacturing took up the issue of a council of arbitrators for Paris on April 8, 1819. Many members of the Council on Manufacturing believed that the establishment of a *conseil de prud'hommes* in Paris presented great difficulties or even insurmountable obstacles. Some argued that it would be unworkable because of the "impossibility" of classifying the diverse types of industry if one wanted to extend the institution to the many production facilities that existed in the city. Members also observed that a *conseil de prud'hommes* would not offer the same advantages to Paris that it had to other locales, and whether there was one council of arbitrators or several, there would be confusion regarding its composition, jurisdiction and attributions. Other members objected that by excessively increasing the number of *conseils de prud'hommes* it was possible that authorities might unwittingly bring back in some fashion the former corporations or at least lead to a perception that this could occur.

One member sought to reassure the Council on Manufacturing on the concerns that had been raised, asserting that if the procedures of the law were followed, a council of arbitrators could be beneficial for Paris. Another member supported him, and pointed out that the town of Reims had long had one and it had proven useful. The council concluded that the issue required greater examination and formed a special subcommittee to consider it.[190]

Although the Council on Manufacturing treated the issue intermittently throughout 1819, the subcommittee did not bring forward a report that year, citing the time required to gain information and the prolonged absence of some members.[191] Clearly, however, opposition remained strong – ultimately, Paris would receive a *conseil de prud'hommes* only in 1844, under the regime of Louis-Philippe and long after any prospect of reestablishing guilds had passed.

Perhaps emboldened by the effort under way in Paris, during the spring of 1819 tradesmen in the Department of Bas-Rhin sent a petition to the Chamber of Deputies seeking the reestablishment of guilds in their trades. Master masons, stonecutters and carpenters in Fontaine asked for the enactment of a law reorganizing corporations for their benefit. The tradesmen based their request on the fact that a large number of outside workers, without domicile, without an occupational license and usually with little skill in the trade, were taking work from master workers. They asked for an inspector who would visit work sites and enforce regulations.

The petition provoked a lively debate in the chamber, the discussion revealing both the rationale and the means by which tradesmen were grouped into guild-like bodies. The unnamed deputy who served as reporter immediately observed that guilds had been abolished, but, he added, unlimited freedom did not extend to all trades. Many, he stated, were subject to ordinances and regulations in the general interest of society. The art of masonry, he noted, required similar precautions because the solidity of buildings guaranteed the

---

[190] AN F¹²* 196, fols. 71–72.
[191] AN F¹²* 196, fols. 96, 98, 101, 140.

safety of individuals – a badly constructed furnace, he said, could incinerate an entire village. The petitioners, he asserted, could not seek the reestablishment of guilds in their favor, but they did seem to have a basis for asking for regulations of public administration. He recommended that the petition be sent to the Ministry of the Interior.

Many members of the left protested, seeking to table the request. The deputy Marie-Louis-Auguste de Martin du Tyrac, Comte de Marcellus, however, an ultra, mounted a defense of corporations and argued for their legal reestablishment – they were useful to any profession "from the most liberal to the lowliest trade." It was for this reason, he said, that one saw "in one of the greatest cities," presumably a reference to Paris, a rebirth of corporations. He supported forwarding the petition to the Ministry of the Interior.

The deputy François-Bernard, Marquis de Chauvelin,[192] a member of the left who fought reactionary tendencies, responded that forwarding the petition would overturn twenty-five years of complete freedom for commerce and industry and added that debates over the restoration of guilds had been conducted previously and that the principle of freedom had always prevailed over their reestablishment. He asked not only that the petition be tabled, but that in the future the chamber not accept any such request for consideration.

The reporter for the petition retorted that if Chauvelin had listened to what the reporter had said, he undoubtedly would not be seeking to table the petition. The commission, he said, had not shown itself favorable to the reestablishment of guilds "for all professions in general," but that there were many that required particular regulations – there were, for example, regulations for pharmacists and other occupations. It seemed useful, he said, to reestablish those that would guarantee the solidity of buildings. He reiterated his proposal to send the request to the Ministry of the Interior, and the chamber voted to do so.[193]

Immediately afterward, the chamber heard a petition from the shoemakers and boot makers of Paris that sought what they called a "definitive organization," the reestablishment of arbitrators (*prud'hommes*) and of a central office at which all those who practiced the trade would have to register in order to be ranked according to their ability. In this instance, however, the reporter for the commission stated that it did not regard this trade as having any influence on the safety of citizens. Moreover, the Prefect of Police was currently developing an organizational structure between masters and workers in the trade to resolve the issue of shoddy workmanship. The commission proposed that the request be tabled and the chamber again followed its recommendation, tabling the measure.[194]

Three days later, on May 6, 1819, at a meeting of the Council on Manufacturing, a member inquired whether the Minister of the Interior had

---

[192] On his electoral background, Alexander, *Re-Writing the French Revolutionary Tradition*, p. 109.
[193] *Gazette nationale, ou le Moniteur universel*, May 3, 1819.
[194] *Ibid.*

authorized the printing of the subcommittee report on the means of assuring strict enforcement of current laws on commerce, manufacturing and workshops. He asked that the request be renewed, and the council approved his proposal.[195] Ultimately, however, it took several months for the subcommittee's report to be printed and given to the council. At the conclusion of a meeting on September 2, 1819, the summary was distributed to council members, but no date for discussion was set.[196]

Between the meetings of May and September, during August, the Council on Manufacturing had been reorganized, and one of the members not appointed to the reorganized council – and who had also been a member of the subcommittee examining the reestablishment of guilds – was de Bray. He sent a letter to the council expressing his regret at not being able to share in its work. The council curtly decided to respond only that it shared his regret – no member offered a tribute to his years of service.[197] Moreover, although Levacher-Duplessis would mount another effort to reestablish guilds, he merely reused his earlier *mémoire* and no topics of discussion by the council appeared publicly again.

THE INDUSTRIAL EXHIBITION OF 1819

As the Council on Manufacturing was considering the issue of restoring guilds or pursuing stricter enforcement of current legislation, the Crown decided to sponsor another industrial exhibition – the first since the massive Napoleonic exhibition of 1806. During December 1818 Louis XVIII had appointed Elie Decazes as Minister of the Interior, and one of his early endeavors was to seek to revive the industrial exhibition, which by now had been dormant for more than a decade.[198] His efforts were successful – on January 13, 1819, after receiving a report from Decazes, Louis XVIII issued a decree proclaiming that the Crown believed that periodic exhibitions of products of French industry would be a means to encourage and bolster its progress. He authorized an exhibition for 1819 and a second for 1821, and decreed that an exhibition should be held at least every four years thereafter.[199]

Shortly afterward, on January 26, the Minister of the Interior initiated preparations for the exhibition by circulating a letter to prefects of departments. He advised them to form juries of men versed in production who would be capable of judging products. Each jury would evaluate all of the items that came before it and admit only those that served as an example of skillful production or great usefulness. Furthermore, products should represent the particular industries of each department.

[195] AN F^{12*} 196, fol. 92.
[196] AN F^{12*} 196, fol. 119.
[197] AN F^{12*} 196, fol. 119.
[198] Louis Costaz, *Rapport du jury central sur les produits de l'industrie française* (Paris: Imprimerie Royale, 1819), p. v.
[199] *Exposition publique des produits de l'industrie française au Palais du Louvre. Année 1819* (Paris: Imprimerie Royale, 1819). There was no exposition in 1821, however – the next one was held during 1823.

The letter also recommended that the jury not reject common items, particularly if they had general usage and were inexpensive. For all of the products selected, the government would pay for the cost of transport to Paris.

The minister also observed that Louis XVIII had not placed a limit on the number of prizes to be awarded – the monarch intended to give support to all those worthy of his munificence. As a result, manufacturers other than those selected for medals who had developed new processes or made important discoveries could be recognized with a Legion of Honor decoration and be presented to the monarch.[200] Some weeks later, the Minister of the Interior reported to Louis that the solicitation had elicited an enthusiastic response in all of the departments, and praised those "who had created new machines" or developed other technical advances.[201]

The authorization of the industrial exhibitions, and particularly the commitment to their continuation, represented a significant statement by the Crown. Mechanization, which was implicit in the notion of "progress of industry," was widely understood as the antithesis of the corporate ideal embodied in guilds. In 1799, for example, Nicolas-Louis Robert patented a method of papermaking that involved "mechanized movements that had been the monopoly of skilled men." Robert's primary goal in creating his machine had not been to increase production, although production did go up markedly. Rather, its invention had been directed against the corporation of paper workers; Robert had simply desired to manufacture paper without the assistance of workers.[202] The support of industry, then, was not solely an economic decision – it was also inseparable from broader principles about the nature of the French state.

In the Department of Seine, the jury that screened entries submitted a report to the prefect of the department. The judges – one of whom was Chaptal, who had revived the exhibition during the Consulate – noted that the announcement of the exhibition had been greeted with enthusiasm by a wide range of producers. The jury believed that the event could produce fortuitous results, particularly because of the inclusion of ordinary, inexpensive objects and because of the decision to award the Legion of Honor to deserving producers.

The Department of Seine had, despite the high standards set by its jury, contributed more products than it had to any of the previous exhibitions, and the products themselves were more noteworthy. The jurors also expressed their hope that Louis XVIII would recognize many of the entrants with decorations, awards or subsidies. The members of the jury observed that even after the disastrous events of 1814 and 1815, French manufacturers appeared to have gained new vigor and chided those who doubted the prosperity of French manufactures.

---

[200] AN F¹ᵃ 34, dossier 1819, circular of January 26, 1819.
[201] *Ibid.*
[202] Leonard M. Rosenband, *Papermaking in Eighteenth-Century France: Management, Labor and Revolution at the Montgolfier Mill, 1761–1805* (Baltimore: The Johns Hopkins University Press, 2000), pp. 147–148.

The jurors expressed concern that during the 1806 exhibition some of the entrants who had been designated as gold medal winners had not actually received the medal because they had been given one at the preceding exhibition. This precedent had discouraged many distinguished manufacturers from entering the competition for the upcoming exhibition, and the jury did not want a repetition of that protocol. After receiving the report of the jury, the prefect, in his letter to the Minister of the Interior, supported the recommendation of the jurors – indeed, he worried that if the protocol of 1806 was followed, then only objects of lesser merit would be entered.[203]

The commitment of the restored Bourbon government to industrialization and mechanization was evident both in the scale of the exhibition and in the actions of Louis XVIII throughout its duration. Held at the Louvre, the 1819 exhibition, which opened on August 25, had 1,662 exhibitors, making it larger than any of the exhibitions of the Napoleonic era – the largest Napoleonic exhibition had been that of 1806, which had had 1,422 exhibitors.[204] The amount of space dedicated to the exhibition was also larger than that of any previous exhibition, enabling participants to display entire sheets of fabric or wallpaper rather than merely samples.[205]

Moreover, Louis XVIII visited the exhibition twice, and princes of the royal family attended several times as well.[206] Louis had been the one to whom those wishing to restore guilds had often directed their efforts, so his two visits, especially the second, sent a powerful message. The first royal visit could be interpreted as primarily ceremonial or the result of curiosity, but the second was clearly an endorsement and was recognized as such, particularly after his failure to visit the exhibition during its opening days was noted by the press.[207] Indeed, as if to make a point, Louis's first visit to the exhibition lasted nearly five hours.[208] Furthermore, the second appears to have been spontaneous – after attending Mass, the monarch simply walked to the Louvre, without an escort or bodyguard. He was joined by a few officials, but none were in their official dress.[209]

In addition, during the exhibition, the monarch received delegations of manufacturers. On September 9, he met with a group of cotton manufacturers, including Emile Oberkampf, the son of the founder of the famous printed

---

[203] L. Héricart de Thury, *Rapport du jury d'admission des produits de l'industrie du Département de la Seine, à l'exposition du Louvre* (Paris: C. Ballard, 1819), pp. x–xv.

[204] *Exposition publique des produits de l'industrie française…1819.*

[205] AN F¹ᵃ 34, dossier 1819, circular of July 10, 1819.

[206] AN F¹² 512, report presented to Minister of the Interior on exposition of French industry by Arnould and Guillard-Senainville, November 9, 1819. See also *Gazette nationale, ou le Moniteur universel*, August 29, 1819, August 31, 1819, September 6, 1819, September 20, 1819.

[207] On Louis's failure to visit, *Gazette nationale, ou le Moniteur universel*, August 27, 1819; on the second visit being recognized as an endorsement of industry, *Gazette nationale, ou le Moniteur universel*, September 20, 1819.

[208] *Le Constitutionnel, journal du commerce, politique et littéraire*, August 30, 1819.

[209] *Le Constitutionnel, journal du commerce, politique et littéraire*, September 19, 1819.

cotton factory, during which he spoke glowingly of his visit to the exhibition, and on September 20 he met with another group of textile producers, including Ternaux, in a special audience. During the first visit, he repeatedly told the deputation of manufacturers that they could rely on his support.[210] In fact, when some members of the group represented by Levacher-Duplessis launched another effort to restore guilds in 1821, the delegation directed its efforts not to the Crown – the monarch or the Ministry of the Interior – but to the legislature.

Every aspect of the awards ceremony was designed to demonstrate the support and respect of Louis XVIII for industry and those engaged in it, beginning with the fact that, at Louis's direction, the ceremony was held in the throne room of the Tuileries palace.[211] After a brief address from the spokesman for the jury and medal winners, Louis XVIII, surrounded by his ministers, proclaimed his respect and admiration for industry, acknowledging that during his youth he had been jealous of the industrial prosperity of "neighboring nations," a clear allusion to Great Britain and the experience of the Eden-Vergennes Treaty. He told the medal winners to "tell my faithful manufacturers that they can rely upon me, as I will rely upon them."[212]

More remarkable than his warm words for industry, however, was the etiquette employed by the monarch during the presentation of the medals. Under the Consulate, the Ministry of the Interior had presented the medals, and Bonaparte, although present, had not spoken.[213] Not only had Louis XVIII spoken, and spoken in the most laudatory terms of industry, but, after the Minister of the Interior called each winner forward, the monarch handed the medal to the recipient himself rather than using an aide. The significance of the gesture was not lost on a society highly conscious of protocol,[214] and was noted in an official report of the exposition.[215] In fact, one commentator asserted that the awards ceremony was more solemn than that of a university because the king himself had presented the awards – indeed, he compared the solemnity of the observance to former protocols for admission to the Legion of Honor under the Napoleonic regime and the Académie Française under the Old Regime.[216] The awards ceremony was extensive, as the monarch bestowed 62 gold medals, 134 silver medals and 80 bronze medals.[217] Furthermore,

---

[210] *Gazette national, ou le Moniteur universel*, September 10, 21, 1819.

[211] *Le Constitutionnel, journal du commerce, politique et littéraire*, September 26, 1819.

[212] Louis Costaz, *Rapport du jury central sur les produits de l'industrie française, présenté à S.E.M. le comte Decazes* (Paris: Imprimerie Royale, 1819), pp. xv–xvi. The phrase of relying on him was the same that he had used during his meeting with cotton producers on September 9.

[213] During the 1806 exposition he had been on campaign.

[214] *Gazette nationale, ou le Moniteur universel*, September 27, 1819, which noted that recipients of the gold, silver and bronze medals received their award "from the very hands of the king."

[215] Louis Costaz, *Rapport du jury central sur les produits de l'industrie française* (Paris: Imprimerie Royale, 1819), p. xvi.

[216] *Le Constitutionnel, journal du commerce, politique et littéraire*, October 1, 1819.

[217] *Le Constitutionnel, journal du commerce, politique et littéraire*, September 26, 1819.

as each winner received his award, Louis offered warm and encouraging remarks.[218] Beginning after the morning Mass, the awarding of medals did not conclude until 1:30 p.m.[219]

Although one should not overstate the change of perspective, nor attribute it altogether to developments under the Restoration – nobles had been involved in enterprise since before the Revolution[220] – it should equally be noted that contemporaries on both sides of the issue remarked on the transformation in outlook. In the foreword to a book on the industrial exhibitions through 1819, the publisher, after extolling producers such as Ternaux and Oberkampf, went on to observe that "today the noble does not disdain to undertake the career of the plebeian. He sets an example, dedicates himself to increasing the industry and commerce of his *patrie*, and after having contributed to meeting its needs, leaving the modest *atelier*, sits in this Chamber of Peers, where he can again contribute to upholding or creating laws that secure public happiness ..." and he cited as examples La Rochefoucault, Polignac and Villeneuve.[221] Indeed, in writing of those on the other side of the issue, a newspaper noted during the exhibition that, three days after Louis's first visit, neither the visit itself nor the words the monarch had offered to the businessmen who surrounded him had been mentioned in royalist newspapers.[222]

The report of the jury also effusively praised the Society for the Encouragement of National Industry, almost certainly seeking to close completely the breach that had opened between it and the Crown in 1815, but which had been healing since 1817. The jury stated that although it had been founded only in 1802, it had contributed to industrial progress in a significant manner. The report also observed that the society was a voluntary association that had never sought financial support from the government.[223]

---

[218] *Ibid.*; *Gazette nationale, ou le Moniteur universel*, September 27, 1819.

[219] *Journal des débats politiques et littéraires*, September 26, 1819. Ultimately, despite the requests of the jury and the prefect of Paris, individuals who had previously received gold medals at preceding expositions were not given medals. In addition, four members of the jury who had won gold medals did not receive them. *Bulletin de la Société pour l'Encouragement de l'Industrie Nationale* 19 (1820): 51.

[220] George V. Taylor, "Types of Capitalism in Eighteenth-Century France," *English Historical Review* 79 (1964): 478–497; and "Noncapitalist Wealth and the Origins of the French Revolution," *The American Historical Review* 72 (1967): 469–496; Guy Chaussinand-Nogaret, *The French Nobility in the Eighteenth Century: From Feudalism to Enlightenment* (Cambridge: Cambridge University Press, 1985), pp. 91–114.

[221] Louis Sébastien Le Normand and Moléon, *Description des expositions des produits de l'industrie française, faites à Paris depuis leur origine jusqu'à celle de 1819 inclusivement* (Paris: Bachelier, 1824), pp. 76–77. Members of the nobility would, in fact, play an important role in modernizing the French economy under the Restoration and beyond. Joël Felix, "Avant-garde Aristocrats? French Noblemen, Patents and the Modernization of France (1815–1848)," in *The French Experience from Republic to Monarchy, 1792–1824: New Dawns in Politics, Knowledge and Culture*, Máire F. Cross and David Williams, eds., (Basingstoke: Palgrave, 2000), pp. 199–203.

[222] *Le Constitutionnel, journal du commerce, politique et littéraire*, September 1, 1819.

[223] Costaz, *Rapport du jury central*, pp. xx–xxi.

The endorsement of the society represented an effort to restore the sense of common purpose between the society and the ministry, especially with the current Minister of the Interior favorable to mechanization. Chaptal, a former Minister of the Interior, was one of the jurors and had been closely associated with the society since its founding.

In addition, the jury's report praised the legislation of the last quarter-century as having contributed to the rise of French industry and lauded the policy of subsidies to industry. The jurors noted that the legislation had brought about order in factories without slowing the rise of industry and at the same time created a salutary situation for workers – an oblique argument against the restoration of guilds.[224]

The report concluded with a strong commendation of the exhibitions – every one of them, it asserted, had had useful and beneficial results. The recognition and reward that the exhibitions accorded to manufacturers or innovators inspired emulation and brought like-minded individuals together in Paris, increasing their knowledge and expanding their horizons. Citing all the elements that they had adduced in their report, the jurors predicted a brilliant future for French industry.[225] In fact, a few years later, during November 1823, Charles Dupin, a member of the Institute and the Academy of Sciences, gave a speech on the progress of French industry since the beginning of the nineteenth century and cited the year 1819 as a turning point.[226]

At the same time, however, the lingering coexistence in Paris of industry and guild-like structures, as well as the relative ease with which many guilds could have been reestablished had such a decision been taken, are evident in a single issue of a major Parisian newspaper, *Gazette nationale, ou le Moniteur universel*. On August 31, 1819, the newspaper provided additional details on the visit of Louis XVIII to the industrial exhibition. On the same page, it noted another event in Paris – the celebration of a solemn Mass at the parish of Saint-Eustache by master wigmakers on the feast day of their patron saint, Saint Louis. The choir and nave of the church, it stated, were filled with artisans and their families.[227] The report is a reminder that concern about the potential reestablishment of guilds was not wholly theoretical or abstract. Indeed, as the exhibition was in progress, another newspaper published a royalist article advocating the reestablishment of corporations as a means to restore order in manufacturing and commerce.[228]

Several weeks later, during the fall of 1819, Louis XVIII offered another significant sign of support for industry when he named many manufacturers to the Legion of Honor.[229] A few weeks after these announcements, the

[224] *Ibid.*, pp. xxv–xxvi.
[225] *Ibid.*, pp. xxii–xxiv.
[226] Charles Dupin, *Progrès de l'industrie française depuis le commencement du XIXe siècle* (Paris: Bachelier, 1824), pp. 19–20, 43–44.
[227] *Gazette nationale, ou le Moniteur universel*, August 31, 1819.
[228] *Journal des débats, politiques et littéraires*, September 4, 1819.
[229] *Gazette nationale, ou le Moniteur universel*, December 4, 1819.

Minister of the Interior revealed an even greater indication of the esteem in which the monarch held industry. Beyond the medals awarded at the exhibition, the minister stated, Louis wanted to reward manufacturers who invented new processes or made important discoveries that served to advance national industry with a more striking sign of royal favor. This had been the basis for the Legion of Honor awards, but Louis now wished to bestow an even greater reward for honorable perseverance. As a result, he granted the textile manufacturers Ternaux and Oberkampf the title of Baron in recognition of their eminent service to French industry. In addition, he made a chemist who had developed processes useful to industry a member of the Order of St. Michael.[230]

A NEW ATTEMPT TO RESTORE GUILDS

Approximately eighteen months later, however, due largely to the change in political climate following the assassination of the Duc de Berri in February 1820, there was a new effort to reestablish guilds. On the day after Berri's death, Jean-Claude Clausel de Coussergues, an ultra, sought to impeach Decazes, the Minister of the Interior, leading to Decaze's ouster and ushering in a period of ascendancy of the extreme Right from February 1820 until December 1821 – a period known as the Royalist Reaction of 1820. Its defining element was the passage of legislation known as the Exceptional Laws that effectively banished the opposition and conferred political power on the royalists.[231] Among other policies, Decazes had been a supporter of mechanization and industry and, after his fall, during the period of dominance by the Right, a group of merchants and artisans from Paris, apparently from the group formerly represented by Levacher-Duplessis, made another effort to have guilds restored.

Several factors coalesced to bring the issue of the reestablishment of corporations forward once again. The economy slowed during the winter and spring of 1820, which led to concern about worker unrest. Gauze makers, many of whom were women and children, were particularly hard hit, and weavers and wallpaper workers were also experiencing high unemployment. A police report from early March 1820, made clear the level of concern the police had about worker unrest because of the assassination of the Duc de Berri the previous month, but, to their relief, the workers were quiescent.[232]

Moreover, although it cannot be ascertained with certainty, the fact that the assassin, Pierre Louvel, was a journeymen saddle maker may have helped prolong the debate on the restoration of guilds, which served as a vehicle for policing

[230] *Gazette nationale, ou le Moniteur universel*, December 6, 1819.
[231] Bertier de Sauvigny, *The Bourbon Restoration*, pp. 164–169; Alexander, *Re-Writing the French Revolutionary Tradition*, p. 89; David Skuy, *Assassination, Politics, and Miracles: France and the Royalist Reaction of 1820* (Montreal: McGill-Queen's University Press, 2003).
[232] AN F⁷ 3874, report of March 7, 1820.

workers. In the wake of Berri's assassination, worker actions, even those that were obviously apolitical, drew heightened attention from the police.[233]

Indeed, David Skuy has examined the coverage of Louvel and the assassination in the newspapers, and one can detect in the language an underlying, if perhaps subconscious, argument for the reestablishment of corporations. A royalist newspaper in Toulouse, for example, attributed Louvel's act to "impious and anarchic doctrines" that were "subversive of religion, morals and legitimacy."[234] To the degree that guilds were viewed as a disciplinary and monarchical institution that helped maintain order and harmony in society, an argument for their reestablishment is not difficult to discern.

The most widely circulated account, the "assassination article," as Skuy characterized it, had a similar tone. It emphasized "the influence of revolutionary doctrines on Louvel's mind." The assassination was portrayed not only as a murder, but as a "revolutionary act," and Louvel gained a public persona as a "fanatical revolutionary."[235] Again, to the extent that guilds were perceived as stable monarchical institutions, their reestablishment could contain revolution, and this equation would not have been lost on contemporaries.

Finally, the wave of reaction to the assassination provided a more favorable climate for the reestablishment of corporations. At the same time, however, there was a fear that worker corporations could be used by liberal interests.[236] Whatever the reason might have been, the debate on restoring guilds continued despite the fact that there was little support for the idea.

Since the elections of September 1816, the ultras had lost ground to moderates, but the assassination of the Duc de Berri galvanized ultraroyalists in the chambers.[237] With the royalists in the ascendancy in the legislature, in March 1821 a group of merchants and artisans, led by ten delegates, submitted a petition to the two chambers asking for the reestablishment of guilds. The fact that the petition was simply a reprint of the one drawn up by Levacher-Duplessis in 1817 suggests that the effort was hastily organized and that it was put forward once again by members of the original group,[238] but whoever the sponsors were, the tactic of the petitioners is evident. With Louis XVIII having made clear his support for mechanization and industry, proponents of the restoration of corporations realized that they could no longer work through the Crown.[239] Rather, with ultras in control of the

---

[233] See, for example, the reports on the cessation of operations and wage disputes at a cloth manufacture in the *faubourg* Saint-Antoine. AN F⁷ 3875, reports of April 25, 26, 27, 28, 1820.

[234] Skuy, *Assassination, Politics, and Miracles*, p. 113.

[235] *Ibid.*, pp. 114, 119, 124.

[236] AN F⁷ 4305, report of prefect of Department of Isère to director of departmental administration, February 21, 1821. On unrest in Grenoble, Alexander, *Re-Writing the French Revolutionary Tradition*, pp. 145–146, 150–156.

[237] Alexander, *Re-Writing the French Revolutionary Tradition*, pp. 63, 86–87, 89; Skuy, *Assassination, Politics, and Miracles*, p. 129.

[238] ACCIP 2 Mi 4, fols. 66–67; *Gazette nationale, ou le Moniteur universel*, March 24, 1821.

[239] Ironically, however, the reprinted petition still read *Requête au Roi*, just as in 1817.

legislature, they calculated that the chambers offered the best opportunity of achieving their goal.

Just as had been the case during 1817, the petition elicited a protest from the Chamber of Commerce of Paris. After asserting that chambers of commerce had been established in particular to make known the needs and wishes of commerce and industry and to call attention to factors that could halt their progress, the chamber cited the statement that it had issued on October 8, 1817, in opposition to the request of Levacher-Duplessis. The chamber noted that its membership had changed significantly since 1817 but its position remained the same: It was strongly and unanimously against the petition submitted to the two chambers of the legislature. The Chamber of Commerce of Paris went on to state that nothing had contributed as much to the progress of French industry as the complete freedom granted to the exercise of industrial undertakings by the abolition of guilds, masterships and corporations of arts and trades.[240]

The declaration by the Chamber of Commerce of Paris reveals the degree to which many contemporaries viewed the destruction of corporations and the progress of industry in France as inextricably linked. The response that the effort to reestablish guilds provoked also indicates that contemporaries regarded the threat as a serious one. On April 3, however, the Chamber of Peers tabled the petition.[241]

During most of the attempts to restore guilds that had been made since 1814, proponents had tried to generate or to follow up on current opinion or pamphlet literature endorsing the idea, but in 1821 there was little discernible sentiment for endorsing the concept. The undertaking did, however, provoke a strong countervailing effort from both unofficial and official quarters.

Among the former was a work by Victor-Joseph Jouy, an author and playwright who had been named to the Académie Française in 1815.[242] In 1821 he published a pamphlet in which he argued that industry had civilized the world and enlarged the intellectual world. The genius of man was no less evident in the invention of a steam engine than in an epic poem, he claimed, and the discovery of printing alone had been more advantageous to the progress of the human spirit than all the lofty intelligence of Aristotle, Plato and Homer.

Entering the debate on the restoration of corporations, Jouy condemned the request to return to the system of guilds and masterships, which he called a shameful institution. He asserted that guilds and masterships were privileges instituted in favor of small communities at the expense of the larger community of the state. Jouy's linkage of the development of guilds to the reign of Henri III, one of the most reviled of all French kings, was an obvious effort to discredit them. As they matured thereafter, he argued, they became detrimental to commerce and industry and a source of abuse and vexation. Turgot had

[240] ACCIP 2 Mi 4, fols. 66–67; *Gazette nationale, ou le Moniteur universel*, March 24, 1821.
[241] *Archives parlementaires*, 2nd series, 30: 574.
[242] *Nouvelle biographie générale*, 27: 89–96.

wisely sought to abolish corporations and to remove limitations on industry, but intrigue led to his ouster and to the reestablishment of guilds. Ultimately, it was the National Assembly that had definitively eradicated them.

Jouy bemoaned the fact that many attacks had been made against industry since the 1819 exhibition. He was especially troubled by assertions that had been made in the Chamber of Deputies concerning the commerce of Lyon, particularly a claim that the suppression of corporations had been catastrophic for that city. Jouy responded that in 1789 there had been only 14,500 looms in Lyon, but that in 1820 there were 24,000. He put forward other figures proving the expansion of industry in Lyon to counter any notion that the suppression of corporations had been inimical to the city and insisted that freedom was the first need of commerce.[243]

On April 24, 1821, the Council on Manufacturing met in an extraordinary session when it learned that the proposal to reestablish guilds and the *corps de marchands* had been sent to the chambers. The vice-president of the council noted that the central commission of the council, a subcommittee, had met to discuss the matter and had submitted a report to the council. The vice-president read the report to the council, and, after an extensive discussion, the council made several changes to craft a definitive statement that was unanimously approved and signed by all those present.

The council's statement took issue with both the form and substance of the petition. The council objected to the impropriety of a request drawn up by a barrister for a group of individuals who arrogated to themselves a mission that they improperly claimed to have received, because the true constituents had never been effectively consulted on the object of the petition. The delegation that had drafted the petition was so inappropriate that this reason alone had seemed sufficient to the Chamber of Peers to reject the petition during its April 3 meeting. The council also denounced the fact that the group had sought to bypass institutions created to advise the government on such issues. The council noted that the Chamber of Commerce of Paris was not, as had been asserted, "... a council on commerce without character, designated by the prefecture." Rather, the statement emphasized in italics "... it is legally instituted, chosen by its peers" and noted that the chamber recruited in succession manufacturers and businessmen who stood out because of their knowledge.

The council then pointedly added that the unanimous opinion of the chamber on the issue, made known at different times, and the principles that had guided the chamber, reflected more favorably on it than on those advocating the reestablishment of corporations. Indeed, the council asserted that the individuals arguing for the reestablishment of guilds and the merchants' body were seeking to become the leaders of these organizations. The men of the Chamber of Commerce, the council asserted, knew how to sacrifice

[243] Jouy, Victor-Joseph-Etienne de, *Etat actuel de l'industrie française, ou coup d'oeil sur l'exposition de ses produits, dans les salles du Louvre, en 1819* (Paris: L'Huillier, 1821).

momentary personal advantages to the well-understood, permanent interests of the laboring classes of society.

The council went on to note that it had debated the question of the reestablishment of guilds on many occasions, particularly during 1818. It stated that, with the exception of one member, it remained convinced that this "ancient institution" could not be reestablished without losing the enormous advantage that industry had gained from thirty years of freedom. The council believed unanimously that to accede to the request would represent a regression toward the infancy of manufacturing, to the great satisfaction of France's rivals.

The facts, the council asserted, were irrefutable – French industry had progressed greatly since it had been freed from the constraints imposed by corporations. The only plausible reason one could offer for restoring guilds was the need to repress or prevent abuses that were now seen in commerce and industry.

The council concluded its statement with the judgment that it believed that current legislation, strictly enforced, would be sufficient to deal with any real or imagined abuses and serve the interests of both manufacturers and the public. All the council members who were in attendance – twenty-six in total – signed the decree, which the vice-president was to send to the Minister of the Interior.[244]

A member of the Council on Commerce also brought to the attention of that body the effort to approach the chambers with the request to reestablish guilds and the *corps de marchands*. The council member asserted that this question was of great importance to commerce in general and that the council should not remain silent on the issue, particularly because the Chamber of Commerce of Paris and the Council on Manufacturing had already offered opinions on the matter. The member put before the council an extract of a letter from Le Havre relating that a wage dispute involving ship caulkers had led the caulkers to form a kind of corporation, with statutes, officers and an employment office, through which employers would have to seek workers, who would then be selected by the office. The group had been denounced and the royal prosecutor had annulled the statutes and set a wage rate.

During the discussion that followed many members agreed that the interests of industry would only suffer from the requested reestablishment of corporations. One member observed how difficult it would be in the current state of affairs to form corporations among diverse industrial professions. As a hypothetical example, he cited a spinning mill in which one might have not only the spinners, but also locksmiths who would tend to the metalwork of the machines and carpenters for the wooden frames – potentially three different corporations in one establishment. He added that similar situations could be imagined in other settings. He believed that it would be impossible to achieve any workable system if corporations were reestablished.

[244] AN F¹²* 196, fols. 265–267.

In a clear reference to Réveillon, another member recalled the many obstacles and limits that had prevented the establishment of a wallpaper factory in Paris, but noted that production of wallpaper had now reached a high degree of perfection and that French wallpaper was well regarded throughout Europe. When corporations were still in existence, however, each innovation was contested by a guild that claimed it was an encroachment on its privileges. The freedom that had come with the abolition of guilds had allowed inventiveness, which in turn had allowed industry to flourish in France.

After further discussion on the reestablishment of guilds, the Council on Commerce decided that on a matter of such importance its opinion should not be quickly improvised. As a result, the council formed a three-member subcommittee to draw up a statement to be presented to the council, after which it would be sent to the Minister of the Interior.[245]

The council convened the following month to consider the statement written by its subcommittee. After a reading of the project, the vice-president of the council invited any member who objected to it to speak. One member asked if he could state the reasons for his dissent from it. He asserted that he understood that corporations could not now be reestablished in the manner in which they had existed under the Old Regime, but he did not believe that this was the goal of those seeking their restoration.

The unnamed member believed that the council should not pronounce its opposition to the reestablishment of guilds in such a general and absolute fashion. He believed that the deficiencies of corporations could be ameliorated and any hindrance they might present to the progress of industry could be avoided. Shorn of any privileges relating to production and with no limit on the number of individuals admitted, corporations, he claimed, could become useful in halting some of the abuses now present.

He cited as an example a situation in Lyon in which corrupted material – false gold – was being used by gilders. The council member said that he did not believe this situation could be dealt with through current legislation, and that the use of false gold had led to the loss of a very important branch of commerce to foreign competition. The speaker asserted that unlimited freedom of industry had not been, as most seemed to believe, the sole cause of the prosperity of the manufactures of Lyon, and contended instead that, as this particular case indicated, the opposite might be true.

He argued that councils of arbitrators could replace the former corporations, and that this could be achieved in a beneficial fashion if their attributions were strengthened through additional legislative and regulatory measures. He concluded by offering a summary of his position with two statements. First, he was in no way seeking the reestablishment of corporations, especially through a general measure. Second, he would be inclined to support the views presented in the report and deliberation if the council expressed its opposition to the return of corporations in a less trenchant manner. He did not want to

---

[245] AN F¹²* 193bis, fols. 12v⁰–13v⁰.

rankle those who held opposite views or reject altogether an examination of the partial reestablishment of corporations when this might be requested by interested parties and deemed useful by the government. He said that with these modifications to the opinion put forward by the council, the statement would gain his assent.

Another member immediately asked if he could argue against these observations. Without disputing the accuracy of the abuses spoken of in Lyon, he pointed out that the current dispersion of workers over a vast territory could facilitate the escape from punishment of those guilty of misconduct. At the same time, he added, the regime of guilds that was being solicited would not be able to extend to isolated workers spread throughout the countryside, which meant that even if a system of corporations were to be reinstated, the same misconduct could continue.

He believed that one could more easily attain the goal of worker discipline by strengthening the powers of and giving a wider range of jurisdiction to the institution of the council of arbitrators. Perhaps realizing that a *conseil de prud'hommes* in Paris could become a surrogate for corporations, he quickly abandoned the point as secondary to the question at hand and more properly within the purview of the Council on Manufacturing. He asserted that the Council on Commerce, asked to offer an opinion on a general question, should declare itself against the reestablishment of corporations because this was the issue that had been submitted for deliberation. He said that he noted with pleasure that the previous speaker himself recognized the danger and the impossibility of the reestablishment of guilds that was being solicited.

The respondent stated that he did not want to conclude without rebutting the observations offered on the current state of affairs in Lyon compared to the past. He argued that during the beginning stages of manufacturing in the city, it was both useful and necessary to establish rules and restrictions on the manufacturing process to guide unskilled or inexperienced workers. Thirty years later, however, with foreign competitors offering such a challenge, if those same regulations had been maintained, French industry would undoubtedly have remained stagnant or even regressed instead of gaining the preeminence and prosperity that it had.

The vice-president queried the council as to whether it should include in its statement the idea on improvement or whether it should take a stance on the *conseil de prud'hommes*. Many members opposed the suggestions, however, noting, among other things, that those issues should be decided by the Council on Manufacturing. The Council on Commerce decided that its mandate was to determine whether or not guilds and the *corps de marchands* should be reestablished. With only one dissenting vote, the council adopted the report and deliberation of its subcommittee. The council also decided to print and distribute the report and deliberation to the Chamber of Peers, the Chamber of Deputies and the chambers of commerce.[246]

---

[246] AN F¹²* 193bis, fols. 15–17. Its deliberation was printed, along with that of the Council on Manufacturing. *Delibérations des Conseils Généraux, du commerce et des manufactures,*

The statement was unusually long, so only major points will be treated here. The Council on Commerce criticized the group seeking the reestablishment of guilds as having no authority to make the request and reaffirmed the council's opposition to guilds as destructive to industry.

The council asserted that industry had increased production and enriched France, particularly through exports. The council stated that it did not fear an increase in the number of producers, which it characterized as "useful and never dangerous for the state." Any deficiencies in production were far less significant than the "inestimable and unhoped for advantages" of this great metamorphosis to industrial production. The report cited as an example the town of Homblières, near St.Quentin, which it claimed had been transformed from a sleepy village with many poor to a thriving and prosperous center of industry and asked rhetorically how many more such villages there were.

The report argued that a reestablishment of corporations would return such villages to the poverty of the past. It also stated that it feared that limits on industry could deprive France of ingenious discoveries that would instead enrich neighboring countries.

The report by the Council on Commerce also cited Richard Arkwright, the Englishman who had made the first steps in the mechanization of cotton spinning. Arkwright was a wigmaker who had worked on his machine until he had perfected it in 1780. The council stated that if he had not been a wigmaker in Manchester, but had instead been in a town with guilds, he would not have been able to contribute to the prosperity of his region, bring about great changes in industry and acquire a vast fortune – he would still have been a wigmaker.

It also mentioned the wallpaper industry and quoted Réveillon, the wallpaper manufacturer whose factory had been destroyed on the eve of the Revolution, on the difficulties that he had had with guilds. All of the innovations that had been made since the Revolution, the council claimed, would have remained buried under a regime of corporations.

The report asserted that the argument that guilds needed to be reestablished to repress abuses in the practice of industrial or commercial professions was utterly specious. It reiterated the government's position that current legislation was sufficient to address problems in the workplace. It also contended that establishing *conseils de prud'hommes*, which had already demonstrated their utility in a number of cities, would be preferable to restoring corporations.

The report denounced the effort by the caulkers of Le Havre to form a corporation and argued that tumultuous scenes and worker revolts, which had formerly been relatively frequent, no longer occurred now that the practice of labor was free. It concluded its arguments by extolling Turgot's abolition of guilds and argued that one should learn from the lessons of history.[247]

établis près du Ministre de l'Intérieur, sur le rétablissement demandé des corps de marchands et des communautés d'arts et métiers (Paris: Hacquart, n.d.).
[247] AN F^{12*} 193bis, fols. 17–24.

The Council on Commerce approved the statement and declared that the requested reestablishment of guilds would be equally contrary to justice and the public interest. The discussion that followed revealed the fundamental agreement of the members with the arguments made in the report.

The council was particularly impressed by the reference to Turgot's edict of 1776. Members believed that the benefits of economic freedom that had resulted from the Revolution demonstrated the wisdom of the measure. The council reiterated its belief in a free labor market and praised the current state of French commerce. The members decided that the report would be signed by all present and sent to the Minister of the Interior.[248] Although the attempt to restore guilds stood little chance of success, and had been tabled by the time each body met, the spirited denunciations of the effort by the Council on Manufacturing and the Council on Commerce, the two principal governmental bodies concerned with economic policy, assured its failure.

During the fall of 1821, Costaz reworked an earlier pamphlet to produce a statement against the reestablishment of guilds, which he also submitted to the Council on Manufacturing.[249] Although the council continued to examine the regulation of factories and workshops, by the time Costaz published and submitted his *mémoire*, the issue of the reestablishment of guilds had largely receded from view.[250] The chambers never again took up a request to reestablish corporations, and the restoration of guilds never again emerged during the Bourbon regime as a matter of public discussion or policy debate. For better or for worse, French industrialization would proceed unimpeded.

With the rejection by the chambers of the petition, the French government, both Crown and legislature, had committed itself to mechanization and industrialization – there would be no looking backward to the model of guilds. Indeed, the forward-looking outlook of the restored Bourbon government is evident in an incident that occurred during the late summer of 1821.

During May 1810, the Napoleonic Ministry of the Interior, inspired by the success of mechanized production of cotton and wool, had offered a one million franc prize to the inventor of the best machine to spin flax. The notice of the competition was translated into many languages and sent to ambassadors, ministers and consuls in foreign countries for dissemination. The competition was to be open for three years, until May 1813.[251]

The competition attracted entrants from across France and the Empire – Saxony, Frankfurt, and Italy. It also drew two Americans from Vermont who,

[248] AN F¹² 193bis, fols. 25–25v°.
[249] Claude-Anthelme Costaz, *Corps de marchands et communautés d'arts et métiers* (Paris: Huzard, 1821); on its submission to the council, AN F¹² 196bis, fol. 24.
[250] On the council working on regulation of factories and workshops, see AN F¹²* 196bis, fols. 20, 23.
[251] AN F¹² 2206^A, dossier Contest for the spinning of flax, extract from minutes of Secretariat of State, Ministry of the Interior, May 7, 1810, attached to circular of Minister of the Interior, November 24, 1810. For another glimpse at this competition, Felix, "Avant-garde Aristocrats?," pp. 204–205.

overcoming "the great danger of capture by the perpetual enemy of mankind," succeeded in transporting their machine to France shortly before the deadline.[252] By the time the deadline had arrived, however, the situation of the Empire had changed considerably, as Bonaparte desperately sought to recover from the debacle in Russia, and no prize was awarded.

Years later, on August 29, 1821, the ministry received an inquiry as to whether the competition remained open. The minister replied that the competition had long been closed and no more entries were possible. The government had no intention of reviving it, instead relying on the fact that France had flax-spinning machines that were becoming more efficient every day.[253] Much to the surprise, and in some cases bitter disappointment,[254] of those who had expected otherwise, France under the Bourbons did not look to restore former production and commercial models, but instead continued the advance into the industrial age.

* * * * * * *

After approximately a decade of desultory debate on the reestablishment of corporations, the creation of the Ministry of Manufacturing and Commerce by the Napoleonic government appeared to represent a clear decision against any restoration of guilds. The establishment of the ministry, however, coincided with a severe economic crisis that continued until the fall of Bonaparte in 1814 and left the commitment to mechanization of production open to question.

The return of the Bourbons in 1814 generated a widespread expectation that the reforms of the Revolution – in which the abolition of guilds figured prominently – would be overturned. The appointment of Montesquiou-Fezensac, a former clerical deputy to the National Assembly who had opposed many revolutionary measures and subsequently emigrated, as Minister of the Interior did little to assuage such fears. Furthermore, the dissolution of the Ministry of Manufacturing only weeks after the Bourbon government returned to power seemed to confirm such fears and to presage the reestablishment of corporations. The Council on Manufacturing and the Society for the Encouragement of National Industry – also bodies that had come into existence under the Napoleonic regime and that were staunch opponents of efforts to restore corporations – similarly feared that they might be suppressed. The Crown, however, did not take any immediate or decisive action, leaving the situation in relation to guilds indeterminate.

Bonaparte's escape from Elba and brief assumption of power during 1815 completely transformed the political climate. Louis XVIII called for elections that same year, which led to the "incomparable chamber," in which extreme

---

[252] AN F¹² 2206ᴬ, letter of Baldwin and Parks to Minister of the Interior, April 5, 1813.

[253] AN F¹² 2206ᴬ, dossier Contest for the spinning of flax, letter of Minister of the Interior to Barbie, September 8, 1821.

[254] See the indignant letter of Bruyard in IISH Bruyard Papers, *liasse* 25.

royalists, known as ultras, achieved a substantial majority. Their ascendancy led to intensified efforts to reestablish guilds.

The Minister of the Interior during late 1815, Vaublanc, was an ultra who allowed some local efforts to reestablish corporations to move forward. On a larger scale, during March 1816, which was the zenith of ultra dominance, the budget committee of the Chamber of Deputies proposed the reestablishment of guilds. In fact, a bill to restore corporations was drawn up but was not presented during the 1816 session, and was never acted upon. After March 1816, however, ultra domination began to recede, due partly to the appointment of Lainé, a moderate, as Minister of the Interior in May 1816.

During late 1817, a group in Paris, led by Levacher-Duplessis, mounted an effort to restore corporations in the city. The attempt became the catalyst for a major consideration of the issue of guilds both inside and outside of government that continued for years. Ultimately, however, the venture launched by Levacher-Duplessis failed and guilds were not restored in Paris.

During early 1819 the Minister of the Interior, Decazes, also a moderate, proposed an industrial exhibition – the first since the Napoleonic era. Louis XVIII gave his approval, stating that periodic exhibitions of products of French industry would be a means to encourage and bolster the progress of industry. Although indirect, the decision of the Crown signified its preference for mechanization and industry over a reversion to a system of guilds – "progress of industry" was widely understood as the antithesis of guilds.

The exhibition of 1819 was the largest yet held, both in terms of the number of exhibitors and the amount of space provided. Louis visited it twice and received delegations of manufacturers during the exhibition. More significantly, the etiquette he employed during the awards ceremony clearly and unambiguously demonstrated his support for industry, and a few months later he ennobled two major industrialists. In the aftermath of the exhibition, royalists were disappointed and advocates of industry were pleased.

As a result of Louis's clear endorsement of industry, when proponents of guilds undertook another attempt to reestablish them, they did not approach the Crown, but instead sought to work through the chambers. In the wake of the assassination of the Duc de Berri, royalists were again ascendant, but the final effort to restore guilds under the Bourbons failed when their petition was tabled in April 1821. The course of French industrialization had been set and would proceed largely unimpeded.[255]

[255] This point was not lost on contemporaries. Louis-Benjamin Francoeur, Louis-Sébastien Lenormand, et al., *Dictionnaire technologique ou nouveau dictionnaire universel des arts et métiers, et de l'économie industrielle et commerciale, par une société des savans et d'artistes,* 26 vols. (Paris: Thomine et Fortie, 1822–1835), 11: 401.

Conclusion

When one considers the strange [collection] of laws and institutions that governed industry before 1789, one is astonished that it was able to gain such importance: corporations, privileges, masterships, manufacturing regulations, pointless impediments – all seemingly intended to hold back development. The first step to take to make progress was therefore to free it (industry) from the shackles that kept it in infancy.

According to the jury named to screen items admitted into the 1819 exhibition, it (this step) contributed to the thriving state of our manufacturing today. We transcribe here its opinion in order to remove all doubts that could remain in the mind of some on the benefits it brought forth.

Claude-Anthelme Costaz
Histoire de l'administration en France

By the eighteenth century guilds had been a prominent feature of urban life for centuries, providing a structure to labor and some degree of control over journeymen and apprentices – in effect, they served as an extension of the police. Corporations had been abolished in 1776, but after only a few months characterized by unnerving unrest among journeymen, they were reorganized. By May 1789, then, as the Estates-General opened, with memories of 1776 still relatively fresh, the position of guilds seemed secure.

Yet, just two months later, on August 4, the National Assembly unexpectedly launched a comprehensive attack on privilege and abolished guilds, which were perceived as beneficiaries of privilege. Even among the cascade of renunciations made during the meeting, stunning deputies and observers alike, the abolition of guilds stood out. In fact, the National Assembly appears to have had doubts about the action because it temporized – in the drawing-up of the August decrees summarizing the renunciations made during the meeting, the Assembly pronounced the reform of guilds rather than their abolition. Ultimately, in early 1791, the National Assembly did do away with corporations, but their dissolution came only after the destruction of provinces, the *parlements* and the nobility, and a fundamental reorganization of the Church.

The Assembly's tentativeness indicates the uncertainty and even apprehensiveness of deputies, but they honored the compact forged on August 4 and eradicated corporations.

The National Assembly dissolved guilds not on the basis of economic doctrine but spontaneously as part of its unanticipated attack on privilege and corporate bodies. The decision to abolish corporations was impulsive, and subsequent policy on guilds was indefinite and contingent. Because guilds had been mentioned, however ambiguously, in the August decrees, measures with respect to them had been anticipated; at the same time, it was equally expected that legislation to carry out the functions formerly fulfilled by corporations would emerge. But the National Assembly not only failed to enact any laws to manage tasks previously carried out by guilds, it did away with all remaining regulations and oversight just before it disbanded, compounding the sense of dislocation caused by the dissolution of corporations.

Although the Assembly vested the Ministry of the Interior with a vague mandate to supervise commerce, the ministry was a new entity seeking to define itself and responsibility for commerce did not become a major priority. The National Assembly delegated responsibility for establishing new laws on commerce and production to the Legislative Assembly, which never acted on the issue. This inaction created a major vacuum soon filled by abuses, which proliferated and accelerated. Responsibility for addressing these problems devolved to municipal officials, who with few resources and numerous obligations, made oversight of commerce a low priority.

In place of guilds, the National Assembly enacted an occupational license (*patente*) that allowed its holder to practice any trade he wished. The establishment of the occupational license was primarily a fiscal measure to produce revenue, and problems quickly arose, to such a degree that the abolition of guilds and the introduction of the occupational license became indelibly associated with a sharp decline of standards in both production and commerce.

Amidst fraud, corruption and declining quality, the Legislative Assembly declared war on Austria during April 1792, beginning nearly a quarter-century of almost continuous conflict. After a favorable beginning, the war went badly for France, and the government – primarily the Committee of Public Safety acting on behalf of the National Convention – placed the country on a war footing, taking extraordinary actions, among which was mass conscription. The *levée-en-masse*, as it was known, raised armies of a size not seen in Europe since the Roman era, and the scale of production needed to outfit and equip the troops far exceeded the capacity of the traditional artisanal system that had heretofore prevailed.

Early efforts at mass production of muskets and boots centered on the requisition and reorganization of labor, but manpower shortages rendered the logic of mechanization of production ineluctable. Indeed, the National Convention endorsed and supported this course when it founded the Conservatoire des Arts et Métiers in the fall of 1794 – its purpose was to expedite and advance mechanization in France.

In terms of production, the efforts of the Committee of Public Safety succeeded, especially in arms – Paris became the largest producer of muskets in the world. Ultimately, however, the government shut down the arms workshops, due largely to labor unrest. Indeed, the manufacturing endeavors of the Convention essentially defined the issues that would frame the ensuing debate on the reestablishment of guilds.

On the one hand, the undertakings revealed the possibilities of mass production, later attached to mechanization of production – the arms program had been driven by a proto-assembly line method rather than mechanization. In the view of those who advocated mechanization, a restoration of guilds could offer workers a platform from which to impede mechanization.

On the other hand, the government ended the program mainly because of worker unrest, and proponents of guilds asserted that reestablishing them would bring an end to "insubordination." They also argued that the reestablishment of guilds would restore quality and trust to manufacturing and commerce.

The debate began in earnest during the National Convention as doubts about the proscription of guilds deepened. As France emerged from the Terror, there was disaffection with the unregulated market, especially in Paris, leading to a rise in opinion favoring corporations. In an indication that the sentiment to return to a system of guilds was more than idle longing, the commission appointed by the National Convention to draft a new constitution believed it necessary to include an article maintaining the abolition of guilds. Although two deputies from different parts of the political spectrum opposed this proposal, the Convention approved it and it became article 355 of the Constitution of the Year III that established the Directory. Conditions in the workplace and market continued to deteriorate, however, and the year after the Constitution of the Year III was adopted, the deputy who claimed to have written and put forward article 355 expressed regret at having done so. The dearth of the early Directory, to an extent unknown in living memory, enabled the favorable recollection of guilds that had formed to gain momentum – indeed, in internal communications republican officials and policymakers acknowledged that the suppression of corporations had substantially contributed to the deplorable state of commerce and manufacturing.

As privation and suffering eased, the issue of the reestablishment of guilds became less trenchant, but misgivings remained and a favorable sentiment toward corporations lingered. During the year VI (1798), however, the Directory sponsored the Exhibition of the Products of French Industry, which generated a positive image of mechanization of production, momentarily stemming the favorable sentiment toward guilds. In his opening speech at the event François de Neufchâteau had drawn an invidious comparison between the regime of corporations and the developing mechanization of production, associating liberty with industry and the former system of guilds with the yoke of despotism. Despite straitened fiscal circumstances, the Directory also sought to assist and encourage the development of industry – indeed, its role in providing a foundation for French industrialization is not as recognized as it perhaps should be.

In November 1799, Napoleon Bonaparte overthrew the Directory, over-turning the Constitution of the Year III and effectively reopening the possibil-ity of more quickly reestablishing guilds. If, in fact, there was a time during the revolutionary and Napoleonic epoch when guilds might have been rees-tablished, it was during Bonaparte's rule. Indeed, under the Consulate the central government reorganized bodies of bakers and butchers in Paris, and the Prefect of Police in Paris, on his own authority, organized various trades into guild-like structures. In addition, Fiévée, a secret counselor of Bonaparte, urged him to reestablish guilds.

The Bonapartist regime was also the first since the dissolution of corpora-tions to address some of the problems that had arisen as a consequence of this. The law of 22 germinal year XI established regulations for apprenticeships, quality control and worker discipline. The last provision, in particular, which required workers to carry a passbook from employer to employer, creating controversy during the nineteenth century, but contemporaries regarded the law as largely ineffective. The government was aware of its deficiencies, which may account for the fact that the Council of State debated larger projects for the reestablishment of guilds on several occasions until 1810. Those who argued for their restoration emphasized in particular that greater order and discipline would result.

At the same time, the Napoleonic regime saw – both inside and outside of Paris – the development of large-scale mechanized production, particularly in the textile sector. The cotton-producing facility of Richard-Lenoir was so vast and so novel that it was mentioned in a major guide to the city. The years between 1815 and 1830 were one of the most rapid periods of gains in cotton production in nineteenth-century France, and the foundation for that increase had been established under the Napoleonic regime.[1] Indeed, French industrial production during the Empire was 50 per cent greater than under the Old Regime, and a key sector in this growth was cotton – in 1789, there were six large-scale mechanized cotton production facilities operating in France, but by 1814 there were 272.[2]

Furthermore, manpower shortages resulting from conscription brought about by the Napoleonic wars virtually mandated mechanization of produc-tion, and those who opposed any restoration of corporations asserted that they could become a platform for mounting opposition to mechanization. Ultimately, increased production trumped the desire to impose order, and the regime did not reestablish guilds.

Bonaparte delayed making a clear and explicit choice between corporations and mechanized production for more than a decade, but a resolution occurred with a major reorganization of the Ministry of the Interior in January 1812.

---

[1] On cotton production between 1815 and 1830, Landes, *The Unbound Prometheus*, p. 160.
[2] Horn, *The Path Not Taken*, p. 223.

A portion of its responsibilities were transferred to an entirely new entity, the Ministry of Manufacturing and Commerce. The restructuring signaled an endorsement of mechanized, industrial production by the Napoleonic regime, but the decision coincided with an industrial crisis that began in 1811 and continued until the end of that regime. The depression was a new experience for the French, and had resulted in great hardship by the time Bonaparte fell from power.

Consequently, when the Bourbons returned in 1814 they came back to an economy in major dislocation, and contemporaries expected the monarchy to undo the reforms of the Revolution, including the abolition of guilds. The restored monarchy soon abolished the Ministry of Manufacturing and Commerce and reintegrated its functions into the Ministry of the Interior. This action, along with the expectation that it would do away with most reforms of the Revolution, created the perception that the government of Louis XVIII would also reestablish guilds. Both the Crown and the Ministry of the Interior received a number of requests to this end, and a spirited debate, both in public and within the government, took place.

The monarchy took no action, but Bonaparte's brief return to power during 1815 transformed the political atmosphere. The elections of 1815 placed extreme royalists, known as ultras, in power, and they used their ascendancy to attempt to restore corporations. In the course of budget hearings during 1816, a member of the budget committee recommended the reestablishment of guilds, and a bill to restore them was drawn up but never presented. Shortly afterward, ultra domination began to wane, signified in part by the appointment of a more moderate centrist, Lainé, as Minister of the Interior in May 1816.

Although he was seeking a return of inspectors of manufacture rather than guilds, Charles-Jean-Baptiste Bruyard, a former inspector of manufactures, undoubtedly spoke for proponents of the reestablishment of corporations when he expressed his frustration during the spring of 1817. In a letter to the Minister of the Interior he wrote that he had hoped that the "return of the legitimate prince" would lead to the "reestablishment of former institutions," but he now believed that this was not going to occur.[3]

During the fall of 1817 a group in Paris undertook a significant effort to reestablish corporations in the city. Their effort became the catalyst for a major debate on the place of guilds in the polity and the economy – a discussion that occurred both within the government and publicly. The debate went on for months, but, in the end, the group failed to achieve the restoration of guilds in Paris.

Once again, as had been the case under Bonaparte, a decision with respect to a restoration of guilds versus mechanization of production came in a somewhat indirect fashion. On this occasion, the Crown announced its intention

---

[3] IISH, Bruyard Papers, *liasse* 25. See also IISH, Bruyard Papers, *liasse* 24, for similar sentiments expressed during the summer of 1816.

to hold an industrial exhibition in 1819, signaling its preference for industry over the restoration of corporations. Larger than any of its four predecessors – from its scale to the site and etiquette of the awards ceremony – the exhibition of 1819 clearly conveyed the Crown's support for modernization. In an added demonstration of its backing of large-scale manufacturing, a few weeks after the exhibition Louis XVIII ennobled two noted textile industrialists. In the aftermath of the exhibition, royalists were disillusioned by the unequivocal support for both industry and industrialists that Louis XVIII demonstrated throughout and after the event.

With Louis XVIII endorsing mechanized industry, proponents of the reorganization of guilds had to seek a path other than through the Crown to achieve their goal. The assassination of the Duc de Berri in 1820 provided them with an opportunity, as the royalist reaction again placed ultras in the ascendancy. Seeking to take advantage of ultra dominance, the group that had attempted to reestablish corporations in 1817 launched another effort in 1821. Resurrecting the petition from 1817 without changing a word, during the spring of 1821 the group, approaching the legislature rather than the Crown, made overtures directly to the chambers. Although the Chamber of Peers discussed whether or not to accept the petition, it tabled it on April 3, 1821, and no serious attempt to reestablish guilds ever occurred again under the Bourbon regime.

Although it cannot, of course, be attributed merely or even primarily to the absence of corporations, it is also true that with the return of peace in 1815, French production experienced a period of growth and development, particularly in textiles. To the degree that advocates of industry saw the restoration of guilds as one of the greatest threats to mechanization, the actions of those who prevented this should be given recognition. As Jeff Horn argued, the overarching goal of the Bourbon regime in the economic sphere was "to permit – over the long term – a defeated and diminished nation to mechanize, to innovate, and to compete with a victorious Britain," and this objective would have been greatly facilitated by the continuing suppression of guilds.[4]

In addition, Robert Alexander contended that the liberal opposition under the Restoration was essentially an ideologically loose coalition made up of disaffected liberals, Bonapartists and republicans. Among liberals in particular, he argued, a unifying principle was opposition to privilege, especially clerical and noble privilege, represented by ultraroyalism – liberals claimed to represent the nation. This study suggests that another core concern – represented in the actions of, among others, such liberals as Ternaux, Chauvelin and Jouy – was economic liberalism, at least with respect to guilds.[5]

Because the abolition of guilds by the National Assembly in 1791 was never reversed, the finality of the act has tended to obscure the debate on

---

[4] Horn, *The Path Not Taken*, p. 240.
[5] Alexander, *Re-Writing the French Revolutionary Tradition*. Many of them did not support free trade, which is why the qualification that it applied to guilds is necessary.

their reestablishment that occurred for decades afterward. In enumerating reforms of the Revolution, for example, Madame de Staël, a particularly incisive observer, simply wrote that the suppression of guilds and masterships and all other restraints on industry had made possible the development of manufacturing, but never mentioned the debates that took place on the reestablishment of corporations.[6] The fact that guilds were not reestablished in any comprehensive fashion should not obscure the efforts made to bring this about – indeed, the wisdom of the liquidation of corporations was at times strongly questioned. To appropriate the apposite phrase of Jeff Horn, the reestablishment of guilds was also a "path not taken" and maintaining their dissolution was the product of extended deliberations and considered decisions, particularly during the Napoleonic and Restoration periods.

In order to grasp the deeper meaning of the debate on guilds, it is instructive to return to the advice given to the Council of State by those preparing projects for its consideration early during the Consulate – that the Council of State should determine its goals for society before resolving the matter of guilds. The destruction of corporations had originally been enacted by the National Assembly as part of its remaking of France between 1789 and 1791, a feature of its effort to eradicate privilege and corporate bodies from French society. The maintenance of their abolition was likewise driven by societal goals – in this instance, the development of a modern, industrialized economy and state.

By examining the debate on the restoration of guilds, this study has attempted to demonstrate that the passage from the eighteenth-century regime of corporations to the unstructured world of the working classes of the nineteenth century was neither seamless nor irreversible. Furthermore, the change in the organization of labor altered its nature as well. After the dissolution of guilds, and the maintenance of that dissolution, work evolved increasingly from a skill developed and ratified by artisans within a hierarchical, regulated system into a commodity offered by independent individuals.[7] Although mechanization is usually associated with textiles, and unquestionably had its most significant impact in that sector, it also affected formerly guild-based trades, from locksmiths to shoemakers. Moreover, even in occupations not overtaken by mechanization, anyone in possession of an occupational license could practice whatever trade he wished, irrespective of his level of skill – again, the dissolution of guilds served to make labor more a product offered by individual practitioners or laborers than an art.

The degree of success of the French economy during the nineteenth century remains a matter of debate,[8] but there can be little doubt that maintaining the

---

[6] Anne-Louise-Germaine de Staël, *Considérations sur les principaux événemens de la Révolution française*, 3 vols. (London: Baldwin, Craddock et Joy, 1818), I: 285.

[7] To be sure, a similar shift had begun before the Revolution, but the abolition of guilds hastened and generalized it in France, and mechanization subsequently influenced it, especially under the Napoleonic regime. Johnson, *The Life and Death of Industrial Languedoc*, pp. 10–11.

[8] Horn, *The Path Not Taken*, is a recent and persuasive favorable assessment.

abolition of guilds could only have aided it. For better or for worse, mechanization would proceed unimpeded by guilds or regulations, generating greater social injustice than the system of corporations had engendered, particularly under the Orléanist regime that succeeded the Bourbons. Indeed, the corporate idiom survived to inspire worker movements throughout the nineteenth century and even into the twentieth.[9] Despite their dissolution in 1791, guilds, as the object of debates, enjoyed a considerable afterlife, but, unlike 1776, after 1791 they were never were able to come back from the oblivion to which they had been consigned.

[9] Matthew H. Elbow, *French Corporative Theory, 1789–1848: A Chapter in the History of Ideas*, reprint ed. (New York: Octagon Books, 1966), pp. 19–22; Johnson, "Economic Change and Artisan Discontent," p. 109; Sewell, *Work and Revolution in France*.

Bibliography

Primary Sources – Unpublished

Archives Nationales (Paris)

Series
AA
    13, 29
AB XIX
    3889, 3994
AD XI
    13, 14, 65, 67, 72, 76
AD XIX
    1, 2
AF I*
    10, 11
AF II
    78
AF III
    21^A, 47, 93,
AF IV
    925, 926, 931, 942, 1019, 1012, 1060, 1088, 1288,
    1290, 1291^A, 1292, 1318, 1329, 1353, 1470, 1471, 1472, 1473, 1475, 1477
AP
    27 AP 1, 349 AP 30
C
    45, 54, 71^1, 98, 124, 127, 232
C* II
    12, 13
D III
    363
D IV
    1, 6, 15, 20, 21, 22, 32, 33, 35, 40, 41, 43,
    46, 49, 51, 53, 55, 56, 57, 61, 63, 64, 65
D XI
    1
D XIII
    1

F¹a

  23, 24, 33, 265¹, 268¹, 270

F¹b I

  56/59,

F¹c I

  13, 70, 91

F¹c IV

  2

F¹d I

  31

F² I

  106²⁴

F⁷

  3024, 3751, 3755, 3759, 3787, 3789, 3829, 3830, 3831, 3834, 3835, 3837, 3864, 3874, 3875, 4219, 4236, 4283, 6861, 9786, 9787

F¹²

  501ᴮ, 506, 507, 508, 509/510, 512, 513, 517ᴬ, 618,
  633/637, 638, 652, 654, 761, 763, 781ᴬ, 786, 922,
  923, 925, 926, 937, 941, 981/984, 985, 1310, 1311, 1391, 1559, 1560, 1561, 1566, 2178, 2179, 2180, 2181, 2182, 2183, 2188, 2194, 2195, 2202ᴬ, 2203, 2204, 2206ᴬ, 2206ᴮ, 2207, 2263, 2333, 2366/2367, 2384, 2386/2387, 2397, 2467, 2469, 2471, 2473, 2474ᴬ, 2491ᴬ, 2495, 2998, 4639, 4648, 4774, 4791, 4792, 4861, 4897, 5118

F¹²*

  111–112, 192, 193ᵇⁱˢ, 194, 195, 196, 196ᵇⁱˢ

F¹³

  508, 521

H¹

  1023

H²

  2103, 2176, 2180

M

  667

T

  51, 1373

T*

  1562/1

W

  363

Y

  9334, 9395ᴮ, 9500, 9509, 9530, 11207ᴮ, 11208ᴬ, 12079ᴮ, 13016ᴮ, 13017, 14437ᴮ

Archives De La Chambre De Commerce Et D'Industrie De Paris

1 Mi 1, 1 Mi 2, 1 Mi 4
2 Mi 1, 2 Mi 2, 2 Mi 3, 2 Mi 4

Archives De La Préfecture De Police (Paris)

DB 1, 123, 305, 402, 403, 513

Archives Départementales

Ain
 1 Mi 1
Côte d'Or
 E* 3366, 3370, 3372, 3473
Dordogne
 O E DEP 5004
Isère
 2 C 86, 88, 90
 L 284, 285, 288
Jura
 1 Mi 167
Nord
 M 557/5, 557/80
Seine-Maritime
 5 E 474, 519, 648, 680, 706
 8 M 2, 34
 10 M 1, 2

Archives Municipales

Bayonne
 AA 51
Bordeaux
 D 85, 86, 89, 90, 91, 92, 139, 227
 I 81
Grenoble
 FF 55, 56
 HH 13, 18, 42, 45
 LL 162, 258
Le Havre
 D^2 1
 D^3 38
Marseille
 AA 7–7
 1 BB 3291, 3292
 4 D 43
 HH 388
Strasbourg
 AA 2005[a]

Bibliothèque Historique De La Ville De Paris

Ms. 35, 713, 737, 742, 768, 769, 775, 786, 790, 796, 799,
    808, 894, 1006, 1013, 1014, 1017, 1024
Ms. CP 4867, 4868, 4869, 6540
Ms. N.A. 22, 108, 152, 192, 477

Bibliothèque Municipale

Grenoble
    Ms. R. 7451
Orléans
    Ms. 1422
Saintes
    25486 MAR

Bibliothèque Nationale

Mss. Fonds Français
6687, 11697, 13713
Mss. Microfilm
4884
Mss. Nouvelles acquisitions françaises
1777

Bibliothèque Nationale Et Universitaire De Strasbourg

Ms. 452
Ms. 559

International Institute Of Social History (Amsterdam)

Bruyard Papers
12, 24, 25, 187, 189, 191, 192, 193, 194, 195, 196, 197, 198, 199, 200, 201, 250, 252, 253, 254,
    260, 262, 263, 265, 1292

Napoleonica.Org

Project numbers 663, 2044bis, 2044ter, 2089, 2163, 2717, 2976

Newspapers

Affiches d'Angers
Annales de la république française
Affiches des Evéchés et Lorraine
Annales patriotiques et littéraires de la France
Annales politiques et littéraires
Bibliothèque de l'homme publique
Bulletin décadaire de la république française

Bulletin de Paris
Bulletin de l'Assemblée Nationale
Bulletin National/Républicain
Chronique de Paris
Code de la Patrie et l'humanité, ou des droits & des devoirs de l'homme et du
    citoyen
Courier de Madon
Courier français
Courier provincial
Courier républicain
Etats-Généraux. Journal de la Correspondance de Nantes.
Gazette National, ou le Moniteur universel
Journal d'Etat et du citoyen
Journal de Toulouse, l'observateur républicain
Journal des décrets de l'Assemblée nationale, pour les habitans des campagnes
Journal des départements, districts et municipalités de la ci-devant province de
    Bretagne; et des amis de la constitution
Journal de la cour et de ville
Journal de la Haute-Garonne
Journal de la ville, par Jean-Pierre-Louis de Luchet
Journal de Perlet
Journal de Toulouse
Journal des débats
Journal des débats et des décrets
Journal des décrets de l'Assemblée Nationale, pour les habitans des campagnes
Journal du Bon-Homme Richard
Journal politique du Maine-et-Loire
L'Abeille politique et littéraire
L'Ami du Peuple
L'Indépendant
La Chronique du mois
La Décade philosophique
Le Conservateur décadaire
Le Constitutionnel
Le Point du Jour
Le Républicain français
Le Spectateur National et le modérateur
Nouvelles de Paris

Primary Sources – Published

Actes de la Commune de Paris pendant la Révolution, Sigismond Lacroix, ed., 7 vols.
    (Paris: L. Cerf, 1894–1898).
Arrêté du directoire du district de Bourg, concernant la suspension de la fabrication
    des souliers et bottes pour l'armée, jusqu'à l'approvisionnement de cuirs forts, du
    18 vendémiaire an III (N.p., n.d.).
Au Directoire Exécutif. Les Entrepreneurs des filatures mécaniques de coton
    (Paris, n.d.).

Bailly, Charles Thomas Désiré. *Observations sur les manufactures de draps adressées à Sa Majesté l'Empereur et Roi* (Paris: Amand König, 1806).

Bailly-Jean Sylvain. *Mémoires d'un témoin de la Révolution*, 3 vols. (Paris: Baudouin, 1822).

Baudin (des Ardennes), P.C.L. *Eclaircissemens sur l'article 355 de la constitution, et sur la liberté de la presse* (Paris: Imprimerie nationale, an IV [1796]).

Berryer, Pierre-Nicolas. *Souvenirs de M. Berryer, doyen des avocats à Paris, de 1774 à 1838*, 2 vols.(Paris: Ambroise Dupont, 1839).

Bosc, Joseph-Antoine. *Essai sur les moyens d'améliorer l'agriculture, les arts et le commerce en France* (Paris: Patris, an VIII).

Bulletin de la société d'encouragement pour l'industrie nationale.

Collection officielle des ordonnances de police, 4 vols.(Paris: Boucquin, 1880–1882).

Catalogue détaillé des produits industriels, exposés au Champ-de-Mars (Paris: Guillemat, n.d.).

Compte-rendu par le Comité révolutionnaire de la Section de l'Observatoire; sur les mesures à prendre pour détruire l'esprit de corps qui règne parmi les boulangers; imprimé par ordre de l'assemblée générale (N.p.,Société typographique, 1793).

Condorcet, Marie-Jean-Antoine-Nicolas Cantat, marquis de. *Mémoires de Condorcet sur la Révolution française, extraits de sa correspondance et de celles de ses amis*, 2 vols. (Paris: Ponthieu,1824).

Costaz, Claude-Anthelme. *Corps de marchands et communautés d'arts et métiers.* (Paris: Huzard,1821).

Essai sur l'administration de l'agriculture, du commerce, des manufactures et des subsistances suivi de l'historique des moyens qui ont amené le grand essor pris par les arts depuis 1793 jusqu'en 1815. (Paris: Huzard, 1818).

Histoire de l'administration en France de l'agriculture, des arts utiles, du commerce, des manufaactures, des subsistances, des mines et des usines accompagnée d'observations et de vues, et terminée par celle des moyens qui ont amené le grand essor pris par l'industrie française, depuis la révolution, 2 vols. (Paris: Huzard, 1832).

Mémoire sur les moyens qui ont amené le grand développement que l'industrie française a pris depuis vingt ans suivi de la législation relative aux fabriques, aux ateliers, aux ouvriers, et aux découvertes dans les arts. (Paris: Huzard,1816).

Déliberation des différentes corporations de Grenoble (Grenoble: Allier, 1790).

Démarches patriotiques de M. de La Fayette, à l'égard des ouvriers de Montmartre (Paris: n.d.).

Deseine, Louis-Pierre. *Mémoire sur la nécessité du rétablissement des maîtrises et corporations comme moyens d'encourager l'industrie et le commerce.* (Paris: Fain, 1815).

(Dinochau, Jacques-Samuel). *Histoire philosophique et politique de l'Assemblée nationale, par un député des communes de B*****, 2 vols. (Paris: Deveaux, 1789).

Directoire Exécutif. Procès-verbal de la fête de la fondation de la république, célébrée à Paris le 1er vendémiaire l'an 7 (Paris: J. Gratiot, n.d.).

Droz, Joseph. *Des lois relatives aux progrès de l'industrie, ou observations sur les maîtrises, les réglemens, les privilèges et les prohibitions.* (Paris: Laran, 1801).

(Duplaine de Saint-Albine). *Lettres à M. le comte de B*** sur la révolution arrivée en 1789.*

Duquesnoy, Adrien-Cyprien. *Journal sur l'Assemblée constituante, 3 mai 1789–3 avril 1790*, Robert de Crevecoeur, ed., 2 vols. Paris: 1894).

Exposition publique des produits de l'industrie française. Catalogue des produits industriels qui ont été exposés au Champ-de-Mars pendant les trois derniers jours complémentaires de l'an VI; avec les noms, départemens et demeures des artistes et manufacturiers qui ont concouru à l'exposition; suivi du procès-verbal du jury nommé pour l'examen de ces produits. (Paris: Imprimerie de la République, year VII).

Extrait des déliberations du corps des cabartiers-hôtelains de la ville de Douai. Du 14 janvier 1791 (Douai: Derbaix, n.d.).

Fiévée, Joseph. *Correspondance et relations de J. Fiévée avec Bonaparte, premier consul et empereur pendant onze années (1802 à 1813). Publiée par l'auteur.* 3 vols. (Paris: A Desrez, 1836).

Francoeur, Louis-Benjamin, Louis-Sébastien Lenormand, et. al., *Dictionnaire technologique ou nouveau dictionnaire universel des arts et métiers, et de l'économie industrielle et commerciale, par une société des savans et d'artistes,* 26 vols. (Paris: Thomine et Fortie, 1822–1835)

(Grégoire, Henri-Baptiste). *Rapport sur l'établissement d'un Conservatoire des Arts et Métiers par Grégoire* (Paris: Imprimerie Nationale, 1794).

Guide des corps des marchands et les communautés des arts et métiers, tant de la ville et faubourgs de Paris, que de royaume (Paris: Veuve Duchesne, 1766).

(Jabin, M. de). *Liberté du commerce, abolition des maîtrises et jurandes, suppression des moines* (Paris: Laurens, n.d.).

Jouy, Victor-Joseph-Etienne de. *Etat actuel de l'industrie française, ou coup d'oeil sur l'exposition de ses produits, dans les salles du Louvre, en 1819.* (Paris: L'Huillier, 1821).

Legret, G.P. *Sur les corporations.* (Paris: Scherff, 1818).

L'Oracle françois, dédié à l'Assemblée Nationale, au Roi et à toute la Nation (Paris, n.d.).

Les Charbonniers de Paris à leurs concitoyens. (Paris: 1794).

Levacher-Duplessis. *Requête au Roi et mémoire sur la nécessité de rétablir les corps de marchands et les communautés des arts et métiers.* (Paris: J. Smith, 1817).

Moléon, Jean-Victor-Gabriel. *Du développement à donner à quelques parties principales et essentielles de notre industrie intérieur.* (Paris: Crapelet, 1819).

Napoléon sténographié au Conseil d'Etat 1804–1805, Alfred Marquiset, ed. (Paris: Honoré Champion, 1913).

Pasquier, Etienne. *Histoire de mon temps: Mémoires du Chancelier Pasquier,* 3 vols. (Paris: Plon-Nourrit, 1894).

Perron, Pierre; Pierre Plasse and Pierre-Honoré Roux. *Au Roi* (Marseille: Eberhart, 1814).

Peuchet, (Jacques). *Vocabulaire des termes de commerce, banque, manufactures, navigation, marchande, finance mercantile et statistique* (Paris: Testu, an IX).

Pilastre de la Brardière, Urbain-Réné, and Leclerc, J. B. *Correspondance de MM. les députés des communes de la province d'Anjou avec leurs commettants relativement aux Etats-Généraux...en 1789,* 10 vols. (Angers: Favie, 1789–1791).

Pillet-Will, Michel-Frédéric. *Réponse au mémoire de M. Levacher-Duplessis, ayant pour titre: "Requête et mémoire sur la nécessité de rétablir les corps des marchands et les communautés des arts et métiers," par Pillet-Will.* (Paris: Didot l'aîné, 1817).

Procès-verbal de la fête anniversaire de la Fondation de la république, célébré à Paris le 1 vendémiaire an 8 (Paris: Imprimerie de la République, an VIII).

Procès-verbaux de l'Assemblée nationale.

Procès-verbaux du Comité des Finances de l'Assemblée constituante, Camille Bloch, ed., 2 vols. (Rennes: Oberthur, 1922–1923).

Projet de constitution, pour la république française; présenté par la commission des onze dans la séance du 5 messidor, l'an 3 (Paris: Imprimerie Nationale, an III [1795]).

Rapport sur les jurandes et maîtrises; et sur un projet de statuts et réglemens pour MM. les marchands de vin de Paris, imprimé par ordre de la Chambre de Commerce du Département de la Seine. (Paris: Stoupe, 1805).

Recueil des lettres circulaires, instructions, programmes, discours et autres actes publics, émanés du C.^{en} François (de Neufchâteau), pendant ses deux exercices du Ministère de l'intérieur..., 2 vols. (Paris: Imprimerie de la République, an VII).

Regnault, Jean-Joseph. *La Constitution française, mis à la portée de tout le monde*, 2 vols. (Bar-le-Duc: Société Typographique, 1792).

Rendez-nous ce que nous avons perdu, c'est ce que nous avions le plus cher (Paris: Lerouge, an V).

Roederer, Pierre-Louis. *Mémoires sur la Révolution, le Consulat et l'Empire*, Octave Aubry, ed. (Paris: Plon, 1942).

Soufflot de Merey. *Considérations sur le rétablissement des jurandes et maîtrises; précédées d'observations sur un rapport fait à la Chambre de Commerce du Département de la Seine sur cette importante question, et sur un Projet de Statuts et Règlemens de MM. les Marchands de Vin.* (Paris: Marchant, 1805).

Stoupe, Jean-Georges-Antoine. *Mémoire sur le rétablissement de la communauté des imprimeurs de Paris; suivi de réflexions sur les contrefaçons en librairie, et sur le stéréotypage* (Paris: chez les Marchands de Nouveautés, 1806).

Thirion, E. *Mémoire à l'Empereur, sur l'amélioration des loix et règlemens commerciaux. Lettres à la Chambre de Commerce de Rouen, et au Ministre de l'Intérieur à ce sujet. Observations sur un rapport fait à la Chambre de Commerce du Département de la Seine, sur les jurandes et maîtrises et sur les considérations, publiées par M. Soufflot de Meret, sur ce rapport.* (Paris: chez l'auteur, 1806).

Secondary Sources

Addington, Larry H. *The Patterns of War since the Eighteenth Century* (Bloomington, IN: Indiana University Press, 1981).

Alder, Ken. *Engineering the Revolution: Arms and Enlightenment in France, 1763–1815* (Princeton: Princeton University Press, 1997).

Alexander, R.S. *Bonaparte and Revolutionary Tradition in France: The Fédérés of 1815* (Cambridge: Cambridge University Press, 1991).

Re-Writing the French Revolutionary Tradition (Cambridge: Cambridge University Press, 2003).

Andress, David. *The French Revolution and the People* (London: Hambledon and London, 2004).

Angleraud, Bernadette. *Les Boulangers lyonnais aux XIXe et XXe siècles* (Paris: Éditions Christian, 1998).

Baczko, Bronislaw. *Ending the Terror: The French Revolution after Robespierre* (Cambridge: Cambridge University Press, 1994).

Ballard, John R. *Continuity During the Storm: Boissy d'Anglas and the Era of the French Revolution* (Westport, CT: Greenwood Press, 2000).

Ballot, Charles. *L'Introduction du machinisme dans l'industrie française* (Paris: F. Rieder, 1923).

Becchia, Alain. *La Draperie d'Elbeuf (des origines à 1870)* (Rouen: Publications de l'Université de Rouen, 2000).

Bergeron, Louis. "Douglas, Ternaux, Cockerill: aux origines de la méchanisation de l'industrie lainière en France," *Revue Historique* 47 (1972): 67–80.

Bergdoll, Barry. "Les Aménagements du prieuré <<nationalisé>> (1798–1819)," in *Le Conservatoire national des Arts et Métiers au coeur de Paris*, Michel Le Moël and Raymond Saint-Paul, eds., (Paris: Délégation à l'Action Artistique de la Ville de Paris, 1994): pp. 51–56.

Bertaud, Jean-Paul. *1799: Bonaparte prend le pouvoir*, 2nd ed. (Brussels: Editions Complexe, 2000).

Bertier de Sauvigny, Guillaume de. *The Bourbon Restoration* (Philadelphia, PA: University of Pennsylvania Press, 1966).

Blanning, T.C.W. *The French Revolutionary Wars 1787–1802* (London: Longman, 1996).

Bossenga, Gail. "Economic Privilege and Government Regulation: Guilds, Public Officials, and the Bourgeoisie in Lille, 1700–1820," *Proceedings of the…Annual Meeting of the Western Society for French History* 11 (1993): 222–230.

"La Révolution française et les corporations: Trois exemples lillois," *Annales: Economies, Sociétés, Civilisations* 43 (1988):405–426.

The Politics of Privilege: Old Regime and Revolution in Lille (Cambridge: Cambridge University Press, 1991).

Bouneau, Christophe. *La Chambre de commerce et d'industrie de Paris (1803–2003): histoire d'un institution* (Geneva: Droz, 2003).

Bourgin, Hubert. *L'Industrie de la boucherie à Paris pendant la Révolution* (Paris: Ernest Leroux, 1911).

Brown, Howard G. *War, Revolution and the Bureaucratic State: Politics and Army Administration in France, 1791–1799* (Oxford: Clarendon Press, 1995).

Burstin, Haim. *Le Faubourg Saint-Marcel à l'Epoque Révolutionnaire: Structure économique et composition sociale* (Paris: Société des Etudes Robespierristes, 1983).

Une revolution à l'oeuvre: le Faubourg Saint-Marcel, 1789–1794 (Seyssel: Champ Vallon, 2005).

"Unskilled Labor in Paris at the End of the Eighteenth Century," in *The Workplace before the Factory: Artisans and Proletarians, 1500–1800*, Thomas Max Safley and Leonard N. Rosenband, eds., (Ithaca, NY: Cornell University Press, 1993): pp. 63–72.

Butrica, Andrew J. "Creating a Past: The Founding of the Société d'Encouragement pour l'Industrie Nationale Yesterday and Today," *The Public Historian* 20 (1998): 21–42.

Chassagne, Serge. *Le Coton et ses patrons: France 1760–1840* (Paris: Editions de l'Ecole des Hautes Etudes en Sciences Sociales, 1991).

Clapham, J.H. *The Causes of the War of 1792*, reprint edition (New York: Octagon, 1969).

Coffin, Judith. *The Politics of Women's Work: The Paris Garment Trades, 1750–1915* (Princeton: Princeton University Press, 1996).

Crook, Malcolm. *Napoleon Comes to Power: Democracy and Dictatorship in France, 1795–1804* (Cardiff: University of Wales Press, 1998).

Crouzet, François. *De la supériorité de l'Angleterre sur la France: économique et l'imaginaire, XVIIᵉ-XXᵉ siècles* (Paris: Librairie académique Perrin, 1985).

Crowston, Claire Haru. *Fabricating Women: The Seamstresses of Old Regime France, 1675–1791.* (Durham, NC: Duke University Press, 2001).

Dakin, Douglas. *Turgot and the Ancien Régime in France*, reprint edition (New York: Octagon Books, 1972).

Daly, Gavin. *Inside Napoleonic France: State and Society in Rouen, 1800–1815*. (Aldershot: Ashgate, 2001).

Des Cilleuls, Alfred. *Histoire de l'administration parisienne au XIXe siècle*, 3 vols. (Paris: Champion, 1900).

Donaghay, Marie. "Calonne and the Anglo-French Commercial Treaty of 1786," *The Journal of Modern History* 50 (On Demand Supplement) (1978): D1157–D1184.

Doyle, William. "The Price of Offices in Pre-Revolutionary France," *Historical Journal* 27 (1984): 831–860.

Venality: The Sale of Offices in Eighteenth-Century France (Oxford: Clarendon Press, 1996).

Dwyer, Philip. *Napoleon: The Path to Power* (New Haven, CT: Yale University Press, 2008).

Ellis, Geoffrey. *Napoleon's Continental Blockade: The Case of Alsace* (Oxford: Clarendon Press, 1981).

Emsley, Clive. "The Impact of War and Military Participation on Britain and France, 1792–1815," in *Artisans, Peasants & Proletarians 1760–1860*, Clive Emsley and James Walvin, eds., (London: Croom Helm, 1985): pp. 57–80.

Farr, James R. *Artisans in Europe, 1300–1914* (Cambridge: Cambridge University Press, 2000).

Faure, Edgar. *12 Mai 1776: La Disgrâce de Turgot* (Paris: Gallimard, 1961).

Felix, Joël. "Avant-garde Aristocrats? French Noblemen, Patents, and the Modernization of France (1815–1848)," in *The French Experience from Republic to Monarchy, 1792–1824: New Dawns in Politics, Knowledge and Culture*, Máire F. Cross and David Williams, ed., (Basingstoke: Palgrave: 2000), pp. 196–211.

Ferguson, Dean T. "The Body, the Corporate Idiom, and the Police of the Unincoporated Worker in Early Modern Lyons," *French Historical Studies* 23 (2000): 545–575.

Fierro, Alfred. *La Vie des Parisiens sous Napoléon* (Saint-Cloud: Napoléon Ier éditions, 2003).

Fitzsimmons, Michael P. *The Night the Old Regime Ended: August 4, 1789, and the French Revolution* (University Park, IL: Pennsylvania State University Press, 2003).

The Parisian Order of Barristers and the French Revolution (Cambridge, MA: Harvard University Press, 1987).

The Remaking of France: The National Assembly and the Constitution of 1791 (Cambridge: Cambridge University Press, 1994).

Forrest, Alan. *Conscripts and Deserters: The Army and French Society During the Revolution and Empire* (New York: Oxford University Press, 1989).

Society and Politics in Revolutionary Bordeaux (Oxford: Oxford University Press, 1975).

The Soldiers of the French Revolution (Durham: Duke University Press, 1990).

Fryer, David M. and John C. Marshall, "The Motives of Jacques de Vaucanson," *Technology and Culture* 20 (1979): 257–269.

Gallinato, Bernard. *Les Corporations à Bordeaux à la fin de l'ancien régime: Vie et mort d'un mode d'organisation du travail* (Bordeaux: Presses Universitaires de Bordeaux, 1992).

Gille, Bertrand. *Documents sur l'état de l'industrie et du commerce de Paris et du département de la Seine (1778–1810)*. (Paris: Imprimerie municipale, 1963).

Le Conseil général des Manufactures. (Inventaire analytique des procès-verbaux.) 1810–1829. (Paris: S.E.V.P.E.N., 1961).

Les Sources statistiques de l'histoire de France: Des enquêtes du XVIIe siècle à 1870 (Geneva and Paris: Librairie Droz, 1980).

Gottschalk, Louis. *Jean-Paul Marat: A Study in Radicalism*, revised edition (Chicago: University of Chicago Press, 1967).

Harris, J. R. *Industrial Espionage and Technology Transfer: Britain and France in the Eighteenth Century* (Aldershot: Ashgate, 1998).

Heimmermann, Daniel. "The Bordeaux Shoemaker's Guild at the End of the Old Regime," *Selected Papers of the Consortium on Revolutionary Europe 1750–1850* (2001): 211–219.

"The Guilds of Bordeaux, les métiers libres and the sauvetats of Saint-Seurin and Saint-André," *Proceedings of the Annual Meeting of the Western Society for French History* 25 (1998): 24–35.

Hesse, Carla. *Publishing and Cultural Politics in Revolutionary Paris, 1789–1810* (Berkeley, CA: University of California Press, 1991).

Hirsch, Jean-Pierre. *Les deux rêves du commerce: Entreprise et institution dans la région lilloise (1780–1860)* (Paris: Editions de l'Ecole des Hautes Etudes en Sciences Sociales, 1991).

"Revolutionary France, Cradle of Free Enterprise," *The American Historical Review* 94 (1989): 1281–1289.

Histoire de Grenoble, Vital Chomel, ed., (Toulouse: Privat, 1976).

Histoire du commerce de Marseille, Gaston Rambert, ed., 4 vols. (Paris: Plon, 1949–1954).

Horn, Jeff. "Machine-breaking in England and France during the Age of Revolution. Controversy/Controverse)," *Labour/Le Travail* 55 (2005): 143–166.

"The Legacy of 14 July 1789 in the Cultural History of French Industrialization," *Proceedings of the Annual Meeting of the Western Society for French History* 28 (2000): 251–260.

The Path Not Taken: French Industrialization in the Age of Revolution, 1750–1830 (Cambridge, MA: The MIT Press, 2006).

Horn, Jeff and Margaret C. Jacob. "Jean-Antoine Chaptal and the Cultural Roots of French Industrialization," *Technology and Culture* 39 (1998): 671–698.

Hyslop, Beatrice Fry. *French Nationalism in 1789 According to the General Cahiers*, reprint edition (New York: Octagon Books, 1968).

Jacob, Margaret C. *Scientific Culture and the Making of the Industrial West* (Oxford: Oxford University Press, 1997).

Jaffé, Grace. *Le Mouvement ouvrier à Paris pendant la Révolution française* (Paris: Librairie Felix Alcan, 1924).

Johnson, Christopher H. "Capitalism and the State: Capital Accumulation and Proletarianization in the Languedocian Woolens Industry, 1700–1789," in *The Workplace before the Factory: Artisans and Proletarians, 1500–1800*, Thomas Max Safley and Leonard N. Rosenband, eds., (Ithaca, NY: Cornell University Press, 1993): pp. 37–62.

"Economic Change and Artisan Discontent: The Tailors' History, 1800–48," in *Revolution and Reaction: 1848 and the Second French Republic*, Roger Price, ed., (London: Croom Helm, 1975): pp. 87–114.

The Life and Death of Industrial Languedoc, 1700–1920 (New York: Oxford Univesity Press, 1995).

Jones, Peter. *Reform and Revolution in France: The Politics of Transition, 1774–1791* (Cambridge: Cambridge University Press, 1995).

Kaplan, Steven L. "Les Corporations, les 'faux ouvriers' et le faubourg Saint-Antoine au XVIIIᵉ siècle," *Annales, Economies, Sociétés, Civilisations* 43 (1988): 353–378.

La Fin des corporations. (Paris: Fayard, 2001).

"Réflexions sur la police du monde du travail, 1700–1815," *Revue historique* 261 (1979): 17–77.

"Social Classification and Representation in the Corporate World of Eighteenth-Century France: Turgot's Carnival," in *Work in France: Representations, Meaning, Organization and Practice*, Steven Laurence Kaplan and Cynthia J. Koepp, eds., (Ithaca, NY: Cornell University Press, 1986): pp. 176–228.

The Bakers of Paris and the Bread Question 1700–1775. (Durham: Duke University Press, 1996).

"The Character and Implications of Strife Among the Masters Inside the Guilds of Eighteenth-Century Paris," *Journal of Social History* 19 (1986): 631–647.

Kaplow, Jeffry. *Elbeuf During the Revolutionary Period: History and Social Structure* (Baltimore, MD: The Johns Hopkins University Press, 1964).

Koehn, Nancy F. *Brand New: How Entrepreneurs Earned Consumers' Trust from Wedgwood to Dell* (Boston, MA: Harvard Business School Press, 2001).

Landes, David S. *The Unbound Prometheus: Technological Change and Industrial Development in Western Europe from 1750 to the Present* (Cambridge: Cambridge University Press, 1969).

Le Conseil d'Etat: son histoire à travers les documents d'époque 1799–1974 (Paris: Editions du CNRS, 1974).

Lefebvre, Georges. *Napoleon*, 2 vols. (New York: Columbia University Press, 1969).

Legrand, Robert. *Révolution et Empire en Picardie: Economie et finances* (Abbeville: F. Paillart, 1995).

Lemay, Edna Hindie. *Dictionnaire des Constituants 1789–1791*, 2 vols. (Oxford: Voltaire Foundation 1991).

Livesey, James. *Making Democracy in the French Revolution* (Cambridge, MA: Harvard University Press, 2001).

Lomüller, L.M. *Guillaume Ternaux 1763–1833: Créateur de la première intégration industrielle française* (Paris: Les Editions de la Cabro d'Or, 1978).

Lyons, Martyn. *France Under the Directory* (Cambridge: Cambridge University Press, 1975).

Margairaz, Dominique. *François de Neufchâteau: Biographie intellectuelle* (Paris: Publications de la Sorbonne, 2005).

Margerison, Kenneth. *P.-L. Roederer: Political Thought and Practice During the French Revolution* (Philadelphia, PA: The American Philosophical Society, 1983).

Mathiez, Albert. "Les corporations ont-elles été supprimées en principe dans la nuit de 4 août 1789?" Annales révolutionnaires 8 (1931): 252–257.

McPhee, Peter. *Living the French Revolution, 1789–99* (Basingstoke: Palgrave Macmillan, 2007).

Minard, Philippe. "Colbertism Continued? The Inspectorate of Manufactures and Strategies of Exchange in Eighteenth-Century France," *French Historical Studies* 23 (2000): 477–496.

Mokyr, Joel. *The Lever of Riches: Technological Creativity and Economic Progress* (New York: Oxford University Press, 1990).

Monnier, Raymonde. *Le Faubourg Saint-Antoine (1789–1815)* (Paris: Société des Etudes Robespierristes, 1981).

Murphy, Orville T. *The Diplomatic Retreat of France and Public Opinion on the Eve of the French Revolution, 1783–1789* (Washington, DC: The Catholic University of America Press, 1998).

"DuPont de Nemours and the Anglo-French Commercial Treaty of 1786," *The Economic History Review*, New Series 19 (1966): 569–580.

Nigeon, René. *Etat financier des corporations parisiennes d'arts et métiers au XVIIIe siècle* (Paris: Bieder, 1934).

Palmer, R.R. *Twelve Who Ruled: The Year of the Terror in the French Revolution* (Princeton: Princeton University Press, 1941).

Parker, Harold T. "Two Administrative Bureaus under the Directory and Napoleon," *French Historical Studies* 4 (1965): 150–169.

Patrick, Alison. "French Revolutionary Local Government, 1789–1792," in *The Political Culture of the French Revolution*, Colin Lucas, ed., (Oxford: Pergamon Press, 1988): 399–420.

Place, Dominique de. "L'Hôtel de Mortagne et les dépôts de l'an II," in *Le Conservatoire National des Arts et Métiers au coeur de Paris,* Michel Le Moël and Raymond Saint-Paul, eds., (Paris: Délégation à l'Action Artistique de la Ville de Paris, 1994): 47–50.

Poitrineau, Abel. *Ils Travaillaient la France: Métiers et mentalités du XVIe au XIXe siècle* (Paris: Armand Colin, 1992).

Reddy, William M. *The Rise of Market Culture: The Textile Trade and French Society, 1750–1900* (Cambridge: Cambridge University Press, 1984).

Rosenband, Leonard N. "Jean-Baptiste Réveillon: A Man on the Make in Old Regime France," *French Historical Studies* 29 (1997): 481–510.

Papermaking in Eighteenth-Century France:Management, Labor, and Revolution at the Montgolfier Mill,1761–1805 (Baltimore, MD: Johns Hopkins University Press, 2000).

Sargentson, Carolyn. *Merchants and Luxury Markets: The Marchands Merciers of Eighteenth-Century Paris* (London: Victoria and Albert Museum, 1996).

Scott, Samuel F. *The Response of the Royal Army to the French Revolution: The Role and Development of the Line Army 1787–1793* (Oxford: Clarendon Press, 1978).

Shepherd, Robert Perry. *Turgot and the Six Edicts* (New York: Columbia University Press, 1903).

Sibalis, Michael. "Corporatism after the Corportions: The Debate on Restoring Guilds under Napoleon I and the Restoration," *French Historical Studies* 15 (1988): 718–730.

"Shoemakers and Fourierism in 19th-Century Paris: The Société Laborieuse des Cordonniers-Bottiers," *Social History/Histoire Sociale* 20 (1987): 24–49.

Skuy, David. *Assassination, Politics, and Miracles: France and the Royalist Reaction of 1820* (Montreal: McGill-Queen's University Press, 2003).

Smith, Angie. "Weighed in the Balance? The Corporation of Apothecaries in Bordeaux, 1690–1790," *The Journal of the Society for the Social History of Medicine* 16 (2003): 17–37.

Sonenscher, Michael. *The Hatters of Eighteenth-Century France* (Berkeley, CA: University of California Press, 1987).

"Journeymen, the Courts and the French Trades 1781–1791," *Past and Present* 114 (1987): 77–109.

Work and Wages: Natural Law, Politics and the Eighteenth -Century French Trades (Cambridge: Cambridge University Press, 1989).

Sydenham, Michael J. *The First French Republic 1792–1804* (Berkeley, CA: University of California Press, 1973).

Truant, Cynthia Marie. *The Rites of Labor: Brotherhoods of Compagnonnage in Old and New Regime France* (Ithaca, NY: Cornell University Press, 1994).

Tulard, Jean. *Joseph Fiévée, conseiller secret de Napoléon* (Paris: Fayard, 1985).

"Le Débat autour du rétablissement des corporations sous le Consulat et l'Empire," in *Histoire du droit social: Mélanges en hommage à Jean Imbert*, Jean-Louis Harouel, ed., (Paris: Presses Universitaires de France, 1989), pp. 537–541.

Vardi, Liana. "The Abolition of the Guilds during the French Revolution," *French Historical Studies* 15 (1988): 704–717.

Velut, Christine. "L'Industrie dans la ville: Les fabriques de papiers peints du faubourg Saint-Antoine (1750–1820)," *Revue de l'histoire moderne et contemporaine* 49 (2002): 115–137.

Viennet, Odette. *Napoléon et l'industrie française: La crise de 1810–1811* (Paris: Plon, 1947).

Wesemall, Pieter van. *Architecture of Instruction and Delight: A Socio-Historical Analysis of World Exhibitions as a Didactic Phenomenon (1798–1851–1970)* (Rotterdam: OIO, 2001).

Williams, Alan. *The Police of Paris 1718–1789* (Baton Rouge, LA: Louisiana State University Press, 1979).

Woloch, Isser. *Napoleon and His Collaborators: The Making of a Dictatorship* (New York: Norton, 2001).

Unpublished Secondary Sources

Heimmermann, Daniel Joseph. "Work and Corporate Life in Old Regime France: The Leather Artisans of Bordeaux (1740–1791)," (Ph.D. Dissertation, Marquette University, 1994).

Livesey, Gerard James Christopher. "An Agent of Enlightenment in the French Revolution: Nicolas-Louis François de Neufchâteau, 1750–1828," (Ph.D. Dissertation, Harvard University, 1994).

Munson, James Robert. "Businessmen, Business Conduct and the Civic Organization of Commercial Life Under the Directory and Napoleon," (Ph.D. Dissertation, Columbia University, 1992).

Potofsky, Allen Samuel. "The Builders of Modern Paris: The Organization of Labor from Turgot to Napoleon," (Ph.D. Dissertation, Columbia University, 1993).

Sibalis, Michael David. "The Workers of Napoleonic Paris, 1800–1815," (Ph.D. Dissertation, Concordia University (Canada), 1979).

Biographical Dictionaries

Arnault, A. V., Jay, A., Jouy, E. Norvins, J. et. al., eds. *Biographie nouvelle des contemporains, ou Dictionnaire historique et raisonné de tous les hommes qui, depuis la Révolution française, ont acquis de la célébrité par leurs actions, leurs écrits, leurs erreurs ou leurs crimes, soit en France, soit dans les pays étrangers.* 20 vols. (Paris: Librairie Historique, 1820–1825).

Michaud, J. F. and L. G. Michaud. eds., *Biographie universelle, ancienne et moderne; ou, Histoire, par ordre alphabétique, de la vie publique et privée de tous les hommes qui se sont fait remarquer par leur écrits, leurs actions, leurs talents, leurs vertus ou leur crimes. Ouvrage entièrement neuf, rédigé par une Société de gens de lettres et de savants...*, 85 vols. (Paris: Michaud Frères, 1811–1828).

Biographie universelle, ancienne et moderne... (Nouvelle édition publiée sous la direction de M. Michaud..., 45 vols. (Paris: Mme. C. Desplaces, 1854–1865).

Dictionnaire de biographie française. (Paris: Letouzey et Ané, 1933-in progress).

Nouvelle biographie générale depuis les temps les plus reculés jusqu'à nos jours... Publiée...sous la direction de M. le docteur Hoefer, 46 vols. (Paris: Firmin Didot frères, 1853–1866).

Robert, Adolphe et Cougny, Gaston. *Dictionnaire des parlementaires français comprennant tous les membres des Assemblées françaises et tous les ministres français depuis le 1ᵉʳ mai 1789 jusqu'au 1ᵉʳ mai 1889; avec leurs noms, état-civil, états de service, actes politiques, votes parlementaires, etc., publié sous la direction de A. Robert et G. Cougny,* 5 vols. (Paris: Bourloton, 1889–1891).

Bibliographical Aids

Fierro, Alfred. *Bibliographie analytique des biographies collectives imprimées de la France contemporaine (1789–1985).* (Geneva: Slatkine, 1986).

Index